1992

University of St. Francis
GEN 807 S598
Simmons, John S.
Teaching literature in middle

3 0301 00085210 9

P9-AQV-968

Teaching Literature in Middle and Secondary Grades

TEACHING LITERATURE IN MIDDLE AND SECONDARY GRADES

JOHN S. SIMMONS
Florida State University
Tallahassee, Florida

H. EDWARD DELUZAIN
A. Crawford Mosley High School
Panama City, Florida

LIBRARY
College of St. Francis
JOLIET, ILLINOIS

ALLYN AND BACON, INC.
Boston   London   Toronto   Sydney   Tokyo   Singapore

Series Editor: Sean W. Wakely
Series Editorial Assistant: Carol L. Chernaik
Production Administrator: Susan McIntyre
Editorial-Production Service: Ruttle, Shaw & Wetherill, Inc.
Cover Administrator: Linda Dickinson
Cover Designer: Suzanne Harbison
Manufacturing Buyer: Megan Cochran

Copyright © 1992 by Allyn and Bacon
A Division of Simon & Schuster, Inc.
160 Gould Street
Needham Heights, MA 02194

All rights reserved. No part of the material protected by
this copyright notice may be reproduced or utilized in
any form or by any means, electronic or mechanical, including photocopying, recording, or by any information
storage and retrieval system, without the written permission of the copyright owner.

Library of Congress Cataloging-in-Publication Data

Simmons, John S.
    Teaching literature in middle and secondary
grades/John S. Simmons, H. Edward Deluzain.
        p.   cm.
    Includes bibliographical references (p.   ) and index.
    ISBN 0–205–13195–6
    1. Literature—Study and teaching (Secondary)—
United States.
I. Deluzain, H. Edward, 1947–   . II. Title.
PN70.S5   1992
807.1′273—dc20   91–4153
                                                        CIP

Printed in the United States of America
10 9 8 7 6 5 4 3 2 1   96 95 94 93 92 91

807
S598

To our wives, Katie and Beth

143, 243

Table of Contents

Chapter One   Introduction 1
What Should Be Promoted 4
    Empathy 4
    Verisimilitude 8
    Willing Suspension of Disbelief 10
    Symbolism 14
Summary 16

**Chapter Two   The Place of Literature in the
      Secondary School Curriculum 18**
Literature through the Ages 18
Dimensions and Options 33
    Critical Reading 34
    Reflection on Correlative Experience 35
    The Cultural Heritage 36
    Pleasure and Recreation 37
    Study of Aesthetics 38
    Preparation for Scholarship 40
Middle School Components 41
Individual Concerns 41

**Chapter Three   Reading and Listening in
      Literature Study 45**
Prereading Activities 48
Some Pertinent Reading Competencies 53
Metaphor 55
Comprehension Elements 57

Culmination of the Reading Discussion:
   A Sample Lesson 59
Listening Capabilities 64

Chapter Four   Reading Interests and Interest in Reading 69

Introduction 69
Factors That Affect Interest in Reading 70
   Reading Ability 70
   Home Environment 74
   The Period of Adolescence 75
   The Influence of Television 76
   Other ``Competitors'' 78
Ways to Stimulate Interest in Reading 82
Reading Interests 84
The Issue of Realism 86
Promoting Interest in the Classroom 88

Chapter Five   Young Adult Fiction 94

A Disclaimer 94
The Transition Concept—Reading to Study 94
The Young Adult Novel 99
The Question of Quality 104
The Question of Literary Realism 111
Summary 115
Appendices for Chapter Five 117

Chapter Six   The Reader-Response Orientation to Teaching Literature 130

Reader-Response Criticism 136
The Response-Centered Curriculum 137
   Social Learning 140
   Cognitive Learning 141
   Affective Learning 147
Response-Centered Teaching 148
   The Response-Centered Lesson 149
   Testing, Evaluating, and Grading in Response-Centered
      Teaching 153
Conclusion 156

Chapter Seven   Expressing Responses Orally and in Writing 157

Oral Language 157

Whole-Group Discussion versus Small-Group
Discussion 158
Oral Reading 160
Readers Theatre 161
Improvised Dramatic Activity 161
Oral Book Reports 164
A Word about Listening 165
Conclusion for Oral Responses 166
Written Expression 166
Writing as a Way of Knowing 167
The Writing Process 168
Types of Writing Assignments 172
Academic Assignments 172
Creative Writing Assignments 178
Conclusion for Written Responses 181

Chapter Eight   Broad-Range Approaches to Curriculum Organization in Literature   183

General Principles for Curriculum Organization 183
Broad-Range Approaches to Curriculum Organization
in Literature 186
Free Reading 186
Chronological Survey 188
Genre Approach 191
The Mythic Approach 198
Conclusion 203

Chapter Nine   Focused Approaches to Curriculum Organization in Literature   205

The Focused Chronological Approach 207
The Major Writer Approach 211
The Major Idea Approach 216
The Thematic Approach 224
Conclusion 235

Chapter Ten   Literary Topics of Special Importance   237

Introduction 237
Coming of Age 237
Types of Coming of Age Fiction 244
Initiation Fiction 244
The Bildungsroman 248
The Uses of Coming of Age Fiction 250
Utopia 251
Social Criticism 254

Literature by and about Women and Minorities   255
Conclusion   258

Chapter Eleven   Teaching Literature to Students with High and Low Academic Ability   259

A Note About Tracking   259
Teaching Literature to High-Ability Students   261
Characteristics of High-Ability Students   262
Principles of Teaching Literature to High-Ability Students   266
Special Courses for High-Ability Students   274
Advanced Placement   274
International Baccalaureate   277
High School–College Dual Enrollment   278
Helping High-Ability Students Deal with Stress   279
Teaching Literature to Low-Ability Students   282
Characteristics of Low-Ability Students   283
Materials for Poor Readers   286
The Language Experience Approach   288
Alternatives to Reading   289
The Nonprint Media   289
Reader-Response with Low-Ability Students   291
Conclusion   294

Chapter Twelve   Censorship and Literature Study   296

Introduction to the Issue   296
Kinds of Censorship   299
Censorship and Young Adult Fiction   313
Some Suggestions for Classroom Teachers   314
Summary   319

Bibliography   321

I. Resources for Book Selection   321

II. Journals in English Education and the Teaching of Literature   322

III. Selected Works of Literary Criticism   322

IV. Selected Texts on the Theory and Practice of Teaching Literature   323

V. Censorship   327

Index   329

Foreword

The appearance of a new book on the teaching of literature in the secondary schools is of itself an event to applaud. To greet a new book of quality is a happy privilege. We have had few books treating comprehensively the teaching of literature in secondary schools during the past two decades. Our predominant concerns in the teaching of English have been elsewhere, notably in the teaching of writing, a justifiable concern. Yet my bias over many years in teaching has remained that literature should occupy a position of centrality in the English curriculum. Perhaps at this time a new book on teaching literature is a harbinger of some shift in priorities. Thus, my feeling of privilege in introducing this volume.

Imaginative literature has a unique importance in the school curriculum, that of generating what I have called "felt knowledge" of human experiences, the human condition. Though long given lip service, this primary function of the study of literature has been obscured in a number of schools by the impediments of historical surveys and technical analyses and other offshoots of the scholarship of literature. While not demeaning these traditional touchstones of literature teaching, this book delineates the principal functions of literary study in secondary schools without resorting to standard pleas for not neglecting the humanities or to vague exhortations on the joys of "appreciation" of literature. The volume maps a needed structure for study of literature in the secondary school that can lead to well-defined outcomes, making it possible to assess in some specific ways student progress and achievement in literary study—the lack of which in the past has been a major weakness in the English curriculum.

An important criterion of a book on teaching in a particular subject is that it have balance between theory and scholarship in the field and practical concerns of the classroom. This volume has such balance. Traditional approaches and methods of organization in the teaching of literature are evaluated along with the newer thrust toward response-centered teaching, which many teachers are at a loss to translate into classroom specifics. Other matters of special practical importance to teachers of literature are treated—the role of young adult or adolescent literature in the program, the thorny issue of censorship, and the problems of teaching literature to students at both ends of the ability continuum.

A baseline for judgment of a book on teaching, in sum, is that it be useful to teachers and prospective teachers and that it distill the scholarship in the field into that which has direct implication for the classroom. This volume succeeds in doing that.

Dwight L. Burton
May 1991

Preface

Writing this book has been a labor of love, one that had its genesis in innumerable conversations over almost twenty years of friendship and professional association. During the years, we have both benefitted from the ideas we've read in professional publications and heard expressed in lectures and presentations at professional conferences. We have attempted to acknowledge these formally in the pages that follow, but we are acutely aware that a full acknowledgment of every source of ideas is impossible. Our friends and colleagues at the middle school, high school, junior college, and university levels have generously shared their insights with us, and four of them—Alice Colvin, ReLeah Hawks, and Ann Williamson, all of A. Crawford Mosley High School, and Donald W. Adams of Chipola Junior College—made valuable comments about sections of the manuscript. Reviewers W. Hugh Agee of the University of Georgia and Jo-Ann Mullen of the University of Northern Colorado provided valuable feedback on the manuscript. Our wives, Katie Simmons and Beth Deluzain, who are both teachers of literature of great experience and sensitivity, have helped us at every phase of the project, and the Deluzain children, Susan and Catherine, contributed to the book in many ways, including graciously allowing their father to monopolize the family computer for the better part of a year. Lt. Philip Mayfield, USAF, made a major and invaluable contribution by patiently helping us with computer applications. Finally, our students—in preservice teacher training programs, in graduate school courses, in college and university literature classes, and in middle school and high school English programs—have motivated us to want to share what we know about teaching literature with others. To these, and to others who have assisted us, we offer a heartfelt *thank you*.

J.S.S.
H.E.D.

CHAPTER ONE

Introduction

As a rule, the teaching of literature in secondary schools, both public and private, will move in one of two directions: up or down. When effectively taught, the study of imaginative literature can be the most exciting event of the adolescent student's day. Young people can become deeply engrossed in what they read. They can respond with intensity and conviction. They can perceive and enthusiastically express relationships between the work they have just read and the meaningful experiences of their past lives—and they often do so with refreshing candor. Even prosaic classroom atmospheres can be charged with the electricity of excited verbal interaction.

Other teaching approaches, however, can produce a totally different atmosphere. An example: During the middle of this century, the secondary school English program of a certain moderately large Northeastern United States community mandated the teaching of *David Copperfield* during the tenth grade year. After a prescribed (by the school district) and lengthy introductory lecture on the life of Charles Dickens, the students were assigned a chapter a night for homework reading, four nights per week. The assigned chapters were then "discussed" in class on each successive day. (On Fridays, of course, the students took a weekly test on twenty spelling words from spelling lists, also prescribed by the district.) After five weeks of this chapter-by-chapter explication, the students took a one-hundred-dred item true–false test on the novel. And it must have been a good test because, at the time the writers of this text became aware of its use, it had been in operation for at least twenty-five years.

Long selections of low-interest, heavy emphasis on rote response assignments, repetitive classroom activities ("... answer questions one through five in the Study Guide"), evaluation instruments which lay stress on trivial dimensions of the text—all of these frequently used approaches can spell doom for the vital teaching of literature in secondary school English classrooms. And that doom occurred just as surely in the "good

1

old days" as it does in the 1990s. Adolescence is a time of restlessness, of becoming, of rebellion or at least of questioning, of irreverence for adults and their institutions, and a lot more overt turbulence. In this emotional, social, and intellectual milieu, literary study can offer some credible, imaginative guidelines for evolving sensibilities, or it can be the lifeless chore that countless young people continue to endure, to slog their way through in order to pass the test, to earn a passing grade, to receive a diploma so that they can get the hell out of that education mill and get on with their lives.

This text offers as its central purpose some means of assisting classroom teachers to go the first rather than the second of the routes described above. It will define the teaching of literature as multidimensional, an effort whose goal is to affect the inner nature of human beings rather than (as some extreme behaviorists propose) to produce someone who can demonstrate certain minimum competencies. A major premise to be found throughout the ensuing chapter is that students aren't products but people. And people are turned on by various selections, various response activities, various expectations, and various levels of tolerance. Multidimensional approaches will be described as alternatives in a kind of *if-then* manner. *If* you, as a teacher, have a certain set of circumstances, *then* we suggest one approach; *if* you have a different teaching milieu, *then* we propose another alternative. To us, the very nature of literary study, analysis, and/or appreciation is antithetical to the lock-step approach. As long as readers are individuals, breadth in teaching strategies seems clearly to be the better way. That's what you'll find herein.

Throughout the chapters that follow, one central thesis will be implicitly, but persistently, present: that the major task of the secondary school teacher of literature is to assist adolescents in a move from the reading of imaginative literature to its study. Because, as we contend, this necessary movement places literature in a unique position in the overall school curriculum, it is worth some further consideration at the outset of this text.

Consider the kinds of subject matter which gradually come to constitute the main bill of fare for both public and private school students throughout the United States and indeed the English-speaking world. Almost all subjects, whether it be "numbers" (mathematics) in the first grade or geography (social studies) in the fourth, start out as serious business. As the middle grade curriculum devolves into a period of earth-science, followed by a period of arithmetic, and then one of language arts, geography, and so forth, the name of the game is serious study. Despite the occasional—and usually whimsical—departures into the "math can be fun" motif, the *tone* of most such curricular enterprises is serious from the very beginning. From their early school years, then, youngsters learn to adopt a businesslike stance when certain components of the subject matter curriculum are posed to them (i.e., "All right, children, it's time for long division."). At that point, in the language of the National Football League, it's time to put on your game face. In the great majority of our schools, this is not so with literature.

From kindergarten through most elementary grades in most school systems, literature is introduced and maintained as a change-of-pace activity. Teachers take off the pressure of study by telling or reading their students a story. Poetry comes through the reciting of short, rhythmical verses or the singing of songs. Children are assigned parts in playlets, always short and frequently used to celebrate such calendar events as Halloween, Thanksgiving, Christmas, Valentine's Day, and Easter (Bunny style, in all probability). Oral and choral presentations become the dominant modes. There is little *silent* reading.

Let's shift the scene abruptly. We're in an English class in a senior high school located in a suburb just north of Chicago (or Philadelphia, or Fort Lauderdale, or Dallas, or San Francisco). The anthologies are on the desks and open to a short lyric poem by William Butler Yeats (or Wallace Stevens, or Ezra Pound, or W. H. Auden). The teacher calls for a brief, written in-class *explication du texte* of the work. Rhetorical style will be counted. References to scholarly sources will be looked on with favor. The class has the rest of the period to complete the work.

What *everybody* needs to consider—students, administrators, counselors, parents, school board members, and most of all English teachers—is that this transition doesn't just come about because these young people get older and move up a grade each year. This transition—from the *reading* to the *study* of literature must be planned for, guided, encouraged, and monitored as it develops through these grade levels.

The secondary school years, where most young people encounter their first professionally trained, certified, interested literature teachers, seem to us to be the logical place for this transition to take place most directly and effectively. For both teachers and students of literature, the middle school to junior high years are those in which a new proposition is made, one which is unique in the students' lives: "Look, folks; for ___ years you've been looking at this stuff (literature) primarily as fun, as a departure from the grind of studying those other things (math, science, etc.). From now on, it is going to take on a more serious tone in class. We're going to study literature for its implied meaning, for its structure, for its place in the world of serious thought." Then, almost as an afterthought, the statement, "Of course, we still want you to like it."

The significance of the ramifications of movement from reading to study of literature cannot be underestimated. Somehow literature must take on this new status, must take its place with those other curricular elements which demand serious thought. Somehow it must shed the cloak of being "just for fun" but at the same time retain that dimension of interest which attracts the committed reader. We would contend that no other curricular element must go through that metamorphosis. And while it is surely true that works of proven high interest will play an important role in effecting this desired change, it is the teacher who, according to research, authoritative statement, and wisdom gained through first hand experience, becomes the vital X in the equation.

What Should Be Promoted

Since the study of literature involves the teaching of *something* to *someone,* and since large numbers of adolescents have consistently resisted some approaches to literary study, English teachers should keep their *someones* in mind as instructional preparations are made. Awareness of the nature of adolescents as readers of literature plus the curricular need to move those students from reading to study have led us to propose that teachers consider four key concepts as they make such preparations. These four are: empathy, verisimilitude, willing suspension of disbelief, and symbolism.

Empathy

One of the probable reasons why many of the "classics" (*Silas Marner, Great Expectations,* "The Lady of the Lake," *The Merchant of Venice,* and so forth) have left so many twentieth century American high school students cold is the fact that the plot, characters, setting, and language of these masterpieces are all far from the sensibilities of that young audience. Much of the work of certain psycholinguists (see Smith, Frank. *Understanding Reading.* 2nd ed. New York: Holt, Rinehart & Winston, 1978) of the past ten to fifteen years has led to the conclusion that without a considerable fund of *correlative experience* most, if not all, readers have real trouble comprehending the texts they attempt or are assigned. Correlative experience is a rather simple concept. It has to do with the backgrounds readers have compiled as these backgrounds relate to the content of what they are reading. Put on a more personal level, readers will constantly ask themselves, "What has happened in my life that I can tie in to what is happening in this text?" as they attempt to follow the narrative line in print before them. Without such a fund of correlative experience, psycholinguists tell us, comprehension is at best difficult and at worst impossible.

As one considers the age and maturity level of secondary school readers, especially those in middle school or junior high, the problem of promoting empathy (i.e., finding those texts with which readers have some correlative experience) becomes an increased necessity. For example, it is quite possible that most American teenagers don't know much about the Wessex countryside in England. They are also, no doubt, pretty light on rural British history of the early nineteenth century. They may well have little acquaintance with elderly hermits who are attempting to cope with their loneliness. These teenagers probably haven't had much to do with out-and-out misers. And they've never thought much about what effect finding and adopting a small child might have on an old hermited skinflint living in a small rural English village. In all probability, then, their interest in the above might well be pretty low, and *Silas Marner,* as an all-class, multiweek study, might well founder to the point of failure.

The world of imaginative literature is broad indeed, and it grows with every publication of a new novel, short story, poem, or play. Teachers, both the new recruits and the old soldiers, often fall into the trap of assuming that what interests them will automatically interest their students. Since we are all products of our experience and we are all different people, this assumption seems false on its face. Clearly, teachers need to be enthusiastic in presenting literary works to their classes. Choosing those works with which a class has a chance to empathize, however, represents an equally important part of the process.

There is some danger, however, in interpreting correlative experience too narrowly. This kind of experience should never be equated one-to-one with literary selections chosen for all-class reading. Dwight Burton, in *Literature Study in the High School,* uses the term "imaginative entry" for empathy or correlative experience.[1] In essence, Burton maintains that, in order to empathize with Holden Caulfield, for example, young people need not travel to New York City, rent a hotel room, and retrace the steps taken by Holden in his three-day odyssey. However, readers *do* need to have had some experiences that relate to Holden's world in a general sense. In this case, readers could have some idea of what it's like to be expelled from something, to be afraid to face their parents over failure, to have the desire and opportunity to hide out for a while and do things that make them feel good and forget their problems temporarily, but all the while to be haunted by fears of what's going to happen next.

Because countless young people have experienced some or all of these situations, often in their teenage years, *The Catcher in the Rye* by J.D. Salinger has been greatly popular for over thirty years. (It has also caused a lot of teachers headaches which have stemmed from parental and community objections; more about that matter in a later chapter.) And, the reading audience for Salinger's novel has ranged far beyond teenagers who live in the New York area.

Correlative experience, as well as being a vital element in the teaching of literature, is also quite broad in scope. Teachers need to be aware of the several sources of such experience.

1. **Family and Neighborhood Activity** The kind of family experience young people have provides an immediate and obvious touchstone. Because of the changing nature of neighborhoods, particularly in urban and suburban areas, as well as the currently high divorce rate affecting families, such correlative experience is broad indeed in late twentieth century America. Works about family and neighborhood lifestyles are numerous today, and they have been for a long time.

2. **Community and Region** America is a vast country replete with thousands of communities, large, small, and in between. The great distances between regions plus the great differences in regional and community lifestyles add to the difficulty teachers face in choosing works with which their students can truly empathize. In the 1960s, a teacher was leading his students through the study of *Swiftwater* by Paul Annixter. The first part of the novel was set in winter in the North Country. Snow. Ice. Subzero temperatures. Heavy clothing. Snowshoes. Frostbite. The students were ninth graders of average ability living in a relatively small (70,000 people) North Florida community. When the teacher asked his students to identify the locale of the work, they replied almost unanimously, "The Everglades." Apparently that great South Florida wilderness was the only one they had at their disposal to correlate with the *Swiftwater* setting—and they obviously couldn't contrast the tropical nature of what they knew with what Annixter was describing. Because of the vastness of America (and indeed the world) mentioned previously, teachers who believe that their students can make automatic imaginative entries into the wide variety of geographical, sociological, and historical settings in imaginative literature are sanguine in the extreme. On many occasions, background must be carefully built by the teacher right there in the classroom.

3. **Television and Other Nonprint Media** We need not reiterate how television has shrunk the universe and brought the remote corners of the world into people's living rooms. To deny the reality of the electronic media's expansion of the correlative experience of young people, however, would be colossally naive. The two-edged-sword nature of current media offerings, however, deserves at least a brief mention. The syndrome of the happy ending, with all problems solved in thirty minutes (minus commercials), has unquestionably infected hordes of kids. It has probably made more difficult the task of teaching such aspects of literature as literary

realism, cause-and-effect relationships, and anti-climactic endings (to name only three). But television is here to stay. It does occupy countless hours of students' time, and it provides them with views of the world they would never otherwise perceive—for better or worse.

4. **Part-Time Employment** Two facts of contemporary American life are (a) a large number of secondary school students work after school, on breaks, and during the summer, and (b) work experiences have a significant effect on these students' awarenesses and attitudes. While the worlds of the professional person, the union boss, or the military leader are still well beyond the ken of our students, their part-time work experiences can play a major role in their attempts to cope with the realities posed by a large number of writers. While parents and teachers may seek to protect these youngsters from some of the harsher, more callous aspects of reality, their employers may well be totally uninterested in providing such protection. The old bromide, "learning the hard way," has real currency in the lives many students lead in their part-time careers after school. There are numerous excerpts from such books as Studs Terkel's *Working* to which many of today's teenagers can quickly and easily relate. Part-time jobs provide an avenue of transition to adulthood, and their impact should be considered carefully by all teachers of secondary school literature.

5. **Travel** Here is another fairly obvious touchstone. Alvin Toffler's old and reputable book *Future Shock* begins with an extended treatment of the mobility of American society and what that movement of people portends for the twenty-first century. Any secondary school teacher who has dealt with the offspring of military personnel will be immediately sensitive to the impact that the constant establishment of new living situations has on adolescents. While it may well have an adverse effect on their sense of security, the travel experience of military offspring has the inevitable effect of increasing their firsthand awareness of the world at large. When, at an earlier grade level (here in the United States) they have been asked to read a story about little Hans of Heidelberg, they may well be familiar with his type, having had him as a next-door neighbor not so long ago. Another old bromide, "Travel broadens one," is ever operative in the process of promoting comprehension of literary works in the classroom.

Verisimilitude

Of the several ways in which adolescents can be contrasted with children as readers of literature, one of the clearest lies in their different preferences for the treatment of reality. Children consistently embrace the fanciful. For them, a story, poem, or play can be as it wants to be. Suffused as they are in early childhood with fairy tales, fables, stories of magic, and the like, they continue to relish "never-never land" as a backdrop for what they read and what is read to them. Concern for carefully developed cause-and-effect sequences are nonexistent. Contrivances and sudden turns of events and character portrayals are just fine. The *deus ex machina* is a welcome intruder. In the people they meet, the good guys *do* wear white hats, and the villains sport handlebar mustaches, wear pointed shoes, and use lots of hair oil.

Part of the passage from childhood to adulthood is marked by a distinct change in this attitude. Adolescents overwhelmingly demand the real in what they read. No more lovely young ladies on gossamer wings or rabbits coming out of hats for them. With the exception of science fiction and fantasy, they seek a kind of literary offering that they can relate to what they perceive as the *real world,* one with outcomes justifying motives, complex characters, potential related to achievement, and terra firma in place of pink clouds. And if that's all there was to it, choice and teaching of texts for the secondary grades would be easy.

An imposing body of evidence, much of it gathered by J. Harlan Shores, indicates conclusively that while the great majority of adolescent readers demand the *real* in what they read, their definitions of reality, when verbalized, differ greatly from one another. The reasons for these widely different conceptions are virtually self-evident: family unity, neighborhood makeup, socioeconomic status, academic motivation, and a few others. Probably worth particular note among these "few others" is that of sex. In their reading interests, attitudes, preferences, and so forth, adolescent boys differ markedly from girls, and the two sexes usually define the real in radically different ways, thus making teachers' tasks of selecting texts for the whole class and deciding on the kinds of responses to solicit all the more difficult.

And then there's commercial television. There is no accurate means of assessing the impact the slick private-eye melodramas, the grin-a-second comedies, and the afternoon and evening soaps have on the way adolescents define the real in the literature they read, but the impact is undoubtedly there. Fed a steady diet of fast-moving plots, bloody incidents, and less than subtle character typing, secondary school students can not help but draw some parallels with their required reading in English classes.

So don't expect students to define realism the way William Dean Howells did. Seek those works which, at the adolescent readers' level, do portray life in less than fantastic but more than utterly dismal terms. Avoid those which depend on abrupt, unexpected shifts in fortunes, which don't portray all human conflicts in terms of Batman–Joker square-offs, which do provide reasonable consequences for major characters' decisions. Make the presence of logical cause-and-effect sequences a criterion of high priority. Allow the variety of expressions of perceptions of reality that come from almost any class, as they relate to reading, to be fully and candidly aired. And try to avoid, from your superior, English-major status, being too derogatorily judgmental of what your students say or write on the matter of verisimilitude.

One potentially valuable means of introducing and reinforcing the verisimilitude ingredient into literary study lies in works that focus on the theme of the adolescent's search for self-definition. While this theme will be treated more fully in a later chapter, it needs to be identified at this point as a most useful vehicle for leading secondary school readers to find credibility in the literary selections they are either assigned or choose from teacher-developed reading lists. Most of these works are fictional, and long fictional examples are far more plentiful than short ones. In fact, a later chapter will deal at length with the large number of well-written novels available for study whose theme is the young person's search for self. There is also a considerable number of excellent short stories based on the theme of self-definition, as well as initiation into adulthood, and they can be found in thematically organized collections as well as in the tables of contents of more general anthologies. There are a few serious plays of high literary quality on this theme, such as Eugene O'Neill's *Ah! Wilderness* and Paul Zindel's *The Effect of Gamma Rays on Man-in-the-Moon Marigolds,* and these are usually popular with adolescent readers. Poetry illustrating this theme is harder to find. Some possible titles are "Cherrylog Road" by James Dickey, "We Real Cool" by Gwendolyn Brooks, and "To the Virgins To Make Much of Time" by Robert Herrick.

Despite the fact that the search for self-definition theme is to be found largely in fictional form, it is one well worth interjecting as teachers help their students find and examine the real in what they are reading. Works on this theme will be further valuable in that they incorporate the correlative experience ingredient with that of verisimilitude. Most adolescents, both younger and older, will be more willing to accept as real the travails of Holden Caulfield (*The Catcher in the Rye*), Gene Forrester (*A Separate Peace*), Adam Farmer (*I Am the Cheese*), or Conrad Jarrett (*Ordinary People*) than they are the cast of characters and the fundamental conflict in, say, Sloan Wilson's *The Man in the Gray Flannel Suit.* Problems of these adolescent characters' lives will probably prove to be a more effective means of providing *the real* in literary study than the problems of their *classic* literary counterparts.

Before leaving the matter of verisimilitude, one cautionary note needs to be made. In the search for those selections which would seem most effective in promoting literary realism, be very careful about offending parental and community mores. This is particularly relevant if you use our suggestions about works which center around the problems faced by adolescents in their search for self-definition. An imposing number of these works dwell on aspects of human experience which large numbers of parents and other concerned citizens feel—and feel very strongly—have no place in a public school program of study. The censorship problem is one without an apparent solution, at least for the English teacher who firmly believes that literature should be a legitimate reflection of human experience. It is also one which has reared its head at some fairly unlikely moments throughout the history of American education. Teachers take some chance every time they assign a literary selection for whole-class reading and study, but sensitivity to community standards can help reduce the risk inherent in the selection of works for study.

While we will devote a subsequent chapter to the issue of censorship in effective literature teaching, which will focus on possible solutions rather than anguished laments, it does strike us as necessary to at least mention it in the context of the search for and promotion of verisimilitude. Works which can really do the job in this area may prove to be more trouble than they are worth. Teachers have in the past been frequently guilty of becoming carried away in their desire to use literature study to acquaint students with sophisticated slants on the facts of life. The Jerry Falwells and the Mel and Norma Gablers of today are truly archetypal figures in our society. They've always been around to harass teachers, from Ichabod Crane, to Wing Bibblebaum, to *you*. In their zeal to promote their true- blue form of orthodoxy in the schools, verisimilitude is going to suffer. We'll deal with effective responses in detail later, but for now suffice it to say that judicious selection is probably the proper ounce of prevention.

Willing Suspension of Disbelief

In a sense, the side of the coin opposite verisimilitude is the establishment of willing suspension of disbelief in secondary school literature study. Dwight Burton used the term *imaginative entry* in proposing the need for the intermingling of correlative experience with literary understanding. The reader's imagination, then, must be reached if much of what is worthwhile in this study is to be realized. For hard-nosed, literal-minded adolescent readers (especially among the academically talented), a large dose of literature which is both reputable and teachable is hard to take. These students have trouble buying Samuel Taylor Coleridge's contention, voiced in the preface to *Lyrical Ballads*, that the fantastic can provide an avenue to truth if the reader will only give it a chance. Some careful prereading activity introduced in class by the teacher is what we suggest as a means of maneuvering those students who may be skeptical into a position where they are willing to accept the authors' interpretations of human experience, no matter how off-the-wall these interpretations may seem initially.

One possible way to insinuate the idea of a willing suspension of disbelief into the thinking of a class is by introducing the proposition that literature is not life itself but a picture of life. This is an argument raised by many literary scholars in their critiques of bizarre descriptions of life as found in certain works of high quality. One of the striking differences between journalism and literature is that the journalist is concerned only with the facts of an event, whereas the writer of imaginative literature seeks to discover the dramatic and/or philosophical significance of that event. To accomplish this, the writer may deliberately distort or exaggerate certain aspects of reality in order to jar readers' sensibilities or cause readers to consider the interaction of their imaginations with their literal perceptions. An analogy to the distortion mirror at an amusement park may provide a concrete illustration. In both cases, viewers will almost invariably take a closer look.

The presentation of the opening paragraphs of Franz Kafka's "The Metamorphosis" may be of further assistance in directing the attention of the class to the role that willing suspension of disbelief plays in literature study. The story begins this way:

> As Gregor Samsa awoke one morning from uneasy dreams he found himself transformed in his bed into a gigantic insect. He was lying on his hard, as it were armor-plated, back and when he lifted his head a little he could see his dome-like brown belly divided into stiff arched segments on top of which the bed quilt could hardly keep in position and was about to slide off completely. His numerous legs, which were pitifully thin compared to the rest of his bulk, waved helplessly before his eyes.
>
> What has happened to me? he thought. It was no dream. His room, a regular human bedroom, only rather too small, lay quiet between the four familiar walls. Above the table on which a collection of cloth samples was unpacked and spread out—Samsa was a commercial traveler—hung the picture which he had recently cut out of an illustrated magazine and put into a pretty gilt frame. It showed a lady, with a fur cap on and a fur stole, sitting upright and holding out to the spectator a huge fur muff into which the whole of her forearm had vanished![2]

Kafka has obviously taken liberties with reality. He has described Gregor Samsa's present insect-like nature in indisputably concrete terms. And he has added the detail that "it was no dream" to further perplex readers.

Readers can either write this story off, saying, "Human beings don't go to sleep people and wake up bugs," or they can go along with the author and see where Gregor's nightmarish situation takes him next. In opting for the latter course, readers have the opportunity for a close-up view of the adaptability of the human mind to the bizarre and the unprecedented. On this journey, they may discover some insights which are provocative indeed. We as teachers should be prepared to listen attentively to the students' reactions and responses and then offer some observations from our own responses and from our familiarity with the responses of literary critics.

Earlier in this discussion, the term *exaggeration* was mentioned. A more careful consideration of the application of the term to willing suspension of disbelief may also come in handy. The use of exaggeration in satire can help establish the need for such suspension. A discussion of the nature and purpose of satire can lead to an understanding of an imaginative writer's selection of details. This discussion can center on almost any short, satiric selection, from a timely editorial by Art Buchwald or Mike Royko all the way to Jonathan Swift's "A Modest Proposal." If the latter were used, such a response as "Give me a break! Why would this guy ever suggest eating one-year-old babies?" might be heard. A little background on the economic plight of eighteenth century Ireland, plus a close and possibly oral reading of the concluding paragraphs of the essay, should provide a reasonably clear, and obviously satiric, answer to the question.

In any event, secondary school students of literature need to become familiar, early on, with the literary device of deliberately selecting details to create exaggeration as they make the reading-to-study transition already delineated in this chapter. Much satire is action-packed, plenty is available, and numerous satirical works can be made relevant to issues within students' correlative experiences. As students move from the obvious to the more subtle exaggeration used in satire, they are more likely to suspend their disbelief in order to discover the target a writer chooses to satirize and why that target was selected. Then they can compare that writer's view with their own.

In order to extend students' willingness to suspend their disbelief, teachers may be able to use works of science fiction. These works have risen to great heights of popularity with young readers during the past four decades, and today such authors as Isaac Asimov, Robert Heinlein, Ray Bradbury, and Arthur C. Clarke are household names with large numbers of young readers. Some modern science fiction may seem vastly improbable, but students today have cut their teeth on the visual electronic marvels that bombard them in movie theaters and on their television screens. In short, the task of selling science fiction has been considerably reduced. Equally influential has been the space exploration of the past several decades, so familiar to today's students that it has become commonplace. To older members of our society, some of the fantastic exploits of Flash Gordon and Buck Rogers have become virtual reality, thus making all contemporary readers more willing to accept the credibility of much science fiction. Nonfiction periodicals which feature the most recent scientific achievement and experimentation reinforce this acceptance. The potential of science fiction for liberalizing the literal constraints of the adolescent imagination is considerable.

Another vehicle for promoting willing suspension of disbelief is the romantic epic. The full-blown study of the epic hero is one which has long been popular in English classes from middle school through college. Hero worship represents a common propensity among adolescents from all socioeconomic levels and all geographic regions. Again, the media, especially through television shows and newspaper and magazine accounts of contemporary heroes and heroines, have made the acceptance of the epic hero of literature more possible. These media have also facilitated the analysis of epic heroes from cultures other than the Anglo-Saxon. As the dreams of the adolescent male and female reader correspond with the exploits of the epic hero in a variety of literary selections, the willingness of these readers to accept these exploits as interesting, if not totally plausible, will give teachers greater leverage in choosing works for study in which the plots, characters, settings, and situations do not coincide exactly with the historical and sociological realities of the contemporary scene.

Of somewhat less widespread value, but still worth considering in this pursuit, are expressionistic plays. In these plays, which are usually rather short and action-oriented, unusual events and characters are featured. Some background for the themes of these plays almost always needs to be built by teachers, but their fast-moving and often humorous nature provides incentives for reading, dramatization, and discussion. Marc Connolly's *Green Pastures* can provide a relatively obvious introduction, and it has been popular for a long time. Another playwright who plays on the imagination is Elmer Rice. His plays will also require some historical background information provided by teachers, but both *Street Scene* and *The Adding Machine* offer thoughtful messages through highly unusual scenarios. More complex and oblique are Eugene O'Neill's *The Emperor Jones* and Maxwell Anderson's *Winterset*. They will both require careful preparation and guidance, but as students grapple with the human interaction in each, they may be more willing to suspend disbelief when confronted with nonrealistic works in subsequent units of study.

More generally, there are virtually countless novels, short stories, plays, and even poems which are surrealistic in nature but which, because of engrossing plots, unique characters, vivid settings and other incentives, can be used to wean the literal minded readers in the class away from their narrow predilections. Teachers need to be prepared with all manner of beguiling approaches to coax these straight-arrow thinkers into the imaginative mode.

Symbolism

There is probably no more significant dimension of the transition from reading to study of imaginative literature than the introduction by teachers of the concept of possible symbolic representation in the selections they assign. The relating of a literary symbol to its referent(s) is without question an advanced reading skill. As such, it will receive direct and extensive attention in a later chapter which looks at literature study from the perspective of critical reading skills. In any event, the adolescent reader's awareness of a possible symbolic relationship between a literary selection and a fundamental proposition about human experience is one which few English teachers should presume. It is a concept which comprises a vital part of the transition between the reading and study of literature. And one of its obvious prerequisites is a degree of maturity on the part of the reader.

If maturity is of such importance, teachers of early adolescents, that is, students in middle or junior high school, should proceed with caution in introducing the symbol-relating process and should choose works in which the relationships between symbols and their referents are fairly obvious. A readiness activity which may be worth trying is the disseminating and discussing of some short stereotyped passages in which the students are asked to see the physical description of the individual as representative of a class of people. Some examples of such stereotypes would be the *dumb jock* student athlete; the hard-line disciplinarian teacher; the bespectacled bookworm student; the fast-talking, wise-cracking disc jockey; and others. Teachers should probably make up their own stereotypes, tailoring their choices to their local school and community situation. Obviously, racial or ethnic stereotypes should be avoided, as should those which unmistakably indicate some known group which is already the object of dislike or ridicule.

These stereotypes should be short, easy to read, and should provide a content whose elements can be analyzed by a class and then related as a whole to an idea which is already part of their correlative experience. A good deal of oral interaction, combined with one-sentence written summaries of symbolic relationships, are profitable activities once the stereotyped passages have been passed out. The teacher, in this introduction to symbolic representation, would do well to make concrete reference to the ways in which the physical details of the passage come together to develop the stereotyped image.

Once the process of moving from symbol to referent in reading has been introduced and practiced with the stereotyped passages, the teacher can introduce the class to some literary selections in which symbolic representation is fairly easy to perceive. Several of the parables from the New Testament would be appropriate. Since a parable usually contains a narrative followed by its intended moral, the symbolic relationship is explicitly described. Another useful type of selection is the exemplum, such as Chaucer's "The Pardoner's Tale," in which the moral is stated directly and then followed by an illustrative anecdote.

A further level of subtlety can follow the parable and exemplum. Aesop's *Fables* presents a series of clearly perceived stories-with-moral. They have the added advantage of being familiar to many in the class. These can be followed by any number of American folk tales. A host of heroes, heroines, and villains in these stories represent the good guy, the American way, and evil-doers-get-their-just-deserts morality of so many folk tales and legends. The symbolic representation is as readily transparent as most of Aesop's best known yarns.

There are numerous stories and poems which can represent the next level of sophistication. Certainly one of the best known stories in the English language, and one which receives widespread television exposure around Christmastime, is *A Christmas Carol* by Charles Dickens. This story has all the ingredients of an unequivocal symbol-to-referent illustration. It has a protagonist who is converted from *bad guy* to *good guy*. It has ghosts who manipulate Scrooge's metamorphosis. It has the poor, hard-working good guy who is finally given a break. It has a pathetic little crippled lad of great spirit who is given hope. It is all set against the backdrop of a season which symbolizes the virtue in charity and the bestowing of peace on people of good will. And, it is not an overtly religious tale.

The next level of instruction should feature works of more subtle symbolism, and these works can be drawn from the genres of fiction, drama, and poetry. It is in these choices that a teacher's own background as a reader and critic of literature will become a factor of considerable importance. Such a background will assist the teacher in making choices of selections which are not beyond the ken and maturity level of the students who must read and interpret them. This background will also play a role in the teacher's development of adequate background material for enhancing students' abilities to perceive relationships between the selection and its referents. This background must be of such depth as to allow the teacher to present clear and effective background material to students. English teachers will never be more dependent on their academic background than in the preparation of that instruction which will introduce, develop, and reinforce the concept of symbolic representation to adolescents in secondary schools.

Teaching Literature Triangle

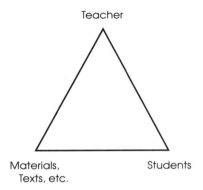

Figure 1.1

One final note about this pedagogical concept: it is truly the culmination of the three concepts described earlier. In order to move from a literary symbol to its general referent, readers must have an adequate fund of correlative experience so that the equation can be completed. Works which symbolize real world values (real to readers, that is) must be representative of that experience which is credible to the reader (i.e., redolent of verisimilitude). Those works which demand willing suspension of disbelief of readers must display a unity of detail which enables those readers to see a message of general and continuing significance through the fantasy and/or improbability of the text. Thus, the search for symbolic meaning in literature has as its prerequisites the kinds of classroom literary experiences which have been presented as meaningful ways of assisting students in their movement from reading to study. There is no clearer indication of success in this transition than in readers' demonstrated ability to relate symbol to referent.

Summary

The most important task faced by teachers of literature in secondary schools is assisting their students in the transition from the reading to the study of literature. Teacher need to accumulate background and experience to become adept in this undertaking. Background and experience come from a knowledge of adolescent psychology. They come from teaching experience at various grade levels and from knowledge of the communities in which teachers live and teach. They come from a broad and intensive personal reading and study of literature and a willingness to elicit personal responses from students.

An indication of these awarenesses will be teachers' choices of literary selections for class study that contain experiences that are truly correlative. Another will be in the balance they establish between selections representing verisimilitude and those which require willing suspension of disbelief. Still another will be reflected in the degree to which teachers balance all-class reading with small group and individual reading activities. Of equal importance is their ability to create response activities which are both varied and genuine. Included in this rubric is the development of evaluation techniques which go beyond the true–false test, six-book-reports-a-year variety. Their ability to guide students to the perception of symbolic meaning will be a true acid test and will require all of the qualities mentioned above. Finally, enthusiasm in the teaching of literature and empathy with honest student response are ingredients without which there will be no real achievement, success, or satisfaction. The most interesting literary selection in the world can go down the tube in the hands of a dull, semi-involved teacher who seems to care little about either the students or the work.

Notes

1. Dwight L. Burton, *Literature Study in the High School*. 3rd ed. New York: Holt, Rinehart & Winston, 1970, p 81.

2. From "The Metamorphosis," from *The Metamorphosis, the Penal Colony, and Other Stories* by Franz Kafka, translated by Willa and Edwin Muir. Copyright 1948 by Schocken Books Inc. Copyright renewed 1975 by Schocken Books Inc. Reprinted by permission of Schocken Books, published by Pantheon Books a division of Random House, Inc.

CHAPTER TWO

The Place of Literature in the Secondary School Curriculum

The well known English educator from the British Isles, John Dixon, made the following statement in the opening chapter of his text *Growth Through English*:

> English is a quicksilver among metals—mobile, living and elusive. Its conflicting emphases challenge us today to look for a new, coherent definition. Its complexity invites the partial and incomplete view, the dangerous simplification that restricts what goes on in the classroom. A map is needed on which the confusing claims and theories can be plotted.[1]

If English is a quicksilver among curricular metals, then literature must be recognized as its most volatile component. To attempt to fix the place of literature study in the public schools of our country, today or any day, is a task which will carry those who are interested all over Dixon's *map*. A brief look at the period from World War I to the present day will provide a clear reflection of that zig-zag journey.

Literature through the Years

As the United States emerged from World War I, substantial changes were both proposed and made in curricula in general and literature in particular. A decreasing preoccupation with Latin and Greek caused a shift in study from the works (in translation, usually) of Cicero, Virgil, Demosthenes, Horace, and others, to such Anglo-Saxon texts as the novels of Sir Walter Scott (*Ivanhoe*), Charles Dickens (*A Tale of Two Cities, Great Expectations*), Robert Louis Stevenson (*Treasure Island, Kidnapped*), and George Eliot (*Silas Marner*). Certain Shakespearean plays also joined the list (*Macbeth, Julius Caesar, A Midsummer Night's Dream*), as did, somewhat surprisingly, a core of genteel American poets: Longfellow, Whittier, Holmes, and Lowell. The rise in popularity of British and American authors represented the growing spirit of nationalism in the United States as well as the country's tradition of both emulating and imitating the literary models penned by authors from the Mother Country.

The spirit of the curriculum was hardly democratic, however. The spirit of classicism still prevailed, as seen in the retention of Latin and Greek in lieu of modern languages, the required study of ancient and medieval history, the presence of enrichment courses in logic and rhetoric, the increasing emphasis on Latinate grammar across the English course of study, and the studied exclusion of American authors (Hawthorne, Melville, Twain, James, Crane), whose works had already gained considerable scholarly esteem abroad. In the form described in the previous paragraph, the literature component of the 1920s to the early 1930s curriculum kept its place in the front ranks, at least in grades 9 through 12.

The Great Depression changed all that. As hard times spread throughout the country and earning a living became a matter of life and death, the entire public school curriculum underwent radical change. Influenced by the reconstructionist theories of John Dewey and by the pragmatism enunciated by William James, the courses of study introduced during the mid 1930s and perpetuated for the twenty years following promoted the survival motive. Consumer mathematics, secretarial courses, vocational education, and health/nutrition offerings appeared in abundance. The English courses reflected this shift. W. Wilbur Hatfield's text, *An Experience Curriculum in English*,[2] sounded the keynote. *Communication for Survival* was its thesis, and this new focus had a profound effect on the status of literature study in the schools. As Dwight Burton notes:

> Practicality and immediacy dominated high school curricula. Literature did not contribute much to the aims of secondary education as then identified. Writers of textbooks on education assigned to literature a vague place in the aesthetic development of the student, or viewed it as a kind of recreational dessert capping the solid nutriment of the really important components of the curriculum. Literature study as such disappeared in many junior high schools, and in some senior high schools. "Core" programs or "common learnings" became widespread, and in the resulting "bloc," literature appeared only when ingenious teachers

could drag it into units of "Modern Transportation" or "Home and Family Problems."[3]

The study of literature stayed pretty much in the background of most English programs through the mid 1950s. Spearheaded by the National Council of Teachers of English (NCTE) Curriculum Commission, under the leadership of Dora V. Smith, the term English Language Arts took center stage in curricular thinking, conferences, and text publication. Communications skills gained a position of top priority, and literature became regarded in many quarters as a frill. Moreover, the English classics mentioned earlier had to move over to make room for modern works by writers such as Hemingway, Fitzgerald, Steinbeck, O'Neill, Frost, Sandburg, and others. A new interest in short fiction and non-Shakespearean drama was beginning to grow, and on the horizon was a new literary form, the well-written Junior Novel (now labelled the Young Adult Novel). This new form was considered by many to be worthy of a place in junior high courses, not just for "leisure reading," but for all-class reading and study. Nevertheless, until the late 1950s, literature study held a back-bench status in the United States.

Three events conspired to change that status in the decade following the year 1957. The first of these, in terms of its curricular impact, was the October 1957 launch of the unmanned space satellite, *Sputnik*, by Soviet scientists. This event had a profound effect on the American psyche—fear, anger, and shock that a *peasant* nation, which had been in existence in its present form of governance for only 40 years, could take the lead in space exploration. One level of society which felt these shock waves most keenly was the education establishment.

Reactions were rapid and significant. The federal government rushed in to establish the National Science Foundation, providing great amounts of money for curricular development projects in science, mathematics, and foreign languages, retaining renowned university scholars to head these projects, and sounding a clarion call for a "return to excellence" in education. That particular war cry echoed through the second Eisenhower administration and was raised to a crescendo during the Kennedy–Johnson years.

This new direction, which was fueled by federal support, was not lost on leaders in the field of English. A year after the Sputnik launch, the executive bodies of the Modern Language Association, College English Association, American Studies Association, and National Council of Teachers of English (NCTE) joined forces to stage a meeting of eminent scholars in the discipline at Carnegie–Mellon University. This meeting quickly became known as the Basic Issues Conference. From it came the demand for a *New English*, decidedly academic in nature, and with that turn of events, the stock of literature study rose almost overnight to a new, unprecedented level of importance.

To catalogue all the manifestos, curricular projects, and federally sponsored programs which emanated from the post-Sputnik frenzy would be digressive. The zeitgeist of that era was probably best stated in the text *Freedom and Discipline in English*,[4] produced by the Commission on English of the College Entrance Examination Board (CEEB). This text articulated or implied several fundamental precepts of the teaching of literature as a big-time player in the movement to excellence:

1. Texts chosen should be of *high quality*.
2. *New Criticism*, in its preference of close-text analysis, provided the guiding principles of literary study.
3. Student response to literary works should be disciplined and scholarly.
4. *Junior books* (their term) should remain wholly apart from classroom literature study.

It can be readily perceived that the place of the literature study had changed drastically from the Deweyan life adjustment era of the two previous decades.

Two other events of that late 1950s period also impacted the study of literature. These events diverged widely from the academic model proposed by the post-*Sputnik* scholar-architects. One which occurred less than two weeks before the *Sputnik* launch was the federally supported, forced integration of Little Rock Central High School, in the Arkansas capital city. This signalled the beginning of massive school integration across the country and eventually promoted an honest examination of the educational needs of Black youth. The term *culturally disadvantaged,* used in the 1960s to characterize this school population, speaks eloquently of educational incapacities and the obvious need to reconcile literature study with that academic plight. Clearly, using works of *high quality* was not the way to begin such a curricular redesign.

A third happening which influenced literature study in the public school was the rapid advance of nonprint media technology. Since *Sputnik,* the effect of commercial television on the whole of American culture has been enormous and, to many concerned social critics, deleterious. "Have you read it?" has been replaced by "Did you see it on TV?" Furthermore, to compete with television, Hollywood film makers have significantly improved the techniques used in their productions. One result of this increased cinematic sophistication can be seen in the incidence of Film Study and Literature on Film courses offered today in hundreds of college English departments. To resist the notion that literature consideration is now multimedia in scope is to be antediluvian in the extreme.

The tenure of literature as a main component of the secondary English curriculum, and one to be presented in full academic form, was short lived. During the period from late 1966 to early 1969, two momentous events, one professional and the other political, sounded the end of this exciting but brief era. The first of these, the professional one, was an August 1966 meeting of British, American, and Canadian English scholars–educators at Dartmouth College in Hanover, New Hampshire. The British educators sharply and eloquently denounced the academically oriented American curricular model, suggesting in its place a more language-experience, student-centered one. John Dixon, quoted earlier, was the United Kingdom representative chosen to write the summary of this three-week seminar from the perspective of the educators from his side of the Atlantic. The two excerpts recorded below, both found in *Growth Through English*, state clearly the contrast in the two approaches as the British viewed them. The United States position appeared thus to these United Kingdom participants:

> Literature itself tended to be treated as a given, a ready-made structure that we imitate and a content that is handed over to us. And this attitude infected composition and all work in language. There was a fatal inattention to the processes involved in everyday activities as talking and thinking things over, writing a diary or a letter home, even enjoying a TV play. Discussion was virtually ignored, as we know to our cost today on both sides of the Atlantic. In other words, the part of the map that relates a man's language to his experience was largely unexplored. . . The purposes and pressures that language serves tended to be reduced to a simple formula—a lump sum view of inheritance.[5]

In the aftermath of the debate at Dartmouth, it was unmistakably clear to most Americans that their British counterparts had made a most persuasive case for their point of view. Literally in its infancy, the academic approach to teaching literature and the place of literary masterpieces at the center of curricular development were rapidly abandoned by scholars, learning theorists, and professional organizations devoted to the teaching of English.

A political event, coming a little more than two years after the showdown at Dartmouth, inflicted a mortal wound in the academic model, but for very different reasons and with equally different results. In November 1968, the American people narrowly elected former Vice-President Richard M. Nixon over the current Vice-President, Hubert H. Humphrey. One of the reasons for this popular decision, as stated by a number of political analysts, was the shape of the public school curriculum of that day and what they felt to be its effect on the rebellious, antiestablishment, "freedom-thinking" youth of the storied 1960s. Early in his administration, President Nixon replaced the literary and historical scholars who had become the educational policy makers of the Kennedy–Johnson reign with a cadre of behavioral psychologists. The direction advocated by these people was labelled "accountability," a term which has been in the forefront of educational thinking ever since.

The accountability model offered a systems approach to curriculum which was tightly prescribed, heavily worksheet driven, and replete with both intermediate and culminating test mechanisms. It emphasized concrete data to be assimilated by students at all levels. Its producers were suspicious of any teaching strategies that didn't produce observable learning activities ("The learner will identify . . . the learner will list . . . the learner will choose. . ." and so on). They also demanded activity which could be precisely tested or measured. Naturally, these behaviorists were suspicious of literature study in most forms with its involvement in interpretation, semantic analysis, and (most suspect of all) aesthetic appreciation.

Soon after this new breed of authorities entered the U.S. Office of Education, systems approaches to English study were being introduced to school districts nationwide. They featured preoccupation with formal grammar, mechanics of written expression, historical elements of linguistics and literary history, and sanitized approaches to reading and writing instruction. They studiously excluded offerings in personal writing and literature study. Corollary innovations in curricula called Career Education and the Right To Read further diminished literature study opportunities in course syllabi. For over ten years, scholarly interpretation was greatly reduced, as was provision for personal, qualitative, affective response to works of any kind, at any level—a dark period indeed for teachers who longed to involve their students in such activity.

The period described above was known as the Back-to-the-Basics time in our public schools. During this period, just as in the Depression era, the goal of education was perceived to be the training of young people for the vocational aspects of adult life. Thus the *content* of reading shifted significantly from literary materials to those which adults needed to understand as employees, as trainees for occupations, as consumers, and as active participants in the community's decision-making process (i.e., as enlightened voters). Those priorities left much less room for teaching and study of literature. The term which was used to indicate the main outcome to be desired from virtually all educational effort was that of Functional Literacy among all soon-to-be adults. A major activity during that period was the statewide testing programs, first put into operation in Florida in fall, 1977, and within a few years, functioning in all fifty states. Virtually all of these basic skills tests concentrated on reading, writing (in several forms), and computation. The Florida program featured tests, all multiple choice for economic reasons, at grades 3, 5, 8, and 11, with a separate one, titled the Functional Literacy Test, tossed in at grade 11.

Perhaps "tossed in" does not accurately characterize the second 11th grade specimen since it was tied, by the Florida legislature, to the granting of the high school diploma (i.e., no pass, no graduate). This decision was soon challenged by several parent groups, but in 1983, the constitutionality of the law was upheld at both the U.S. District and Circuit Court levels. More germane to the focus of this chapter, however, was the fact that its reading component contained twenty-eight items, more than one-third of the test, which centered on critical reading abilities. Resourceful high school teachers, in attempting to prepare their students for this phase of the test, turned to literary works, especially short stories and poems, for their content. In the battle to keep literature's place in the curriculum a viable one, its use as a vehicle for teaching critical reading took on increased value.

Since education is a reflection of society, and much of the movement of society is cyclical, the Back-to-the-Basics, Functional Literacy, Individually Prescribed Instruction mania began to give way in the early 1980s to another cry of alarm raised by several highly visible educational observers and critics of the day. In August 1981, President Ronald Reagan's Education Secretary, Terrell H. Bell, appointed a National Commission on Excellence in Education chaired by Dr. David Gardner, then president-elect of the University of California, Berkeley. Less than two years later, the Commission published its report titled *A Nation at Risk*. This relatively brief document proclaimed that public education in the United States was "adrift in a sea of mediocrity." With this catch phrase, the Gardner report signalled the beginning of the major trend of that decade, which was the effort to improve the quality of the curriculum. Most state education leaders, in an effort to respond to the gauntlet laid down in the report, began to take steps to "improve" the curricula, particularly in secondary schools. The direction taken in most of these efforts was to return to a decidedly academic form of curriculum.

The implications for the new look in literature treatment in those curricula would seem almost self-evident. Two findings in the Gardner Report, under the title *Indicators of the Risk*, provided part of the rationale for such a change:

> The College Board's Scholastic Aptitude Tests (SAT) demonstrate a virtually unbroken decline from 1963 to 1980. Average verbal scores fell over 50 points and average mathematics scores dropped nearly 40 points.

College Board achievement tests also reveal consistent declines in recent years in such subjects as physics and English.[6]

In two other places, the report indicated the need for a heightened emphasis on literature study. In "Findings," the report states:

Too few experienced teachers and scholars are involved in writing textbooks. During the past decade or so a large number of texts have been "written down" by their publishers to ever-lower reading levels in response to perceived market demands. . . .[7]

In many schools, the time spent learning how to cook and drive counts as much toward a high school diploma as the time spent studying mathematics, English, chemistry, U.S. history, or biology.[8]

In the first point made in "Recommendations," the report further states:

The teaching of ENGLISH in high school should equip graduates to: (a) comprehend, interpret, evaluate, and use what they read; (b) write well-organized, effective papers; (c) listen effectively and discuss ideas intelligently; and (d) know our literary heritage and how it enhances imagination and ethical understanding, and how it relates to the customs, ideas, and values of today's life and culture.[9]

Thus an influential commission study once again catalyzed a new role of literature study in the public schools.

Also in 1983, the Carnegie Commission published the report of a study, begun in 1980 and chaired by the charismatic former U.S. Commissioner of Education, Ernest Boyer, succinctly titled *High School*.[10] Because of the comprehensiveness of the project and the status of its participants, the Carnegie Report had an even greater impact on public education officials nationwide than did the Gardner Commission's report. It was no less critical of public school curricula than its counterpart but, because of its narrower focus, had a stronger influence on those responsible for secondary school programs of study. Here are the four essential goals proposed by Boyer and his committee:

First, the high school should help all students develop the capacity to think critically and communicate effectively through a mastery of language.

Second, the high school should help all students learn about themselves, the human heritage, and the interdependent world in which they live through a core curriculum based upon consequential human experiences common to all people.

143,243

LIBRARY
College of St. Francis
JOLIET. ILLINOIS

Third, the high school should prepare all students for work and further education through a program of electives that develop individual aptitudes and interests.

Fourth, the high school should help all students fulfill their social and civic obligations through school and community service.[11]

Later in this lengthy document, the following statement of recommendation on literature teaching can be found:

Literature. As a first step we recommend that all students, through a study of literature, discover our common literary heritage and learn about the power and beauty of the written word.

At the turn of the century, there was, in this country, what amounted to a core curriculum in literature. In more than 25 percent of the public schools, the following works were included: *The Merchant of Venice, Julius Caesar*, "First Bunker Hill Oration," *The Sketch Book, Evangeline*, "The Vision of Sir Launfal," "Snow-Bound," *Macbeth, The Lady of the Lake, Hamlet*, "The Deserted Village," "Gray's Elegy," Thanatopsis," *As You Like It*. Today, most students take at least one literature course to meet the English graduation requirements, but rarely do they encounter, in depth, enduring works of literature.

We do not propose a national great books curriculum. We do propose, however, a one-year literature course in which all students discover that creative writers are, as Abrams said, both the mirror and the lamp of the time. Through comedies and tragedies of ancient Greek playwrights, the plays of Shakespeare, as well as the work of contemporary authors, students should be introduced to basic human questions and dilemmas and be inspired to return to great literature time and time again.

In one school we visited, a group of high school teachers spoke of using literature to help students better understand life's deeper meanings. A teacher with master's degrees in both English literature and psychology said:

"My background in literature is more useful [than my psychology background] in helping students understand human motivations and in making them more sensitive people... They need to feel, through literature, a relationship and kinship with the human family."

Many literature classes we visited were not inspired. Language skills, not great literature, were being taught. Poetry was used to teach punctuation. Course guides spoke only vaguely about the contributions of great writers. Rarely were great books listed as required reading.

Still more discouraging was the inclination to introduce only "gifted" students to great literature. At Garfield High, college preparatory students were reading Milton's *Paradise Lost* and e.e. cummings's "in Just-spring". These treasures were not being taught to students in the general and vocational program.

Literature addresses the emotional part of the human experience. It provides another perspective on historical events, telling us what matters and what has mattered to people in the past. Literature transmits from generation to generation enduring spiritual and ethical values. As an art form, literature can bring delight and re-creation. As a vehicle for illustrating moral behavior by specific example (Job, Odysseus, Oedipus, Hamlet, Billy Budd, Captain Queeg) it speaks to all. As great literature speaks to all people, it must be available to all students.[12]

It could be reasonably concluded that the two reports described above could well have returned the study of literature to the place it held during the days following the *Sputnik* revelation and the 1958 Basic Issues Conference manifesto, and in some ways it did. There were, and are, some significant differences in the current place of literature study in the schools. Some factors which have created this distinctive (from the 1960s) position are as follows:

1. The accountability philosophy which still has a stranglehold on most state programs.
2. The *Great Testing Movement* which is far from over and which remains the main instrument for making school districts *accountable*.
3. The demand for multi-ethnic and feminist literary elements which have had a profound impact on all literature texts published in the last twenty years.
4. The current awareness of the inadequate critical reading abilities of adolescents—revealed to some extent by statewide testing results.

To the above factors must be added the current (as this text is written) concern of education watchers for the Cultural Literacy, or lack thereof, of our young people.

A great deal has been written since 1985 about the lack of cultural awareness found among teen-age Americans. In this summary, however, only two will be cited. (To overlook documentary influences, however, would be inexcusable in this chapter; it is the Cultural Literacy movement which has had the greatest influence of any on the way in which literature study in the schools is being viewed today.) Most of the proponents, and indeed architects, of the Cultural Literacy paradigm have been, or now are, in the ranks of leadership in the National Endowment for the Humanities (NEH), a federally sponsored organization which has become the most prominent critic of literature study in public schools in the present day.

In the Foreword (written by Ms. Lynn Cheney, chairperson of the Advisory Group on History and Literature) to *American Memory*, published by NEH in 1987, the following statement is made:

> We at NEH undertook this study enthusiastically. In 1984, under the chairmanship of my predecessor William Bennett, NEH had issued *To Reclaim a Legacy*, a report on the humanities in higher education. It was time for us to consider elementary and secondary schools. Indeed, for many reasons, it seemed urgent to do so. A number of thoughtful observers were expressing alarm about the state of the humanities in our schools, but history and literature were not emerging as central concerns in the various state, regional, and national commissions looking at education. Educational reform was in the air, but the humanities were seldom a part of it.
>
> And so it was with the sense of being about an important task that an advisory group on history and literature first met on March 2, 1987. I convened this group twice more. Our discussions were informed by readings, statistical data, short presentations by outside experts, and by the results of an NEH-funded nationwide test of what seventeen-year-olds know about history and literature.[13]

This statement reveals two important facts: (1) the goal of the study undertaken by this Advisory Group and (2) the spiritual founder of the Cultural Literacy movement. Since his tour of duty at NEH, Mr. Bennett has, as history records, gone on to positions of major responsibility in the U.S. Government, first as U.S. Commissioner of Education in the (second) Reagan administration, and later as the Drug Czar under President George Bush. The ongoing influence of Cultural Literacy on curricular change is, to a considerable degree, testimony of the stature of this energetic, often confrontational, public figure.

American Memory voices dismay at the current lack of awareness rampant among young people of the major facets of Western civilization, both in its history and literature. Once this dismay has been articulated, Ms. Cheney and her group make some proposals for change which are clearly worth noting. The former perception/concern is voiced in the opening statement:

> Cultural memory flourishes or declines for many reasons, but among the most important is what happens in our schools. Long relied upon to transmit knowledge of the past to upcoming generations, our schools today appear to be about a different task. Instead of preserving the past, they more often disregard it, sometimes in the name of "progress"—the idea that today has little to learn from yesterday. But usually the culprit is "process"—the belief that we can teach our children HOW to think without troubling them to learn anything worth thinking about, the belief

that we can teach them HOW to understand the world in which they live without conveying to them the events and ideas that have brought them into existence.[14]

Another follows shortly:

> Current reformers have emphasized the necessity of paying close attention to WHAT our children learn as well as to HOW they learn, but their message has proved difficult to translate into the classroom. In Texas, new "Rules for Curriculum" have been issued that set forth "essential elements" for three English/language arts courses required in high schools: how "to vary rate of reading according to purpose," how "to recognize relevant details," for example. Among the essential elements—more than one hundred in all—there is just one mention of major literary works and authors.[15]

The Group then offers a number of suggestions for dealing with the problem at the classroom level. Here are two noteworthy ones:

> By their nature, the humanities disciplines ought to be the easiest to bring to everyone. While some students will need more help than others with the language of Shakespeare's plays, for example, the themes that animate the plays—love, honor, betrayal, revenge—are familiar to all and interesting to all. Moreover, once the case for humanities education has been made, the conclusion that it is for every student seems inevitable. If history gives us perspective on our lives, then shouldn't every young person be encouraged to study it? If literature connects us to permanent concerns, then shouldn't every young person read it? "To make the best that has been thought and known in the world current everywhere" is the way Matthew Arnold stated the goal. No other ambition suits a democracy well.[16]
>
> One step that should be taken is to assign textbooks a less important role. Let teachers enlighten their students with real books—real works by real authors in the same form in which they are read by the rest of us. Many teachers do this now, often paying for real books out of their own pockets since their schools' book budgets are consumed by textbooks.[17]

In 1988, the California Assembly (legislature) passed some exacting legislation demanding that "real literature" replace several of the "watered down" language arts texts in current use, an unmistakable result of the pressure being applied by NEH leaders to restore quality to the literature curriculum in the final decade of this century.

A much more popular influence on the current place of literature in the curriculum, however, can be found in a text titled *Cultural Literacy: What Every American Needs to Know,* by E. D. Hirsch, Jr.[18] Dr. Hirsch, who was a

Historical Development of English Curriculum

1930s **Great Depression**	1940s **World War II**	1950s **School Desegregation Sputnik**	1960s **The Great Society Vietnam**	1970s **Accountability Watergate**	1980s **Japan's and Germany's Ascendancy Technology Explosion**
→	→	→	→	→	→
Experience Curriculum in English	Emergence of Junior High Young-Adult Fiction	Basic Issues Conference Curricula for the Disadvantaged	Tripod Curriculum Dartmouth Conference	Behavioral Objectives Functional Literacy Minimum Competencies	Quality Curriculum Cultural Literacy

Figure 2.1

senior fellow at NEH (his name appears on the roster of Ms. Cheney's advisory group), teaches at the University of Virginia. His text, written partially to report the results of research he had conducted in the cultural backgrounds of a large sample of American teenagers, has become the most widely read book on education since Jerome Bruner's *Process of Education* (1960), and Postman and Weingartner's *Teaching as a Subversive Activity* (1969).

To editorialize about the thesis of *Cultural Literacy* would seem unnecessary. What follows is the presentation of a few excerpts; the inferences to be drawn regarding their relation to proposed literature teaching are self-evident.

From the Preface:

> To be culturally literate is to possess the basic information needed to thrive in the modern world. The breadth of that information is great, extending over the major domains of human activity from sports to science. It is by no means confined to "culture" narrowly understood as an acquaintance with the arts. Nor is it confined to one social class. Quite the contrary. Cultural literacy constitutes the only sure avenue of opportunity for disadvantaged children, the only reliable way of combating the social determinism that now condemns them to remain in the same social and educational condition as their parents. That children from poor and illiterate homes tend to remain poor and illiterate is an unacceptable failure of our schools, one which has occurred not because our teachers are inept but chiefly because they are compelled to teach a fragmented curriculum based on faulty educational theories. Some say that our schools by themselves are powerless to change the cycle of poverty and illiteracy. I do not agree. They *can* break the cycle, but only if they themselves break fundamentally with some of the theories and practices that education professors and school administrators have followed over the past fifty years.[19]

And from his opening chapter:

> We Americans have long accepted literacy as a paramount aim of schooling, but only recently have some of us who have done research in the field begun to realize that literacy is far more than a skill and that it requires large amounts of specific information. That new insight is central to this book.
>
> Professor Chall is one of several reading specialists who have observed that "world knowledge" is essential to the development of reading and writing skills. What she calls world knowledge I call cultural literacy, namely, the network of information that all competent readers possess. It is the background information, stored in their minds, that enables them to take up a newspaper and read it with an adequate level

of comprehension, getting the point, grasping the implications, relating what they read to the unstated context which alone gives meaning to what they read. In describing the contents of this neglected domain of background information, I try to direct attention to a new opening that can help our schools make the significant improvement in education that has so far eluded us. The achievement of high universal literacy is the key to all other fundamental improvements in American education.[20]

One of Hirsch's more controversial positions lies in his fervent support of memorization in the classroom. Later in the same chapter, he states:

Children also need to understand elements of our literary and mythic heritage that are often alluded to without explanation, for example, Adam and Eve, Cain and Abel, Noah and the Flood, David and Goliath, the Twenty-third Psalm, Humpty Dumpty, Jack Sprat, Mary had a little lamb, Peter Pan, and Pinocchio. Also Achilles, Robin Hood, Paul Bunyan, Satan, Sleeping Beauty, Sodom and Gomorrah, the Ten Commandments, and Tweedledum and Tweedledee.

Our current distaste for memorization is more pious than realistic. At an early age when their memories are most retentive, children have an almost instinctive urge to learn specific tribal traditions. At that age they seem to be fascinated by catalogues of information and are eager to master the materials that authenticate their membership in adult society. Observe for example how they memorize the rather complex materials of football, baseball, and basketball, even without benefit of formal avenues by which that information is inculcated.[21]

The author identifies a number of implications for his description of the current status and needs of the culture-deficient curriculum. He leads off this discussion with:

Having traced the nature of cultural literacy and shown its importance to national education, I want to consider the practical implications of the ideas I have set forth.

One immediate implication is that we have an obligation to identify and publish the contents of cultural literacy. It is reasonable to think that those contents can be identified explicitly, since they are identified **implicitly** by every writer or speaker who addresses the general public. If writers did not make tacit assumptions about the knowledge they could take for granted in their audience, their writing would be so cumbersome as to defeat the aim of communication.

It is true that the specific content of the national literate vocabulary changes from year to year, even from day to day, as striking events catch the national attention. But such changes are few when compared to the words and associations that stay the same. Of course, one literate person's sense of the shared national vocabulary is not precisely identical with another's; individual experiences produce different assumptions in different people about shared knowledge. But these differences are insignificant compared to what is common in the systems of associations that we acquire by daily experiences of literate culture.

It's also true that we adapt our conjectures about what others know to particular circumstances. Obviously, the knowledge we assume when we talk to a young child is substantially different from that which we take for granted in addressing an educated adult, and we constantly make other adjustments to our audiences. But when we address a general audience we must assume that we are addressing a "common reader," that is, a literate person who shares with us a common body of knowledge and associations. Since we so frequently have to posit a common reader in writing or public speaking, it should be possible to reach a large measure of agreement about what that common reader knows.[22]

As this text is being composed, the influence of Hirsch's view of Cultural Literacy remains a significant one on the shaping of the current literature programs of study. Not the only force, however. The residue of these past seventy-five years or so clings to the current structure in a number of ways. It seems reasonable for us to look next at some of the more prominent aspects of both the rationale and purpose of the literature curriculum as it exists today in American secondary schools.

Dimensions and Options

In part, the foregoing historical review should provide teachers of literature with a series of options. While the Cultural Literacy preoccupation of many contemporary educational theorists is undoubtedly having an effect on programs through the fifty states, the several trends and emphases previously recounted reveal the number of ways in which the literature component can take its rightful place. It must be kept in mind that public education in America is first and foremost a locally directed enterprise. Unlike many European countries, there is no national program of studies. Each school district, therefore, is left with the decision on how its curriculum should be developed. Unquestionably, the statewide testing programs introduced during the late 1970s have influenced and continue to influence curricula established in school districts. Just how those curricula are established, however, remains in the hands of local school boards and the program specialists they hire.

Before embarking on a description of teachers' options, which are based on the dimensions of literature appropriate for investigation, a definition of *literature* is needed. The definition offered by the noted scholars Ren Wellek and Austin Warren in their text *Theory of Literature* is an appropriate one. It limits works to be considered as *literature* to those which deal with the "world of fiction, of imagination."[23] We contend that such a definition limits the study of literature to such works as those that represent the genres of fiction, drama, and poetry. Such a definition, logically, excludes such forms as biography, essay, editorial, sermon, epistle, and so forth, and allows teachers and scholars to focus their attention accordingly. Such a delimitation will govern most of the discussion which follows.

Despite the constraints placed on literary study in the preceding statement, today's secondary school English teachers who are given the freedom to do so can place literature in several positions in their course of study. The six described below are those which the authors of this text support most enthusiastically. One reason for this enthusiasm lies in the flexibility which these perspectives provide. With them, teachers can work within the frameworks provided by most departments and districts and, at the same time, retain their sense of individuality in designing literary instruction.

It is in that spirit of flexibility that the options are presented in an *If . . . then* format (i.e., the teachers finding themselves in a particular construct can reconcile one of these positions to the current state of affairs).

Critical Reading

If the espoused goal is to promote critical reading abilities, then literature offers an excellent vehicle for such promotion. In reading instructional parlance, the main ideas in virtually all literary works are implied rather than expressed. It seems patently absurd to expect to find an author's theme expressed directly in any work of literature, certainly in any work of high quality. Thus, in finding central meaning in any literary selection, the student will face the need to draw inferences, make judgments, arrive at (individual) conclusions, create and test hypotheses, make predictions, analyze data for their interrelatedness, and establish connections between symbols and their referents. All of those processes represent facets of the critical reading process. The carry-over value of this process into *real world* materials, for example, political tracts, advertising blurbs, propagandistic pieces, proposed bureaucratic and legislative mandates, product warranties/guarantees, and so forth, would seem self-evident. From the critical reading perspective, literature can be viewed as excellent *training material*.

Not to appear Machiavellian, we feel that the critical reading option is one which can be readily sold to school administrators, school board members, and skeptical parent groups (the latter often categorizing literature as a frill). The results of Functional Literacy Test data analyses, now twelve years' worth as this chapter is being written, point to a consistent pattern of weakness in tenth graders' critical reading capacities in the large and diverse state of Florida. These data have revealed persistent student difficulty in responding to items which reflect the following four reading objectives:

1. To infer an idea from a selection
2. To infer a cause or effect of an action
3. To identify a fact or an opinion and to distinguish between a fact and an opinion
4. To recognize an unstated opinion

Difficulties in dealing with such items have been found in students enrolled in schools from Pensacola to Key West, and across, proportionately, all ability levels. Such results constitute a persuasive argument for increased use of literature in the Florida secondary school curriculum and the selection of works containing central meanings which are subtly expressed.

Teachers' effective inclusion of critical reading strategies will be discussed later in this text, principally in Chapters Three and Six. Unquestionably, the recent emphases on Reader-Response orientation to literary consideration can be especially helpful to teachers who count among their major goals the establishment of independent critical judgement among their middle school, junior high, and senior high school students. This is the perspective which can be most clearly associated with the continuing demand for Accountability in the public school curriculum.

Reflection on Correlative Experience

If young readers are to be encouraged to consider human concerns, problems, and values which often pertain to their own lives, then literature offers a commodity in which the human situation can be examined. And, unlike such examination of problems as considered by counselors in the school guidance suite, they can be studied and evaluated in a nonthreatening environment. The crises, both major and minor, faced by characters in novels, plays, poems, and short stories offer situations which can be studied and reacted to by students from a detached angle of vision. They are spectators and commentators on these dramatic situations. The manner and degree to which they correlate these vicarious experiences with those in their own background is up to them. Through the assistance of teachers who are sensitive to such possible correlates but still judicious enough not to play the role of Sigmund Freud in the classroom, these correlative realizations can be meaningful indeed.

In "The Red Pony" by John Steinbeck, for example, Jody's desire to possess a colt of his very own allows him to place his friend and role model, Billy Buck, in an untenable position (i.e., having to deliver the impossible in order to maintain his image as the all-wise, omnipotent adult). Billy's initial failure and subsequent triumph, both selfless in nature, provide a powerful opportunity for students to consider human strengths and limitations during their own maturation process.

In *The Glass Menagerie* by Tennessee Williams, Laura ultimately realizes that to venture out of the world of her small but precious collection of tiny, delicate artifacts constitutes a risk that can have disastrous consequences and, at the play's end, that she's not yet ready to step out into the world beyond her limited but reassuring microcosm.

In *Lord of the Flies* by William Golding, Ralph struggles to maintain a sense of order among his peers. He confronts the need to reconcile the use of reason with the use of force and passion as he vies for the leadership role. He clearly sees, as he decides whether or not to confront the violent and contentious Jack, what is at stake in making this reconciliation, as well as the possible losses to be sustained by total capitulation.

In *A Separate Peace* by John Knowles, Gene Forrester finally comes to grips, after a long period of unwillingness to do so, with his mixed feelings—admiration and envy, loyalty and exasperation—for his friend and hero, Phineas. The gradual but inexorable manner in which he discovers his true feelings toward this intimate companion causes him a great deal of dismay and self-deprecation but ultimately provides him with a powerful lesson in honest self-assessment.

In all four of these literary instances, significant problems of self-awareness and definition are to be found at the core of the text. The issues are usually painfully compelling, the need for careful and candid examination of the problems is unavoidable, and the potential for increased self-awareness by young people encountering these issues is great.

The Cultural Heritage

Related to the pronouncements in the Cheney and Hirsch texts cited previously is the fact that literature does offer students opportunities to examine backgrounds—political, social, economic, and recreational—to which they have fallen heir. It is a unique opportunity because authors of imaginative literature view the past not through the hard data compiled by the census taker, the historian, or the sociologist, but through the prism of imagination. If, therefore, students want to know more and *different* things about the Great Depression, they can read The *Grapes of Wrath* or *The Bluest Eye* (Toni Morrison, 1970). If they want to inspect World War I from the soldier's point of view, they can read *A Farewell to Arms* or *All Quiet on the Western Front.* If they want to become acquainted with the direction earlier writers felt that technology was dictating, they can read *Gulliver's Travels, Erewhon, Brave New World,* or *The Adding Machine.* If they want to look at some forerunners to the Feminist Movement, they can read *The Awakening* or *A Doll's House.* If they want to consider the manner and degree to which the New England Puritan society affected individual fears and aspirations, they can read *The Scarlet Letter* or *The Crucible.*

All of the above are mentioned primarily to whet the appetite of those teachers who would assist students in developing an awareness of "the way it was back then," whether "back then" refers to the frustrations caused by the Korean War as seen in Michener's *The Bridge at Toko-Ri* or the glory that was the Roman Empire as seen in *Julius Caesar* and *Antony and Cleopatra.*

Pleasure and Recreation

If teachers wish to provide their students with the wherewithal to use their leisure time constructively, then the introduction of literature as recreational reading activity is well worth considering. In this sense, the reading of books for enrichment and pleasure can pose a viable alternative to watching television, attending rock concerts, or viewing vapid films. If the goal is pleasure and recreation, some of the conventional approaches to all-class, intensive reading of selections, for example, recitations, essay exams, book reports, graded activities, and so forth, must be replaced with a more informal, individualized style. Beyond that, *choice* from wide reading lists must replace mandates as a criterion for student involvement. The teacher must also reconsider, in a certain sense, the imposition of narrow, elitist views on taste (i.e., the so-called academic canon of Great Books must be temporarily abandoned as one of the course requirements). Several other guidelines should be considered if this use of literature is to be attempted:

1. The usual attempt at finding profound metaphysical revelations in reading literature must be temporarily suspended.
2. Adequate time to reflect individually on what has just been read, an opportunity not usually accompanying television or commercial films, probably must be built in. For some excellent suggestions on ways to do so, see Fader, Daniel N. and Elton B. McNeil. *Hooked on Books: Program & Proof.* New York: Berkley, 1968.
3. Catharsis in and from reading can take the form of joy and sadness as well as in intellectual enlightenment, and it should be valued.

4. The teacher must keep in mind that, at times, to empathize is to enjoy and that enjoyment can be spontaneous and even somewhat mindless (e.g., the sudden belly laugh).

5. Opportunities for students to share their responses to what they have read in a leisurely manner, both with their peers and their teacher, are to be encouraged.

6. Even in this era of prolonged Accountability, free reading time, occasionally built into class schedules, continues to be a very good idea.

Even though such reading activities need to be relatively free from restrictions, the teacher should not abandon a commitment to literary quality in developing reading lists or advising students on choices. Some choices, reflective of such judiciousness, are offered below:

1. Kaufman and Hart, *You Can't Take It with You* (play)—a light-hearted treatment of a businessman's escape from the rat-race

2. *The Hobbit* and its fellow exotica—an exciting and still popular jaunt through the strange, bizarre, and improbable

3. Novels of Daphne du Maurier—sentimentalized views of romantic life, to be sure, but still a cut above the formulaic stuff in the "Silhouette" and "Harlequin" series, and in no way comparable to the many semipornographic novels available today

4. The short pieces, both fictional and nonfictional, of E. B. White and James Thurber, in which the authors poke gentle fun at human institutions and at a variety of human frailties

5. The Stephen King novels—a little violent in spots but still highly popular and clearly lacking in sadism, brutality, and prurience

6. The plays of Neil Simon—some care in choice of titles may be necessary in order to avoid censorship problems; some clever treatment of contemporary life, including adolescent coming of age in *Brighton Beach Memoirs* and *Biloxi Blues*

If reading of literature is to become a truly life-long experience, some contribution by the high school curriculum probably needs to be made. It is well worth the effort.

Study of Aesthetics

It is hard to argue with the contention that works of literature can and probably should be placed alongside such creations as music, painting, photography, sculpture, architecture, and dance as being worthy of assessment for their beauty. Courses in art and music appreciation can be found in a large number of secondary schools today, as well as school-sponsored activity in photography, various kinds of music, and dance. Appreciation of literature may not be very easy to teach, especially by those accountability-oriented teachers who live and die by cause and effect activities and whose passion is to put lots of grades in the grade book, but it *happens* and should be promoted in the classroom.

Beauty is the outcome of the manipulation of language and exists in physical (through description), intellectual, emotional, and tonal dimensions. It does so with words rather than with space, color, or (usually) sound. The meticulously careful placement of juxtaposed words, phrases, and metaphors to produce certain aesthetic effects should not be ignored. What has done violence to such pursuits has been the relentless, metronomic review by some teachers of rhyme schemes and metrical patterns in lyric poetry, usually before any attempt to deal with meaning has been made. A great deal of sharing of aesthetic responses, often spontaneous, by students and teachers would also help the cause. And *new* works, that is, those which are not anthologized to death, should be presented on regular occasions to see what reactions they engender.

While much of the aesthetic preoccupation in literature study will necessarily occur with poetic and dramatic selections, short fiction and excerpts from novels should not be overlooked. It was Flaubert who expressed his desire to fashion his prose in such a manner that it would be as poetry—unchangeable. In this endeavor, he served as a source of inspiration to many of the renowned novelists of the twentieth century. Segments of the works of James Joyce (the last section of his story "The Dead" comes to mind), Virginia Woolf, Albert Camus, William Faulkner, Ernest Hemingway, Walker Percy, Doris Lessing, and John Updike make for such aesthetic review. Their incorporation of lucid physical image, tonal resonance, and inner reflection are worth a closer look. And this list of prose fiction artists is barely representative.

Obviously, poetic selections, far too numerous to mention, will figure prominently in applying aesthetics to literature study. There is also plenty of drama to consider, as in some of the choruses in Greek tragedy, a plethora of soliloquies from Shakespeare, the lyrical passages found in *Cyrano de Bergerac*, much of the verse created by Maxwell Anderson in such plays as *Winterset* and *Elizabeth the Queen*, and even the epitaph uttered by Uncle Charley at the end of *Death of a Salesman*. Language has beauty, and as Keats said, "beauty is truth." That may not be all one ever needs to know, but the beauty in the printed words of imaginative literature needs attention, enthusiastic attention, and strategic emphasis. Its impact may last in both the active and subconscious minds of some students for a very long time. And teachers can't always predict which students are the most impressionable.

Preparation for Scholarship

Literature is a subject that students will encounter in institutions of higher education. Most of them will face it as part of their required work during those first two arduous years, usually labelled as *Basic Liberal Studies*. It occurs regularly as one of the components of freshman English, often one whole term's work, and it comprises part of the *Humanities and the Arts* component often prescribed for the first two-year sequence. Whether students who graduate from high school enter a two-year community college, a four-year college, or a university with its elaborate graduate programs of study, they will most likely find some form of literature study awaiting them upon arrival. Thus some attention to more scholarly approaches to the study of literature needs to be included in whatever poses as college preparation programs in today's high schools. Many college freshmen and sophomores also elect to take college courses in humanities, theater, and oral interpretation. These courses also contain elements of literary study for which well-designed, effectively taught high school literature components can help to prepare them well.

Beyond these first two years, it is a fact that some students take a college major in English, which usually means they opt to major in literature. And that number has risen dramatically in institutions coast to coast since 1985. Many of those majors, when asked why they chose this major, identify high school English teachers who had inspired them with their approach to works of literature, and this inspiration has led them to study literature in greater depth. A smaller number of college students pursue this study on into graduate school, a few going all the way to the Ph.D. degree. Wherever their formal literary study comes to an end, a significant number trace its origins back to the high school teachers (not courses, authors, or works) who have motivated this serious decision.

The most helpful preparation for the serious study of literature is almost invariably found in the Advanced Placement English courses. Since they will be described in some detail later in this text, no attempt will be made at this point to do more than note their presence and purpose. There are several other course offerings, variously titled, "Advanced," "Accelerated," and "Honors," which are designed expressly for the college-bound and whose main emphasis is on literature study.

For those who will study English beyond high school, literature will be perceived as a component of the higher education curriculum. To study it successfully at that level, students need background in its history, especially as it occurs in the Anglo-Saxon culture, its forms, modes, archetypal patterns, and great authors. They will also profit from intensive study of a representative group of its most renowned selections and from some passing acquaintance with critical and scholarly statements written about some of its featured selections. In a significant number of high schools, these college prep literature courses can provide an introduction through which the students' chances for success in college are increased.

Middle School Components

Middle school curricular leaders have taken a different direction from the high schools. This direction is basically student (early adolescent) centered and eschews the establishment of separate courses in the traditional content areas in favor of a more integrated content approach. To put such an approach into operation, teachers at the several middle school grade levels have been formed into *teams,* and their curricula take the form of integrated learning. Thus an instructional must in "the family" may include some sociological and historical considerations (from social studies teachers), some physiological and health considerations (from science teachers), some consumer considerations (from math teachers), and some language-oriented considerations (from English teachers). English teachers will probably be asked to provide some instruction featuring literary works emphasizing family life, problems, aspirations, and so forth. Thus the thematic approach to literary study would be the one probably most compatible with this recent, and initially popular, development. Since the thematic scheme will be described in the chapter on focused approaches to organization of literature study, no attempt will be made to amplify it here. It is worth maintaining, however, that future teachers of English in many middle schools will be asked to teach literature in a considerably broader context than has been taught to them in their earlier school years.

Individual Concerns

The foregoing discussion emphasized the broader elements of English components and their place in the broader curricular spectrum. Some attention should be given the individual teacher's role in the process. For reasons of direct communication (avoiding his/her or their), this chapter will address you, the teacher.

As you plan to teach literature to young people, keep the following aspects of the task in mind:

1. **You and Them** *You* are, typically, an English major, which is to say that you are a literature major. *They* are younger, less mature, have read much less, and have certainly not read with the same degree of intensity as you have. Don't use yourself, your abilities, your background, your analytic powers, or your skill as a reader as measuring sticks when dealing with *them* in the classroom.

2. **Classics and Junk** You may have a great temptation to force some unreasonably long, subtle, mature, sophisticated texts on your students in the name of exposing them to *the best.* Find out what *they* like, what *they* read, and how *they* read before making decisions about what works to assign. Never forget how important correlative experience is in literary understanding.

3. **Multiethnic Materials** Whenever possible, try to supplement or even balance the Anglo-Saxon texts you choose with those by and about African-Americans, Hispanics, Native Americans, Asians, and those of other cultures. This is particularly important in classes which include minority students. In doing so, however, retain your literary standards.

4. **Old versus New** Try to maintain some equilibrium between the older works you choose to teach and more contemporary ones. Too many selections from the distant past may bore, confuse, or irritate your students. It helps when students have some prior awareness of the events described in a work of literature.

5. **Nature of Student Involvement** Consider choices which include works studied by the entire class, those which can be studied through group involvement, and those which become individual choices made by your students from wide reading lists you compose. Try to avoid constant use of one text with the entire class.

6. **Print and Nonprint Selections** Don't stick your head in the sand when it comes to modes of presentation in literature study. People who use audio cassettes, video tapes, films, and/or slides to complement, reinforce, and extend their reading tasks and assignments are not necessarily compromising their standards. Many text messages are clarified, and many visual impressions are intensified, when they are heard and seen as well as read. Once again, proportion of use is a determining factor.

7. **Use of the Anthology** Avoid making the assigned anthology your course of study. If you do, you will be using someone else's ideas and giving their assignments, with little or no original decisions of your own. You teach best what you like best, and while you can't turn your literature course into a review of your favorite selections, it's always a good idea to work them in when the

context is appropriate. It's also wise to be on the lookout for new (to you) texts which will extend, vitalize, and deepen the concepts you are trying to present to your students through literature study. By passively accepting the anthology as your September-to-June literary resource, you'll become deadly prosaic far more quickly than you may realize.

8. **Staying in Touch** Keep a check on your own literary preferences and values. Try having your fellow English teachers list the five (arbitrary number) selections they either enjoy teaching most or would like to teach. Then compare lists through the group. The similarities, differences, and reasons for choices should prove most interesting to you and your colleagues. Establishing new patterns of study based on these choices could also be engrossing when, of course, a cooperative spirit prevails.

Thus the suggestions to you as you endeavor to fit your course of study into its most coherent slot in the overall picture. Literature study continues to be a versatile and significant element in any secondary curriculum. Developing your own perspectives and integrating them into that course of study would be a most refreshing and professionally sound starting point.

Notes

1. John Dixon. *Growth Through English*. Reading: National Association for the Teaching of English, 1967, p 1.

2. W. Wilbur Hatfield, Chairman. *An Experience Curriculum in English*. A Report of the Curriculum Commission of the National Council of Teachers of English. New York: Appleton-Century Co., 1935.

3. Dwight L. Burton. *Literature Study in the High Schools*. 3rd ed. New York: Holt, Rinehart & Winston, 1970, p 4.

4. Commission on English. *Freedom and Discipline in English*. New York: College Entrance Examination Board, 1965.

5. Dixon, *Growth Through English*, p 4.

6. National Commission on Excellence in Education. *A Nation at Risk*. Washington, D.C.: U. S. Department of Education, 1983, p 9.

7. National Commission on Excellence in Education, *A Nation at Risk*, p 21.

8. National Commission on Excellence in Education, *A Nation at Risk*, p 22.

9. National Commission on Excellence in Education, *A Nation at Risk*, p 25.

10. Ernest L. Boyer. *High School*. A Report on Secondary Education in America. The Carnegie Foundation for the Advancement of Teaching. New York: Harper & Row, 1983.

11. Boyer, *High School*, pp 66–67.

12. Boyer, *High School*, pp 96–97.

13. Lynn V. Cheney. *American Memory: A Report on Humanities in the Nation's Schools*. Washington, D.C.: National Endowment for the Humanities, 1987, p v.

14. Cheney, *American Memory*, p 5.

15. Cheney, *American Memory*, p 9.

16. Cheney, *American Memory*, p 10.

17. Cheney, *American Memory*, p 19.

18. Excerpts from *Cultural Literacy* by E. D. Hirsch. Copyright (c) 1987 by Houghton Mifflin Co. Reprinted by permission of Houghton Mifflin Co.

19. Hirsch, *Cultural Literacy*, p xiii.

20. Hirsch, *Cultural Literacy*, p 2.

21. Hirsch, *Cultural Literacy*, p 30.

22. Hirsch, *Cultural Literacy*, pp 134–135.

23. Ren Welleck and Austin Warren. *Theory of Literature*. 2nd ed. New York: Harcourt, Brace & World, 1956, p 14.

CHAPTER THREE

Reading and Listening in Literature Study

During this century, much has been written about the teaching of reading. Until the age of electronics in education exerted powerful influences on classroom instruction in all subject areas, "reading" was synonymous with "literature" in secondary level English classes. The development of multimedia capabilities, however, has assigned reading to a somewhat different place in the curriculum in general and in the study of literature in particular. Revolutions in educational technology have also affected the manner in which listening strategies can be implemented by literature teachers. Not until later in this discussion, however, will the "new place" of reading be the focal point of description, analysis, and suggestion.

Obviously, students who don't read well will not be very good readers of literature. Behind this self-evident assertion, however, lies the fact that the nationwide testing programs of the past twenty years have been largely devoted to the assessment of basic educational skills. Of these skills, reading was the most basic and the most comprehensively tested. In fact, reading ability was identified as the key to students' ability to perform in objectively tested language, writing, and even computation components. It seems unnecessary, therefore, to present any lengthy rationale for the claim that the ability to read is a vital factor in students' attaining literary competence.

What follows will not be an attempt to provide an elaborate treatise on reading skills and adolescent readers of literature. Instead, emphasis will be placed on those aspects of the developmental reading process which will most likely assist English teachers in creating certain classroom experi-

45

ences. These experiences will help their students read texts which are aimed at revealing the world of imagination (i.e., fiction, drama, and poetry).

The term "developmental" can be one of the slipperiest—and most misused—words in the pedagogical lexicon. In this context, it concerns those special competencies which young readers who already possess basic skills in word recognition and comprehension need to acquire, extend, and refine in order to deal actively with literary meaning. Thus, the needs of seriously disabled readers will not be be treated. Teachers who are seeking instructional techniques to use with these readers can find pertinent literature in any number of professional sources. Students in need of such assistance will undoubtedly have tremendous difficulty in meeting the demands of most high school English teachers in the area of literary understanding, interpretation, and appreciation. It is to the reading situations of students with some ability that we now turn our attention.

Ironically, it is not in the students' ability to read that most secondary school teachers will probably experience their greatest frustration. Rather, it is the degree to which today's young people are willing to read at all, let alone do so with any measure of enthusiasm that will frustrate teachers. Literary works approached without enthusiasm should probably not be read at all. The "age of television" as described by Neil Postman in his persuasive book *Amusing Ourselves to Death* has so permeated American sensibilities in this final quarter of the twentieth century that it dominates every phase of all citizens' lives. And students in public schools are among those most profoundly affected.

> We face the rapid dissolution of the assumptions of an education organized around the slow-moving printed word, and the equally rapid emergence of a new education based on the speed-of-light electronic image. The classroom is, at the moment, still tied to the printed word, although that connection is rapidly weakening. Meanwhile, television forges ahead, making no concessions to its great technological predecessor, creating new conceptions of knowledge and how it is acquired. One is entirely justified in saying that the major education enterprise now being undertaken in the United States is not happening in its classrooms but in the home, in front of the television set, and under the jurisdiction not of school administrators and teachers but of network executives and entertainers. I don't mean to imply that those who control television want this responsibility. I mean only to say that, like the alphabet or the printing press, television has by its power to control the time, attention and cognitive habits of our youth gained the power to control their education. . . .[1]

Coming to grips with the insidiously patent influence of television on the entire educational establishment would seem to be an important prerequisite to decision making by literature teachers in three areas: (1) what selections to teach, (2) when to teach them, and (3) what classroom strategies to use in teaching them.

A likely place to start in consideration of potential effective teaching approaches is through reflection on the not-so-startling revelation that, "You don't read reading; you read something." The content of reading, quite apart from the skills needed to understand that content, needs careful attention as a point of departure for planning instruction. First, literary selections are about something; they depict some aspect of human experience and, most frequently, do so with imagination. Thus readers of such works must come to the task with some experiences which they can correlate with those presented in the text. The nature of this correlation is worth noting. Readers must be able to relate, to some degree, the experience described in the work to that which they have undergone. The "to some degree" is a vital factor in this first phase of understanding. Young readers do not have to have literally experienced that which occurs in the story they have read; they need only to be able to call up experiences in the general area of the subject represented.

Obviously, then, works must be within the emotional range of readers in order for them to have any chance of making such an entry. In light of this, one of the teacher's important functions in promoting empathy between reader and work is to "select" for study those works which offer a legitimate chance for students to use their experiences as touchstones for imaginative entry.

This assertion is one which has aroused controversy for over half a century and will no doubt continue to do so whenever the selection of appropriate literary texts is at issue. The enthusiasm for many "classic" works, such as those mentioned in the previous chapter, remains low as we head toward the twenty-first century. In fact, such works, while extolled by literary scholars, have been egregious turn-offs to secondary school readers since English educators started keeping score.

If one accepts the significance of the correlative experience factor in literary understanding and appreciation as a valid perception, then it is small wonder that some of the traditionally touted, taught, and (sometimes) tortured masterpieces elicit little more than groans from legions of suffering secondary school students. In the first place, most of them were *too long*. (Both authors have arrived at the conclusion, after years of observation, that an imposing number of such students want to weigh assigned texts before they read them.) Second, the language they were presented in was anything but late twentieth century, U.S.A. patois, for example, *forsooth, wormwood, ergo*. Third, and most unappealing, they described *other* people doing *other* things, at *other* places, in *other* eras. Because of these, the readers in the high school classrooms had a hard time making real contact with these "masterpieces." And, as Postman argues, the growing preoccupation of all of us with television has created a gap between the students and the written "masterpieces" which is swiftly widening.

In addition to these problems, consider the fact that many, if not most, adolescent readers struggle with long passages which are purely descriptive. Getting into novels which begin with extended descriptions—such as *The Scarlet Letter, A Tale of Two Cities,* and *The Return of the Native*—is tedious for all but the most avid literature students and is even harder for today's youngsters, conditioned as they are to the action-packed, rapid fire delivery of contemporary media.

So the nature and style of a number of critically acclaimed literary works constitute problems for teachers who would include them in their program of study. It is hardly adequate, however, to do nothing more than bemoan the frequent remoteness of major literary texts from the sensibilities of secondary school students. The backgrounds and experiences of these young people can be used as an effective medium for leading them to an active involvement with a broad range of texts. This can be so if teachers can induce their students to inventory and then reflect on particular phases of their past experiences before reading tasks are assigned to them.

Prereading Activities

Harold Herber, a noted reading educator from Syracuse University, has created a most useful technique for assisting students in relating their backgrounds and experiences to texts subsequently read.[2] His approach, called by some an "advance organizer,"[3] can be applied to a great number of content area text passages (e.g., biology, civics, health, art appreciation, geography). The application here is to works of literature, in this case a poem. A poem is useful because of its brevity. Herber's activity, however, can be used with works from any genre and, in terms of secondary school students, at any grade level and with students of any ability level. The author of this chapter, for example, once used it as a means of introducing college juniors and seniors to the study of Shakespeare's *Antony and Cleopatra.* On another occasion, he used it to assist a class of lower ability seventh graders to a simple but moving short story titled "The Cub" by Lois Dykmann Kleihauer.

In addition to this flexibility, the Herber exercise provides an excellent means of integrating literature study with reading instruction. Many content area teachers resist including reading instructional activity because of the irrelevancy of the subject matter found in the reading workbooks to their content. In using this activity, such teachers "get two for the price of one." Finally, the Herber exercises offer teachers a most effective means of beginning work in reading comprehension. Some high school content area teachers, untrained in reading instructional strategy, complain that they don't know where to start in the reading process. They are also reluctant to sacrifice too much time away from their syllabi. What follows represents a most likely strategy to get the ball rolling.

The exercise takes the form of group work and includes five steps. The forming of the groups, in terms of who works with whom, is up to the teacher. Group sizes should range between three and five. Three persons per group is an absolute minimum; groups of more than five tend to be unwieldy. It is perfectly acceptable to have groups of slightly uneven sizes (e.g., there may be four groups of four each and one group of five in a class of twenty-one students).

Once the groups have been established, the teacher appoints one member of each one as a recorder, not a leader. (The recorder's duties are purely clerical.) The individuals chosen need a pencil or pen and a blank piece of paper on which they are instructed to draw lines down the middle. When those details have been completed, the class is ready to begin the five-step procedure.

Step One

The teacher draws a line down the center of a segment of the chalk-board and places the word "Struggles" near the top of that segment and to the left of the center line. The recorders place the same word at the top left of the blank sheets of paper. Then, consulting a watch, the teacher gives all groups the "go" signal. At that signal, students all give to their recorders any word that comes into their heads which relates in any way to "Struggles." Recorders transcribe these words under "Struggles" to the left of the center line. They also add whatever words they can think of as related to "Struggles." The groups are given a short period of time, three to four minutes for senior high students, four to five for middle schoolers. When that period expires, the teacher stops them and asks the recorders to total the words which their groups have compiled. The results are then announced to the entire class. (Note: If teachers wish to award some small prize to the winning groups, they may; this is not a vital dimension of the exercise, however.) Finally, in terms of this step, the teacher asks each recorder to read aloud a few of the words which that group has contributed.

Step Two

A repeat of the procedure in Step One, this time placing the word "Youth" to the right of the center line. The same time limits are used. The recorders are once again asked to read aloud to the class a few words from their "Youth" list.

Step Three

The teacher asks each group to choose five words (an arbitrary number) from the list under "Struggles" and relate them logically to another set of five words from the "Youth" list. One example might be "contest-athletes." The recorders should write down these matched pairs of words on the sheet they have used to compile their two lists. No time limits should be prescribed, although the students should be told to complete the pairings without hesitation. A prize will not be offered for the "best" set of matched pairs. When all groups have finished their pairings, the teacher asks the recorders to place their sets on the board, asking the rest of the class to write down the matched pairs of words from groups other than their own on scrap paper. All students should then review briefly these matched pairs.

Step Four

The teacher passes out to each class member a set of sentences labelled "Predictive Statements." Once the students receive them, they should mark each one "A" if they agree with it, or "D" if they disagree. While they remain in their group setting for this step, their decision to agree or disagree with each statement is individual. Discussion within the groups is permissible; in fact, it is to be encouraged, but the ultimate agreements or disagreements rest with each person. Once again, no time limits are established for this step, but the teacher should urge all class members to get on with their choices. When all students have made those choices, the teacher can ask several of them what they decided on each of the *predictive statements*. Following are the statements:

1. War is a terrifying experience to many.
2. Young men once went to war with great spirit.
3. People usually return from their first taste of war unchanged.
4. War experience does much to increase morale and self-confidence.
5. A person holds the same belief in a cause before a war experience as after.

Step Five

When the review of the students' responses to the Predictive Statements has been completed, the teacher passes out the passage to be read, in this case a poem by Ezra Pound, and asks the students to read it carefully. He/She further asks them to review silently the ideas they generated during their participation in the preceding four steps. When that reading has been completed, the students may return to their original class seating arrangement. The poem:

THE RETURN

–by Ezra Pound

See, they return; ah, see the tentative
Movements, and the slow feet,
The trouble in the pace and the uncertain
Wavering!

See, they return, one, and by one,
With fear, as half-awakened;
As if the snow should hesitate
And murmur in the wind,
   and half turn back;
These were the "Wing'd-with-Awe,"
   Inviolable.

Gods of the winged shoe!
With them the silver hounds,
   sniffing the trace of air!

Haie! Haie!
   These were the swift to harry;
These were the keen-scented;
These were the souls of blood.

Slow on the leash,
   pallid the leash-men!

SOURCE: from *Personae*, copyright 1926 by Ezra Pound. Reprinted by permission of New Directions Publishing Corporation.

Rationale for, and Nature of, the Herber Exercise

The Herber exercise provides a logical introduction to the study of literary works with adolescent readers, both in middle schools (and younger) and senior high schools (and older). The exercise takes as its point of departure the experiences accumulated by each reader rather than an abrupt, "Here kids, read this" assignment of the selection. During the five steps, teachers lead the students through a systematic inventorying, sharing, analyzing, relating, and evaluating of their experiences. In short, shared experience is featured throughout. Step Three includes the vital cognitive process of perceiving relationships. (A word under "Struggles" related to one under "Youth.") This aids students in forming an awareness of the core of meaning in the work. Step Four is a pivotal one; it moves the students from a concentration on their experiences (Steps One through Three) to experiences featured in the text (Step Five). In doing so, it personalizes the reflections of the students on those features. During the five steps, students should not be intimidated; there should be no answers judged as "wrong."

Whether veterans or beginners, teachers can develop a Herber exercise. Since all works are about something, the exercise can be done with any literary selection. To create one, teachers need to follow these five steps:

1. Choose the selection. It can fit into any organizational pattern used in literature study: chronological, thematic, genre, author, or other.

2. Read the selection or (as is often the case) re-read it silently. If the selection is a poem, read it aloud. Before going on with this development, one more close, thoughtful reading is well worth the time and effort.

3. Write one sentence which represents the best inference as to the main idea (theme, message, controlling idea, hidden meaning, etc.) of the work.

4. Choose from the sentence (#3) the two words, or word clusters (e.g., power base, front runner, soap opera, couch potato, etc.) which, when related to each other, form the core of that main idea. (In the Pound poem above, the core is formed from the relationship between struggles and youth, at least in the mind of the writer.) Note that, with the choice of these words, the elements needed to perform Steps One, Two, and Three in the process are present.

5. Write a series of predictive statements. They should be short, direct declarative sentences which reflect significant events, elements, or anecdotes found during the reading. In addition, these statements should be arranged in the order of the appearance of those words in the text. The inclusion of certain "buzz words" (i.e., "usually," "for many," "often," or "seldom") is worth considering because these words stimulate thought and discussion.

Herber exercises are relatively easy to create. Furthermore, the five-step process can be readily remembered and put into operation. With short works, especially lyric poems and short stories or plays, the entire process can be completed in a class period and still offer some time for student response. Speaking of response, the question is often raised, "What do I do after the students complete Step Five, the reading of the text?" The answer is, "Any kind of response you'd prefer." The nature and variety of such activities will be discussed in considerable detail later in this text. (See Chapter Six.)

Some Pertinent Reading Competencies

To catalogue, let alone describe, the entire range of reading skills which enable students to deal with printed material successfully would require a book-length treatise. Indeed, during the Accountability, Basic Skills, Right-To-Read era of the 1970s, discussed in Chapter Two, a large number of State Departments of Education produced taxonomies of reading skills so extensive and so meticulous that they bewildered teachers who were attempting to shore up the reading capacities of their less able students. Since it is a tenet in the philosophy of this text to avoid possible workbook overkill in promoting literacy among young students, what follows will be a sharply limited description of some pertinent enabling skills. For those teachers who wish to build a more elaborate pattern of reading instructional schema into their courses of study, the bibliography found in the Appendices of this text cites a number of highly regarded, comprehensive resources on the subject of teaching reading in middle and secondary schools.

Unfortunately, the vocabulary component offered in many contemporary American secondary schools is too often sterile, redundant, and heavily dependent on memorization. That is, the time honored practice of assigning twenty words on Monday, whose meanings need to be discovered in the classroom dictionary, and then testing students on the meanings of those items on Friday, still flourishes. Such an approach deals almost inevitably with lexical development as an isolated experience. More inappropriately, it depends almost totally on memorization for successful task completion. Any surprise, delayed post-test inventory will almost without exception reveal that the meanings of the "sacred twenty" will have been wholly or largely forgotten, even when such a test is administered first thing on the following Monday morning. Thus, English teachers wishing to add vocabulary activity to their literature instructional framework should pick their spots, ever mindful of the fact that frequent inventories of, and reflections upon, correlative experience in the classroom will probably do more to enhance the reading vocabularies of their students than endless sessions featuring skills and drills. Focusing on a few pertinent techniques can be helpful, however, and here they are:

1. **Discussion, Illustration, and Application of Abstract Nouns**   In the reading of literary works, secondary school students will inev-

itably encounter thousands of abstract nouns. The ability to deduce relevant, that is to say contextual, meanings for these nouns is vital to the comprehension process. To repeat a deeply felt concern, however, memorization of *any* definition, be it from the dictionary, a glossary, or even a teacher-created listing, won't do the job. In his chapter on "Classification," in *Language in Thought and Action*, Hayakawa makes a persuasive case for the ineffectual nature of superficial treatment of lexical meaning.[4] To be useful, key abstract nouns must be identified, discussed, illustrated, and turned back on the students to investigate their own sense of meaning. This procedure takes time; thus, the approach must be highly selective (i.e., the key nouns chosen must truly be *key*). Abstract nouns are labels for events, incidents, attitudes, processes, realizations, and the like, which befall characters in literary works. These words must not be glossed over by readers who are attempting to discern meaning in those texts. Both the judicious choice of those nouns and a response-based treatment of them constitute the best advice for teachers who are concerned about expanding their students' vocabularies.

2. **Word Clusters** Mentioned earlier, these are lexical constructs overlooked by many vocabularists. In fact, one of the ways in which concept developers create new meaning for the ideas they create is juxtaposing two words to form such a cluster. In putting them together, the "inventor" cares little about the original, normally accepted meanings for each word. Therefore, knowing what they usually mean doesn't provide the reader with much help. Again, the broad experience of the reader is an important factor in finding meaning for the cluster. Clusters come into being because of new, significant events which transpire. Thus, readers need to "keep up with the news" in order to determine meaning. Here are a few which have been created in the last fifty or so years: fellow traveler (communist sympathizer, 1940s); hit man (assassin, 1950s); asphalt jungle (ghetto, 1950s); slum lord (owner of ghetto property, 1960s); free fire zone (Vietnam battleground, 1960s); couch potato (compulsive television viewer, 1970s); and spin control (political consultant work, 1980s).

Because they employ common words, and thus give the appearance of being "easy," word clusters merit the close attention of teachers as they choose and review works for class study.

3. **Meaning through Context** This is probably as important a word study skill as any on any list. Briefly stated, readers who encounter a word that is hard or unfamiliar peruse the text which surrounds

that word in trying to determine its meaning. The length of the search varies: sometimes clues are in the immediate vicinity; at other times, they are farther removed; sometimes the direction of search must be modified; sometimes clues exist before the appearance of the word in question and at other times they appear after the word; on still other occasions, they can be found on both sides. Literary works, especially fictional pieces, need to be examined carefully for the presence of context clues. When students develop the capacity to use them habitually, they become more independent readers in that they don't have to rely on reference sources, in either printed or human form.

4. **Cross Referencing** In learning to use most reference sources, be they footnotes, glossaries (in the text), dictionaries, or one of several library resources, students need to work on the skill of cross referencing. This set of moves represents an interruption in students' normal linear, left-to-right, top-to-bottom approach to reading a page. Using a footnote on a page as an example, the sequence of activity goes like this: When readers encounter an unfamiliar, but footnoted word on a page, they:

1. *Stop* at that point in the text, alerted by the raised arabic number;
2. *Move* to the bottom of the page, locate the corresponding number, and read the information which follows it;
3. *Return* to the original text passage and RELATE the data found in the footnote;
4. *Continue* to read the text beyond the footnote.

Cross referencing with sources in the back of the book (e.g., glossaries), in forms other than print (e.g., text graphics), or in separate sources (e.g., dictionaries) will call for a more elaborate set of moves. In any event, the almost reflexive use of cross referencing, when needed, will come in handy in a large number of content area reading tasks. Literature study, of course, is one of these tasks.

Metaphor

As readers attempt to find meaning in subtly stated, sophisticated literary works, particularly older ones, they will find the need to discover meaning in metaphor on a regular basis. Some high school students think that a metaphor is a word or phrase they must find in a poem. It is much more general than that; it is a basic linguistic device that speakers or writers use to convey meaning to their audiences. Newspapers, magazines, and texts contain large numbers of metaphors. Finding meaning in these metaphors represents a critical thinking process that involves three steps:

1. **Finding the Metaphor** As they are reading, students note places where authors compare one of their topics with something they hope is familiar to their readers. When students find these words or phrases with which the authors are comparing the topic, they have completed the first step.

2. **Trying Its Literal Meaning** Students attempt to insert the first, most familiar meaning for the word used in the metaphoric expression. Almost without exception, they will discover that this meaning is totally inadequate as a solution to the problem at hand.

3. **Finding Its Intended Meaning** Now the students must search the immediate context surrounding the metaphor. They must also inventory their own experience that is relevant to the situation in the text. By relating these elements, they should be able to infer the metaphoric meaning of the figure of speech in question.

Sometimes, however, the metaphorical allusions used by speakers or writers aren't in the students' experience. For example, in the final chapter of *A Christmas Carol* by Charles Dickens, Scrooge has had a terrifying dream; the ghost of Christmas Yet to Come leads Scrooge to a deteriorated cemetery. There they find a gravestone bearing Scrooge's name. When Scrooge wakes up, he realizes that he is not dead, that it is Christmas Day, and that he does have a chance to mend his miserly, misanthropic ways. Dickens describes him in this manner: "He frisked into the sitting room, making a perfect Laocoon of himself in his stockings."

Students may ask themselves how Scrooge looked when he realized that he wasn't dead and had a chance for redemption. He looked like Laocoon. The difficulty for readers may lie in figuring out this metaphoric allusion to Laocoon. They may use the three-step process described above. It's easy to complete the first step because the metaphor obviously is "Laocoon." The key, however, is the second step: "try its literal meaning." Most people cannot accomplish this because there are possibly two unknowns: (1) the appearance of the subject, Scrooge and (2) the supposedly familiar person that the subject is compared to—Laocoon. When students encounter two unknowns in a metaphor, they may have serious comprehension problems.

What should they do? First, they have to find out about the things to which the subject is compared. Who is Laocoon? Through research, they learn that he was a priest, a holy man in the myth of the Trojan War. During the ten-year war, Laocoon was performing a religious ceremony in his temple on a hill outside Troy. Because he had supernatural powers, he realized that enemy Greek soldiers were housed inside the huge gift horse. To warn his fellow Trojans, he ran down from the hill, waving his arms and yelling, "Don't take the wooden horse into the city! I fear the Greeks even when they bear gifts!" When he reached the bottom of the hill, two large snakes emerged from the sea, entwined themselves around Laocoon and his two young sons, and dragged the three to their deaths in the sea. Believing that this event was a sign that Laocoon was wrong, the Trojans hauled the horse into the city. That night the Greek soldiers slipped out of the horse, opened the gates to their fellow Greek soldiers, and destroyed Troy.

Next, students find the intended meaning of the metaphor. Their thought processes might go something like this: "How did Scrooge look on Christmas morning? He looked just like Laocoon. How did Laocoon look? He struggled frantically with the sea serpent's coils, trying to free himself. That's the way the excited Scrooge looked—all tangled in his long stockings." There are further relationships which can be seen by examining more closely these unusual metaphoric partners. Both men are provided with extraordinary insights and truths: Laocoon's awareness that the horse is really a trap, and Scrooge's revelation that true happiness lies in love and generosity, rather than piling up material wealth. Both gained their knowledge through spiritual means; Laocoon through his priesthood, Scrooge through his ghostly encounters. Furthermore, both men attempted to share their knowledge with others: Laocoon by warning the Trojans, Scrooge during his Christmas Day visit. Using the three-step process helps students unlock the meaning of metaphors. When they have trouble with step two, they must find the information they need to fill in the picture.

Thus, working successfully with metaphor requires attention to correlative experience and critical thinking. Helping students refine their skills in unlocking the meaning of metaphors may require a great deal of concentration as well as class time, but it is well worth the effort.

Comprehension Elements

Since a great deal of attention is going to be given the critical reading aspects of comprehension in later chapters, the discussion of the basic elements here will be brief. Those mentioned can be enabling ones that assist readers of literature in dealing with the more demanding tasks of interpretation, analysis, appreciation, and application of those three elements to correlative issues in their own lives.

1. **Finding Facts and Details** It was Robert Frost who said, "A poet must lean on his facts." Similarly, readers must pay close attention to the facts, details, events, statements, and other concrete elements selected by writers. This is especially pertinent to short fiction and poetry, where language is often cryptic, and in drama where details often appear in unusual structures and formats (e.g., stage settings, directions, italicized movements of characters, asides, and so on). Lack of attention to and/or misperception of those elements can cause confusion. James Squire, in a celebrated study of tenth graders' reading of short stories, presented among his significant findings that "gross misreading leads to gross misinterpretation." In their search for central meaning, careful readers must be able to perceive details clearly and recall them accurately.

2. **Finding Order and Sequence** In any serious literary selection, the ordering of data is never random; there is a reason for each juxtaposition of elements. Discovering the nature of that positioning and inferring the rationale for it are two more responsibilities of thoughtful literature students.

    Some sequences are regular, following chronological order. In other cases, however, such stylistic features as flashbacks, prophecies, interior monologues, and simultaneous plot development can cause casual readers both bewilderment and misunderstanding. In preparing to provide students with opportunities to sharpen their ability to follow order and sequence, teachers should realize that one of the most important critical reading skills is discerning cause and effect relationships. In order to discern these relationships, however, students must be able to deal with many kinds of sequences.

3. **Sustaining Comprehension** In the reading of a lengthy text for its implied main ideas and impressions, students must be able to recall what went on in the earlier passages of a given text as they are moving toward the reading of its later ones. Content area study in the upper grades (i.e., grades six through twelve) features longer selections than do those used at early childhood levels. Thus, students must keep track of, and recall, earlier characters, settings, details, events, and so on, when they complete the reading of those longer passages. An attendant problem lies in the fact that the students' preoccupation with television and other contemporary media (Postman's theory was discussed earlier in this chapter) has generally shortened the attention span of many American adolescents. Moreover, there are few if any group survey reading tests

for secondary grade levels which provide any data on the ability to sustain comprehension. Conducting ongoing discussions, assigning reading notes, and springing pop quizzes during the study of longer works may help. In short, teachers should keep in mind that the sustaining capacity is a most important one in fostering comprehension skills.

Culmination of the Reading Discussion: A Sample Lesson

Several years ago, the author of this chapter asked for and received the assignment of teaching a lower ability class of seventh graders at the Developmental Research School (K–12) of Florida State University. The nominal subject matter of that course was "English," but since the average level of reading ability among those twenty-two class members, as measured by the Gates-MacInitie Reading Test, was 3.6, the use of "regular" approaches and texts materials was out of the question. Thus, after some initial class periods spent in rather free-wheeling discussion, mostly on their perceptions of what "English" was all about, the author/teacher took the students through the lesson described below. This lesson is presented here as an example of ways in which several of the reading and language skills described earlier can be integrated into a systematic instructional offering to early adolescents whose reading abilities clearly prohibit the use of independent silent reading and interpretive response tasks as the sole means of dealing with literary works in the classroom. Here, then, is the "Lottery Lesson." The "teacher" referred to is the writer.

Since the students were relatively immature and had limited reading ability, the teacher developed two kinds of readiness activities: word attack and experiential. The word attack exercises were using context clues and finding meaning in metaphor, both of which were done orally. The teacher put on the board sentences such as "She laughed. She jumped. She shouted. She had never been so happy. She was simply buoyant." The clues to the meaning of the difficult words were identified. Then the teacher passed out some other context-clues sentences, which the students worked on individually. The sentences, taken from the story, contained increasingly harder words and fewer clues: (Boldface type identifies the special words.)

The morning of June 27th was clear and sunny, with the fresh warmth of a full-summer day; the flowers were blossoming **PROFUSELY** and the grass was richly green.

School was recently over for the summer, and the feeling of liberty sat uneasily on most of them; they tended to gather together quietly for a while before they broke into **BOISTEROUS** play, and their talk was still of the classroom and the teacher, of books and reprimands.

The lottery was conducted—as were the square dances, the teen-age club, the Halloween program—by Mr. Summers, who had time and energy to devote to **CIVIC** activities.

There was a story that the present box had been made with some pieces of the box that had **PRECEDED** it, the one that had been constructed when the first people settled down to make a village here.

There was the proper swearing-in of Mr. Summers by the postmaster, as the official of the lottery; at one time, some people remembered, there had been a recital of some sort, performed by the official of the lottery, a **PERFUNCTORY**, tuneless chant that had been rattled off duly each year; some people believed that the official of the lottery used to stand just so when he said or sang it, others believed that he was supposed to walk among the people, but years and years ago this part of the **RITUAL** had been allowed to lapse.

She hesitated for a minute, looking around **DEFIANTLY,** and then set her lips and went up to the box. She snatched a paper out and held it behind her.

SOURCE: Excerpts from "The Lottery," from *The Lottery* by Shirley Jackson. Copyright (c) 1948, 1949 by Shirley Jackson. Renewal copyright (c) 1976, 1977 by Laurence Hyman, Barry Hyman, Mrs. Sarah Webster and Mrs. Joanne Schnurer. Reprinted by permission of Farrar, Straus & Giroux, Inc.

After the context work had been completed, the teacher introduced the students to metaphor. He put a sentence on the board: "I really fell for that used car salesman's line." Through discussion the students demonstrated their awareness of the metaphoric nature of this statement and the difference between the literal and the intended meaning. Then, material was passed out which contained metaphoric expressions composed by the teacher. After the students worked through identifying intended meanings, the teacher asked the class to consider quotes from the story: (Boldface type indicates phrases that should be underlined by the teacher.)

1. The rest of the year, the box was put away, sometimes one place, sometimes another; it had **SPENT ONE YEAR** in Mr. Grave's barn and **ANOTHER YEAR UNDERFOOT** in the post office, and sometimes it was set on a shelf in the Martin grocery and left there.

2. Mrs. Hutchinson **CRANED HER NECK** to see through the crowd and found her husband and children standing near the front.

3. "Horace's not but sixteen yet," Mrs. Dunbar said regretfully. "Guess I **GOTTA FILL IN FOR THE OLD MAN** this year."

4. A sudden hush **FELL OVER THE CROWD.**

5. Nancy and Bill, Jr. opened theirs at the same time, and **BOTH BEAMED**, and laughed, turning around to the crowd and holding their slips of paper above their heads.

SOURCE: "The Lottery," by Shirley Jackson; from *The Lottery*, copyright 1948, 1949 by Shirley Jackson; by permission of Farrar, Straus, & Giroux, Inc.

After the work on word attack skills and metaphor, the teacher put this question on the board, asking the students to think about it:

Suppose you lived in a place where they had a custom which could hurt people badly. The people in that place had been doing it for years, but you thought it was wrong. What would you do?

This question was the focus of animated discussion, providing a second kind of readiness—that of an experiential nature. The students thought about, visualized, and discussed a hypothetical experience which was correlative to that they would discover in "The Lottery." They dealt, then, with a human problem and proposed their solutions, comparing these solutions with those of other class members. Among other things, the text provided them with the problem and a solution played out in dramatic terms.

At the conclusion of this discussion, the teacher passed out copies of the story and gave the students the entire period to read it silently, encouraging them to finish, reread, or review the story after class. At the next class meeting, he played a recording of Shirley Jackson's reading of her story. During the recording, the students could follow along in the text or not, as they wished. (The attempt to follow an oral reading in the text can be confusing to some students, especially those with reading disabilities.)

The recording was the first of a series of reinforcement activities conducted by the teacher. Impressions gained through silent reading were broadened and intensified through the use of an adept, oral interpretation. Following this, the teacher displayed a large drawing of an incident. This drawing, the first of five to be exhibited, was done by a senior high art student who, at the teacher's request, identified five striking visual images in the story and then drew his impressions. The students were asked if the drawing represented a scene from the story they had just read and heard read. They agreed that it did, and then the teacher asked them to find the words that represented to them the drawing.

As a reinforcement activity, drawings (paintings, photographs, cartoons, slides, and so on) have three potentially valuable uses: (1) They provide an opportunity for students to relate the verbal to the visual. (Most of today's students are highly oriented to visual media.) (2) They get the student to examine the text for evidence, a habit badly needed in the qualifying of generalizations. The students had to find the exact words representing the drawing, which served as an introductory exercise in reading to analyze. (3) The students were asked to compare their visual impression to another classmate's, thus introducing the reading of material for inferences. This shows students that the same words can often create different impressions from reader to reader.

Each of the five drawings was shown in turn, and the students searched the text for the verbal representations. When this was completed, the teacher replaced all five on the board but out of the order in which they occurred in the story. The students were asked to rearrange them in the order in which they had actually occurred. This exercise stressed reading to identify order or establish sequence, a skill often overlooked.

When the pictures had been removed, the teacher passed out the following exercise:

Directions: Put the Following Events in the Order in Which They Actually Occur in the Story

1. Mrs. Hutchinson arrives at the square.
2. Five slips of paper are returned to the black box.
3. All the villagers open their slips of paper.
4. The villagers begin to throw the stones.
5. The townspeople, first the children, then the elders, gather in the town square.
6. The first men come forward to draw slips of paper from the box.
7. Mr. Summers arrives with the black wooden box.

In this exercise, the students were asked to establish proper sequence of events as seen in print. The movement in the sequence exercise was, again, from visual to verbal, thus capitalizing on early adolescents' potential strength in perception.

Following this comprehension reinforcement, the teacher divided the class into four groups of unequal numbers and passed out this set of activities:

Role Playing Activities—"The Lottery"

1. Assume that we have a young person who lives in the town join with another young person from a town that has dropped the Lottery. These two confront Old Man Warner about the advisability of continuing the custom.

2. Assume that Mr. Summers has become less henpecked and suddenly takes on a more rebellious nature. What would he say to his wife and a group of village residents?

3. Assume that a group of five or more townsfolk got together to discuss the stoning of Tessie Hutchinson after the event had taken place. Recreate their conversation.

4. Recreate the discussions that might have taken place between Mr. Hutchinson and his children in the privacy of their home after Mrs. Hutchinson was stoned to death.

Each of the four situations was discussed briefly, and then each group was given a situation to act out via an improvised drama. The teacher allowed the groups to work an entire period on their presentations, working with each group in turn. This was a purely oral activity with no written scripts. Each group gave its presentation, and the rest of the class was asked to react.

Although the teacher did not use written exercises, the following are examples of some items that require various degrees of involvement and imagination, asking the students to relate the work to life as they perceive it. Of course, these questions can be handled orally as well.

Written Statements — "The Lottery"

1. Change the handling of the story to the way it might appear in a television serial.

2. Suppose you were a person (your same age) living in the town and that you opposed this custom. What arguments would you use with your parents? Your peers?

3. Do you think this story could take place in the 1990s or at the beginning of the twenty-first century? Why or why not?

4. What might happen if all the children of the village lined up together and opposed their parents on continuing the lottery?

5. (For urban students) Would the lottery be a likely custom in a city of this size? Why or why not?

The use of readiness and reinforcement activities, then, aided these students in developing a meaningful context for the story, "The Lottery." If students' limitations and needs are seriously considered by teachers, and if contexts for reading are carefully established, the transition teachers ask them to make from reading to the study of literature may not be so difficult after all.

Reading Instruction in English (Literary) Content

Reading Readiness Activities	→	Silent Reading	→	Reinforcement Activities
Skills				Audio
Correlative Experiences				Visual
Improvised Drama				Sequencing
Pantomine				Response
				Discussion
				Written Work
				Role Playing

Figure 3.1

Listening Capabilities

Development of listening capabilities as part of the study of literature will be taken up in the subsequent chapter on "Expressing Responses." Thus the treatment of those abilities in this segment of the chapter will be somewhat brief.

Listening becomes a vital element of student reaction to works offered and will be considered as an integral part of the entire response discussion. Students must, at times, listen to works read aloud, to media presentations, and to oral statements about the works in order to formulate any thoughtful response. Thus, throughout the text, attention will be paid to the promotion of the act of listening.

Several of the abilities just described in the reading discussion obviously rely on listening. Some of the ensuing comments, therefore, will be in a sense a series of reminders. For example, correlative experience, without which little or no comprehension can occur, will be accumulated through listening as well as reading. In fact, many educators would insist that more content for comprehension comes through nonprint media that demands listening skills than through print media. In many instances, word clusters become familiar auditorily before students ever see them in print. Consider, for example, young peoples' familiarity with "soap operas" and, more recently, "sound bites," which probably came about through radio and television programming. The same can be said for a large number of nonliterary metaphoric expressions such as "he can hit the bricks" and "the judge's ruling was way off base." The listening vocabulary is an indispensable forerunner to the expansion of the reading vocabulary.

Those who work with the severely hearing impaired attest to this highly important dimension of early childhood education.

Similarly, much that has been said about basic comprehension skill development can be said about listening. Sustaining comprehension of long oral statements depends to a considerable degree on peoples' factual recall capacities as well as their attention spans. Reasoning ability, such as that allowing individuals to follow complex sequences of details or events, comes through listening before it is developed in reading. Good listeners zero in on key details in oral discussion just as readers identify them in texts. Therefore, many points that are made about reading comprehension are applicable to listening comprehension.

One aspect of language as a powerful factor in oral comprehension activity merits particular notice: that of dialect. All native users of any language speak and write that language in a dialect. Dialects are manifested in syntactic patterns as well as in undefined idiomatic inclusions. The New Englander, for example, may ask for a bottle of "tonic" on a hot day, whereas a Midwesterner may request a bottle of "pop." A third dimension of dialect, phonology, is far more pertinent to understanding through listening than it is to reading. To be able to "dig" what a teacher or peer has to say in introducing or reacting to a work of literature depends heavily on the readers' abilities to deal with the way people pronounce words. The sounds of vowels and diphthongs, as well as the pace and cadence of oral language, either facilitate or impede understanding of the message, and this fact is relevant to various age, intelligence, and educational levels among the listeners. The heavy use of dialect can be found in imaginative literature, especially in fiction and drama. (Eugene O'Neil's frequent use of "eiyuh" in his New England plays comes to mind.) But dialect in these texts is no more than the writers' attempts to represent the oral language of particular geographic regions or social classes which they have first heard. Thus students need to be sensitized initially to the way that language is supposed to sound.

In any discussion of listening activities, oral interpretation of literature plays a significant role. Whether that interpretation takes the form of individual reading, choral presentation, or the acting out of dramatic literature, the refinement of listening capacities of students not involved in such presentations will be a main instructional goal. Not only can these performances offer students opportunities to expand their abilities to draw inferences, make judgements, and establish comparisons and contrasts, but they can have a marked effect of the students' appreciation of literature. (For example, notice the students' interest in hearing poets such as Dylan Thomas reading their own poetry.) Such presentations can also assist students' critical listening abilities through their awareness of the presence of a third agent in oral interpretive presentations—that of readers or actors.

These individuals (or groups) can have a decided impact on students' comprehension of the meaning implicit in virtually any passage from an imaginative work. The treatment of Macbeth's "Is this a dagger I see before me?" soliloquy depends heavily on how that speech is intoned by an actor playing the role. Sensitivity to the several ways in which key passages can be interpreted orally by recordings, live presentations, or student readers should be part of any set of teaching strategies prepared by the literature teacher.

In oral presentations, teachers must decide whether or not to have their students follow the lines in their textbooks. One guideline in making this decision should be the comprehension goals for the reading. If teachers wish to focus on basic elements of comprehension (meanings of key words; identification of facts, details, events; establishment of order/sequence), then it is probably helpful to have the students follow in their texts. If, however, the focus is critical assessment of the passage as a whole, it is better to ask the class to listen only. The ability level of the students is a factor also; slower students will usually benefit more from integrating reading with listening to the more concrete elements in the text. A review of the audio reinforcement activity described earlier as part of the "Lottery" lesson can serve as a further correlate.

When oral presentations are provided as part of group activity, teachers should assign specific listening responsibilities to each group. That is, they can assign Group Two to be the designated listeners to the oral performance of Group One. Group Two, then, will be asked to make an oral, critical response to Group One. Then Group Three will be the critical listeners to Group Two, and so forth. This does not mean that all other class members should be allowed to tune out. They should be given opportunities to respond to all oral presentations at some point. In this approach, however, the responsibility for providing some manner of reaction/critique to any oral presentation becomes fixed.

Some response activity should also be encouraged during all activities in which groups are functioning as groups, especially in preparation sessions. Young people who are reluctant to give oral responses in all-class settings are usually more willing to speak out in small groups which provide a less threatening atmosphere. Reactions within small group interactions must be encouraged. They may create a classroom climate which some principals condemn as *noisy*, but the perpetuation of these opportunities can only enhance literary comprehension, interpretation, and appreciation. Teachers should enthusiastically defend this kind of "noise."

Undeniably, evaluation of listening abilities of students is no easy, fool-proof task. Some advice is offered regarding the assessment of these capacities:

1. **Avoid formal, pressure-laden experiences** The "I talk–you listen–I test" procedure should be conducted, if at all, in an atmosphere as free from rigidity and urgency as possible. Teachers can and do create such tensions by their manner of soliciting responses to various aspects of orally presented selection. Avoid that demeanor.

2. **Use peer evaluation** Establish small group or all-class interaction situations in which the students' contributions are assessed by their peers. Make the criteria clear, and stick mostly to questions which demand concrete, specific aspects of comprehension.

3. **Whenever possible, record oral segments which are to be evaluated** Then either teachers or peers who are involved can avail themselves of the playback capability whenever they want to review a given statement.

4. **Integrate note-taking into the component to be evaluated** Occasionally allow the students to use these notes, and evaluate their efforts, whether they are presented orally or in writing.

5. **Ask questions of what students are required to listen and respond to in loud, clear, deliberate tones** Make these questions short and direct, purging them of difficult terminology and unnecessarily obscure abstractions.

6. **At strategic intervals during the "live" performance or taped (audio or video) version of a long work, use a *progressive exercise*** That is, at the end of a chapter or act, teachers can take a time-out to ask orally these three questions:

   a. What has been happening so far?
   b. What effect have these events had on the principal characters involved?
   c. What do you think will happen next?

Assess the accuracy of student responses, taping them whenever possible. Then, play the tapes of these intermediate responses selectively at the end of the text presentation to elicit further feedback responses.

Finally, as teachers prepare to include classroom activities which emphasize listening skills, they should keep a few procedures in mind:

1. **Teachers should practice any oral reading which they, themselves, plan to offer** Teachers are models for oral presentations, and the students' listening sessions should be enjoyable.

2. **Teachers should carefully state all directions, assignments, and questions** These oral products should be in the teachers' language, not that of literary artists, especially since teachers are aware of the linguistic and academic limitations of their own students.

3. **Students' oral responses should be taped whenever possible** Teachers should listen to these responses to literary selections privately, after school, at home, etc.

4. **Teachers should ask some questions based on contextual meaning of key words, basic comprehension, and so forth,** *before* **asking more "difficult" questions on works the students have just heard**—that is, questions that are based on critical thinking requiring inferences, judgments, hypotheses, and others. (Recall the "Lottery" exercise as an example.) The answers to readiness questions become the building blocks for more abstract responses.

At the heart of literature study lies the students' ability to read, and to a somewhat lesser degree, to listen. Teachers should persevere in their attempts to facilitate such reading and listening. Classrooms in which such activities are going on may not be nearly so quiet and neatly organized as those in which grammar workbooks and literature worksheets are distributed day after day, *ad nauseam,* but the end product—students who are interested and even excited about what they are learning and who are actually eager to get to class—makes it well worth the effort.

Notes

1. Neil Postman. *Amusing Ourselves to Death.* New York: Viking Penguine, 1985, p 146.

2. Harold Herber. *Reading in Content Areas.* 3rd ed. Englewood Cliffs, NJ: Prentice-Hall, 1989.

3. D. R. Ausubel. *Educational Psychology: A Cognitive View* New York: Holt, Rinehart & Winston, Inc., 1968.

4. S. I. Hayakawa. *Language in Thought and Action.* 3rd ed. New York: Harcourt Brace Jovanovich, Inc., 1972.

5. James R. Squire. *The Responses of Adolescents While Reading Four Short Stories.* Research Report No. 2. Champaign: National Council of Teachers of English, 1964, p 40.

CHAPTER FOUR

Reading Interests and Interest in Reading

Introduction

In leading young people toward increased literary awareness, teachers used to consider the nature and extent of the interest factor on those efforts. Interests are a two-edged sword. When positive, they can enhance teachers' efforts to involve their students in the concern with literary pieces and do so most significantly. When negative, however, they present a formidable obstacle to meaningful transactions taking place between texts and readers. Experienced teachers have witnessed the degree to which motivation, whatever its origins, can lead to overlearning by students who otherwise lack needed reading skills or broad sophistication in facing certain works of literature. When they're genuinely turned on, it is amazing what some youngsters can accomplish in the classroom. Conversely, well prepared teachers usually find only frustration when they present works to indifferent groups, no matter how high the quality of those works are.

Interests as factors in genuinely productive literature study are slippery elements indeed. Inventories provided to students in an attempt to discover what they prefer in reading materials can be, and often are, faked by the inventory takers. ("Oh, yes, I love to read books like that, Miss Fiddich. Now, can I have my 'A'?") Thus, the discrepancy between what some young people claim they enjoy reading and what they will actually interact with can be a significant one. Furthermore, teachers must be ever mindful of the differences between their interests, tastes, and enthusiasms for certain literary selections and those of their students. The 24-year-old first year teacher, fresh from a successfully completed M.A. in English Literature, from a major university, for example, will view the value of such study in a vastly different light from that of her ninth grade "basics,"

69

whether they reside in Podunk or in the inner city. The reconciliation of that difference is an absolute prerequisite to any successful encounters with literature in such a classroom.

And when such teachers find it possible to suspend their prejudices upon entering the ninth graders' classroom lair, they must also be vigilant that, in trying to "reach" the students, they don't sacrifice literary understanding for entertainment. There is, indeed there *must* be, more to literature teaching than keeping a class titillated or convulsed in gales of laughter. Striving to achieve such a balance is no easy task, but teachers need to learn about, come to grips with, and ultimately use the interest factor to their advantage. To avoid doing so is to invite disaster.

In attempting to provide such positive experiences, teachers also need to keep in mind the frequently burdensome realities of adolescent temperament. Middle school and high school students often balk at displays of overt enthusiasm for the selections they are asked to read in class precisely because they are adolescents. To many of them, the fact that a work is on the required list means that it simply *cannot* be interesting. To hammer this point home, they will doggedly refrain from any display of enthusiastic or appreciative response despite the teachers' creative efforts and/or the actual effect the work has had on them. "Boring" becomes the operative judgment. In rendering that categorical, implacable judgment, they retain their "cool" demeanor, one which they value above all else. When faced with such studied, often melodramatic indifference (the big sigh, the rolling of the eyes, the feigned anguish), teachers must be careful not to lose their cool. In the final analysis, they must come to an awareness of what adolescent reading interests and tastes tend to be: complex, delicate, volatile, and sporadic—just like adolescents themselves.

Factors that Affect Interest in Reading

The differences between successful and ineffective instructional undertakings are vast, especially between those to which students react with interest and those which they complete only because they have to. What follows is a series of brief descriptions of some of those factors which seem to control these diverse responses:

Reading Ability

While the previous chapter touched on a number of issues in the reading of literature from the perspective of reading ability, some links need to be established between that ability and the interest element. Obviously, there will be many students who will turn away from the task of studying literature because of inadequate competence in the necessary reading skills. Metaphoric expressions, for example, abound in all literary works, whether they are fictional, poetic, or dramatic. Such expressions are placed in those works to clarify, indeed intensify, the meanings of those works. When students are unable to establish precise relationships between metaphors and their referents, however, what was put there to clarify produces confusion instead. It doesn't take many such experiences in missed communication to discourage or to vex less able readers. Given the additional problem of these students' probably limited attention spans, the option of giving up on a selection which is heavily metaphoric is often the one taken.

The ability to follow a narrative is obviously a basic one to reading in general and to the reading of many literary works in particular. Problems which readers have with that ability sometimes manifest themselves when a lengthy narrative is part of the reading assignment (i.e., a full length novel or a three- to five-act play). Then the problem of sustaining comprehension, as described in the previous chapter, becomes a significant one. And sustaining comprehension can be a function of a reader's attention span, which is a capacity often affected by lack of interest. Shorter attention spans are common among readers of lesser ability at all grade levels; this problem increases dramatically, however, in the senior high grades where every content-area assignment tends to be much longer. Such readers often give up totally on school-assigned reading, which in turn exacerbates their academic status and their hostility toward the curriculum.

Irregularities in narrative structure pose potential comprehension problems to poor readers in the English class. The novel, which begins *in medias res* and which, as is usually the case, includes a number of flashbacks (both brief and extended) can confuse these readers. The result is that many of them give up long before they complete the reading of the work or consider its central meaning. The presence of passages of prophecy, those interludes in which one or more characters are given a look at the hypothetical future (as in Philip Roth's award-winning short novel *Goodbye, Columbus*) can cause further confusion. Add to those interruptions in the sequence of events such stylistic features as shift in narrators, multiple narrators, stream of consciousness, interior monologues, and unexpected shifts from outer to inner action, and it's clear why many of these unskilled readers balk when teachers ask them to draw inferences or make judgments of those works taken as total entities.

An even more prevalent potential reading problem lies in the majority of well written short stories and poems which are found in abundance throughout the pages of secondary school literature anthologies. These shorter selections feature compression of meaning. That is, all the details in them must be noted by the reader. Such details are frequently subtle and/or understated. In any number of instances, they represent foreshadowing details. Good readers of literature, as I.A. Richards states in *Practical Criticism*,[1] are distinguished by the fact that they continue to make predictions as they move through a given selection. They are able to make accurate predictions because they have both noted and assimilated the subtle, understated details within that selection. Having done so, they are better able to deal with an implied meaning. Poorer readers, by contrast, usually overlook such details and therefore come to some very eccentric conclusions about that implied meaning. When these failures to perceive meaning occur consistently, some very negative attitudes toward the reading of literature can emerge and grow.

Unfortunately, these negative attitudes can be helped along by teachers who approach all-class considerations of literary works in a totally prescriptive manner. When such teachers allow little room for, or show little patience with, individual response to assigned texts, poorer readers tend to opt out of any attempt to express their reactions in class discussion. When such readers come to believe that only the teacher's perceptions of meaning, supplemented occasionally by the contribution of some "smart kid," will be tolerated, they often refrain from even beginning the reading of texts assigned. And the failures described above feed on themselves. When many of these poor readers reach tenth, eleventh, or twelfth grade, their interest in the established literature curriculum is dead.

While poor readers often lack a consistent interest in reading, the converse is not always the case: that good readers, as measured by any one of the numerous test instruments in use today, display a rapt, or even moderate interest in reading literature. Many of these gifted students come to the task of reading literature with a spirit of independence and view the selections they choose or are assigned to read in that spirit. In other words, they want to have it their way. Students with distinctly creative thinking approaches often possess the same attitude, only more so. When the tactics used by the teacher demand conformity in response, gifted and creative students are most likely to resist, one way or another. Moreover, these students may be among the most vocal in their criticisms of selections (especially long ones) which they are forced to read in all-class or group settings. "Why do we have to read *that*?" is a question commonly raised by such students, and they will not usually be placated by such overused reasons as "It's important in terms of your background," etc., etc.

Many gifted students have considerable talent and interest in mathematics and physical sciences. Their perspective on what is important to learn in terms of academic components may not include English. They will put out a great amount of effort and concentration in physics, calculus, and computer science, but when faced with the requirement of reading literary works, they may question the value of such involvement, ignore assignments, or treat them in a superficial manner. Moreover, these and other gifted students sometimes display a certain cynicism to any study of the humanities. Their sense of pragmatism may tell them that the road to success (usually material) in life does not include a serious preoccupation with renowned works of literature, art, or music. "How will it prepare me for business (or law or medical) school?" is an all too common question posed by these students to English teachers' demands/requests that they "get serious" about the study of literature.

Thus whether the students are inadequate readers or are superior readers they may evince little or no interest in reading when the reading to be done is of literary texts. Before leaving the study of reading skill and interest in reading, however, some mention needs to be made of the sex factor in problems teachers may face in promoting that interest. Studies dating all the way back into the late 1930s and early 1940s demonstrate clearly that boys represent a significantly greater challenge to teachers than girls do in terms of developing and sustaining a genuine interest in reading and willingness to read worthwhile literary selections in the classroom and outside it.

Virtually from their early school years, boys, on average, prove to be less able and more reluctant readers than girls. As the reading curriculum divides into content-area reading, this negative reaction to the task can be seen most vividly in boys' attitudes toward the reading of literary texts. They tend to be less tolerant of the material they are assigned; they voice more criticism; they quit on these texts sooner; and they refuse to read more than do their female counterparts. In many communities, they are led to believe that boys should be interested in athletic, not studious, pursuits. From this belief sometimes grows the notion that the serious study of literature is somewhat effeminate. (It's just not cool for guys to be turned on by works of literature.) This attitude is demonstrated most flagrantly when poetry is the genre selected for classroom consideration. To many boys, this study is only fit for females or gay males; He-men, that macho term once labelled by Gertrude Stein as a vulgar redundancy, should scorn such study in order to preserve their virility. As an English teacher for over thirty years and a swimming coach for twenty, the author of this chapter has come to believe that this attitude is an institutionalized rationalization: the facts are that many adolescent boys are poor readers, and that much poetry, especially lyric poetry, is hard to read.

In any event, persuading great numbers of young adult males to become genuinely involved in literature study may prove to be a challenge. They don't much like long works. They may refuse to read selections in which the protagonist is female and/or the activities described are in any way feminine. (Try *Pride and Prejudice* on most senior boys, for example.) They often refuse to see the value in studying literature at all. Thus, when teachers assign them responses to literary texts, they may plagiarize, either from book jackets, Cliff's Notes, or the papers of other students; they may "analyze" an issue of Classic Comics; they may coerce a girlfriend or an older sister to write the paper; or they may seek other, more creative means of avoiding their own serious insights. In short, it behooves any secondary school literature teacher to consider the propensities of male students in choosing texts, in designing approaches, and in structuring response tasks.

Home Environment

The attitudes of parents—toward reading, school and its importance, literacy as a personal need, teachers and the value of literature as part of the schooling experience—are all matters for teachers to discover whenever the opportunity arises. It isn't always possible, but an awareness of which books are to be found in the home is one well worth having. The same is true of the nature and amount of periodical literature (all the way from *Harper's* to the *National Enquirer*) collected and read there. It would also be helpful to gain an insight into the nature, quality, and frequency of conversation in the family living room. What topics are entertained? How are they perceived? How much genuine interaction takes place (i.e., are the children allowed to contribute, or do they only listen to adult revelations and pronouncements?) These data could provide helpful insights into the kinds of experiences which are of interest to those families as well as the kinds of reflection pursued on those experiences. Such deliberations have significant correlates in the literary themes investigated in classroom study and analysis.

Informal conversations among parents (or other relatives, guardians, and the like) and teachers can provide even more telling insights. As revealing as such conversations can be, however, they may not tell teachers as much as does the absence of these adults. It's those who do not show up whose kids are frequently having the most difficulty in school, academic and otherwise. Since literature is about human experience, and all young people are the products of some adult or familial experience, it is usually helpful to shed light on what the background profiles really are.

One parental attitude about school in general and literature study in particular which sometimes manifests itself dramatically is found in parents' objection to the texts their children have been assigned to read. These objections are so far-ranging as to be mind boggling on occasion. The history of the censorship struggle leads to the fairly indisputable conclusion that, in a given school situation, no text is safe from attack by some parent or concerned citizen. When such attacks are mounted, teachers of literature find out firsthand, often to their horror and dismay, what literary values are held in the home. The chapter on school censorship will provide a substantive review and analysis of that issue.

The Period of Adolescence

Volumes have been written on the nature of the vagaries and self-identity crises that take place during the adolescent years. While these factors cannot be undervalued, teachers who wish to study that multifaceted stage can find vast amounts of material on the topic, both in professional libraries and in the popular print media.

Interest in reading fluctuates widely before the age of sixteen, an age at which many students begin to think seriously about choices affecting their future: college, military service, industrial careers, dropping out of the academic scene altogether, and so forth. For most young people, interest in reading usually peaks between the ages of twelve and fourteen, although for many boys, it peaks long before that age (or never peaks at all). This is an age at which many adolescents of both sexes become withdrawn, at least temporarily. It is a period of intense, prolonged introspection in which the desire to raise and organize problems about self is at its height. It's a kind of limbo between a lost childhood and approaching adulthood. People at this age tend to be more interested in being alone with their thoughts and emotions than at any time earlier or later in their lives. For some, reading fiction, especially novels which delve into the teenage experience, can be a source of comfort, challenge, stimulation, and/or escape. The chapter that follows, on Young Adult Literature, focuses on the nature and availability of literature with which youngsters at that difficult stage of their lives can identify.

People in these years are also capable of, and often involved in, deeper reflection that centers on abstract concepts: love, loyalty, fear, justice, betrayal, and the like. Obviously, their reading can feed this preoccupation, but the fare must be nourishing. In short, abstract thinking may contain a profound concern with interpersonal relationships, and reading can provide countless opportunities for them to view their problems from the detached prism of fiction.[2]

Some of these interpersonal problems will be quite obvious. Some mention of them should be made, however, because they have implications for teachers who search for works which deal with correlative experiences:

1. Problems related to the need for reconciling relationships with parents and a growing sense of independence (i.e., the desire to assume the adult roles without the wherewithal to do so);
2. Problems related to communication with younger siblings, partially stemming from thirteen-year-olds' desire that the "little

people" regard them as adults—and these younger children's
irritating reluctance to cooperate;
3. Problems related to the conflicting need to establish individuality
   as opposed to an equally strong need to be accepted into a peer
   group;
4. Problems which reside in thirteen-year-olds' ambivalence toward
   members of the opposite sex (i.e., culture and peer pressure, clash
   with hormones). The gap between girls' and boys' relative imma-
   turity exacerbates this greatly.[3]

In all of the above, imaginative literature can become a source of excitement,
revelation, guidance, and/or solace. Teachers as *guidance counselors* can be
of great personal assistance to adolescents in their struggles. The movement
of middle school curricula toward an emphasis on the personal and social
identities of early adolescents, rather than on the cultural heritage into
which they will someday be assimilated, provides a whole new niche for
literature to occupy, one in which its relevance to the nature of the early
teenage years can be maximized.

The Influence of Television

Our concern with television as a factor, mostly a negative one, has
been voiced earlier (Chapter Three). As one considers what affects young
people's interest in reading, however, this issue cannot be glossed over.
Because its influence is so pervasive in American culture, the degree to
which commercial television distracts young people from literature study
is only one of its questionable values. Since this book is about literature
study for and by young people, some clarification is in order.

One of the great goals of literature study in secondary schools is to
lead students to serious reflection on human experience. That is to say,
desirable literary encounters in the English classroom will always extend
beyond mere entertainment. Yet in his provocative book, *Amusing Ourselves to Death*, Neil Postman argues persuasively that the obsession Americans of all ages have with television has reduced to "show business" their
relationship with their major institutions—politics, religion, current affairs,
and education. In his chapter titled "The Peek-a-boo World," Postman
states:

> Together, this ensemble of electronic techniques (telegraph, phonograph,
> radio, film) called into being a new world—a peek-a-boo world, where
> now this event, now that, pops into view for a moment, then vanishes
> again. It is a world without much coherence or sense; a world that does
> not ask us, indeed, does not permit us to do anything; a world that is, like

the child's game of peek-a-boo, entirely self-contained. But like peek-a-boo, it is also endlessly entertaining.

Of course, there is nothing wrong with playing peek-a-boo. And there is nothing wrong with entertainment. As some psychiatrist once put it, we all build castles in the air. The problems come when we try to *live* in them. The communications media of the late nineteenth and early twentieth centuries, with telegraphy and photography at their center, called the peek-a-boo world into existence, but we did not come to live there until television. Television gave the epistemological biases of the telegraph and the photograph their most potent expression, raising the interplay of image and instancy to an exquisite and dangerous perfection. And it brought them into the home. We are by now well into a second generation of children for whom television has been their first and most accessible teacher and, for many, their most reliable companion and friend. To put it plainly, television is the command center of the new epistemology. There is no audience so young that it is barred from television. There is no poverty so abject that it must forgo television. And most important of all, there is no subject of public interest—politics, news, education, religion, science, sports—that does not find its way to television. Which means that all public understanding of these subjects is shaped by the biases of television.[4]

The grim fact is that many teachers believe, or more accurately, are driven to the belief, that they must constantly entertain their students in order to hold their attention. This attempt is rather pathetic since commercial television has creative electronic resources, almost without number, with which to dazzle viewers. Teachers, on the other hand, typically have to plead for *any* resources—electronic included. Logically, then, teachers of literature must realize that they simply cannot compete with the appeal of television as they plan and implement their strategies for the teaching of literature. They must sell their main product, the reading (usually silently and independently) of worthwhile literary selections, for what it is: a significant component of the public school curriculum. Their ultimate goals must be to use literary works as vehicles to involve their students in some of the major areas of philosophical speculation: metaphysics, axiology, epistemology, and aesthetics. To consider the watering down of the choices, let's say, to Teen Age Romances, or the nature of study—let's say to compare works of short fiction to television sitcoms—is to debase the meaning and value of the whole endeavor. If teachers don't separate education from "show biz," they will indeed achieve the end result of amusing themselves—and their students—to death.

Postman is probably right when he contends that the only hope is for our culture to escape its drowning in a sea of trivia. In his final chapter, he states,

And yet there is reason to suppose that the situation is not hopeless. Educators are not unaware of the effects of television on their students.

Stimulated by the arrival of the computer, they discuss it a great deal—which is to say, they have become somewhat "media conscious." It is true enough that much of their consciousness centers on the question, How can we use television (or the computer, or word processor) to control education? They have not yet got to the question, How can we use education to control television (or the computer, or word processor)? But our reach for solutions ought to exceed our present grasp, or what's our dreaming for? Besides, it is an acknowledged task of the schools to assist the young in learning how to interpret the symbols of their culture. That this task should now require that they learn how to distance themselves from their forms of information is not so bizarre an enterprise that we cannot hope for its inclusion in the curriculum; even hope that it will be placed at the center of education.[5]

If we are to take Postman at his word, literature study in the schools indeed becomes an undertaking of great significance.

Other "Competitors"

As teachers make an effort to read and study literature as a means of both using leisure time profitably and reflecting on some of the more significant aspects of the human situation, they must face commercial television as a major competitor for the time which such reading and study will require. There are others, however, and most adolescents are well aware of them even if their teachers are not. Here, briefly, are several of them.

1. **Teen Age Romances** Published in cheap paperback editions, these simplistic, often mushy/sentimental love stories are born by the hundreds every year. Since they are expected to follow a rigid formula, most of their authors are truly nonentities. The plots are totally predictable, endlessly redundant, and utterly divorced from reality. They represent *escape* reading in the extreme. *But they are enormously popular with female readers at all age groups.* Some series target adult audiences and, more recently, several have been aimed at teenage readers, even further dividing their focus between either younger or older teens. These romances can, hopefully, be balanced by Young Adult novels (whose focus may or may not be romantic interests) as well as by more mature works.

2. **Girlie Magazines** Since the publication of *Esquire* in the 1940s, with its Varga Girl centerfold, magazines which display rather than discuss flesh have flooded the magazine spindles of this

country. Years after *Esquire* (actually a publication containing some well-written articles on various cultural issues), Hugh Hefner's *Playboy* came on the scene showing more flesh, in more provocative poses. The more permissive standards of the past quarter century have witnessed the addition of the Guccione-type magazines such as *Oui* and *Penthouse*. As this text is being written, organized antipornography groups nationwide are seeking to oust them from supermarkets, convenience stores, airport stalls, and other spots of easy access. Take a peek behind the large, hardback textbooks your students are allegedly studying in class, and you may find one of those monthly titillators as the real object of scrutiny.

3. **Comic Books** One of the older, enduring traditions in the leisure reading habits of young people is the comic book. Before television took over, comic books (actually magazines) and their predecessors, the "Big Little Books," were a major commodity in the popular entertainment marketplace. Now that Superman, Batman, and the worthy sons of Buck Rogers have made the switch into television and Hollywood film productions, the widespread preoccupation with comic books has diminished somewhat. They do exist, however, usually in a different trim size (the "Archie" series, for example) and can be found in many secondary students' lockers from Maine to California. Magazines devoted to surfing and skating are also popular today, as are those describing the wonders of computers.

4. **Rock and Roll, Soul, and Country Music Lyrics and Videos** If it's poetry you want, the popular music of this century has plenty to offer. And the young people of America have always eaten it up, all the way from the Rudy Vallee, Bing Crosby, early Sinatra moon-June-croon-spoon numbers to the Hard Rock, Acid Rock, Punk Rock ear-splitters of the moment. While most teenagers would object violently to this pronouncement, the quality of poetic pieces is often low.

By careful listening, however, teachers can find some lyrics in this music which have literary merit. To find it, we must often suspend our (sometimes generational) disbelief and give the lyrics a chance. The songs of the group Rush, for example, often are quite poetic, and other groups even set major poems to music. (Iron Maiden's version of *The Rime of the Ancient Mariner* is notable in this regard.) To categorically and caustically dismiss them all is both counterproductive to the establishment of rapport and, to a degree, intellectually dishonest.

There was a time in the late 1960s and early 1970s when the "message" in those lyrics did contain a modicum of substance. Certainly they did address the several ills of the times in a forthright, if not terribly artistic manner. The songs of Pete Seeger, Joan Baez, Bob Dylan, Simon and Garfunkel, and other pop crusaders gave voice to the issues of Vietnam and Watergate America in a style which sometimes approached eloquence. Where open-minded teachers were on duty, several of these pieces became the object of classroom deliberation. The writer of this chapter recalls vividly observing student teachers as they challenged their students with "Those Were the Days, My Friend" or "Where Have All the Flowers Gone?" contrasting "Richard Cory" by E. A. Robinson with the one composed by Simon and Garfunkel. But, as the song says, the times they are a-changing. For the most part, today's rock, soul, and country lyrics abound with a mixture of sentimentality, anger, platitude, and/or obscenity. Add to this the graphic, often violent and/or lewd video interpretations that accompany them on the "teen music" channels of cable television, and you have a hypnotic fix for teenagers almost any time of day or night.

5. **Thriller Movies** Not much has to be said on this one, does it? By the time this text appears, the movie-going public will probably be in the throes of "Psycho XX," "Nightmare on Elm Street XV," and "Indiana Jones Marches On, Encore." A sizable portion of the public has been captivated by this technologically driven adventure madness, and there is probably no end in sight. Plot gives way to mannerism and sensation; extended cause and effect chronology ceases to exist; and subtlety is a dirty word. While teachers involved in Film-as-Literature courses give these noisy spectacles a wide berth in their syllabi, the kids continue to crave them, which is, obviously, why they continue to appear in abundance. Working with longer, high quality works of literature is not easy when the students are hooked on cinematic monstrosities. Teachers need to keep in mind that, for the present, they are neither gone nor forgotten.

6. **Simplified Classics** The revised, reduced, usually gutted works of literature found in such text publications as the Lyons/Carnahan Classmate editions, the Landmark Series, the Globe Book Literature materials, and certain *Reader's Digest* editions represent a somewhat different kind of competitor to meaningful literature study. They are written primarily for, and usually found in, secondary school classrooms. Middle school and junior high English

Reading Interest Factor Wheel

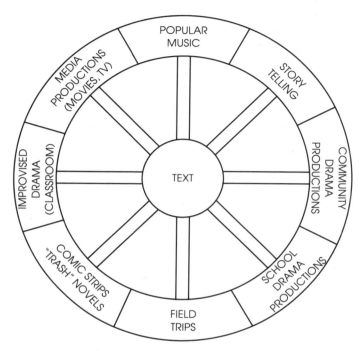

Figure 4.1

teachers are particularly prone to including them in classroom instructional designs. These books drastically reduce plots, exclude most extended metaphoric expression, eliminate such stylistic features as flashbacks, prophecies, and interior monologues, and in general downplay those text segments which dwell on the inner nature of characters. Teachers of basic students and coordinators of reading laboratories continue to find them useful and often emphasize their use in promoting reading with reluctant and less able students. To this effort, no objections here. What must be remembered is that these selections are not literature and should not be represented as such. The differences between Homer's *Odyssey* and Globe Books' *The Story of Ulysses,* for example, are legion and momentous. Students who come to know the story, recognize characters, and can identify where it all took place have some awareness of the skeletal elements of such works. However, they aren't *studying literature,* nor should they ever be led to believe that they are.

Some of the competitors for the attention of young people, as those listed above, have a vague resemblance to literary works (some very vague). These competitors, however, are widespread, accessible, potent, and commercially attractive. They cannot be ignored, and, in fact, must be recognized and transcended.

Ways to Stimulate Interest in Reading

Briefly, before moving on to reading interests, a few ideas on how to stimulate interest in reading would seem to be in order.

1. **Book Talks** Classroom teachers can provide these, discussing recent books, those known to be perennially popular, or those related to a topic under study. Librarians are often most eager to enter English classrooms to discuss books, be they new acquisitions or old favorites. And members of the community who have some particular attachment to likely texts can be invited to present. There are few better ways to stimulate book selection than by such enthusiastic reviews.

2. **Classroom Libraries** Most experienced English teachers support the notion that proximity is a most important factor in book selection. Thus it is usually a better idea to offer choices from books found in the classroom than to request that students go to the library, whether it is school or public. Large collections of literary texts, mostly paperback, have proven over the years to be an effective addition to anthology and single, required selections. Often these collections can be implemented in a particular unit of study, adding the individualized reading component to that unit.

   The paperback classroom library is relatively easy to assemble and manage. If money is available within the school, then paperbacks can be bought with these funds. If money is a problem, friends, neighbors, colleagues, parents of students, and students themselves are often eager to "get rid" of books they no longer want. The books should be displayed with their covers in full view; publishers spend a great deal of money designing covers to sell books, and there is no reason the teacher can't take advantage of this to "sell" books to kids. It is a good idea from time to time to allow students to browse the classroom library; even if they don't choose a book to read, they are at least coming into contact with books and are learning titles and authors painlessly. The classroom library will probably do its biggest business, though, in the three or four minutes before the "tardy" bell rings to signal the start of the class period. Some sort of check-out system is helpful (an index card with the title and a place for students to sign their names is sufficient), but teachers who opt for classroom libraries should face the fact at the start that books will disappear. This is unfortunate, of course, but when students have the freedom they need to examine books in an unrestricted manner, this is one of the risks.

There are basically two types of classroom libraries: those that contain books for leisure reading that aren't particularly related to the curriculum, and those that are supplemental to the curriculum. The first kind obviously contains a variety of books that students are interested in reading for fun, both fiction and nonfiction. The second kind can contain additional titles by authors studied in the course and books that deal with themes that are studied as part of the curriculum. In Chapter Nine we will discuss the thematic approach to curriculum organization in literature, and a classroom library is a *sine qua non* for using this approach.

3. **Book Clubs** Several large commercial publishing companies offer book clubs as means of stimulating wide reading. They generally provide catalogues of very inexpensive paperback books which can be ordered during the school year. For the most part, teachers collect money from students, allow them to order their books, and send in the orders periodically. Clubs often give bonuses of various kinds to their regular subscribers. A great deal of enrichment reading takes place through these clubs.

4. **Parent-Child Cooperation** Several school systems have experimented successfully with programs in which children and their parents read the same book, usually together at home. These selections are sometimes all-class reading assignments. At other times, they are chosen from a wide reading list. Parents and children discuss what they have read both during their reading and when they have completed the book under mutual study. On some occasions, the parents come to the classroom and add to the discussion of certain texts. This is an innovative and positive way to involve parents in the process of their children's education.

5. **"Fifty-two Pick-up"** This idea was originated by Ms. Alyne Farrell, a middle school teacher in Sarasota, Florida. At the beginning of a period, each student is provided with a book from an established reading list or from the classroom library. The teacher then has the students begin to read their books and continue to do so

for five minutes. When the teacher signals the end of the five-minute period, the students pass their books to the student next to (behind or in front of) them. The five-minute reading session is repeated five or six times in a class period. Then the teacher asks the students to choose the book they found most potentially interesting, and the remainder of the class period is spent reading. Active student choice in reading is virtually guaranteed through this approach.

There are a great many other ways to stimulate interest in reading. For example, bookstores are usually happy to sponsor book fairs at schools, and the school usually gets a percentage of the profits. These work particularly well before holidays that are gift-giving occasions or at the end of the school year if students are given summer reading assignments. Also, schools can sponsor book swaps, in which students bring books they no longer want and swap them with other students. Finally, if administrators are willing to cooperate, one or two class periods a week can be set aside for reading by *everyone* in the school. When teachers set their minds to the serious business of encouraging reading, ideas on how to do it come fast.

Reading Interests

Since the reading interests of young people are a function of their development, several facts must be kept in mind by those teachers of literature who recognize the importance of such interests in designing course offerings. The first of these is that interests will change as the individual matures. A preference for the weird, bizarre, exotic, and improbable in literary selections today may be abandoned tomorrow in the pursuit of works which emphasize hard-nosed realistic or naturalistic themes and topics. A commitment to stories about animals among sixth graders may turn into contempt for such stories once these students reach seventh grade. What engrosses them at the moment may soon bore them. When these changes take place is largely unpredictable, but their manifestations will be evident, even to the most unobservant English teacher.

Reading interests may be very nonacademic, a fact that irritates many inexperienced teachers. Students who turn up their noses at the selections in the anthology often embrace Archie comics avidly and will be perfectly willing to flaunt this preference before those teachers who overtly display their irritation. Teachers who try to force their perceptions of quality literature on such students will usually do no more than exacerbate the problem. This is not to say that such preferences should be accepted or, worse, incorporated into all-class literary considerations. They must be recognized and counterbalanced with selections on generally similar topics but ones which can legitimately be called works of literature. More on that in a later section of this chapter.

Reading interests are the result of the multifaceted nature of adolescent development and, since several of these aspects have been discussed already, they will simply be listed here, by way of reminders:

Personal Characteristics of Adolescents

1. Their emotional development—sporadic, unpredictable, often volatile.
2. Their development of self-awareness—a constant, intensive search.
3. Their need for and preoccupation with interpersonal relationships—the ongoing search for "best friends" and the angry response to their "enemies" of the moment. Add family here which is, indeed, a wild card.
4. Their development of a sense of ethics—often inconsistent, frequently self-serving, always intense.
5. Their embryonic development of a philosophical outlook—with respect to death and deity, reflected to a significant degree in the poetry which they (both sexes) write in abundance.

All of these developments are churning within young people during the years they are students in secondary English classes. As described earlier, age thirteen is usually the flashpoint of these changes. They all interact with reading interests, which in turn affect, often in a pronounced manner, the relative success teachers have when they introduce any literary selection for all-class consideration.

Dr. Margaret Early, a distinguished educator in English and reading, has posed a paradigm for the development of appreciation of literature among adolescent readers. The primary importance of this paradigm lies in its recognition of the reading interests of such individuals as a governing factor. Here are stages Dr. Early isolates:

1. **The Stage of Unconscious Enjoyment** Often referred to as the *turn on;* the spontaneous, visceral reaction to the imagery evoked by some works.
2. **The Stage of Self-conscious Appreciation** Largely an intellectual process, it is manifested by voluntary response, participation

in classroom discussion, allusion to key passages, perception of relationships, recognition of symbolic meaning. (Strategic guidance by the teacher is a big factor here.)

3. **The Stage of Unconscious Delight** The long-lasting impact of a particular work, often manifested by repeated allusion to that text, by voluntary memorization of key lines, by searching for other works of that author, by purchasing a copy for personal rereading.[6]

The stages occur because of reading interests and not because of externally imposed edicts or critical judgments. The teacher's role as indirect, subtle leader of consideration, response, and sharing of perceptions becomes a significant factor here, one way or another.

The Issue of Realism

A review of the reading interests of students reveals, as amply stated previously, volatility, inconsistency, and obstinacy. These elements of interest take on increased significance when teachers attempt to reconcile genuine student involvement with their desire to introduce quality texts in the classroom.

A factor of adolescent reading interests is the desire, indeed the demand, of these young people for the *real* in what they choose or are assigned to read. To repeat, the definition of what is *real* may differ widely, virtually from student to student. In recognizing this need and in attempting to use it as a positive force in promoting literary sophistication among their relatively immature students, teachers should be apprised of a series of concerns attendant to the realism demand:

1. **The Search for Certainty** Despite the desire for realism in what they read, adolescents search for, and expect to find, certainty in the selections they encounter. If not the happy ending, they expect the loose ends to be neatly tied up; this usually means virtue rewarded and evil punished. James Squire, in his classic study of tenth graders' responses to four short stories, corroborates this claim.[7] Such expectations can cause frustration among students who encounter endings which are tentative, abrupt, ambiguous, or anticlimactic. The ending in Ernest Hemingway's famous story ''The Killers'' provides an excellent example. Many readers are puzzled, even frustrated by the stoic resignation to catastrophe found in the story's conclusion. Still another example can be seen in the manner in which people turn away from the tragic death of

a boy in Robert Frost's poem "Out, Out—." Those readers are nonplussed by the almost casual manner in which the others in the poem go about their business once they learn about the boy's death.

2. **The Demand for Overt Physical Activity** Reality can be inner in nature as well as outer, but that fact isn't always accepted by young readers as they become involved with a selection that is somewhat cerebral. This preference is probably the cause of Henry James's manifest lack of popularity with most senior high students; why Willa Cather's "Paul's Case" and Herman Melville's "Benito Cereno" are hard sells in the teaching of fiction. Many English educators have, over the years, been most unwilling to accept the popularity of Crane's *The Red Badge of Courage* with secondary school students. The mixture of outer and inner action, predominantly outer (plus the adolescent protagonist and the brevity of the novel), is probably the the reason for its enduring popularity.

3. **The Acceptance of Sensationalism** Despite many disclaimers, young readers still crave the unusual, even the slick, in what they read. They may argue vigorously that certain action-packed, adventure-laden texts retain their realism credentials, and they will usually be hard to dissuade in this belief. As this text is written, the works of Stephen King remain extremely popular with a youthful reading audience. Teachers should be careful as they approach what *they* sense to be the line between reality and sensationalism. With skill and tact, they may lead their students to the acceptance of some bona fide criteria for judgement of such texts.

4. **Contrivance versus Irony** Some works have quirky endings, ones which don't seem to stack up with the cause and effect sequence of events developed throughout the text. Judgment is an all-important factor here, and teachers must take care not to be too overbearing in foisting *their* perceptions and judgments on their students. Plots sometimes turn on the inclusion of seemingly minor events by the author, and readers who miss them may draw some totally inaccurate conclusions from those elements in the text that they *do* note. Conversely, one of the features of poorly written literature is the degree of credibility at the outcomes and revelations presented by an author (i.e., whether or not they hold up to careful, objective scrutiny). Thus this crucial question which must be posed by all critical readers: Are the details there, or aren't they? Teacher-student interaction with such texts can make or break the legitimate judgments which come as a result of careful reading of the work. When students are not genuinely convinced that a

particular judgment is a sound one, the distinction between contrivance and literary craftsmanship may well be blurred.

5. **Potential of the Adolescent** Both James Squire and Stephen Dun-
    ning (the latter will be discussed more fully in Chapter Five)
    concluded in their research that one of the weaknesses of some
    fiction that is popular with young readers lies in the unrealistic
    portrayal of youthful protagonists as *superboy/supergirl* figures.[8]
    While they ostensibly demand the *real* in what they read, a large
    number of these youngsters cling determinedly to certain beliefs
    about the ability of teenagers (at least in fiction) to leap tall build-
    ings at a single bound. While such potential can be easily pointed
    out by teachers during class discussions, it is the manner of such
    pronouncements that represent the horns of the dilemma. Those
    teachers must keep in mind that they are the only adults in the
    room. What seems to them to appeal to logic and reason may be
    perceived as put-downs by teenage students who have difficulty
    in reconciling their often subconscious romantic beliefs with their
    stated demands for the real. The best course of action for teachers
    is to encourage students to relate concrete elements of the text to
    the imagined overall character perceptions these same students
    have already formed.

6. **The Censorship Potential** While *real* may be the stated criterion
    for acceptance by students and reality may be an important factor
    in getting students honestly involved in a literary work, the same
    text may be unacceptable to certain parents, citizens, administra-
    tors, and even fellow teachers. The search for the real can uncover
    some topics which may engross students but simultaneously
    arouse the animosity of those who feel the need to monitor mate-
    rials used in the schools within their community. Taboos are many
    and varied, so much so that an entire chapter will be devoted to
    the censorship issue. (See Chapter Eleven.) For the moment, let it
    be sufficient to caution teachers about the nature and extent to
    which reality is treated in texts they use in the classroom. Enthu-
    siasm for literature study is a great thing to arouse, but creating it
    for certain selections can get teachers fired.

Promoting Interest in the Classroom

Teachers can do a great deal to enhance the interest of literature study in
their classrooms. Being cognizant of the several factors affecting the
students' potential interest, as just described, is important. Beyond that,

however, teachers can consider a series of decisions about the nature of study in their classrooms which can make further differences.

One significant set of decisions concerns establishing balance in the manner in which they ask students to deal with literary selections. A fundamental aspect of such balance rests with teachers' decisions as to who reads what. During a school year, teachers (1) can assign some texts as all-class reading. In other instances, they (2) can choose a few works related to each other in some way (genre, author, mode, theme), and assign each to a small group for reading and sharing responses. Allowing groups to have input about those choices, on occasion, will vary the pattern even further. Finally, teachers (3) can develop a series of wide reading lists, allowing students to make individual choices within their reading assignments. In developing such lists, teachers can almost invariably count on the assistance of the school librarian or media specialist to provide information as to what's available, what's good, and what's relevant to the goals of a particular unit of instruction. Beyond assistance available within the school, public libraries offer a wealth of up-to-date information about their resources. Several professional organizations offer information on quality literary texts and where they can be obtained. Notable among these organizations are the National Council of Teachers of English (NCTE), its active sub-group, the Assembly on Literature for Adolescents National (ALAN), and the American Library Association (ALA). Individualized reading components, with lots of student-choice opportunities (with guidance from the teachers), provide teachers with the best means of relating students' reading interests with course objectives. It takes time and effort to compose appropriate lists for such individual components, but help is available; and in terms of student motivation, the results usually make that effort worthwhile.

Teachers can add another dimension of variety to literary engagement: the assignment of tasks to be completed both within and outside of class time. In considering the latter approach, the book report comes immediately to mind. Little evidence indicates that students have ever been positively motivated by the assignment of a series of periodically rendered book reports stretching from September to June. In and of itself, such a system is fraught with potential negatives, most of which relate to the interest factor. In the first place, the number of such reports over a period of time (the six-weeks grading period, the semester, the year) puts a distinctly quantitative overtone on the experience of reading literature. Students can easily fall into the habit of ticking reports off their lists of things to do, much as they would their after-school chores. Second, book reports, done wholly as outside-of-class tasks, can easily be faked. This is where the desire to find book jackets can grow in appeal to those students who perceive these reports as little more than hurdles to surmount on the way to a passing grade in English. Third, seldom is any attempt made to relate that kind of reading task to what is going on in class. Finally, most book reports are written to no audience in particular. Thus, the relation of the speaking voice cannot be applied to this writing experience unless an unusually enterprising student chooses to do so.

The speaking voice aspect of the writing process relates to the agents present in any written statement. The first of these is the element of *voice*—the identity, indeed the *persona*—of the individual who is making the written statement. Just as all speakers portray a certain kind of identity, so do writers. One of the goals of effective writing instruction should include attention to the question, "Who am I?" asked by writers before they begin to compose. The second element is *tone*—the identification of the intended audience, once again deliberately chosen by writers before the writing is under way. Personae are almost always chosen in relation to the audience for the written piece. The third element of the speaking voice, *attitude*, concerns the manner in which writers will treat their subject matter, again predetermined. Briefly stated, writers decide here (1) what and how much they know about the subject and what and how much of that knowledge they will reveal to (2) what particular audience on what particular occasion, for (3) what purpose(s).[9]

The book report assignment commonly lacks the inclusion of these three elements, and they are significant oversights if the report is ever to be approached with any degree of enthusiasm by students. In particular, the issue of audience needs to be addressed. Before embarking on their first paragraphs, students need to consider the following questions:

1. How many people am I addressing, one or more?
2. Who is my audience; specifically, is it a teacher, a classmate, a peer, a particular adult, etc.?
3. What does my audience already know about this book?
   a. Have they read it?
   b. Have they heard anything about it, such as its plot?
   c. Have they seen a movie version of it?
   d. Have they read a Classic Comics version?
4. Is my task simply to discuss the book in neutral terms, or should my report include personal judgments?
5. Do I discuss only the book, or should I compare it with texts we have read somewhere else, especially in class?
6. Am I expected to have read anything about the book, (e.g., critical commentaries), and share these with my audience?

7. Is the subject matter of the book something my audience is familiar with or not?

8. If the members of my audience are familiar with the subject matter, are they likely to be supportive of or hostile to the theme of the book?

9. Will I have to read my report aloud to some audience?

10. If I read aloud, will my audience be given the opportunity to ask me about my report or be asked to respond in any way?

These are some of the questions seldom posed by teachers to their book reporters. At least some of them should be raised, discussed, and/or chosen by the reporters in every writing task of this nature which students are obliged to generate.

Teachers must make other textual decisions which are closely related to student interest. These decisions involve all-class and small-group instruction. For the most part, the following points have been touched on earlier; therefore, they will be summarized briefly here:

1. **Popular Literature versus Established Texts** Since no national curriculum exists in this country, there is no universally accepted canon of Great Books in high schools and, more obviously, in middle schools. The choices are largely left to the departments and teachers. Popular literature probably represents the most difficult choice since teachers who are considering such texts are largely on their own; they don't have the literary scholarship of the ages on which to rely.

2. **Contemporary Texts versus Classics** Closely associated with #1, above, these choices have to do primarily with the degree to which teachers keep up with current literary publication in their personal reading, as well as their awareness of ongoing book reviews in such magazines as *Saturday Review, Atlantic Monthly, Harper's, The New York Times Book Review*, their own Sunday newspapers, and other pertinent book review periodicals.

3. **Taste versus Entertainment** A balance between *serious* literature and that which is largely entertaining is desirable. The latter should be used primarily as a change of pace from more subtle, challenging works. Obviously, it should not occupy center stage despite its appeal, especially to those students who adhere to the belief that encounters with any literary selections are now, have always been, and should always be fun.

4. **Interrelating Print Versions with Nonprint Ones** Literary texts presented on audio cassette, disc, video tape, 35 mm film, or other electronic reproduction serve as an excellent supplement to printed texts. They should be used occasionally and judiciously. *Never*, however, should they become a wholesale substitute for the reading of literature; a vital goal in the literature curriculum is to develop within young people the ability to assess meaning and aesthetic elements on their own and without the interposition of actors, actresses, directions, editor, special effects, and so forth.

5. **Student Response** The time-honored, read-respond sequence is one to be perpetuated at all levels. In order to satisfy the range of attention spans, reading abilities, reading interests, and the teachers' goals, however, the pattern of student responses should be varied. This can be accomplished in a number of ways: the publication of students' creative attempts in school or class literary magazines; student performance in the form of oral reading; choral presentations; and dramatic productions. One kind of dramatic production is improvised drama, usually performed in the class-rooms (and not at all-school assemblies), which can provide excellent vehicles for anticipating literary selections and eliciting reactions to them. Those students gifted in drawing, painting, photography, and crafts should be encouraged to present some response through visual products; those who lack that talent should be allowed to gather and share those examples of visual art which they feel express relevant meanings. Writing papers and answering questions raised during class discussions remain desirable approaches to response. All of these teaching strategies can break the monotony for often jaded secondary school youngsters.

One last suggestion which is, in a sense, a restatement of an earlier one: all English teachers should stay alive as readers of literature. With the press of duties and the equally important need to remain vital in a personal, familial, and social sense, teachers may forget one of the primary reasons, probably, that they majored in English: the love of *reading imaginative literature*. There will always be many new works which intrigue English teachers as well as those works they have always meant to read. Returning occasionally to this reading is a most desirable means of broadening backgrounds as well as revitalizing enthusiasm. It pays another dividend as well: doing so will further demonstrate to young readers that encounters with literature go beyond entertainment to the evocation of serious, reflective thought—a task tougher today than ever before, but one still well worth the effort. Students should observe that their teachers are not just *preachers* who are admonishing them to read; instead, they are genuinely enthusiastic readers, as reflected in selections on the desk and their eagerness to discuss them.

Notes

1. I. A. Richards. *Practical Criticism: A Study of Literary Judgment.* San Diego: Harcourt Brace Jovanovich, first published 1929.

2. Arnold Gesell, et al. *Youth: The Years from Ten to Sixteen.* New York: Harper & Row, 1956; and the follow-up to that study, Louise Bates Ames. *Your Ten- to Fourteen-Year-Old.* New York: Delacorte Press, 1988. These works report the research conducted at the Gesell Institute for Human Development in New Haven, Connecticut, and they offer invaluable insight to teachers and parents on the developmental tasks of adolescence.

3. Gesell, passim.

4. Neil Postman. *Amusing Ourselves to Death.* London: Heinemann, 1986, pp 77–78.

5. Postman, *Amusing Ourselves,* pp 162–163.

6. Margaret J. Early, "Stages in Growth in Literary Appreciation," *English Journal* 49: 161–167, March 1960.

7. James R. Squire. *The Responses of Adolescents While Reading Four Short Stories.* Research Report No. 2. Champaign: National Council of Teachers of English, 1964.

8. Stephen Dunning. "A Definition of the Role of the Junior Novel Based on Analyses of Thirty Selected Novels." Unpublished Ph.D. dissertation, Florida State University, 1959.

9. For a more complete explanation of the speaking voice approach see D. Bruce Lockerbie, "The 'Speaking Voice' Approach," *English Journal,* 52: 596–600, November 1963.

CHAPTER FIVE

Young Adult Fiction

A Disclaimer

A major purpose of this text is to assist teachers of literature in considering their role from a variety of perspectives. Two of those perspectives directly concern knowledge about and use of *young adult* (YA) fiction in secondary programs of study. Teachers in middle and junior high schools are usually responsible for introducing the serious study of literature to their students; YA fiction can serve as an excellent vehicle for such an introduction. Teachers in senior high schools who deal with students of lower ability, nonacademic motivations, and limited cultural backgrounds should also consider the use of YA fiction to provide insight into the nature of literature study with those individuals.

YA fiction is a commodity whose presence in the literature course of study can prove of great value. Having stated that belief, a disclaimer is in order: this text is not, and does not pretend to provide, an extensive treatment of this literary genre. To study YA fiction in depth, teachers should consult such texts as *Literature for Today's Young Adults* (third edition) by Kenneth Donelson and Alleen Nilsen (Scott-Foresman, 1989); it provides an encyclopedic treatment of YA literature. This chapter, however, will attempt to present the salient features of the genre.

The Transition Concept—Reading to Study

Professional literature on the middle school curriculum, directed to teacher educators, curriculum specialists, and classroom teachers, suggests that the middle school years (roughly grades 6 through 8) should serve as a transition period. The view of this chapter on YA fiction aligns itself with that opinion.

Teachers might consider some of the more clearly detectable tenets of literature teaching in the early childhood years:

1. **Reading for Enjoyment** While most subject matter elements are perceived, both by teachers and students, as hard work from the word *go* (arithmetic, geography, earth science, grammar), literature is usually considered a change of pace. It is an experience which provides pleasure, excitement, even fun.

2. **Frequent Use of Oral Reading** Teachers and students present a large number of literary works through the repeated use of individual and group oral reading. This is particularly true of poems and playlets.

3. **Selections Are Usually Quite Short** Few full-length novels or three-to-five act plays are included. Furthermore, the need for students to sustain comprehension, as described in the previous chapter, is largely unnecessary.

4. **Selections Are Usually Random** There is seldom any attempt made to present patterns of literature, such as genres, modes, or national cultures.

5. **Use of Stories of Fantasy, Whimsy, and the Improbable** A considerable number of fairy tales, simple folk tales, legends, and light supernatural stories will be introduced in abundance.

6. **Topics from Childhood** Beyond the fanciful selections mentioned above, life experiences presented tend to focus on the pleasant, exciting ones of a certain level of childhood (in the sociological sense) (i.e., lives of migrant children and those living on Indian reservations in the West are not common).

7. **Lots of Pictures** To create interest and reinforce understanding of meaning among children, most stories, poems, and so forth will be augmented by the presence of photographs, sketches, drawings, portraits, or cartoons. With most children's texts, these illustrations are an integral part of the publication.

8. **Easy Reading** In the light of items 3, 5, 6, and 7 above, it should be obvious that the ease of reading is a clearly identifiable characteristic of children's literary works. In most of them, stylistic complexity is conspicuous by its absence.

9. **Little or No Symbolism** Another fairly obvious deduction to be drawn from several of the characteristics mentioned above is the absence of symbolic events, characters, settings, or conflicts. Stories are stories per se.

10. **Nature of Response** When teachers ask for class responses to the selections presented, these responses tend to be ones of simple, unqualified appreciation. Literary analysis, interpretations, or associations are seldom demanded, nor are they expected from the children.

This is a review of the literature curriculum of the early school years. What follows are the characteristics of the senior high school, at least the school that seems to be the target in programs of study for average and above average students:

1. **Cultural Awareness** Literature is seen to be linked with historical, mythological, sociological, political, and philosophical dimensions of a given national culture.

2. **Long Works** An imposing number of full-length novels and three-to-five act plays, studied intensively and assigned for book-report type tasks, are commonplace among texts included in courses at this level.

3. **Silent Reading** In senior high literature activity, silent reading is the *modus operandi*. Oral reading is included only occasionally in all-class or group approaches.

4. **Few Pictures** Most literature anthologies used in senior high contain a few pictures, but print is far more abundant in them. Those pictures which are included are usually there for decorative purposes (The Lake Country, Westminster Abbey, and so forth).

5. **Critical Reading** Tasks for students in these courses include lots of questions which call for inferences to be drawn and judgments to be made. Comparisons and contrasts to be made between and among works are also commonplace.

6. **The Symbol Hunt** An imposing number of critical reading tasks, cited in the characteristic noted above, demands that students perceive relationships between referents and symbols in the selections they are assigned to read.

7. **Written Responses** Whether responses solicited reflect basic comprehension (as in plot summaries) or critical assessment (as in stating the *hidden meaning*), they take the form of both written and oral statements, the majority of which are probably written.

8. **Correlative Experience** Most texts assigned are to be correlated with *real life* and focus on experiences of adults in the throes of making major decisions or experiencing other adult crises.

9. **Examination of Stylistics** Students are frequently called on to make judgments, both orally and in writing, on the aesthetic quality of the works assigned and to relate them to the aesthetic tenets of a particular movement (e.g., romanticism).

10. **Scholarly Texts** Students are sometimes asked to read critical and/or scholarly treatises about the literary works they are studying. This kind of assignment can often be found as part of the task of producing research papers.

It should be clear that the two sets of curricular characteristics described above stand in sharp contrast with each other. Given that reality, teachers in the middle grades should pay some attention to bridging the gap between literary involvement of early childhood and senior high school. Some of these means are to be found in teaching approaches (See the "Herber Exercise," p. 48 and the "Lottery Lesson," p. 59). The focus of this chapter, however, will be on YA fiction as the most likely medium through which an effective transition can be made, essentially from *reading* to *study* of literary works, during these middle years. Because of its distinctive literary characteristics, YA fiction seems to offer an abundant and valuable resource to teachers who want to guide their students through this transition rather than stand by while they float aimlessly from one shore to another without such guidance; a sea of confusion may well exist between such shores.

Before embarking on a comprehensive description of YA fiction (*comprehensive* insofar as space in this chapter allows), three further contextual statements must be made:

1. This is a transition unique in all curricular developments. Most subject matter study begins as serious business, a fact already noted. Literature starts out as an enjoyable change of pace between periods of "hard" subjects. Then, somewhere along the way, it moves from a matter of reading to one of study—and with students at ages ten, eleven, twelve, or thirteen. Then, to compound the potential confusion, most teachers try to find works that feature some degree of interest. In presenting these selections, teachers seem to be saying to their classes: "This used to be fun. Now, it's serious. But, don't forget, as you study these novels, short stories, poems, and plays, we still want you to like them." This is an odd schizophrenic twist that requires tact, patience, and creativity from teachers who are trying to be credible to their students.

2. A second statement of caution is actually a reminder. In Chapter One, the value of the thoughtful inclusion of four key terms into

Transitional Literature Diagram

| Children's Literature Experiences | Transitional Period | Literature Study |

Elementary Grades · Middle School · Senior High/College

Stories	Young-Adult Fiction	Renowned Novels
Fairy Tales	Novel of Initiation	Classic Poetry
Rhyming Poetry	Poetry of Correlative Experience	Shakespearean Drama

Figure 5.1

the teaching of literature in secondary schools was discussed: empathy, verisimilitude, willing suspension of disbelief, and symbolism. This inclusion is all-important in designing and delivering literature instruction during the transition period.

As early adolescents begin to study literature, they need the assistance of imaginative entry in order that those encounters be something more than drudgery. Research on reading interests and tastes of young people reveals that most of them, on emerging from childhood, eschew anything that smacks of the fanciful, such as fairy tales, and opt for reading about *real life* in the texts they are offered. Thus, verisimilitude is a vital element at this curricular juncture. Continued interest in science fiction and the works of Tolkien, Stephen King, and the like demonstrates the fact that they are still willing to suspend belief when the context is skillfully crafted; and, their intense preoccupation with self permits openings for teachers to imply that some stories represent truths of a universal nature (i.e., with symbolic significances). Thoughtful recollection of the relevance of those four terms will assist teachers as they plan their transitional strategies.

3. Finally, there is an important element to be considered in the development of this transition phase: that of including the Novel of Initiation in the instructional framework. The initiation into adulthood theme has proven to be a compelling one to early adolescent readers. This theme stretches from *Huckleberry Finn* to Judith Guest's *Ordinary People,* and is probably most familiarly represented in J.D. Salinger's *Catcher in the Rye.* The initiation novel possesses many of the characteristics of YA fiction but differs from it, particularly in the often complex nature of its style and in the breadth of its thematic considerations. Since a chapter later in the text will be devoted in part to a closer scrutiny of these novels as they represent likely classroom additions (See Chapter Ten), no more will be said about them at this time. Together with YA novels, however, they provide teachers with positive means of guiding students through the period of transition.

The Young Adult Novel

Stephen Dunning, in his 1959 study of the YA novel, defines it as "an extended piece of prose fiction written for adolescents which has known adolescent activities or interest as central elements of the plot. It pretends to treat life truthfully."[1] Within that definition, a number of significant characteristics are implied. Several of them have to do with thematic aspects; others are related to the structure of such works. The following summary covers those aspects and more. The YA novel is:

1. **Part of a Long Tradition** The long tradition is that of popular fiction. Evidence offered by classical scholars asserts that popular fiction dates back to the Golden Age of Athens. Throughout the centuries of recorded literature are found innumerable works of literature written largely for a massive, unscholarly audience. In more recent times, since the availability of cheap paperback edi-

tions, those kinds of books have proliferated and are widely read. Seldom profound and metaphysically limited, the works nevertheless exist at a number of quality levels. YA novels represent a form of popular fiction at one level. Their popularity—especially with teenage readers—does not preclude them from representing literary quality (a judgment which some of their critics would categorically deny). The discerning teacher, then, becomes a vital factor in the process of finding those works which are worthy of classroom discussion.

2. **Easy to Read** While not controlled by the readability formulas used to place some school text materials into graded categories, the YA novel generally lacks both the length and stylistic complexity of its adult counterpart. This feature will be delineated later in this summary. The ease-of-reading feature, however, does make the novel more appealing to an audience which is less mature and less sophisticated.

3. **Full of Action, Suspense, and Adventure** These elements, heavily descriptive of outer, physical activity, increase both the appeal and the clarity of the novels with a younger reading audience. They also allow readers to get into novels in the structural sense with less reluctance and thus with less difficulty. In an earlier chapter, allusions were made to the tedious, heavily descriptive introductory chapters of *The Scarlet Letter* and *A Tale of Two Cities*. In the YA novel *Goodbye, My Lady* by James Street, the opening description of the bayou, by contrast, is enlivened by the narration of a search being carried on there for a mysterious animal. Similarly, the Harlem setting of Robert Lipsyte's *The Contender* comes across more dramatically because it is blended with the fears expressed by the protagonist who awaits the arrival of some hoodlum peers. In each case, the setting of the YA novel is established more vividly for younger readers because of this intermingling of setting with action, suspense, and/or adventure.

4. **Directly Related to the Adolescent Situation** The locus of activity, as stated in Dunning's definition, is the world of adolescence. This feature represents a kind of two-edged sword for teachers who are attempting to select YA novels for class consideration. The positive side of the feature is the high interest usually found in the literary development of settings, characters, events, and issues closely related to the lives of young readers. With this promise, however, comes at least two problems, the first of which is the rapidity of change in adolescent interests, fashions, and commitments. (For decades, young people have used the term "boring"

to cover a number of reactions to tasks, demands, and materials presented to them in secondary school classrooms.) Trying to keep up with changes in their preferences is a Herculean task, to say the least. Secondly, the pursuit of such interests through book selection may result in clashes with administrators, parents, or aroused citizens. These confrontations come under the category of censorship, an issue which will be discussed at length later (See Chapter Eleven). Thus the teacher who would choose YA novels which reflect the adolescent milieu must somehow navigate between the Scylla of youthful boredom and the Charybdis of adult meddling.

5. **Dedicated to a Valid Portrayal of the Adolescent Search for Self-definition** Dunning identifies the YA novel's protagonist as being an adolescent. Dorothy J. Petitt's excellent study on the well-written YA novel came to the important conclusion that in all the novels reviewed in the study which were well-written, the protagonists were in search of themselves. A further characteristic of these novels lay in the process of self-definition described in them. The young people had never reached closure in self-realization by the final chapter; they were still making discoveries and adjustments. Accomplishments were balanced by setbacks; insights were gained, but doubts persisted. Old problems were solved, but new ones arose.[2] The valid portrayal of this ongoing quest for the answer to the questions posed so long ago by Oedipus ("Who am I? Why am I here? Where am I going?") continues to be central in the newest YA novels appearing on book racks and in journal reviews. The perpetuation of the YA novel worthy of use in the classroom will continue to depend on the presence of this characteristic into the foreseeable future.

6. **Reflective of Both Historical and Contemporary Situations and Settings** Historical YA novels have waxed and waned in popularity, both with novelists and their readers, over the past half-century. They were quite prevalent throughout the 1940s and 1950s; about half of Petitt's list of twenty-five well-written YA novels (published through 1959) were historical in nature. Such titles as *Johnny Tremaine* by Esther Forbes, *Banners at Shenandoah* by Bruce Catton, and *The Light in the Forest* by Conrad Richter reflect this high level of popularity. From the mid 1960s to the early 1980s, however, historically based novels were largely out of fashion and seldom evident on lists of celebrated new works. More recently, the works of writers such as Sue Ellen Bridgers, Katherine Patterson, and Robert Newton Peck have led a comeback of novels based on some past era. Today, they do not dominate, but they represent

a visible proportion of recently written, well-regarded YA novels.

Actually, the historical novels do not reflect one of the greatest problems of this entire genre: that of creating language that is credible. The writer who deals with the present teenage milieu must strive to recreate adolescent patois and idioms which represent the true state of linguistic affairs. (Think of young readers' reactions today to a kid who used the term "groovy" to express euphoria.) The fact is that teenage language features, like styles of dress, hair length, television shows, and so forth, move in and out of vogue with what approaches dizzying rapidity. Many books, highly popular in the previous decade, lie unread today. The obsolescence of their language has done them in, an ever-present danger when writers of YA novels seek to create the here and now in those works.

7. **Available in Abundance** This may cause teachers who are potential users of YA novels their greatest problem. By contrast, teachers of some senior high courses do not have to worry about selection; *Macbeth* is still way up there on twelfth grade reading lists. The same is true with *The Scarlet Letter* and *Our Town* in the eleventh. *Lord of the Flies* is of a more recent vintage than the three works mentioned before it, but Golding's novel has become solidly entrenched as the turn of the century approaches.

By contrast, there are few standbys among the YA novels available to secondary school teachers. Needless to say, it is well nigh impossible for most teachers, already overburdened with the daily demands of the job, to maintain a schedule of personal reading that would permit basic awareness, let alone thoughtful assessment, of the scores of YA novels published each year. To proclaim that these novels exist at several levels of literary quality is to state the obvious. And, unlike the great traditional works mentioned above, YA novels aren't accompanied by large amounts of scholarly criticism so helpful to teachers. Advice from experienced colleagues, input from school and community librarians, analyses found in the *English Journal*, the *ALAN Review*, and several publications of the American Library Association can be of service. The sheer volume of available YA novels, however, can represent one of the great frustrations to teachers who want to provide their students with YA texts of high quality. Given the abundance of them and the ongoing quest for the *right book* by teachers, this is a problem with no easy solution.

8. **Stylistic Conventions/Complexity** As the YA novel has evolved over the past fifty years, the question of stylistics has been the focus

of great attention. The *easy to read* feature has been an attractive one, both to young readers and those teachers who have taken seriously the *transition function* of the genre. However, the trend in YA stylistics has been more toward complexity than conventionality during the final quarter of this century. Dunning's 1959 study concluded that the YA novel of that era was carefully and narrowly structured. Twenty-five years later, Muller's analysis included the contention that the YA novel, while retaining some of its structural conventionality, had become noticeably more complex, at least in the twenty-five *well-written* novels he chose as representative.[3] Thus, today this genre continues to be more stylistically regular than does the *serious* or *artistic* (as opposed to *pulp*) novels of our time. Some specific stylistic characteristics are:

A. For the most part, the progression of events tends to be regular. There are few flashbacks and fewer prophecies in evidence. Thus these novels proceed directly from beginning to end.

B. Characters continue to speak in clearly recognizable statements in these novels. That is, they talk to each other, and their statements are usually punctuated by quotation marks as well as conventions such as "he said," "she replied," and so forth. Outside statements can be distinguished from inner thoughts, and the inclusion of interior monologue is still quite rare.

C. As stated earlier in this chapter, settings are seldom overextended. They tend to be mixed in with the action in order to grab the reader's attention from the outset. The settings also tend to be characterized by ample concrete detail. Surrealistic atmospheres (common in works by Faulkner and Kafka) are uncommon.

D. The point of view, or angle of vision has moved from one which was largely third person omniscient to a balance between third person limited and first person limited. In more recently written YA novels, teachers will find more narrators being identified as characters, often protagonists, in those works. This limited point of view is represented by the use of both the first and third persons. Readers will generally become aware of the narrator's position in the story by careful reading of the opening paragraphs.

E. The length of the novels continues to be what Dunning identified over thirty years ago: about sixty percent as long as that of their adult counterparts. Few young adult novels published today exceed two hundred pages, which may (and probably does) reflect the continuing influence of television on attention spans of young adults. Suffice it to say that Henry Fielding, Charles Dickens, and Theodore Dreiser would never make it as YA novelists today.

F. Thematic focus continues to be on concerns which are readily discernible by young readers. Of the *big four* conflicts found in most works of fiction—man versus man, man versus nature, man versus fate, man versus self—the emphases in YA novels are the last two, man versus fate and man versus self. This is not surprising given the YA novelists' desire to reach the sensibilities of a less-than-mature audience. The novels of Judy Blume do emphasize the endless self-examination young people engage in, and Robert Cormier's novels almost invariably include some involvement with cosmic forces. The well-written YA novel, in short, provides an excellent vehicle for examination of implied central meaning, a vital component of the reading-to-study transition process.

G. Generally, the endings of YA novels continue to be as Dunning found them—mixed. That is, they still retain the "you win some; you lose some" character. Petitt, incidentally, made a similar conclusion, but she stressed the fact that the gradually increased self-awareness which protagonists experienced by the last page was far more important than whether they scored the big touchdown or got the girl. One consistently redeeming feature of most well-regarded YA novels of this half-century is the absence of a "Leave It to Beaver" triumphal resolution in the concluding chapter. Many YA novels of the past ten years are a bit more pessimistic in their auguries, but almost all of them radiate some hope by the end.

The Question of Quality

Much of the foregoing description of the YA novel has provided a number of implications for a serious literary judgment of the genre overall. Can it be legitimately touted as quality fiction? As this text is written that argument is far from being resolved. The very choice to use or not to use YA novels will depend heavily on which side individual teachers take in this debate, and whether any of the various censorship groups are breathing down their necks.

The elevation of the YA novel to the point at which it holds a place in the literature curriculum took some time, and with good reason. Earlier in the century, books written for and by young people were of undeniably inferior literary quality. The *little men, little women* works of the 1920s, 1930s, and 1940s, written by such popular authors as Zane Grey and Edgar Rice Burroughs (for the boys) and Emily Loring and Grace Livingston Luce Hill (for the girls) were shot through with contrivances, stereotypes, sentimentality, and melodrama. No serious English educator considered them worth discussing in classes or scholarly articles which dealt with the teaching of literature to young people.

During the early 1950s, however, increasing attention was paid to an emerging cadre of serious writers of books for an early adolescent reading audience. The eminent English educator of that era, Dora V. Smith, led a new wave of teacher educators, curriculum specialists, and authorities in library science to take a closer, more scholarly look at the YA texts of that decade. To some extent, she used her position as chairperson of the National Council of Teachers of English (NCTE) Curriculum Commission to do so. In 1952, one of her outstanding University of Minnesota doctoral students, Dwight L. Burton, became the editor of the *English Journal* and quickly turned some of the focus of that widely read, professional publication to the evolution of YA fiction as a bona fide art form.

Negative response to this perception came quickly and not without vituperation. Leaders of the Council for Basic Education, a group of editors, literature scholars, and public figures who denounced *progressive education*, saw this genre as one more example of the deterioration of standards in the schools. In the December 1956 issue of *English Journal,* Burton included an article titled "Literature for Adolescents—Pap or Protein" by Frank Jennings.[4] The thrust of Jennings' argument was that (1) YA novels were, for the most part, devoid of literary value and (2) the only kind of literature which should be considered in the process of introducing adolescent students to literature study should be what he (and others) loosely referred to as *the classics.* Thus, long before the turbulent 1960s came along, this educational battle was raging.

Despite the reactionary statements by Jennings and the Council for Basic Education proponents, interest in and support for YA fiction as having potential for classroom use was growing. In 1958, the same year that Dunning's study was completed, Burton published a college text titled *Literature Study in the High Schools* (Holt, Rinehart, & Winston). He gave considerable attention to the whole range of YA literature in this text, which was to go through three editions before fading in the Back-to-Basics onslaught of the 1970s. As support for the genre grew, so did the strident tone of those who objected to its use in anything but *wide reading* lists to be distributed to low ability youngsters in the junior highs throughout the country. For any other kids, a fervent "No way!"

In early 1960, Dorothy Petitt completed her exhaustive and meticulously scholarly doctoral dissertation on the well written YA novel. For starters, Petitt read and analyzed twenty scholarly treatises on long fiction. Titles included Percy Lubbock's *The Craft of Fiction*, Wellek and Warren's *Theory of Literature*, Forster's *Aspects of the Novel*, Henry James' *The Art of the Novel*, and the like. From that reading, she synthesized a set of criteria for judging fiction. (See Appendix A.) While completing this analysis/synthesis, Petitt developed a list of some 500+ YA novels currently in print. She sent that list to eighteen critics to evaluate. These critics were (1) teachers of courses in literature for young people, (2) editors in publishing houses which produced and sold books for young people, and (3) curators of public library sections on books for young people. Petitt asked the critics (1) to review her list of YA titles, adding any they felt she had left out, and (2) to rank each title with which they were familiar in the following manner: 3 = the book is neither popular nor well written; 2 = the book is popular but not well written; 1 = the book is both popular and well written.

Petitt then took the twenty-five YA novels which received the most 1 ratings and analyzed them using the criteria she had previous synthesized as her yardstick. (See Appendix B.) She concluded that, to one degree or another, all twenty-five generally conformed to those scholarly criteria. In her study, a careful evaluation of the quality of this genre had taken place.[5]

In 1961, William R. Evans assigned two tenth grade classes of equal academic qualifications to read a different novel as part of their literary course of study. The first of these was *Silas Marner*, which Evans claimed was being studied in over ninety percent of the senior high schools in the country at that time. The second was YA novel, *Swiftwater* by Paul Annixter, published in 1950, and acclaimed both by Petitt and Evans's doctoral advisor, Dwight Burton. Both classes studied the novels from a stylistic perspective (i.e., for their plots, character portrayals, settings, and themes). Once the two groups had finished the reading and study of these novels, they were introduced to a third, short novel titled *The Pearl* by John Steinbeck. They studied this work once again from the perspective of its major stylistic elements. In a post-test instrument prepared for both groups by Evans, the class which had first studied *Swiftwater* did slightly better (although the differences were not statistically significant) than did the class which had studied *Silas Marner*. Evans concluded that a well written YA novel can provide students in that age group *at least* as useful a vehicle for teaching the structure of long fiction.[6] Two years later, another of Burton's students, Nathan S. Blount, completed a follow-up study, this time on three novels from YA fiction and three from traditionally accepted fiction. His results were similar to those of Evans.[7]

To many of the critics of YA fiction, the research described above either went unnoticed or was not accepted as legitimate scholarship. Their objections to the use of this genre continued unchecked throughout the decade of the 1960s and beyond. And their position was given a boost by many of the vocal authorities on the public school English curriculum who rose to prominence after the Basic Issues Conference of 1958. One such group of authorities was the Commission on English of the College Entrance Examination Board. In their major position statement on the ideal secondary English program of studies, *Freedom and Discipline in English* (1965), the Commission members make their position clear:

> Claims are frequently advanced for the use of so-called "junior books," a "literature of adolescence," on the ground that they ease the young reader into a frame of mind in which he will be ready to tackle something stronger, harder, more adult. The Commission has serious doubts that it does anything of the sort. For classes in remedial reading a resort to such books may be necessary, but to make them a considerable part of the curriculum for most students is to subvert the purposes for which literature is included in the first place. In the high school years, the aim should be not to find the students' level so much as to raise it, and such books rarely elevate. For college-bound students, particularly, no such concessions as they imply are justified. Maturity of thought, vocabulary, syntax, and construction is the criterion of excellence in literature, and that criterion must not be abandoned for apparent expediency. The competent teacher can bridge the distances between good books and the immaturity of his students; that is, in fact, his primary duty as a teacher of literature.[8]

Even today, this statement is one which expresses the attitude of a sizable number of English scholars and public school professionals toward the place of YA fiction in the classroom.

Despite persistent opposition, however, the use of YA fiction has increased in classrooms all over America. The amount of new YA literature has increased geometrically during that period, as has scholarly attention to the genre. As mentioned previously in this chapter, in the early 1970s, the NCTE leadership approved the establishment of the Assembly on Literature for Adolescents, National (ALAN), an organization whose membership has grown rapidly in the past two decades. The group promptly instituted postconvention workshops at which large numbers of teachers, supervisors, and teacher educators enthusiastically meet after each annual NCTE convention. Concern about the quality of the YA novel was instrumental in the decision of the ALAN executive committee to authorize the publication of the *ALAN Review* in 1978, a journal published three times annually and dedicated to presenting a variety of scholarly and critical analyses of YA fiction and related materials for young people. As this text is written, the *ALAN Review* is one of the most popular periodicals read by English teachers throughout the country.

A significant reflection on the quality of YA fiction, taken as a whole, was made in 1982 by W. Geiger Ellis, a University of Georgia educator, and the first editor of *ALAN Review*. In considering the notable trends of the genre, Ellis stated:

> For many years, adolescent literature was a kind of second-class citizen in the world of literature, and deservedly so. While many books classified as adolescent literature had their pedagogical uses, little could be said for their literary quality. Those books had appeal for some youthful readers, and reading *something* is usually better than not reading at all.
>
> But that was in the past. The world of adolescent literature has been changing and growing, sometimes painfully, as in the case of adolescents themselves. We are emerging from a time in which the range of subjects, such as sexual experiences, abortion, and divorce in adolescent literature, expanded to the same breadth found in literature for adults. This period of shocking realism has passed. It was necessary in order to establish new boundaries, but now that they have been established, the challenge to authors is to create artistic works worthy of their audience, which is better informed and freer than previous generations of adolescents.
>
> The single most notable trend has been the improving literary quality of *some* of the books in the adolescent literature market. There is more adolescent literature overall because it has been shown to be financially rewarding. Indeed, many publishers now have Young Adult divisions. This financial incentive has attracted better writers, such as Robert Cormier, Sue Ellen Bridgers, Katherine Paterson, Robin Brancato, resulting in more adolescent literature of *quality*.
>
> It is ironic that the next trend I should mention features a plethora of books absolutely lacking in quality. I speak, of course, of that publisher's gold mine—teen romance. The "formula" romance, exemplified by the Silhouette and Harlequin series for adults, has gained nearly a third of mass market paperback sales. Inspired by such success at the adult level, publishers have turned to a more youthful audience, which is ever ready to be titillated by the trite. Scholastic took in 1.8 million dollars last year on romances in their "Wild Fire" series. "Wishing Star," a new series, is being added to further exploit this market. Bantam has followed with their "Sweet Dreams" series, and Simon and Schuster has its "First Love" series.
>
> Another recent trend in the field has been the increased critical and professional attention given Young Adult literature. Evidence of this attention is most evident in professional publications, a number of which have come into being in recent years. These include *Signal, Yarns, The Advocate,* and the *ALAN Review*. Also, *established* journals such as *The Arizona English Bulletin, Connecticut English Journals,* and *Texas Tech Journal of Education,* have published issues focused exclusively on adolescent fiction.

Among his predictions for the future of the genre, Ellis states the following:

More adolescent literature will be found in school literature programs. It will be there, in part, simply because it exists, but more importantly because it will be deserving of its place by reason of its quality and because it will be accessible to students. This accessibility is a dual function of the literature's readability for the students and its relevance to students' lives, for it causes the reader to give thought to human matters deserving thought. As for its quality, the best adolescent literature is deftly wrought by artists who employ the language with sensitivity and style.

The best of adolescent literature will more closely resemble the best of contemporary literature for adults. To a certain extent, good literature is good literature. For, regardless of its audience, good literature will cause readers to think on human matters that are deserving of thought. This growing similarity is owing, in part, to the expansion of boundaries for adolescent literature during the past decade. However, while adolescent and adult literature will become more similar in some respects, certain characteristics of the former will remain. For example, adolescent literature is generally shorter, and there usually is a youthful protagonist.

The popularity of the teen romance will wane but never disappear entirely. This form will always have some appeal, whether we like it or not. And it will experience periodic revivals as the ever-changing climate of our society returns in its cycle to its current state. That is to say, I would not expect teen romance novels to be popular in times when our national government is involved heavily in social programs. This type of literature will experience popularity when the social climate is more conservative and less oriented toward the immediate needs of the people. It seems almost as if this kind of fantasy literature—for that's what it is—takes its firmest hold when a society has its attention firmly fixed upon the supposed glories of the past rather than on the dreams and possibilities of future greatness yet to be achieved.[9]

Two issues raised by Ellis merit particular attention in the context of concern about the literary quality of the YA novel. The first of these lies in his noting a series of authors who have risen to prominence in recent years. To an increasing number of literary scholars, the works of Sue Ellen Bridgers, Robin Brancato, Richard Peck, Norma Fox Mazer, Robert Newton Peck, Katherine Paterson, and Robert Cormier have been held up to critical scrutiny. Many of them have been accorded solid acclaim by these scholars, the works of Cormier probably receiving the highest praise. His work has been the made the subject of a 1985 text, *Presenting Robert Cormier* by Patricia Campbell, a publication in the celebrated Twayne United States Authors series. This widely read series has featured texts on the likes of Hemingway, Fitzgerald, Steinbeck, Buck, and other outstanding literary figures. Their decision to present a full-length scholarly treatment of a YA author is a significant reflection on the quality of some of the current YA works.

Another, vastly different aspect of the quality issue can be noted in Ellis' allusions to the status of the Teen Age Romance among young readers. Publishers of literary texts, especially those who specialize in inexpensive paperbound editions, have recognized in recent years the potential marketability of these formulaic, coquettishly titillating love stories. Inspired by the dramatic financial success of the two major adult teen romance series, the Harlequin and Silhouette books, publishers from the late 1970s onward expanded their production of these novels to encompass a teen reading audience. These formula romance stories have been wildly successful in augmenting the bottom lines of their publishing firms.

The companies which publish teenage romance series may have had another motive in embarking on this venture. Since the late 1960s, a number of YA authors have published texts which have violated, some flagrantly, the taboos against depicting certain life experiences of young people. The resulting backlash of censorship activity, mentioned previously and dealt with extensively in a later chapter, caused a number of publishers of YA novels either to back off completely from the publication of *objectionable* novels or to balance them with the addition of those tightly controlled, largely bowdlerized works labelled by Ken Donelson of Arizona State University as *squeaky clean*. Regardless of their indisputably low literary quality, these novels are selling in a big way at the moment. Some publishing executives go so far as to claim that the profit made on Teen Age Romance series allows them to *risk* publication of more sophisticated and realistic YA novels. This prompts the question, Where is George Orwell now that we need him?

The issue of low quality, highly popular love novels is one which all literature teachers need to face as they attempt to promote genuine awareness of literary quality among their students. If teachers look closely, they may find many of their students reading a Sweet Valley High romance concealed behind the assigned copy of *Great Expectations* or Johnny Tremaine. To deal with the problem, teachers must first understand the nature of such materials. In a 1989 doctoral study, Carolyn L. Irvine investigated the attitudes, values, and literary quality of recently written teenage romance novels. Her conclusions are helpful in defining this genre and placing it in the context of literature assessment, broadly conceived. One of these is stated below:

> In terms of quality young adult fiction, romance series novels were discovered to be "inferior" to many "great" young adult books. These romances were easy to read. They had simple vocabulary, short sentences, and uncomplicated ideas. Sutton (1985) pointed out that these books were written on a fifth grade reading level. Each story repeated a familiar pattern, making the plot "trite" and predictable. Since a major aim of

quality young adult literature is to challenge its readers in order to expand their minds and to help them develop critical thinking skills in order to function more efficiently in society, romance series novels cannot be considered quality young adult literature. They were enjoyable to read but were not challenging.[10]

Thus the debate over the quality, and thus the curricular status, of the YA novel rages on undiminished. One major reason for the intensity of this debate can be found in an appraisal of the degree of literary realism to be found in such works, especially those written in more recent years.

The Question of Literary Realism

One of Dunnings' conclusions about the YA novel was that it was "insistently wholesome and rigidly didactic." He found, among the then popular novels that he analyzed, both distortion and selection in their authors' treatment of reality. Taboos on descriptions of sexual activity were strictly observed. Profanity was almost never included in the speech of characters. Poverty, squalor, and class conflict were studiously omitted. Focus was carefully restricted to suburban and rural settings. The white middle and upper-middle classes were the solid economic groups which generally took center stage. The potential of adolescent protagonists was often exaggerated, their achievements sometimes marginally credible.

Coincidentally, in the same year, Mary Tingle completed a research study of family life in YA novels. Her conclusions, although based on a much narrower thematic scope, parallel Dunning's rather closely. Only white and upper-middle class families were involved. Serious conflicts between parents and children, among siblings, and within the extended family were virtually nonexistent. Sexual problems were never the cause for concern or scrutiny. No divorced adults could be found in the eight novels she analyzed. Absent, too, were any incidents of marital unfaithfulness; in fact, all married couples lived in near perfect bliss and harmony. Woman's, that is to say wife/mother's, place was in the home, and she knew it.[11]

While Dorothy Petitt's major conclusion was that the YA novel was well written, she also labelled it *subliterary*. The first reason for this identification was the focus these works placed on the period of adolescence, that is, *becoming*, as has been discussed earlier in this chapter. The second reason, however, had to do with the consistent, deliberate choice of subject matter by YA authors who, in those days, knew that their books would be carefully screened before being chosen for class study or placed on school library shelves. Because her main concern was the well-written novel, Petitt chose to conclude that those books tended to select rather than distort reality. In any event, she classified her entire sample as *subliterary* in part because of the fact that their authors doggedly avoided treating a wide range of "sensitive" topics, most of which have been noted in the summaries of the Dunning and Tingle studies; the remainder can easily be inferred by any thoughtful reader of this chapter.

Of all the inferences which can be drawn from the research findings and conclusions of Dunning, Tingle, and Petitt, one comes through loud, clear, and pertinent: that the pictures of life created by a number of YA novelists of the 1930s, 1940s, and 1950s did not offer a comprehensive and valid picture of life in general and the adolescent experience in particular. (It is interesting to note at this point that J.D. Salinger's novel, *Catcher in the Rye*, published in 1951, enjoyed immediate and continuing popularity among young readers. And this novel violated a number of taboos, the most notable of which was the use of an extremely objectionable word, no less than six times.)

This highly limited view of reality persisted in YA fiction in the early years of the 1960s. In 1966, James E. Davis, at present an English professor at Ohio University and former chairman of ALAN, was then a graduate student at Florida State University. He completed a follow-up of the Petitt study. Davis's study was informal (that is, not a doctoral dissertation) and limited, but he did use the Petitt criteria, and he did send a list of eighty-eight YA novel titles, which were written from 1960 to 1965, to six authorities, asking them to use the 1, 2, 3 rankings Petitt had employed. All six authorities responded. From his analysis of their responses, Davis was able to produce a list of twenty-three well written works. In analyzing their content, he concluded that the selection and, to a lesser degree, the same distortions of reality noted by the previously mentioned researchers were still, undeniably, present. The list of well written YA novels can be found in the appendix of this chapter. Davis's contribution carries us into the latter half of the decade when significant changes took place.

During the academic year 1967 to 1968, three YA novels were published which changed the course of that genre, probably forever. First, a seventeen year old high school student named Susan E. Hinton brought out *The Outsiders*, which gained the immediate attention of adolescent readers and as well as teachers, English educators, and library science specialists who attempt to keep up with young adult interests. The protagonist of the novel, Ponyboy, is a fourteen-year-old lower-class youngster. He lives in a home run by his older brother, Darry, who works at a menial job to make ends meet and is himself barely beyond adolescence. Both parents are dead. Ponyboy belongs to a gang of what in the 1960s was referred to as "disadvantaged youth" called "the Greasers." This gang is in constant struggle with a gang of upper-middle class boys called "The Socs," which is no less violent or cruel because of the members' relatively comfortable economic means. The novel includes treatment of alcohol consumption, brutality, hatred, despair, contempt for the authority of various adults, and violent death. It is told from Ponyboy's point of view and reflects his fears, shock, and frequent disillusionment, as is characteristic of Huck Finn and Holden Caulfield. For close to twenty-five years, Hinton's novel has ranked near the top of all reading interest inventories among young readers. Moreover, Theodore Hipple, an English educator at the University of Tennessee and a member of long standing of ALAN, reported the results of his 1989 survey in which a group of seventy-six English teachers, English educators, and various past and present officers of ALAN identified *The Outsiders* as one of the top three most important adolescent novels they wanted all English teachers to know about. (The other two were *The Chocolate War* by Robert Cormier and *The Pigman* by Paul Zindel.)[12] The taboos *The Outsiders* ignored were many, its tone was harsh, and its popularity endures.

Later in 1967, a syndicated New York sports columnist named Robert Lipsyte published his first attempt at fiction writing, the YA text *The Contender*. In it, Lipsyte created Alfred Brooks, the first teenage African-American protagonist in the genre. The setting was the Harlem ghetto, and the theme was a young adult's search for survival, a further example of self-definition. The novel fits most of the stylistic characteristics described earlier in the chapter and, as has been stated, followed the theme which Petitt claimed has characterized all of the best written YA novels in her analysis. Lipsyte, however, violated a number of the taboos observed by earlier YA novelists. The story was set in urban squalor. It dealt with the concerns ("known areas of interest") of a minority group. Throughout the text, the reader finds instances of racial hatred, distrust for police and other white authority figures, violence, cruelty, contempt for adults, both flaunting and breaking of the law, anti-Semitism, teenage sexual encounters, and drug and alcohol abuse. Yet Lipsyte handled these elements with considerable restraint, to the degree that, to this date, *The Contender* has not been mentioned in any of the reports of censorship attempts by any individual or pressure group. While the novel has not remained as popular as *The Outsiders*, it has, according to Hipple's research, stayed in the top fifteen YA novels.

Early in 1968, the popular YA novelist Paul Zindel completed *The Pigman*, a book that gained the instant, enthusiastic attention of the teenage reading audience. While it too conformed with the theme of search for self-definition as well as most of the stylistic constraints previously noted, the probable reason for its great popularity lay in its ignoring of several taboos. The narration was presented in an epistolary form which had each of the two teenage protagonists appear as alternating narrators. The flash-back was also a significant stylistic feature in its chronology. The protago-nists were involved in a teenage romance in which sexual involvement was evident, as was unwanted pregnancy. Alcohol abuse was a popular teenage group activity, another prominent element of the plot. Probably the most flagrant violation of taboos, however, lay in the attitudes of the teenage co-protagonists. Both harbored contempt and profound dislike for their parents. Their search for guidance and affection from adults lead them to a chance meeting with Mr. Pignati, an elderly loner who is desperate for companionship, affection, and admiration. The young couple appear to befriend Mr. Pignati (the Pigman) but choose ultimately to exploit their relationship with him for their own material ends. They return his kindli-ness and generosity with scorn and abuse. When he eventually becomes a murder victim, they attempt first to repress their sense of responsibility for the act and then to rationalize it. In the final analysis, they both come across as willful, devious, self-centered, and blatantly cruel. Zindel's book does violence to the good-kid-under-it-all thesis of many YA texts of earlier times. There are no winners in *The Pigman.*

Thus, as the end of the fabled decade of the 1960s approached, the themes and stylistic features of YA fiction began to display unmistakable signs of radical change. Concern for the no-no's so characteristic of almost all earlier works largely vanished. After the watershed year 1967 to 1968, a veritable avalanche of works appeared whose themes probed several of the social and psychological ills of the times, those faced by young people and indeed by an entire society traumatized by Vietnam, Watergate, urban revolt, shortages in vital resources, and the like. Such previously avoided topics as sexual activity, drug and alcohol abuse, teenage pregnancy, abortion, divorce, parental promiscuity, gang violence, brutality, torture and murder, homosexuality, adult hypocrisy, racial intolerance, and con-tempt for all authority now became the focal point of literally hundreds of works. Most prevalent among these were the themes of adolescent alien-ation from (and distrust of) the adult world which they realized that they must someday enter. Holden Caulfield's blanket term for the adults with whom he associated was *phony*. In the YA novels which followed 1967 to 1968, that term of disparagement for adults became the watchword.

In his 1973 doctoral study, Al Muller completed a careful follow-up of Petitt's research, using her criteria as well as her sampling procedures. He analyzed the twenty-five novels which received the highest number of 1 ratings, found them once again to be well written, and confirmed the fact that they continued to reflect the adolescents' search for self-definition. His study also confirmed Dunning's conclusion that the YA novel continued to enjoy great popularity with young readers. Muller's most significant *new* finding, however, had to do with the radical shift in choice of subject matter which current writers of the genre had elected to make. Historical YA novels all but disappeared. Almost without exception, the current social milieu became the center of concern. Lighthearted treatments of human experience were almost nonexistent. The emphasis within the novels on Muller's list was contemporary reality, generally harsh in nature. Unquestionably, the goal of the YA novelists on Muller's list was to present literary realism in scrupulous detail. The goal of their teenage protagonists was not usually to succeed but to cope and survive. (Muller's list can be found in the appendix of this chapter.)[13]

While that perspective on young adult experience and aspiration has softened somewhat since Muller presented his research, the tone continues to be implicit in a large number of YA novels published since, including those described in the *ALAN Review* as being well written. In today's YA novels, English teachers can be assured of finding heavy doses of literary realism. They should also be prepared to find reflected a deeply pessimistic view of the world. And they also need to be aware of the presence of those topics to which an increasing number of reactionary individuals, pressure groups, and whole communities have found, and are finding, objectionable. The results of these objections will be discussed in a later chapter on censorship. If ever teachers of young adults need to be judicious in their choice of novels for all-class consideration, it is now.

Summary

Those who teach literature to young people in the middle and junior high school, as as well as those who teach basic students of any age in secondary schools, should adopt strategies and texts which will help them guide students from the reading to the study of literature. Among the most effective text materials available to teachers who want to aid that transition are the Young Adult Novel and the Novel of Initiation (the latter genre to be treated at length in Chapter Ten.) The YA novel is, in general, easy to read and presents topics correlative with adolescent life experiences. It exists in abundance, thus teachers need to be judicious in their choice of appropriate texts for class study. There is an imposing number of well written YA novels in print today, and the main elements of this genre, that is, plot, character, and so forth, can be used effectively in leading early adolescents to an awareness of the presence of certain formal and thematic elements in serious literature. The quality of YA fiction is an issue which continues to be studied, analyzed, and discussed by teachers, supervisors, and teacher educators. To assist those individuals on the topic of such literary quality, there is an abundance of research data and contemporary scholarship now available. During the past quarter century, thematic concerns in YA fiction have expanded and will be, in many communities, the object of concern and even censorship. All teachers must be ready to defend their choices of those YA works which are well written but which lay stress on literary realism.

Notes

1. Stephen Dunning. "A Definition of the Role of the Junior Novel Based on Analyses of Thirty Selected Novels." Unpublished Ph.D. dissertation, Florida State University, 1959, p 61.

2. Dorothy J. Petitt. "A Study of the Qualities of Literary Excellence Which Characterizes Selected Fiction for Younger Adolescents." Unpublished Ph.D. dissertation, University of Minnesota, 1961.

3. Alfred P. Muller. "The Currently Popular Adolescent Novel as Transitional Literature." Unpublished Ph.D. dissertation, Florida State University, 1973.

4. Frank Jennings. "Literature for Adolescents—Pap or Protein," *English Journal* 65: 526–531, December 1956.

5. Petitt, "Literature for Adolescents," passim.

6. William R. Evans. "Superior Junior Novel Versus *Silas Marner.*" Unpublished Ph.D. dissertation, Florida State University, 1961.

7. Nathan S. Blount. "Student Attitudes Toward the 'Ideal' Novel." Unpublished Ph.D. dissertation, Florida State University, 1963.

8. Commission on English. *Freedom and Discipline in English.* New York: College Entrance Examination Board, 1965, pp 49–50.

9. W. Geiger Ellis. Taped statement prepared for the National Association of Teachers of English (United Kingdom). York University, United Kingdom, April 1982.

10. Carolyn L. Irvine. "An Analysis of Attitudes, Values, and Literary Quality of Contemporary Young Adult Romance Series Novels." Unpublished Ph.D. dissertation, Florida State University, 1989, pp 89–90. The Sutton citation is Sutton, Sutton. "Librarians and the Paperback Romance." *School Library Journal* 31(9): 000, 1952.

11. Mary Tingle. "The Image of the Family in Selected Junior Novels." Unpublished Ph.D. dissertation, University of Minnesota, 1958.

12. Ted Hipple. "Have You Read . . .? (Parts 2 and 3)." *English Journal* 78(8): 79, December 1989.

13. Muller, "Currently Popular Adolescent Novel," passim.

Criteria for Judging Fiction for Adolescents

by Dorothy J. Petitt

I. Definition: Is this a novel?
   A. Is it extensive enough to qualify? (at least 50,000 words)
   B. Does its length reveal change?
   C. Is it structured without having its vital qualities destroyed?
   D. Is it fiction, an invented story, or is it history or some other form of prose?
   E. Does it, as fiction, have the individuality characteristic of the novel which immediately sets this novel off as different from any other novel?
   F. Are values communicated by indirection?

II. Unity: Is the novel unified?
   A. Do all technical aspects work together to present the whole?
   B. Is the totality of the novel achieved through the presence of alternatives or opposition?

III. Theme: Does the theme emerge as the controlling element to which all other aspects can be seen finally to contribute?
   A. Is the theme a facet of the general theme of all fiction—the individual in society?
   B. At the same time is the individual facet of the theme unique because of the way it has been developed?
   C. Is the theme skillfully developed?
      1. Do the characters signify some universal truth beyond the meaning of their own existence?
      2. Does the theme have a mythic kinship which universalizes its particularity?

    D. Is the theme developed rhythmically?

        1. Are repetitions and variations in time, in action, in minor themes, and in symbols without monotony?

        2. Does the rhythm of repetitions and variations cause an expansion of meaning beyond the particular people, events or objects?

IV. Plot: Is the plot a purposively directed pattern of events?

    A. Does the story, a series of events, dominate?

    B. Is there a plot which links inner and outer experience by telling why events came about?

    C. Does the plot have a mythic similarity to other plots?

    D. At the same time is it unique?

    E. Do the events of the plot reveal the characters?

    F. At the same time are the events partly shaped by the characters?

    G. Is the structure of the plot self-contained?

        1. Does foreshadowing operate to make the plot coherent?

        2. If used, is coincidence used to develop theme?

    H. Has the author solved the central technical problem of all novelists—the choice of point of view?

        1. Is it clear from what point of view, on whose authority, the story is told?

            a. Is the point of view at all times clearly defined?

            b. Is it convincing, apart from the authority of the author's assertion of validity?

        2. Has the author fully exploited the advantages of his/her choice and contrived to turn the disadvantages into virtues?

            a. If he/she has chosen to speak in the first person, has the author achieved unity, immediacy, and significance while compensating for the limited authority?

                (1) Is the single mind telling the story a believably individual one?

                (2) Does it have a believable depth of insight sufficient to be capable of probing beneath the surface?

                (3) Do the events told in the first person acquire a dramatic immediacy?

                (4) Are the limitations of the single mind compensated for?

                    (a) Are events outside the scope of the first person narrator's observations adequately handled?

(b) Is his/her bias recognized?

(c) Is his/her bias used to reveal him/her as well as the events?

b. If he/she has chosen to speak in the third person, has the author chosen the most appropriate was of revealing his/her theme?

(1) If he/she has chosen to be omniscient, has he/she been able to show the minute human scene as well as the vast scope of human life?

(2) If he/she has chosen to limit omniscience to action, is his/her theme a limited one in which action contains feeling?

(3) If he/she has chosen the method of the effaced narrator, has he/she exercised sufficient subtlety in moving from the limited physical sight of the narrator to his/her own omniscient moral sight?

c. Has the choice of point of view been violated?

(1) Has the author intruded disruptively?

(2) If shifted, has the point of view been shifted skillfully?

I. Have scene and summary been developed in proportion and for effects appropriate to the matter so treated?

V. Characterization: Are the individual characters fully enough developed to become the focus of the reader's interest?

A. Are plot and characterization mutually interdependent? (Is that act inevitable on the part of that actor?)

B. Is the fully developed character—the round character—felt to have an existence independent of the events of the plot?

1. Does the novelist give the impression of knowing more about him/her than he/she chooses to tell?

a. Does the novelist implicitly or explicitly seem to know his/her inner life?

b. Is the character capable of surprising in a convincing way?

c. Is there a pull and play of alternatives of action?

d. Does the author seem to know the past and perhaps the future of his/her character?

2. Is the sense of complete knowledge conveyed through the partial revelations of the novelist's technique?

a. Are physical description and analytic author comment subordinate means of characterization?

b. Is character action?

    C. Does the round character change in the course of the novel?
      1. Is the change significant?
      2. Is the degree of change in keeping with the scope of the novel?
    D. Does the flat character serve as a medium to reveal the complex change of round characters?

VI. Dialogue: Does the dialogue simultaneously further plot and express character?
    A. Is the voice of each character individual?
    B. Does the interaction of speech between characters reveal their relationships to each other?
    C. Does the dialogue advance the story?
    D. Is the dialogue reserved for culminating scenes?
    E. Is the dialogue artistically valid?
      1. Does it imitate without transcribing?
      2. If it attempts to make the inarticulate articulate, does it do so always as a means of clarifying character (never as a vehicle to express abstract ideas for their own sake)?

VII. Setting: Is particularity given to character and event through descriptions of setting?
    A. Is the setting subordinated to the human element?
    B. Does the setting have dramatic use to reveal character?
    C. Does the setting have dramatic use to synthesize place and events?

VIII. Style: Do the elements of style all reveal theme?
    A. Is the sentence structure relevant to the theme?
    B. Do the metaphors reveal the individuality of the novel and thus of its theme?
    C. Are symbols relevant projections of the material?
      1. Do they exist believably on a literal level?
      2. Do they serve as a means to disclose the meaning of the literal level of existence?
    D. Is the tone, the attitude of the author toward the material of the novel, established by a consistent use of language?
      1. Does overdone language or editorializing produce a sentimental or condescending tone?
      2. Does the tone allow character and event to make their own case?

Books for Adolescents Ranked as Those "Best Written"

By Dorothy J. Petitt

Title	Author
1. Johnny Tremaine	Esther Forbes
2. The Yearling	Marjorie Rawlings
3. Seventeenth Summer	Maureen Daly
4. My Friend Flicka	Mary Sture-Vasa
5. Goodbye, My Lady	James Street
6. Lassie Come Home	Eric Knight
7. Winter Wheat	Mildred Walker
8. Swiftwater	Paul Annixter
9. Caddie Woodlawn	Carol Brink
10. Leon Feather	Iola Fuller
11. The Ark	Margot Benary-Isbert
12. Ready or Not	Mary Stolz
13. Adam of the Road	Elizabeth J. Gray
14. Banner in the Sky	James R. Ullman
15. Light in the Forest	Conrad Richter
16. Old Yeller	Fred Gipson
17. Smoky the Cowhorse	Will James
18. Patterns on the Wall	Elizabeth Yates
19. Sarah	Marguerite Bro
20. Banners at Shenandoah	Bruce Catton
21. Innocent Wayfaring	Marchette Chute

Title	*Author*
22. Santiago	Anne Nolan Clark
23. Trumpeter of Krakow	Eric P. Kelly
24. And Now Miguel	Joseph Krumgold
25. Thunderhead	Mary Sture-Vasa

Twenty-three Selected Junior Novels

by James Davis

Title	*Author*
Windigo	Paul and Jane Annixter
Bristle Face	Zachary Ball
Jamie	Jack Bennett
Snow in the River	Carol Brink
The Far-Off Land	Rebecca Caudill
Almost Like Sisters	Betty Cavanna
Pitcher and I	Stephen Cole
Classmates by Request	Hila Colman
Drop-Out	Janette Eyerly
Boy Gets Car	Henry Gregor Felson
Savage Sam	Fred Gipson
A Wrinkle in Time	Madeleine L'Engle
The Pond	Robert Murphy
It's Like This, Cat	Emily Neville
Catseye	Andre Norton
Lord of Thunder	Andre Norton
Raymond and Me That Summer	Dick Perry
Dugout Tycoon	Jackson Scholz
River and Her Feet	Zoa Sherburne
Roosevelt Grady	Louisa R. Shotwell
Who Wants Music on Monday?	Mary Stolz
The Shelter Trap	James L. Summers
Silence Over Dunkerque	John R. Tunis

The Muller List

by Al Muller

Title	Author
Sounder	William Armstrong
Durango Street	Frank Bonham
The Nitty Gritty	Frank Bonham
It Could Happen to Anyone	Margret Craig
Phoebe	Patricia Dizenzo
A Girl Like Me	Jeanette Everly
Drop-Out	Jeanette Everly
Mrs. Mike	B. and N. Freedman
Mr. & Mrs. Bo Jo Jones	Ann Head
The Outsiders	S. E. Hinton
That Was Then: This Is Now	S. E. Hinton
I'm Really Dragged But Nothing Gets Me Down	Nat Hentoff
Jazz Country	Nat Hentoff
Soul Brother and Sister Lou	Kristin Hunter
The Peter Pan Bag	Lee Kingman
Ask Me If I Love You Now	Frederick Laing
Just Dial a Number	Edith Maxwell
Lisa, Bright and Dark	John Neufeld
It's Like This, Cat	Emily Neville
Too Bad About the Haines Girl	Zoa Sherburne
Witch of Blackbird Pond	Elizabeth Speare
You Would If You Loved Me	Nora Stirling
Bless the Beasts and the Children	Glendon Smarthout
Tuned Out	Maia Wojeiechowski
I Never Loved Your Mind	Paul Zindel
My Darling, My Hamburger	Paul Zindel
The Pigman	Paul Zindel

Honor Sampling

by Kenneth L. Donelson and Alleen Pace Nilsen

Title	*Author*
1987	
After the Rain	Norma Fox Mazer
The Crazy Horse Electric Game	Chris Crutcher
The Goats	Brock Cole
Permanent Connections	Sue Ellen Bridgers
Princess Ashley	Richard Peck
Sons from Afar	Cynthia Voigt
The Tricksters	Margaret Mahy
1986	
All God's Children Need Traveling Shoes	Maya Angelou
A Band of Angels	Julian Thompson
Cat, Herself	Mollie Hunter
The Catalogue of the Universe	Margaret Mahy
Izzy, Willy-Nilly	Cynthia Voigt
Midnight Hour Encores	Bruce Brooks
1985	
Betsey Brown	Ntozake Shange
Beyond the Chocolate War	Robert Cormier
Dogsong	Gary Paulsen
In Country	Bobbie Ann Mason
The Moonlight Man	Paula Fox
Pocket Poems: Selected for a Journey	Paul Janeczko, ed.
Remembering the Good Times	Richard Peck
Wolf of Shadows	Whitley Strieber

Title	*Author*

1984

The Changeover: A Supernatural Romance	Margaret Mahy
Cold Sassy Tree	Olive Ann Burns
Downtown	Norma Fox Mazer
Interstellar Pig	William Sleator
A Little Love	Virginia Hamilton
The Moves Make the Man	Bruce Brooks
One-Eyed Cat	Paula Fox
Sixteen: Short Stories by Outstanding Writers for Young Adults	Donald R. Gallo, ed.

1983

Beyond the Divide	Kathryn Lasky
The Bumblebee Flies Away	Robert Cormier
A Gathering of Old Men	Ernest J. Gaines
Poetspeak: In Their Work, About Their Work	Paul Janeczko, ed.
A Solitary Blue	Cynthia Voigt

1982

The Blue Sword	Robin McKinley
Class Dismissed! High School Poems	Mel Glenn
The Darkangel	Meredith Ann Pierce
A Formal Feeling	Zibby Oneal
Homesick: My Own Story	Jean Fritz
A Midnight Clear	William Wharton
Sweet Whispers, Brother Rush	Virginia Hamilton

1981

Let the Circle Be Unbroken	Mildred D. Taylor
Little Little	M. E. Kerr
Notes for Another Life	Sue Ellen Bridgers
Rainbow Jordan	Alice Childress
Stranger with My Face	Lois Duncan
Tiger Eyes	Judy Blume
Westmark	Lloyd Alexander

1980

The Beginning Place	Ursula K. Le Guin
Jacob Have I Loved	Katherine Paterson
A Matter of Feeling	Janine Boissard
The Quartzsite Trip	William Hogan

Title	*Author*
1979	
After the First Death	Robert Cormier
All Together Now	Sue Ellen Bridgers
Birdy	William Wharton
The Disappearance	Rosa Guy
The Last Mission	Harry Mazer
Tex	S. E. Hinton
Words by Heart	Ouida Sebestyen
1978	
Beauty: A Retelling of the Story of Beauty and the Beast	Robin McKinley
The Book of the Dun Cow	Walter Wangerin, Jr.
Dreamsnake	Vonda N. McIntyre
Father Figure	Richard Peck
Gentlehands	M. E. Kerr
1977	
Hard Feelings	Don Bredes
I Am the Cheese	Robert Cormier
I'll Love You When You're More Like Me	M. E. Kerr
Ludell & Willie	Brenda Wilkinson
One Fat Summer	Robert Lipsyte
Trial Valley	Vera and Bill Cleaver
Winning	Robin Brancato
1976	
Are You in the House Alone?	Richard Peck
Dear Bill, Remember Me?	Norma Fox Mazer
The Distant Summer	Sarah Patterson
Home Before Dark	Sue Ellen Bridgers
Never to Forget	Milton Meltzer
Ordinary People	Judith Guest
1975	
Dragonwings	Laurence Yep
Feral	Berton Roueche
Is That You Miss Blue?	M. E. Kerr
The Lion's Paw	D. R. Sherman
The Massacre at Fall Creek	Jessamyn West
Rumble Fish	S. E. Hinton
Z for Zachariah	Robert C. O'Brien

Title	*Author*

1974

The Chocolate War	Robert Cormier
House of Stairs	William Sleator
If Beale Street Could Talk	James Baldwin
M. C. Higgins, the Great	Virginia Hamilton

1973

A Day No Pigs Would Die	Robert Newton Peck
The Friends	Rosa Guy
A Hero Ain't Nothing But a Sandwich	Alice Childress
The Slave Dancer	Paula Fox
Summer of My German Soldier	Bette Greene

1972

Deathwatch	Robb White
Dinky Hocker Shoots Smack!	M. E. Kerr
Dove	Robin L. Graham
The Man Without a Face	Lisbelle Holland
My Name is Asher Lev	Chaim Potok
Soul Catcher	Frank Herbert
Sticks and Stones	Lynn Hall
Teacup Full of Roses	Sharon Bell Mathis

1971

The Autobiography of Miss Jane Pittman	Ernest Gaines
The Bell Jar	Sylvia Plath
Go Ask Alice	Anonymous
His Own Where	June Jordan
Wild in the World	John Donovan

1970

Bless the Beasts and Children	Glendon Swarthout
I Know Why the Caged Bird Sings	Maya Angelou
Love Story	Erich Segal
Run Softly, Go Fast	Barbara Wersba

1969

I'll Get There. It Better Be Worth the Trip	John Donovan
My Darling, My Hamburger	Paul Zindel
Sounder	William Armstrong
Where the Lilies Bloom	Vera and Bill Cleaver

Title	*Author*

1968

The Pigman	Paul Zindel
Red Sky at Morning	Richard Bradford
Soul on Ice	Eldridge Cleaver

1967

The Chosen	Chaim Potok
The Contender	Robert Lipsyte
Mr. and Mrs. Bo Jo Jones	Ann Head
The Outsiders	S. E. Hinton
Reflections on a Gift of Watermelon Pickle	Stephen Dunning and others

CHAPTER SIX

The Reader-Response Orientation to Teaching Literature

After the prereading activities are accomplished and the reading is done, the work of what is traditionally thought of as *teaching* literature must begin. That is to say, at this point in the sequence of instruction students and teachers must begin to do something with the literature in class. In far too many classrooms this involves little more than asking and answering simple recall questions about the plot of the work under consideration and the use of mindless worksheets on vocabulary, figurative language, or some other aspect of the work. We have seen these methods turn classes of bright, eager students who enter the room excited about the terrific story they've read into semicomatose masses of indifferent souls who end the class period more convinced than they were before that school, and especially English, is dull and disconnected from their lives.

The reasons many teachers rely on teaching methods that are guaranteed to create boredom and diminish students' enthusiasm for literature are numerous and complex. In some cases teachers who treat imaginative literature as though it were a set of facts to be memorized or a quagmire to be waded through would genuinely like to do a better job. Often these people are painfully aware of their students' lack of interest in their teaching, and they daily endure the frustration of lifeless classes because they don't realize that they can teach differently. Or, if they know things can be better, they have no idea of where to start to make them better. Many of these people were not English majors in college, and their own fund of experience with literature is inadequate to begin to provide them with a model of how exciting literature study can be. Since they're not particularly interested in literature, these people aren't willing to devote personal time and resources to reading professional publications on the teaching of English or to attending conferences in the field.

In many instances, the fault lies more with the institution of the school than with the character of the teacher. The middle school movement, despite its many strengths, has sometimes tended to concentrate more on the developmental needs of younger adolescents than on the integrity of the content of the academic disciplines. In many middle schools academic departments have been replaced by teams of teachers who together teach all subjects to a relatively small group of students. In some cases, a teacher may have the same group of students for social studies, reading, and language arts, with another teacher having the same group for math and science. If the person teaching the social studies-reading-language arts module happens to have been educated as an English teacher, then the language arts component may be handled well. If the person happens to have been educated as a history teacher, though, the component in language arts may suffer.

In any case, a great many English teachers in middle schools owe their allegiance to their teams rather than to a department peopled by individuals of like interest and training. Because no English department exists in such schools, there is often very little interaction with others who are teaching English. The result is a sense of isolation, and there are few opportunities to exchange ideas, to share successes, to seek advice from more experienced colleagues on how to teach a particular aspect of the curriculum, and to challenge one another to do a better job. We know of one junior high with grades 7, 8, and 9 that had a dynamic English department of ten members in the fall of 1985. In November of that year this department was named a National Center of Excellence in English by the National Council of Teachers of English in recognition of the outstanding curriculum the members had developed. When school opened in the fall of 1986, the junior high school had become a middle school of grades 7 and 8. That year, only four of the ten English teachers of the previous year were still on the faculty. By the fall of 1987, only one of the original ten English teachers was still at the school. The program that the ten had developed and that the National Council of Teachers of English (NCTE) had recognized had effectively disappeared. A number of the teachers hired to replace those who left were trained teachers of English, but the common sense of purpose and the desire for excellence the ten original teachers had developed over several years of intensive reading, dialogue, mutual support, and experimentation was gone. And, since academic departments had been replaced by grade-based teams, it seemed unlikely that the spirit that once characterized the English teachers at that school would ever be rekindled.

While it may be tempting to place all the blame on institutional constraints, there are other reasons why much instruction in literature is lifeless. One of these reasons is the mistaken notion, widely subscribed to among the educational and political power structure of the United States, that literature study should take second place to the more specific, concrete, and measurable language arts skills. The so-called accountability movement of the 1970s, with its emphasis on behavioral objectives, embodied this notion and put a great deal of pressure on English teachers to describe the goals of their teaching in terms of observable behaviors. Clearly, identifying the parts of speech, correcting mechanical errors in sentences, and describing the differences among various types of figurative language are eminently more observable and quantifiable than, say, developing a love for reading, gaining insight into human motivation, or enjoying the humor of a funny story. Teachers were never told not to work on these affective goals, but the emphasis up and down the hierarchical ladder of school systems was on teaching objectives that produced observable, measurable outcomes. Because of this pressure, many teachers tended to emphasize relatively trivial aspects of English, and in no area was this problem more acute than the literature curriculum.

The great push for the use of behavioral objectives was immediately followed by the "back to basics" movement of the early 1980s. Many states mandated lists of minimum skills, and they enforced the use of these lists with statewide standardized testing programs. The effect of these new mandates was to distract teachers, and especially curriculum decision makers, from the teaching of literature. The money that was available to English teachers had to be spent on materials to teach the skills that would be tested at the end of the year. The emphasis in reading instruction in English classes was on vocabulary and comprehension skills, and the enjoyment and appreciation of literature was viewed with suspicion. Teachers who wanted to engage their students with works of literature met questions from colleagues, administrators, and parents like, "Are you *sure* your students have mastered the basic skills?" In some schools, the reading of a story or play was reserved for Friday as a reward for students *if* they applied themselves to the real work of skill mastery during the rest of the week.

Lurking behind both the behavioral objectives and basic skills movements was the question, "How will literature study help these students get a job and earn a living?" A few clever teachers we know retorted with, "Literature study may not directly help students get jobs, but it just might make them want to *try* to get them." However, most teachers of English merely set their anthologies and paperbacks aside and waited for better times. In many schools that better time still has not arrived.

While institutional problems and political issues like accountability and basic skills account for a great deal of the poor teaching that occurs in many classrooms, some of the blame can be traced directly back to the English establishment. Like any other academic discipline, the principles that direct the study of literature have been codified into a number of theories or approaches to literature. The history of literary criticism reveals periodic shifts in emphasis from one aspect of literature to another. At one time, the literary text was almost ignored by critics in favor of historical facts about the period when the text was written and biographical facts about the author. To study literature meant to memorize facts that had virtually nothing to do with the text.

The historical-biographical approach gave way in the 1930s to a new approach called formalism. The general principle of formalism is that the content of a work of literature by itself isn't art; only the content shaped into a particular form is worthy of that name. In practice this means that a critic must not only understand what Wellek and Warren call the "aesthetic effect"[1] of a work of literature, he or she must also understand how the effect is produced. In order to accomplish this, the critic must analyze the work carefully, paying attention to diction, syntax, figures of speech, tone, allusions, and a great many other devices the author uses. This kind of close reading is carried out under the assumption that there is only one *correct* reading of a text.

In the United States formalistic criticism was practiced by people who were generally known as the New Critics, and their particular brand of formalism was known as the New Criticism. The New Critics tried to achieve an almost scientific objectivity in their reading of a text, and for them there were clearly right and wrong answers about the meaning of a literary work.

The New Critics exercised a great deal of influence in how literature was studied and taught in colleges and schools. In addition to the fact that most teachers of English were (and perhaps still are) trained in New Critical methodology, their ideas are still incorporated into the teaching apparatus of contemporary middle school and high school textbooks.[2]

The ways in which New Criticism is partly responsible for bad teaching in schools today are related to the idea that it is necessary to understand *how* a work produces its effect and that there is only one correct reading of a text. In the first instance, the effect a work produces can vary enormously from person to person and, within a person, from time to time. We know a man who had a very direct experience with this phenomenon in connection with William Wharton's novel *Dad*. When he first read the novel, he was moved by the situation of a middle aged man standing by helplessly while his father underwent steady physical and mental deterioration before his death. When he tried to reread this novel shortly after his own father's death under similar circumstances, the emotional pain was too great for him even to finish the rereading. We also know from our teaching and from discussions with friends that the effects of works of literature vary enormously, to the point that people of similar background and disposition sometimes disagree strongly on whether a novel, story, poem, or play is "good" or not.

These examples suggest that how a work produces its effect is at least in part a function of the background, emotional state, and maturity of the person reading it. The text of the novel *Dad* didn't undergo any changes between the time our friend read it the first time and the time he tried to reread it. But, he underwent the physically demanding experience of long hours spent sitting with his father in hospital rooms and the emotionally disturbing experience of watching his father die. Since his first experience with the novel had been enjoyable and inspiring, he assumed a rereading would provide consolation and help in accepting his own father's death. In fact, though, a text which had had a positive effect on him at one time in his life was unbearable at another time.

The assumptions that the New Critics worked under ignored what the reader brings to the act of reading. When they asked how a work produced its effects, they meant which aspects of the plot, setting, characterizations, syntax, tone, diction, organization, imagery, and the like produced the work's effect. This led naturally to detailed analyses of minute aspects of works of literature. It is sometimes useful to readers to have patterns of imagery, symbols, shifts in diction, and the like pointed out because these aspects of texts are often easy to overlook in a first reading and because an awareness of these aspects can sometimes enhance a reader's enjoyment. The problem is that this type of analysis became a model for teaching works of literature in school, and in many, many cases more time and energy were spent discussing *how* the work created its effect than were spent discussing the effect itself.

A second aspect of the New Criticism that helped produce bad teaching was the assumption that there exists only one correct reading of a text. We certainly don't claim that any reading of a text is as valid as any other, but we do acknowledge that it is possible for two equally intelligent, mature, and experienced readers to arrive at different, and even contradictory, interpretations of the same work. The New Critics themselves tacitly acknowledged this by producing a great many different interpretations of texts, presumably in the search for the elusive "perfect" reading.

When the concept of the single correct reading is applied in the classroom, class discussion can easily become a game of "guess what I'm thinking." In this kind of classroom, the teacher has all the answers, and students are reduced to passive receptors of information. When the infrequent student in this kind of classroom insists on a different interpretation that even the teacher thinks makes sense, the teacher doesn't know how to respond. If the teacher agrees that the student's reading is entirely justified by the text, then the whole house of cards of correct interpretation crumbles. If the teacher denies the validity of the student's argument when it is obviously as good as, or better than, the received interpretation, then the teacher risks the deserved ridicule of the class. Many teachers of the strict New Critical persuasion fear genuine insights of the type we've been discussing, and when teachers fear good ideas in their students, everyone is in serious trouble.

This discussion of the weaknesses of the New Criticism is designed to lead into our discussion of reader-response criticism and reader-response oriented teaching in the next section of this chapter. We have pointed out the ways in which a total reliance on New Critical principles can lead to bad teaching when they are applied (misapplied?) in the classroom. Before moving on, though, we have to ask ourselves if New Criticism, which revolutionized the study of literature and which held the attention of the best minds in the field of English for fifty years, has anything to offer to teachers today. Put another way, do such New Critics as Cleanth Brooks, T. S. Eliot, Caroline Gordon, John Crowe Ransom, Allen Tate, and Robert Penn Warren have anything to offer teachers of English? Our answer to both of these questions is a solid yes, and we find a bit presumptuous those who answer no.

We made the point earlier that a preoccupation with how a work produces its effect can lead to petty analysis that bores most students and turns class discussion into exercises in detective work. Yet, aren't literary devices present in literary works? Don't authors choose some words over others because of their connotative value? Isn't an understanding of peculiarities of syntax essential to the comprehension of some poems? Doesn't an awareness of the process of foreshadowing enhance a reader's enjoyment of a story? Isn't the perception of symbolism a help to the understanding and enjoyment of some novels and plays?

On another level, we have to answer questions about the benefits of the process of analysis. Does learning to analyze a literary work help students analyze other, nonliterary texts? Is analysis a worthwhile skill that can focus and sharpen a student's emotional response to a work of art? Can literature be a vehicle for teaching students how to think?

Our answer to all of these questions is again a solid yes. Later we will argue that analysis of the kind the New Critics advocated, called close reading, and the technical vocabulary that goes along with it, has a significant part to play in reader-response oriented teaching.

Earlier we also made the point that adherence to the idea of a single correct reading of a work leads to dogmatic teaching and passive learning.

This aspect of New Critical theory offers very little to the teacher except two reminders. First, this idea reminds teachers that not every interpretation is as good as every other one. Second, it reminds us that responses to literature should lead somewhere (i.e., to interpretation).

Reader-Response Criticism

Throughout the twentieth century, a variety of approaches to literature have been proposed. Some, like New Criticism, have caught on and have had substantial influence on the way people read, think about, and discuss literature. Others, such as neo-Aristotelian criticism of the "Chicago School," never developed much of a following.[3] The one thing that seems certain, though, is that the search for new and better ways to read, think about, talk about, and understand literature continues.

One of the most widely discussed of the newer approaches to literature since the beginning of the 1970s is reader-response criticism. In the New Criticism, the focus was almost exclusively on the text, and meaning was said to reside in the words printed on the page. Naturally, with this focus the personality of the reader was of little importance, and, in fact, the reader was expected to subordinate his or her personality to objectivity in reading. The shift in focus from New Criticism to reader-response criticism is away from the text and onto the reader.

It is obvious that readers differ from one another in a host of ways. Such factors as intelligence, maturity, breadth of experience, education, emotional state, familiarity with other works of literature, and the like all influence the way readers read. Just as different people react to the same person or event in different ways, so too do readers react differently to what they read. In a sense, because readers notice different aspects of a text and respond to what they notice on the basis of their own life experience, each reader "creates" a work of literature that is different from works created by other readers using the same text.

The critic and theorist Louise Rosenblatt speaks of an encounter with a text as a transaction between the text and the reader.[4] Rosenblatt sees a "poem"—the term she uses to refer to any text that has been transformed by a reader from black marks on a page to a work of literature—as an event.[5] All events, including the poem–event, elicit responses from their participants, and these responses can be discussed and understood by others. Just as people watching an accident from different places and different points of view have unique insights to contribute to a description of what happened (in effect, because they each experienced different events), so too do readers reading the same text have unique insights to share. The class discussion of a text—a short story, for example—should allow and encourage the sharing of the "different" stories each class member experienced.

Reader-response theory draws heavily on psychology and philosophy to develop and support the basic premise that the real business of literature teaching lies somewhere other than in an attempt to discover the perfect reading of a poem or story. Reader-response critics differ with one another about the relative importance of the text and the reader, but they all recognize the reader as the center of the process of literature study. Given this premise, the question becomes one of how to conduct instruction in middle school and high school in ways that respect this principle and bring about genuine learning. In other words, what does all of the theory mean for the teacher of literature?

The Response-Centered Curriculum

The first way in which a reader-response orientation affects the teaching of literature is in the way works are chosen for class study. We have maintained throughout this book that works of literature that interest students should be given priority over so-called worthwhile works that are dull or beyond the grasp of students because of difficult language or themes of little or no interest to adolescents. Obviously, if teachers want their students to engage in a transaction with a text and then to articulate their responses orally or in writing, students have to have texts that are accessible to them, at least at some level. However, if students are able to respond fully to a work on their own without the benefit of guidance from the teacher or the responses of their classmates, why teach it? Why not simply make the text available to students and encourage them to read it on their own?

Rather than select only easy works in the name of reader-response, the reader-response orientation encourages teachers to select works of literature because of their potential to provide new experiences that students might not otherwise have and that they are capable of benefitting from. In other words, teachers must anticipate, on the basis of what they know about their students, the kind of experience most students are likely to have with the work.

One of our colleagues, brand new to the school, decided to use S. E. Hinton's classic Young Adult novel *The Outsiders* with a group of lower-ability tenth graders on the assumption that the novel's high-interest subject matter and relatively low readability level would make it accessible to his students. In making the choice, he did not take into consideration that most of the students in the class came from the same low socioeconomic level as the "Greasers" in the book. Without prior experience, one would assume that students would like a novel with characters similar to themselves, but our colleague discovered quite the opposite. The novel is clearly directed to a middle class audience, and Hinton's apparent intention is to show that Greasers have feelings, value, talent, and so forth, too. Our colleague's students reacted negatively to the novel, and quite strongly so, because the book describes a picture of their world they would just as soon not have confirmed in print. In reading the novel they learned that other people have the same picture of them that they have of themselves, and it confirmed the contempt with which the middle class generally views their world. While it's true Hinton's intention is to show the dignity and courage of the Greasers, her approach apparently does not appeal to all adolescent readers, including those who are real Greasers. Because our colleague wasn't in a position to know his students, he wasn't in a position to predict what kind of experience his students' transaction with *The Outsiders* would likely produce. The result was a bad experience for his students that he had to work the rest of the year to overcome. By way of contrast, we have used *The Outsiders* with low-ability students from middle class homes, and the students have loved it. In fact, when one class learned that Hinton wrote the novel when she was seventeen, they insisted on trying one of their own as a group. Theirs was never finished, but the experience of trying to write a novel taught them a great deal about writing and about themselves.

It isn't ever possible to predict with perfect accuracy the kind of experience students will have when they enter a transaction with a work of literature, and this fact underscores how much more valuable the reader-response orientation is for teachers. If the "poem" were merely an object, as the New Critics contend, it wouldn't be capable of producing any more of a response than any other object. Indeed, looking at a verse text, but not reading it, leaves most people as cold as looking at a telephone pole or a paperclip. The fact is, though, that reading does produce responses, and teachers can then use those responses as the starting point for their teaching. Sensitive teachers—and even insensitive ones with their survival instinct intact—learn to read texts to anticipate the kind of responses their students are likely to have, and these teachers don't hesitate to abandon even their most cherished novel or play when they sense it producing experiences for their students that are beyond them.

Besides affecting how decisions are made about which works to teach, the reader-response orientation also helps teachers set the tone for the way they conduct class. Adherents to the belief that a work of literature has only one correct reading will establish a tone in their classes that reflects their belief. When this happens, literature study becomes little more than rote learning. Skillful teachers of this orientation will lead their students to the correct interpretation through dialogue and Socratic questioning. Many students will enjoy this kind of mental exercise. But, learning to live with the ambiguity of not being able to arrive at a single right answer about the meaning of a work of literature is ultimately more valuable than "knowing" what a text means.

We are saying, of course, that a reader-response orientation helps the teacher create an atmosphere of open and honest inquiry in the classroom. Students in such an environment feel free to try out theories about the meanings of works without fear of being ridiculed by the teacher or, more likely, other students. Teachers feel free to admit they had never thought about the work in the way a student has, and they are even free to admit they don't know what a work means.

As an aside on this point, we take issue with some advocates of the reader-response orientation who imply that in a response-oriented classroom the teacher should be a learner on a par with students. That the teacher is a learner in the class is undeniable; that the teacher should be on a par with the students is as naive as it is potentially dangerous. It is naive for two reasons. First, the teacher's greater age, greater maturity, and greater fund of life experience make the teacher a different kind of responder than the students. Second, even if the teacher has never read or thought about the work in question before, he or she has read and thought about and studied a great many other works of literature, so the teacher should be more confident in his or her approach to the work than less experienced readers.

The idea that teachers should see themselves as learners on a par with students is potentially dangerous because it encourages the kind of lack of lesson preparation that is often at the heart of the worst educational experiences many students have in school. Our belief is that a teacher should never enter a classroom without specific plans for what will occur. Planning obviously includes reading and thinking about in advance the literature that is to be discussed.

In addition to the selection of works and the establishment of tone, the reader-response orientation offers guidance in helping teachers decide what it is that students are supposed to learn through the study of literature. The history of literature study in the schools of the United States is in large part a record of attempts by teachers and others in positions of leadership in the profession of English to arrive at a meaningful answer to the question of why study literature. As Arthur N. Applebee has observed, "the teaching of literature has from the beginning been under considerable pressure to formulate itself as a body of knowledge, a recognized content to be acquired by the student."[6] There is not, nor should there ever be, a standardized list of works that every student should read, and it is obvious from a glance at the transcripts of any randomly chosen group of English majors that it is quite possible for two people to both have excellent literary educations without necessarily reading the same works. There are a number of literary terms that most sophisticated readers, teachers, and critics use, but these are hardly numerous enough or important enough to warrant the amount of time spent in the middle school and high school years on literature. Literature study probably improves reading ability, but the same or greater improvement could be produced using other means. Finally, there is a certain amount of cultural polish that comes from studying literature, but, the advocates of the so-called cultural literacy notwithstanding, that, too, isn't worth the time and money that are spent teaching literature. The question, then, is why teach literature?

The reader-response orientation to the teaching of literature places emphasis in instruction on the transaction that occurs between reader and text. We believe that it is the process of entering the transaction, articulating responses to the experience of the "poem," clarifying and sharpening those responses, and arriving at an interpretation of the "poem" in the company of other readers that is instructive. Further, we believe that learning occurs that benefits the student socially, cognitively, and affectively.

Social Learning

The subject matter of literature is human behavior. Novels, plays, and short stories always have characters who do things, who act, who behave. Lyric poems often have characters who do things, but even those lyrics that don't describe humans acting have a speaker, a fictional "I" created by the poet for the purpose of making some observation about an aspect of reality. These facts are obvious, but what may not be so obvious is that readers enter into relationships with characters when they enter into transactions with texts.

At first glance the relationship seems entirely one-sided: characters have an effect on readers by boring them, amusing them, angering them, frustrating them, confusing them, or delighting them. However, readers have an even more profound effect on characters by actually creating them under the guidance of the text, as Rosenblatt would say.[7] Our students illustrated their ability to create characters when we asked them to write a brief composition about the character in *Wuthering Heights* for whom they had the greatest sympathy or admiration. Most of the students wrote about Heathcliff or Catherine Earnshaw or Hareton, but a surprising number chose to write about Isabella. In their minds she is an archetype of the independent woman who marries Heathcliff against the advice and wishes of virtually everyone in the novel, who doesn't hesitate to escape a terrible marriage when Heathcliff's abuse becomes intolerable, and who survives on her own in London, raising her son Linton alone and apparently without male assistance until she dies. We had read *Wuthering Heights* well over a dozen times but had never seen Isabella as anything but a minor character whose only real function in the novel is to produce her son. Our students created someone very different, and we will never be able to read the novel again without being aware of Isabella's strength, courage, and determined independence.

Once a relationship is established with a fictional character, interpretation begins. Readers ask themselves why characters behave the way they do, and the answer to this question is interpretation of human behavior and of literature. When readers share their interpretations with other readers, they learn that other people answer the question "Why?" in different ways, and ultimately they see that human behavior is usually the result of myriad motives and not of a single motive.

Insofar as characters' motives are genuine human motives, by interpreting characters students learn the important social skill of interpreting why real people act the way they do. More importantly, by sharing their interpretations and by listening to or reading the interpretations of others, they begin to grasp the limitations of their own visions of other people. Some characters—Hamlet is an obvious example—are so complex that their motives defy easy interpretation, and the fact that people like Hamlet cannot be fully understood or neatly categorized is perhaps the most important social lesson of all.

Another aspect of the social learning that occurs is what students can learn about themselves when they interpret a character. People often see in others what they like or dislike most in themselves. The boy who sees Heathcliff as virile and commanding, while overlooking the character's rather obvious cruelty and bitterness, probably sees himself as virile and commanding, or at least potentially so. The girl who sees Isabella as independent and self-confident probably cherishes those qualities in herself, or at least wishes she possessed them. By asking students to reflect on their interpretations and to think about the aspects of their own personalities that may have made them respond in the way they did, teachers can help students get to know themselves better. Such reflection is, of course, very private, and most students are unwilling to share their insights about themselves with anyone. Naturally teachers should never insist that students make personal revelations in any form. But whether the insights are shared or not, the act of reflecting is instructive.

Cognitive Learning

Reading literature and responding to it involves thought, and literature classes based on reader-response principles are ideally suited to help students develop mental and intellectual habits that have far-reaching consequences throughout their lives. The five cognitive skills/habits that students can learn from studying literature are as follows: 1. close reading;

2. a tolerance for ambiguity; 3. intellectual honesty; 4. scientific thinking; and 5. logical argumentation.

Close reading is a method of reading advocated by the New Critics in which the reader pays careful attention to every word and every nuance of meaning. It involves taking note of the connotations of words, the tone of a passage or a whole text, the syntax of a piece of writing, the diction used in the work, and any other aspect of the text that conveys meaning. The New Critics used close reading as a method of arriving at both the correct reading of a work and an awareness of how a work produces its effect. Used for these purposes close reading can become a kind of obsession or end in itself, and it can give rise to the kind of nit-picking that most students abhor. However, when used in the context of the reader-response orientation, close reading can be a valuable tool in helping students sharpen their responses and understand which elements of the text caused them to respond the way they did.

One of the first books for teachers on the principles of the reader-response orientation to teaching literature offered the following objective for a response-centered curriculum:

> An individual will know why he responds the way he does to a poem— what in him causes that response and what in the poem causes that response. He will get to know himself.[8]

This objective seems to us to be as valid today as it was when it was first published in 1972. In meeting this objective teachers will have to teach students how to read closely and to encourage them to use that technique.

We have already touched on the first part of this objective—the "what in him causes that response?" part—in the preceding section on social learning, and what we said there applies equally here. Our concern under the heading of cognitive learning is with the second part—"what in the poem causes that response?"

It is a fact that the various elements of literature—such elements as setting, techniques of characterization, figurative language, symbols, and so forth—produce an effect on readers without their being aware of the elements. This represents the lowest level of cognitive involvement with a text, and it is relatively unconscious. It is probably the way most readers approach escapist fiction and even more serious works during their first encounter with them, and it is probably the way young readers transact with every text. In the next highest level of involvement, readers become aware of aspects of the work—the conch shell and the pig's head on the stick in *Lord of the Flies*, for example—as obviously meaningful and worthy of some attention. At this level, readers are perhaps unable to identify literary elements by type, and they perhaps are unaware of the technical terms that have been devised to describe the elements. However, their awareness of important aspects of the work is conscious. At the highest level of involvement, readers are consciously aware that the writer is employing certain devices to achieve effects in the work, and they may even know literary terms to describe the devices. In any case, though, they have available to them some sort of vocabulary that enables them to share their awareness with others.

We believe that a very important part of the job of the teacher of literature in middle school and high school is to facilitate students' progress from the lowest to the highest levels of cognitive involvement with texts *so that students have a way of knowing what in the text causes them to respond to the text the way they do.* The way to accomplish this is to teach the skill of close reading and to encourage its use. At first glance this may appear to be no different from the position of the New Critics. However, it differs substantially from the New Critics' position in both the reason it is done (i.e., to provide students, ultimately, with a tool to promote self-knowledge) and with the methods that the purpose suggests.

Under the New Critical dispensation, students would typically study a definition of a literary device (e.g., personification) and then read sample texts in which the device is used in order to practice identifying it. The poetry sections of most school literature anthologies employ this strategy, and the poems in these sections are presented as a series of practice exercises that are useful in developing a skill. They are not selected primarily to foster meaningful reading experiences. In other words, the ability to identify a literary device is given priority over the transaction between the reader and the text.

In the reader-response orientation, students read poems selected because of the kind of experience the transaction between reader and text is likely to produce. In the course of discussion the teacher may ask students to identify the word, event, person, or idea in the poem that made them respond the way they did. With younger students, this process may go no further; with older students the teacher may identify the device by name and ask students to supply other examples of the device from past reading. In any event, though, the focus is on why the device produced the response, not on an awareness of the device for its own sake or for some possible transfer value this awareness may have in other reading encounters.

Close reading of this type has the goal of enhancing the reader's experience with the "poem" in two ways: first, it is a way to clear up misreadings and misunderstandings that prevent an authentic encounter with the text; second, it forces students to examine their experience in order to understand it better. To illustrate the effect reading error can have on a reader's response, Robert E. Probst describes a discussion of Donald Jones's poem "As Best She Could." The poem concerns an elderly widow's encounter with a welfare caseworker. One student responded negatively to the old woman in the poem because he felt that the woman's husband, instead of the welfare system, should provide for her needs. The problem was that the student didn't know the meaning of the word *widow*, and he assumed that since the woman is described as having children, she must also have a husband.[9] Obviously, once the reading error is cleared up the student's response to the entire poem is likely to change. This is a fairly elementary application of close reading, but it serves to demonstrate how attention to the words of the text serves to enhance response.

Close reading also forces students to examine their experience with a "poem" in order to understand the experience better. In a discussion of chapter eight ("Gift for the Darkness") of William Golding's *Lord of the Flies*, one of our students once commented that she felt somehow unclean or contaminated after reading the description of how the boys killed the pig. We asked the class to look at the particular passage the student was referring to, and other students agreed that the way the pig was slaughtered seemed particularly evil. The paragraph in question is as follows:

> Here, struck down by the heat, the sow fell and the hunters hurled themselves at her. This dreadful eruption from an unknown world made her frantic; she squealed and bucked and the air was full of sweat and noise and blood and terror. Roger ran round the heap, prodding with his spear whenever pigflesh appeared. Jack was on top of the sow stabbing downward with his knife. Roger found a lodgment for his point and began to push till he was leaning with his whole weight. The spear moved forward inch by inch and the terrified squealing became a high-pitched scream. Then Jack found the throat and the hot blood spouted over his hands. The sow collapsed under them and they were heavy and fulfilled upon her. The butterflies still danced, preoccupied in the center of the clearing.[10]

Quite clearly, all of the imagery in the paragraph is sexual, from Jack on top of the pig stabbing downward with his knife to the rather biblical-sounding clause, "they were heavy and fulfilled upon her." Under the lens of close reading, the slaughter of the pig becomes a rape, which in turn becomes a violation of nature of the grossest kind. The text had worked its magic on the students without their realizing why. However, a close reading of the text helped them understand their own repugnance more clearly, and it made them see the characters in a different light. In short, close reading enabled these students to identify what in the text made them respond the way they did.

It should be obvious that not everything people read is worthy of close reading, and students must be encouraged to vary the degree of closeness they use to suit their purpose in reading. However, close reading can be valuable in life situations, and the ability to read closely is learned, not acquired naturally. The literature classroom is the place to learn it.

A second cognitive skill/habit students develop in a response-oriented literature curriculum is a tolerance for ambiguity. Adults know from experience that the most important questions in life rarely have clear-cut right or wrong answers, and they know, too, that there are usually several valid interpretations of any given sample of human behavior. Adolescents, on the other hand, don't necessarily realize these facts, and they tend to demand definitive answers to every question. The New Critics' insistence on a single correct reading of a work plays into this tendency of adolescents, but the reader-response orientation requires students to live with the possibility of numerous equally valid interpretations. At first, some students may find this disconcerting and frustrating, but as they begin to elaborate responses of their own, especially if they are forced to address the issue of what in the work causes their response, they will come to accept the fact that ambiguity exists everywhere in life. To the extent that real life, not to mention most areas of scholarly inquiry, is ambiguous, the skill/habit of living with ambiguity will serve them well.

A third cognitive skill/habit that grows directly out of response-centered teaching is intellectual honesty. We don't want to imply that other orientations to literature study foster intellectual dishonesty, but the reader-response orientation clearly does encourage students to be honest with themselves and with others as they develop and share their responses. This occurs in large measure because there is no single correct reading that has authority over everyone's responses. Some interpretations of texts make more sense than others, and students must learn to accept the fact that all interpretations, no matter how dearly they may be cherished, are not equal. Apart from reading errors, which can create major misunderstandings, the quality of responses or interpretations depends on the extent to which responders make use of all aspects of the text in formulating their responses. For example, to call Hamlet a man of action because he kills Polonius, switches letters to the King of England, and wrestles with Laertes in Ophelia's grave is to ignore a great deal else about his personality. It isn't *wrong* to call him a man of action because of both the evidence we just cited and other details we might mention, but obviously there is much more to Hamlet than the things he does. If they are honest, in the course of class discussion students who begin by thinking Hamlet acts meaningfully and appropriately will broaden their responses to include other aspects of the character's behavior and personality. Likewise, honesty will compel students who start out thinking that Hamlet can't act at all to revise their response to include the fact that at times he *does* act. The result will be a fuller interpretation of the character. If there were only one correct interpretation, obedience to the authority of that reading, instead of honesty, would have to apply.

As students mature and become more experienced readers and responders, they can learn to apply the standards of intellectual honesty to their own responses. It is easy and tempting to ignore details on purpose in formulating an interpretive response, especially if the response one has in mind is particularly neat and ingenious. Furthermore, it is easy and tempting to dismiss as irrelevant or shortsighted contradictory responses of others that force a rethinking of one's position. In both of these cases, though, a failure to incorporate details or to consider opposing ideas is essentially dishonest. Students who are encouraged to do so can learn to apply these standards to their own thinking and to recognize their application in the thinking of others. The skill/habit of intellectual honesty will benefit individuals for the rest of their lives.

The fourth cognitive benefit of the reader-response orientation, namely scientific thinking, is closely related to an emphasis on intellectual honesty. As the critic David Bleich points out in *Readings and Feelings: An Introduction to Subjective Criticism*, a reader's first response to a text will be emotional,[11] but the emotional response is only the beginning. In order for the reader to find out "what in the poem caused that response," he or she must think, and thinking of the type required here must be based on data, on evidence, on facts. The data will come from the reader's experience and/or from the text, but come it must.

In a real sense, the thinking that is involved in responding to literature is similar to the kind of thinking done by scientists or anyone else who is in the process of creating knowledge. The statement of response is a kind of theory or hypothesis about the text, and the facts of the reader's experience and of the text are raw data upon which the response is based. Just as scientists test their hypotheses by subjecting them to new data, readers test their responses against their data. At times hypotheses have to be revised when they don't accommodate all of the phenomena they should be able to explain, and responses change when previously unnoticed aspects of the text are pointed out or when new personal experiences occur. This process can continue repeatedly for both individual readers and whole classes, and by using this process students actually engage in scientific thinking. Besides being an exciting way to read, this method of thinking in a literature class may even transfer to thought in other areas of life.

The final cognitive skill/habit that response-oriented teaching can help produce is skill in logical argumentation. As students formulate their responses and express them to others, they are frequently called upon by their classmates to explain why they respond the way they do. In other words, they are required to argue their positions, and their arguments must be logical if anyone else is to accept them or even understand them. There are relatively few school subjects that permit, let alone encourage, this kind of discourse, so learning to employ logical arguments in the literature classroom takes on added significance insofar as the ability to argue logically is valuable in life.

The cognitive benefits of literature study are significant and far-reaching. While they in no way represent a body of knowledge in the ordinary sense of that expression, they constitute a set of fundamental skills or habits of mind that are in many ways prerequisites for mature living and productive work. Literature study is perhaps not the only way these benefits can be obtained, but they clearly do result from a reader-response orientation to teaching literature.

Affective Learning

In addition to social and cognitive learning, the reader-response orientation also fosters affective learning. By *affective* we mean the kind of learning that provides insights that may, over a long period of time, improve the way people lead their lives. This kind of learning is probably unmeasurable, and it may be only one of many complex and interactive antecedents of how people live. It is nevertheless one of the most important outcomes of the study of literature.

When schooled readers approach a work of literature, they typically employ what Jonathan Culler calls "the rule of significance." That is, these readers assume they should "read the poem as expressing a significant attitude to some problem concerning man and/or his relation to the universe."[12] Another way of saying this is that the basic assumption behind literature, and the idea that draws serious people to it, is that a literary work has some insight to offer readers about their own lives. In this sense, every work of literature attempts to burn away the fog of illusion and to present reality more clearly.

In many instances characters in literary works are presented as living in a world of illusion, and frequently writers employ some concrete object to symbolize illusion. For example, Blanche Dubois, Tennessee Williams' tragic heroine in *A Streetcar Named Desire*, pretends to be an innocent upperclass Southern belle when she is, in fact, anything but that. Blanche hides her age, or thinks she does, by refusing to appear in sunlight, and she covers the lightbulb with a paper lantern to shield herself from the harsh light of reality. Blanche's tragic downfall occurs when she loses her sanity completely and enters the world of total illusion.

While the theme of illusion versus reality is overtly presented in *A Streetcar Named Desire* and a host of other works, it lies beneath the surface in others. Nevertheless, it serves as the basis for Culler's rule of significance, and it ultimately is what makes literature worth studying.

In the reader-response orientation to teaching literature, one of the teacher's primary responsibilities is to help students grasp the rule of significance and to understand that literature can help them strip away their illusions so that they see reality more clearly. By beginning with students' responses, and by helping them clarify and sharpen those responses, teachers can enable students to learn to obtain from their reading insights that can affect them for the rest of their lives.

We have outlined some of the social, cognitive, and affective outcomes that can result from the study of literature undertaken with a reader-response orientation. Learning in literature is quite different from learning in most other school subjects, but it is learning of the most basic and most important kind. While pressure to formulate literature as a body of transmitted knowledge still exists, the nature of literature and of the reading of literature makes such a formulation impossible.

Response-Centered Teaching

Thus far in this chapter we have described the reader-response orientation in theoretical terms with little attention to specific teaching methods. In this section we will attempt to describe methods that can help both beginning and experienced teachers implement the ideas of reader-response teaching in their classes. We must note at the outset that we have been careful to refer to the implementation of reader-response ideas as an orientation rather than a technique, a method, a system, or an approach. We chose the term *orientation* to emphasize that reader-response is a way of looking at the reading and study of literature rather than as a systematic step-by-step method of teaching. Like any good theory, the reader-response orientation will serve its adherents best by suggesting strategies and techniques that are consistent with its principles and by providing a set of implicit standards against which teachers can evaluate teaching methods. However, reader-response is not a cookbook of winning recipes.

The Response-Centered Lesson

The first step in a response-centered lesson is to determine how students have perceived what they have read. We have already discussed how misreadings can affect a reader's ability to respond authentically to a text, and eliciting perceptions can uncover serious misreadings. More importantly, though, the beginning of the lesson can yield responses that basically form the lesson's subject matter. Eliciting responses of this type can be accomplished in a number of ways.

One way to accomplish this is to follow David Bleich's lead and ask students to select the most important word in a literary work and to explain why it is important.[13] Students should be given ten or fifteen minutes to select the word and to write a brief explanation of why they think it is important. It isn't a bad idea to have students write their words in the upper right hand corner of their paper for ease in sorting later. After students have written their response, the responses become the topic for class discussion, and this can be handled in one of several ways. One way is to simply ask students to reveal orally the word they chose and to explain why they thought it was important. Another way is to ask volunteers to read what they have written. In either case the responses can lead to discussion by asking other members of the class to respond to their classmates' responses.

An alternative strategy is to collect the papers and sort them by word. In the event several students select the same word, ask them to work together as a committee to discuss their reasons and to report to the rest of the class, either orally or in writing, on the conclusions they arrive at. If there is no substantial agreement, the responses can be typed for distribution as a handout the next day. The discussion should focus on which word or words, as well as which reasons, the class as a group thinks best serves to capture the essence of the work's meaning.

We have used the most important word technique successfully with short stories and poems. Obviously, the point of the activity isn't to identify single words. Rather, in explaining why a word is important students actually engage in interpretation of the text. At first students may, as ours did, ask which word really is the most important, as though the question had a right answer. With experience, though, they learn that there is no single *correct* most important word, and they enjoy the activity because each of them has as much to contribute as anyone else. The same sort of experience occurs when Bleich's other techniques are used, namely identifying the most important passage[14] and the most important aspect of the work.[15]

Another way to determine how students perceive works and to begin the process of discussing responses is to ask students to identify the character they have the greatest sympathy for and to explain why. This technique is better suited than the most important word to novels and full-length plays. Again, in discussing a character students frequently end up offering interpretations of the entire work.

A third way to determine how students perceive a work and whether there are misreadings to be cleared up is to employ response-generating questions. In large measure the work itself will suggest questions that can begin eliciting responses. The following list of questions related to characters and plot are likely to generate responses. The list is intended to be illustrative of reader-response oriented questions.

1. Did you trust or mistrust any character in particular? Why?
2. If you could be any character in the work, who would it be? Why?
3. If you were casting a movie of the work, which real-life actors would you select to play the various characters? Why?
4. Did any of the characters remind you of people you know or of characters in other works you've read? Who? Why?
5. Did any characters annoy you or make you angry? Which ones? Why?
6. Would you kick any characters out of the work, if you could? Which ones? Why?
7. Did any event take you by surprise when it happened? Which one? Why?
8. Did any event seem to be out of character for the person who was responsible for it? Which one? Why?
9. Could any events be left out without destroying the story? Which ones? Why?
10. Did any events scare you? Which ones? Why?

A fourth method of eliciting responses involves what Leila Christenbury and Patricia P. Kelly call "the Questioning Circle".[16] Recognizing that teachers of literature rely heavily on questioning in their classes, Christenbury and Kelly reviewed the available research literature on questioning in an attempt to locate a questioning system that is suited to the reader-response orientation. They found none of the existing questioning models, or schema, entirely adequate, so they developed their own. The Questioning Circle technique taps three distinct areas of experience, namely *The Matter, Personal Reality*, and *External Reality*. When the technique is applied to literature, these three areas become *The Text, The Reader*, and *The World and Other Literature*, respectively. The technique can be visualized as three overlapping circles, which correspond to the areas that enter into responses to literature.[17]

Questions can be drawn from the *white areas* that deal with the matter, personal reality, and external reality independently. For *The Adventures of*

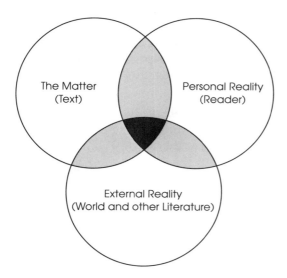

Figure 6.1 The Questioning Circle[17]
SOURCE: Adapted from Christenbury, Leila and Patricia P. Kelly. *Questioning: A Path to Critical Thinking.* Theory and Research into practice Series. Urbana: ERIC Clearinghouse on Reading and Communication and National Council of Teachers of English, 1983, Figs. 1 and 2, pp 13 and 15, with permission.

Huckleberry Finn, Christenbury and Kelly offer the following white questions:

The Matter: What does Huck say when he decides not to turn Jim in to the authorities?

Personal Reality: When would you support a friend when everyone else thought he or she was wrong?

External Reality: What was the responsibility of persons finding runaway slaves?

Questions can also be drawn from the *shaded areas* where two circles overlap. Christenbury and Kelly give these examples:

Matter/Personal Reality: In what situations might someone be less than willing to take the consequences for his or her actions?

Personal Reality/External Reality: Given the social and political circumstances, to what extent would you have done as Huck did?

Matter/External Reality: What were the issues during that time which caused both Huck's and Jim's actions to be viewed as wrong?

Finally, the Questioning Circle technique can produce a *dense question* at the point of overlap of all three circles. Christenbury and Kelly's dense question on *Huckleberry Finn* is as follows:

The Matter/Personal Reality/External Reality: When is it right to go against the social and/or political structures of the time as Huck did when he refused to turn Jim in to the authorities?[18]

Christenbury and Kelly suggest posing the dense question early in the discussion and using it as a kind of focus for what follows. In attempting to arrive at a response to this question, students will probably deal with the issues raised by the white and shaded questions.[19] Consider, for example, this dense question based on Ibsen's play *A Doll's House.*

> Is Nora morally justified in abandoning her husband and children when she walks out at the end of the play?

Obviously, the only possible answers are "yes," "no," and "sort of." However, in explaining each of these responses, students have to consider the text insofar as it presents the events and attitudes of the characters that lead up to Nora's departure. They also have to examine their own experiences as members of families and their beliefs about the inviolability of the marriage bond. Finally, they have to consider prevailing ideas about a woman's responsibility to herself versus her responsibility to her children. When we've used this question with students, we've participated in some of the most lively and sensitive discussions we've ever experienced. Invariably we've found students returning to the text for closer readings as they clarify points. Invariably, too, we've heard students speak of family life and the effects of divorce on children in ways so personal and so authentic as to elicit genuine sympathy and concern from their classmates. As far as we remember, no class of ours has ever arrived at consensus on this question, but the amount of thought and emotion expended in discussion has been amazing.

Our discussion to this point has presupposed that students have actually read the assignment before the discussion begins. We are well aware, however, that some students do not always enter a discussion prepared to participate, even if they had been given time in class to read the text. This is a perennial problem, and we don't have a surefire solution. However, if students know that their feelings and ideas will be the subject matter of the discussion, and if they know that their responses will be taken seriously, they are likely to read in advance. Many teachers give pop quizzes of literal reading comprehension as a way of motivating students to read. Sometimes this technique works and sometimes it doesn't. The danger of a factual quiz is that it sets the wrong tone for a discussion because factual quizzes have right and wrong answers. If grades are an issue, as surely they must be sooner or later, teachers can have students write their initial responses and can then evaluate them to determine whether students have read the text. After all, it would be impossible for students to write about whether or not Nora is justified in walking out if they know nothing about the plot of *A Doll's House*. At any rate, teaching in a way that makes students want to read is possible and preferable to the use of external threats.

Testing, Evaluating, and Grading in a Response-Centered Curriculum

In a perfect world, this section of this chapter wouldn't have to exist. In a perfect world students would throw themselves into their work with the full measure of their energy and talent, and learning would be the most enjoyable form of fun. In that world parents would trust their children to do their best in school, and college admissions officers and employers would know intuitively that students had learned well in school. In short, in a perfect world this section wouldn't exist because tests and grades wouldn't exist.

Unfortunately, such a world is a long way off, and teachers have to face the fact that evaluation, usually in the form of tests, and grades are a very important part of their jobs and of the lives of students. We know of no high school where teachers are not expected to give tests and to assign students grades—even if only *pass* or *fail*. The teacher of literature is no different from any other teacher in this regard.

It should go without saying that the material that is taught should be the material that is tested. Furthermore, it should go without saying that if an English teacher spends fifty percent of the class's instructional time teaching literature, then fifty percent of a student's grade should be drawn from an evaluation of the student's learning in literature. Because so much of the learning that takes place through literature study is untestable in the traditional sense, some English teachers we know base their students' grades exclusively on such areas as spelling, vocabulary study, conformity to the conventions of standard usage, and so forth, and ignore grading in literature altogether. While we understand these teachers' motivation, this practice strikes us as slightly dishonest and a bit unfair to students.

Before we discuss how to test in literature, we must discuss two ideas about how *not* to test. First, literature tests should rarely ask for a simple recall of literal details from the works students have read. There may be times when testing literal reading comprehension is important, but a test or examination in literature is probably not one of those times. As we said earlier, testing of this type implies that knowing what the text says is all that is important about literature, and these kinds of tests suggest that responding to literature is simply a matter of getting answers right. This is not to say that tests on background information, literary terms, the author's biography, and the like might not sometimes be appropriate, but, since all of these concerns are at best of secondary importance in a response-centered curriculum, they should be used very sparingly and even then never as the source of the student's entire grade in literature.

Second, the so-called *objective* testing methods, that is, true-false items, multiple choice questions, fill-in-the-blanks exercises, and so forth, are inadequate for testing in a response-centered curriculum. Besides reducing literature study to a series of right and wrong answers, these kinds of tests don't permit students to make personal responses. Quite clearly, objective tests are much easier and quicker to score than tests that require a free written response, and we are acutely aware that there are times, especially at the ends of semesters, when teachers are required to administer exams, grade them, average grades, and turn in final grade reports all in a matter of a few hours. Nevertheless, the constraints of unreasonable deadlines cannot determine what *should* be done.

If tests of literal recall are inappropriate, and if objective item tests are unacceptable, what's left? Obviously, our answer to this question is the essay, or essaylike, test. We use the term *essaylike* to refer to test items which require a free written response that is shorter and less structured than an essay. The tests we propose focus on the content of the course: the responses of students to the literature they read.

Earlier in this chapter we suggested in some detail how to elicit responses and how to use them for class discussions. In the course of these discussions students sharpen their responses by stating them and by examining and reexamining them in the light of the responses of others in the class. At times a consensus regarding the interpretation of a work will emerge, and at other times the discussion will end with several equally plausible interpretations competing in the marketplace of ideas within the classroom. In both instances, though, these interpretations may serve as matter for testing.

As an example, consider the hypothetical class in which the following statements emerged in discussion to explain Hamlet's delay.

1. Hamlet delays because if he had killed the king when he first knew from the ghost that Claudius murdered his father, there wouldn't have been a play.

2. Hamlet delays because he is consumed with melancholy, and this condition makes it impossible for him to perform any act, much less something as significant as killing a king.

3. Hamlet delays because he identifies subconsciously with Claudius as a result of his (Hamlet's) Oedipus complex, and to kill Claudius would have been to commit psychological suicide.

A test on *Hamlet* might have the following questions:

1. Consider the three statements and explain why all three are plausible explanations of Hamlet's delay.

2. Select the statement that most closely matches your own view and explain why you like it better than the other two.

Another kind of test item on *Hamlet* might ask students to compare how they felt about Hamlet at the start of class discussion with how they felt about him when the discussion was complete and to explain why they changed their minds (if indeed they did) or why they continued to feel the same about him in light of how others felt.

All of these questions have the common advantage of allowing students to respond to the work and to the responses of their classmates. In the course of writing their responses, students will have to think about the play, about themselves, and about the discussion they participated in. The teacher will be able to evaluate these responses in terms of how much thought the student put into the answers and how well the student understands the play. Most importantly, though, the student will have an opportunity to express his or her own feelings about the work of literature and about the ideas of fellow students.

There are a host of less formal ways of evaluating students in literature, including individual conferences, check lists, and student self-assessments. Any of these methods is valuable to both students and teacher, and we encourage their use in situations where they are practical. Whatever the method, though, the principle remains the same: teachers must evaluate what they teach. In a response-centered curriculum, that means the responses themselves.

Conclusion

In this chapter we have described the reader-response orientation, discussed its benefits, suggested methods for eliciting response, and considered how responses can be evaluated. In the next chapter we will turn our attention to ways of permitting students to express their responses, especially in writing.

Notes

1. Rene Wellek and Austin Warren. *Theory of Literature.* 2nd ed. New York: Harcourt, Brace & World, Inc., 1956, p 128.

2. Jane Ann Zaharias. "Literature Anthologies in the US: Impediments to Good Teaching Practice." *English Journal,* 78(6): October 1989.

3. Wilfred L. Guerin, et al. *A Handbook of Critical Approaches to Literature.* 2nd ed. New York: Harper & Row, 1979, p 244.

4. Louise M. Rosenblatt. *The Reader, the Text, the Poem.* Carbondale: Southern Illinois University Press, 1978, p 16.

5. Rosenblatt, *The Reader,* p 12.

6. Arthur N. Applebee. *Tradition and Reform in the Teaching of English: A History.* Urbana: National Council of Teachers of English, 1974, p 245.

7. Rosenblatt, *The Reader,* p 12.

8. Alan C. Purves, ed. *How Porcupines Make Love: Notes on a Response-Centered Curriculum.* Lexington, MA: Xerox College Publishing, 1972, p 31.

9. Robert E. Probst. *Response and Analysis: Teaching Literature in Junior and Senior High School.* Portsmouth: Boynton/Cook, 1988, p 17.

10. Reprinted by permission of The Putnam Publishing Group from *Lord of the Flies* by William Golding. Copyright (C) 1954 by William Golding, p. 125.

11. David Bleich. *Readings and Feelings: An Introduction to Subjective Criticism.* Urbana: National Council of Teachers of English, 1975, p 3.

12. Jonathan Culler. *Structuralist Poetics.* Ithaca: Cornell University Press, 1975. Reprinted in Jane P. Tompkins, ed. *Reader-Response Criticism: From Formalism to Post-Structuralism* Baltimore: Johns Hopkins University Press, 1980, p 103.

13. Bleich, *Readings and Feelings,* pp 49.

14. Bleich, *Readings and Feelings,* pp 63.

15. Bleich, *Readings and Feelings,* pp 70.

16. Leila Christenbury and Patricia P. Kelly. *Questioning: A Path to Critical Thinking.* Theory and Research into Practice Series. Urbana: ERIC Clearinghouse on Reading and Communication and National Council of Teachers of English, 1983, p 15.

17. Adapted from Leila Christenbury and Patricia P. Kelly. *Questioning: A Path to Critical Thinking.* Theory and Research into Practice Series. Urbana: ERIC Clearinghouse on Reading and Communication and National Council of Teachers of English, 1983, Figs. 1 and 2, pp 13 and 15, with permission.

18. Christenbury and Kelly, *Questioning,* p 16.

19. Christenbury and Kelly, *Questioning,* p 17.

CHAPTER SEVEN

Expressing Responses Orally and in Writing

The study of English in the middle and high school years has always involved much more than the study of literature. English teachers are expected to provide instruction in a variety of language arts areas, including listening, speaking, and, of course, writing. The reader-response oriented curriculum in literature can serve as a natural vehicle to create opportunities and possibilities for instruction in all areas of the English curriculum, and particularly in the areas of oral language use and writing. In this chapter we will discuss ways in which students can express their responses to the literature they read and hone their skills in self-expression.

Oral Language

As we said repeatedly in Chapter Six, most of what occurs in a response-oriented classroom will involve class discussion of students' responses to the literature they read. In addition to the obvious fact that discussion enables students to share their responses with one another and with the teacher, discussion also provides an opportunity for thought. The original response that a reader has to a text is emotional, as David Bleich points out,[1] but in order to examine that response and to sharpen it, it must be expressed in words. The act of sharing a response through language is actually the act of creating the response on the cognitive level. When a student struggles to find the words to express how he or she feels about a character or an event in a work, the student actually discovers what his or her response really is. It is possible for people to think about emotions when those emotions are given names, and it is possible to evaluate those emotions when they are expressed in words. Discussion makes it possible for people to objectify

157

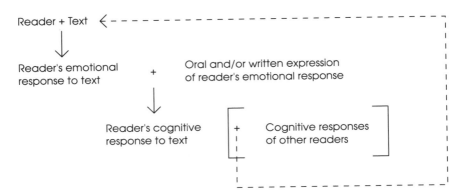

Figure 7.1 The Response-Expression Cycle. The role of oral and written expression of responses to a text can be thought of as part of a kind of cycle, as illustrated in Figure 7.1. The bracket and dotted line indicate optional, but desirable, parts of the cycle. When the optional parts are included, the cycle becomes recursive.

their emotional responses to a text and to understand how they feel and why they feel the way they do.

In a very real sense, class discussion is a way for students to create knowledge. Over and over we have observed students in discussion who begin to express an idea, only to stop halfway through their comment to start all over from a completely different point of view. What occurs in those situations is simple: students begin to examine their ideas as they are speaking and realize that their ideas are wrong, or at least inaccurate for how they feel. The words they say are what they feel, and what they feel is the content of the lesson.

Whole-Group Discussion versus Small-Group Discussion

Most discussion that occurs in most literature classes takes place with the entire class. This happens because when the whole class is involved, the teacher can better monitor what's going on and make sure that the discussion remains on task. Also, much discussion depends on questions from the teacher to stimulate thought, to clarify ideas, and to emphasize important points. Obviously, when the class is divided into small groups of four or five members, it isn't possible for the teacher to know at every moment what each group is discussing or even if they are dealing with the assigned material. For these reasons, many teachers favor large-group discussion over small-group discussion for most of the basic discussion of responses.

Small-group discussion can be very effective, however, for several kinds of activities. Discussion in groups of three, four, or five works best when some kind of decision has to be made. In Chapter Six we described the *most important word* activity, and we said then that if several students select the same word as the most important they can be allowed to work together to select the reason or reasons why the word they chose is the most important. This is an example of a small-group discussion in which a decision has to be made. The task is very specific, and the directions are clear. Under these circumstances most students, even those in the middle school grades, can work well, provided they aren't given more time than they need to accomplish the task.

Another kind of task that can be handled in a small group is to decide which interpretation of a work the group likes best from a set of interpretations provided. The biggest problem here is the difficulty students will have in trying to arrive at a consensus. For this reason the teacher should probably specify in the directions to the group that minority reports are acceptable. Otherwise, the discussion can quickly turn into a game of guessing the right answer. Yet another activity that works well in a small group is to ask students to compile a list of their initial responses to a work and to write a report of their discussion for the rest of the class.

Small-group work can be very challenging to both teacher and students, and students who are perhaps reluctant to speak out before the entire class often feel more secure and are more willing to articulate their responses to a group of four or five than they are to a class of twenty-five or thirty. Other students may dislike small-group work because they like the security that comes from having the teacher watch over them as they present and discuss ideas. These students may consider small-group work a waste of time and may even resent the fact that they don't have the opportunity to share their thoughts with the teacher. In general, teachers find small-group discussions more demanding on them because of the need to move from group to group and to constantly refocus their attention from one topic to another. Despite this possible drawback, most teachers who use small groups realize that they are able to spend valuable time in one-to-one interaction with individual students as they visit the various groups at work in the classroom.

There are good reasons for and against the use of small-group discussions in a literature class, and each individual teacher must make up his or her mind about whether to use them. We believe that small groups can be very effective if they are given concrete, specific assignments, and small-group discussions can add variety to classroom routine. Since there is generally more noise in the classroom when small groups are in session than there is in large-group discussions where only one student is allowed to talk at a time, small-group work may take some getting used to. However, this is a relatively minor problem that both students and teacher learn to cope with.

Oral Reading

Another valuable technique for eliciting responses from students involves oral reading by either individuals or groups. A well-prepared oral reading is actually an interpretation of a text, and in this sense the reading incorporates the student's response to the text. In preparing to read a poem or a passage from a longer work to the class, the reader has to come to understand the text well enough to communicate his or her understanding to the audience. This is really what actors do when they create roles.

The emphasis in oral reading is on a communication of meaning rather than on acting skill. Some students with a flare for the dramatic will be willing and able to present readings that are quite good as entertainment, but oral reading is a valuable activity for every student. One way to overcome the shyness that some students may feel in reading before a group is to allow students to read their selections into a tape recorder. When readings by several students of the same text are taped, they can be played in succession, and the similarities and differences among them can be discussed in class just as any other response is discussed.

Any number of works of literature are well suited to oral reading activities, but some care should be taken to select passages from longer works that lend themselves to this kind of treatment. Long descriptive passages, for example, probably offer relatively less potential for good oral reading than soliloquies or narrative passages. Poems, especially dramatic monologues, are also excellent sources of material for oral reading, and of course virtually any play contains scenes that groups of students can read orally.

The key to successful oral reading activities is preparation. Many teachers routinely call on students to read orally without giving them any time to prepare their interpretations ahead of time. This practice can be useful if the teacher knows that the students called on read well enough "cold" not to distract others and if the passage chosen for this kind of oral reading has a great many trouble spots that the teacher will want to comment on as they are being read. As a general rule, though, unprepared oral reading in class slows down faster readers, and it takes away the pleasure that reading provides. After all, it is almost impossible for a student to go back to a passage for rereading or even to stop to think about what is being read if the class reader is forging ahead regardless of individual reading needs.

Readers Theatre

Another oral language activity that is useful in a response-oriented literature curriculum is Readers Theatre. Readers Theatre involves creating scripts based on works of literature of every genre and presenting dramatic readings of those scripts before an audience. This necessarily involves groups of students working together, although one or more students may be given responsibility for creating the script, while others are given responsibility for performing it.

There are almost no limits on which works can be used for Readers Theatre, although dramatic works, that is, plays, short stories, poems, and so forth, that feature a fairly large amount of dialogue work better than works that contain very little dialogue. In some instances, it may be necessary for the script writers to invent a narrator or storyteller to fill in exposition or to provide linkages that aren't accommodated by the dialogue. We will deal with script writing in more detail later in this chapter. For now, suffice it to say that almost any work of literature has potential for a Readers Theatre presentation.

Like any other oral reading activity, the Readers Theatre presentation must be prepared ahead of time. Students are not expected to memorize lines (in fact, they usually hold their scripts during the presentation), but they certainly must be familiar with their lines in order to be able to deliver them meaningfully. Some Readers Theatre presentations involve almost no movement of the actors on the stage, and it is not uncommon for the readers to be seated on chairs or stools. Other presentations do feature movement. In either case, there are almost no props, scenery, or costumes to complicate matters. Instead, meaning must be communicated by the reading.

A Readers Theatre presentation can be used as a culminating activity for a unit of study for a work the entire class has read and discussed, or it can be used as a kind of group book report for a work that only a small group of students has read. On this last point, Shirlee Sloyer has noted that "experience demonstrates that those who hear dramatized material are inspired to seek out the selections in the future for recreational reading."[2] Because it demands a carefully developed response in the performers, Readers Theatre is ideally suited for use in the reader-response oriented literature curriculum.

Improvised Dramatic Activity

During the summer of 1966, a group of scholars and teachers from the United States and Great Britain met in seminar on the campus of Dartmouth College for a month-long series of discussions about the teaching of English. During that meeting, American participants learned

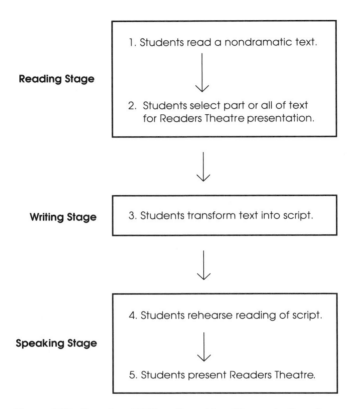

Figure 7.2 Reading-Writing-Speaking Stages in Readers Theatre

of the heavy emphasis on the use of dramatic activities in English classes in Britain, and thus began a wave of interest in the use of drama in American classes.

The rationale for the use of impromptu dramatizations in the literature classroom comes from psychological theory and research regarding the role of play in the lives of children. The British professor of English education Frank Whitehead quotes Peter Slade's assessment of what children accomplish through play:

> . . . by observing children and talking to them like human beings, you learn that their life is based on Play, and that is what they like better than anything else. This is not a way of avoiding unpopular duties; it is their way of trying out bits of real life before it comes to them, and living again bits of life they like.[3]

With respect to children using play to try out aspects of real life before they experience them, Whitehead describes how a child who is frightened of a new situation, for example, going to the dentist, might well play dentist in order to rehearse the experience before it occurs.[4] In this way the children anticipate how they will feel and behave in the dreaded situation, and they prepare the role they will take when the situation actually occurs. In other words, they prepare themselves emotionally through play. Likewise, children often reenact pleasurable experiences, a first train ride, in Whitehead's example, in order to savor them and to come to grips with their meaning for them.[5] In either case, acting out an experience in play enables children, in Dwight Burton's term, to "enter imaginatively"[6] into a real or imagined experience.

These ideas apply to the use of improvised dramatic activities in the classroom. When students improvise a scene from a novel or short story, they have the opportunity to try out what it's like to be the characters behaving in the way the characters behave. In a very real sense, the students *become* the characters of the work. Whether there is an audience or not makes no difference; in fact, students are probably more likely to enter fully into a role if they know that no one is watching and that they won't be evaluated by the teacher or their peers. The way they move, speak, gesture, and comport themselves is a genuine response to the character and/or situation they're portraying. Scripts only get in the way in this kind of activity, and since the students have already read the text, scripts are unnecessary.

Improvised drama need not always involve the reenactment of a work; it can also be based on the situation that is likely to exist after the work is completed. For example, the play *A Doll's House* ends with the main character, Nora, walking out on her husband and children. Some students will agree that Nora did the right thing and others will not. A worthwhile dramatic activity at that point might be a court trial in which Nora faces charges for abandoning her family. One student can play the part of Nora, another the part of her husband, another the prosecuting attorney, and so forth. The whole class can participate as witnesses and jurors. In this situation, students can incorporate their ideas in testimony, questions for witnesses, and the other dialogue that occurs in the trial.

Improvised drama can also be used as a preparation for reading. In this instance the teacher can set the scene and describe a situation that is the same as, or similar to, one that students will encounter in their reading. As students act out how they think a character in this situation would act, they build a familiarity with the emotions the characters in the work are likely to experience.

Improvised dramatics can be used in other ways, as well. For example, students can be asked to act out vocabulary words after they have been given the meanings of the words. This provides a whole range of experiences with the word that no paper and pencil exercise could possibly duplicate. Likewise, improvised drama can be used to review concepts and works of literature that students have studied in the past.

As a general rule, the older the student the more reluctant he or she will likely be to try improvised dramatic activities. However, with encouragement and the assurance that "no one will be watching," even high school seniors can be led to try them. As a means of expressing responses to literature of all types, dramatic activities offer enormous potential.

Oral Book Reports

Oral book reports have long been a part of the teaching repertoire of many English teachers. Sometimes these reports are simply summaries of novels or other books that students have read, and sometimes the reports include evaluations of the books and recommendations about whether the reporters think others in the class would enjoy them. Unfortunately, most of the time these reports are dull, and the members of the audience find them boring. However, there are ways to make oral book reports fun for the reporters and interesting to the audience.

One way to improve oral book reports is to follow the suggestions of Madeleine Myers of MacArthur High School in Irving, Texas, and assign oral book reports in the format of a television talk show.[7] Myers divides her class into groups of six, seven, or eight members and requires that each group select a talk show host. The host must interview three or four guests who role-play characters in the novel. Other members of the group prepare commercials based on products or services that are found in the novel, and still other members of the group prepare news items based on events in the novel for a brief news segment. Myers uses this technique with *Great Expectations* by Charles Dickens, but the talk show format is flexible enough to accommodate any novel, play, or short story. The guests on the show obviously focus on characterization, the products or services on elements of the setting, and the news items on elements of the plot.

Another oral book report idea involves having students enact television commercials to "sell" a book to the class. We have used this technique successfully with junior high school students, who enjoyed performing the commercials and who enjoyed watching the commercials of others. To enhance audience participation, several commercials can be presented in succession during the same class period, and class members can "vote" for the commercial they like best by "buying" the book using play money made up for the occasion.

A Word about Listening

Class discussion and oral activities of other types obviously imply that someone is listening, and listening with interest and comprehension. Apart from such factors as distracting background noise and a failure on the part of the speaker to speak loudly enough to be heard by everyone in the audience, the chief factor that keeps students from listening to what is being said in a discussion or oral presentation is lack of attention. Lack of attention in a discussion, of course, usually is the result of lack of interest on the part of the listener, but sometimes it is the result of the listener's preoccupation with his or her own thoughts.

One technique that often helps increase attention is to require students to recapitulate in summary form the comments of the student who spoke immediately before them. In addition to making sure that the speaker was listening to what was just said, this technique also helps keep the discussion focused on ideas as they come up in the comments of the students who choose to speak. Unfortunately, though, this technique also has some serious drawbacks. For example, a student may hear an idea expressed by another member of the class, and this idea may stimulate a whole train of thought in the listener. This technique requires that these ideas be expressed next in turn, but in most classes that are truly engaged in a discussion, there will probably be several other students who have been patiently waiting their turns to speak. By the time the student who was stimulated to think by the first speaker gets a chance to speak, several intervening comments may have occurred, and these intervening comments may have nothing whatever to do with what the student wants to say. To force this student to recapitulate the last comment even though it is irrelevant to what he or she wants to say seems contrived and rather pointless.

Furthermore, students may appear not to be listening when, in fact, they really are. We are repeatedly amazed at this phenomenon, but it happens every day in our classes.

Our experience has been that students listen best when they are most interested in what is being said. In the response-oriented literature classroom, the subject matter of the class discussion is the responses of the students. If students know that their ideas will be taken seriously and that others will give them honest consideration, their interest in the discussion will be high. One of the teacher's roles in class discussion is to help focus the attention of the rest of the class on what is being said. When the teacher notices that students are not paying attention, then the teacher should decide if the discussion has gone on long enough. If it has, then it should be ended. If it has not, then the teacher should overtly refocus attention. This can be accomplished in several ways. First, the teacher can simply ask the class to pay attention. Second, if the teacher is speaking and attention seems to be waning, he or she can change posture or move to another point in the classroom. We usually sit in a chair pulled up to the front of an empty student desk during class discussions. When we notice that attention is beginning to fall off, we simply stand to make the next point. If we're standing behind the podium in the front of the class, we walk to the chalkboard or into the middle of the classroom. These techniques are simple, but they are usually quite effective in refocusing the attention of the class.

Conclusion for Oral Responses

Talk is an essential means of making learning occur in the literature classroom, and oral activities of all sorts should be a part of the stockpile of teaching methods of every English teacher. In addition to helping students move their responses to literature from the emotional to the cognitive levels, talk of all kinds helps build what Andrew M. Wilkinson calls "oracy."[8] This term refers to receptive and expressive oral language skills, that is, listening and speaking, and is the oral language equivalent of *literacy*. In a response-centered curriculum, oracy and literacy go hand in hand.

Written Expression

Written composition has always been a part of the English curriculum; in fact, the study of rhetoric has had an honored place in schools much longer than the study of literature. In the past (and perhaps the present in far too many schools), composition and literature were thought of as separate components of the English curriculum, and it was not at all uncommon for schools to require a one-semester course in composition and a one-semester course in literature each of the high school years. Since approximately 1970, though, the situation has changed, and composition, or "writing," as it is more commonly called, has taken its rightful place as part of an integrated English curriculum which sees writing as a vital part of the study of literature.

This is not a book on the teaching of writing, and no attempt will be made to present a comprehensive discussion of the theory and practice of teaching writing in middle and high school. Instead, in the sections that follow we will concentrate on how writing can and should be used as a means of eliciting and sharpening students' responses to the literature they read and study. This is not to say that suggestions will not be made from time to time that teachers can use to help their students become better writers.

Writing as a Way of Knowing

Before we consider specific suggestions about the use of writing in the literature curriculum, some theoretical considerations about writing as an intellectual activity must be discussed. We have borrowed the title of this section from James M. McCrimmon's 1970 National Council of Teachers of English (NCTE) Distinguished Lecture.[9] In this lecture McCrimmon distinguishes between writing as a way of telling and writing as a way of knowing. When teachers speak of writing as a way of telling, they are talking about what is generally thought of as style, and this aspect of writing is what usually gets most of the attention in courses on written composition. McCrimmon suggests that English teachers give more emphasis to writing as a way of knowing because this concept focuses on content, on ideas, on what writing is about. This idea seems to us to be ideally suited to our discussion of writing as part of the literature curriculum because our chief contention is that through writing students best discover what their responses to literature really are and that through writing they can best examine their emotional reactions to what they read.

In the previous section of this chapter that dealt with oral discussion, we made the point that people are not able to think about and share their experiences until they are able to express their ideas in words. What often happens is that students will express opinions about something they have read in rather global terms, for example, this character made me angry, without really thinking through all of the reasons for their opinions and without understanding all of the implications that these opinions carry with them. In other words, students have made a beginning at understanding how they feel about the character, but the students' understanding is anything but complete. In the course of the discussion, students hear the comments of others and then modify their initial reactions. All of this occurs in a situation in which students are able to take advantage of the nonverbal, as well as the verbal, messages of the rest of the class.

The same process occurs when students write about their reactions to the character, but the context is very different. As students write, they struggle to find the words that genuinely describe their feelings. This process forces them to think in a way that is more intense and more specific than is required in oral discussion. As students write, they have to constantly evaluate ideas to determine whether they are consistent with what has already been written and with the facts that they have at their disposal. As they make these evaluations, new ideas constantly present themselves, and students *discover* what they know about their topics.

A good many writers have commented on the nature of writing as a process of discovery. The American playwright Edward Albee, for example, said, "Writing has got to be an act of discovery . . . I write to find out what I'm thinking about." The poet W. H. Auden described the relationship between language and thought in these words: "Language is the mother, not the handmaiden, of thought," and he went on to describe how this concept applies in writing: "words will tell you things you never thought or felt before." And the American novelist Frank Conroy echoed Albee and Auden when he said, "Most often I come to an understanding of what I am writing about as I write it (like the lady who doesn't know what she thinks until she says it)."[10]

Donald M. Murray shares these sentiments when he defines writing as "the process of using language to discover meaning in experience and to communicate it."[11] This, of course, is also the basic goal of the reader-response orientation to the teaching of literature. Readers' transactions with texts constitute experiences which have meaning for them, and their responses constitute their attempts to discover this meaning. Insofar as these responses are expressed in words, meaning is communicated to others. In a real sense, then, writing about literature is a way of understanding what the literature means to the person writing about it. In essence, it is a way of knowing the literature, but, more importantly, it is a way of knowing one's responses, of knowing oneself.

The Writing Process

The biggest advance in the teaching of writing in the twentieth century—some would say the biggest advance in the teaching of English—was the rediscovery of the writing process. Aristotle had defined stages of the writing process 2400 years before, but it wasn't until approximately 1970 that English educators began to think in terms of the process with any kind of coherence. The writing process began to have a real effect on the teaching of writing in the schools in the 1980s when textbook publishers began using the stages of the process as structural elements in school rhetoric texts.

Various textbooks define the stages of the writing process in various ways, but there is general agreement that it consists, at least, of a prewriting (or invention) stage, a writing (or drafting) stage, and a postwriting (or revision) stage. The postwriting stage is often subdivided into revision, editing, and proofreading, and some texts also include publication as part of postwriting. In the discussion that follows, we will focus on the two elements of the writing process that are most crucial to responding to literature, namely prewriting and revision.

Prewriting is the stage in the process where ideas are generated. In classical rhetoric, this is a discrete stage that occurs before writing begins. In more modern concepts, prewriting also occurs before writing starts, but it occurs recursively throughout the time people write and revise. As Donald Murray says, ". . . writing will, at times, seem to skip over one part of the writing process and linger on another, and the stages of the process also overlap. The writing process is too experimental and exploratory to be contained in a rigid definition; writers move back and forth through all stages of the writing process as they search for meaning and then attempt to clarify it."[12] The recursive nature of prewriting is what makes writing a way of knowing, and it is also what makes writing ideally suited for expressing and clarifying responses to literature.

The most important prewriting *activity* is, of course, the reading of the text. Throughout this book we have insisted on the importance of helping students identify correlative experience, and in Chapter Three we described a series of exercises that can be used to accomplish this. Identifying correlative experience is also prewriting activity, as is the oral discussion of literature in class. In fact, in the response-oriented curriculum, everything that is done before writing occurs is prewriting activity of the best sort.

In the early grades of middle school and high school, teachers should make it a point to work students through all of the prereading and prewriting activities we have described. In the later grades of high school, though, some students may be ready to write about literature without detailed group prewriting activity. Students in this situation should be taught how to perform their own prewriting activities before they write. Composition textbooks typically suggest several prewriting activities that students can use on their own. These usually include brainstorming, clustering, questioning (i.e., who, what, when, where, why, and how), and perhaps others. Good composition textbooks also emphasize a consideration of purpose, audience, and tone as part of prewriting. These prewriting activities are often useful to students as they go about the business of selecting and narrowing a topic in preparation for writing. In our experience with high school composition textbooks, few, if any, emphasize the recursiveness of the prewriting stage, so it is incumbent upon teachers to make sure their students understand that prewriting occurs throughout the process of writing.

Another major responsibility that teachers have in preparing students to write about literature is to make sure that the assignments they give are clear and specific. Vague and nonspecific assignments tend to produce vague and nonspecific writing. An assignment like "Discuss the symbolism in *Lord of the Flies*" will leave students floundering. A far better assignment on the same subject is one like the following:

Most readers of William Golding's *Lord of the Flies* agree with the author's assessment that Ralph, Jack, Simon, Piggy, and perhaps other characters, are symbolic. As symbolic characters, these boys are thought to represent types of people or aspects of human nature. In a well-developed essay, explain how one or more of these characters can be said to function as symbols. Make sure you identify the character(s), what they symbolize, and what evidence in the novel makes people think they are symbolic. If you disagree with the conventional wisdom about the symbolic nature of the characters, you should attempt to prove that point. If you choose this approach, you should briefly summarize the argument in favor of the symbolic nature of the character(s) before you refute it. Do not simply summarize the plot. In fact, consider your audience for this essay to be a student on your grade level who has read the novel but who has not really thought about the characters' functions.

An assignment of this type makes it very clear what students are expected to do in their essays. This assignment should be given to students in writing, and class time should be spent allowing students to ask questions about the assignment to make sure they understand it. If students are expected to write this essay without benefit of class discussion of their responses to the novel (which seems unreasonable for all but perhaps the most advanced students), then the assignment should be given before students begin reading the novel. More likely, this assignment would serve as a culminating activity after the novel has been thoroughly discussed. In this case, the assignment can be distributed after class discussion is completed.

Another important responsibility of teachers as part of the prewriting phase of the writing process is to specify the criteria that will be used to evaluate students' writing. The following is an example of a set of criteria that could be used for the assignment on *Lord of the Flies:*

An excellent paper on this topic will include the following characteristics:

1. A discussion of at least one of the characters as symbolic.
2. Evidence that the writer considered all of the relevant aspects of the work in developing the arguments of the paper and that the writer did not ignore any relevant details.
3. Quotations from the text and/or references to events in the story to support all of the claims made in the paper.
4. Language that is clear and that engages the reader. This kind of language will employ specific and concrete nouns and adjectives and action verbs that say precisely what the writer intends to say.
5. An organizational plan that helps the reader follow the points that the writer makes.
6. A consistent tone that the writer uses throughout the paper.

In addition, students should remember to follow the conventions of stating the title and author early in the paper and of using present tense. They should also avoid nonstandard usage and mechanics.

These criteria should be distributed to students with the assignment, and students should be encouraged to use them as they go about the process of thinking about their topics and revising their work.

The second aspect of the writing process that teachers of literature should emphasize is revision. Revision is a very personal task that different writers handle in different ways. Many textbooks suggest that writers should write as fast as they can during the drafting or *writing* phase of the process and then devote a good bit more time to revision. Undoubtedly this is good advice for many students, but it sometimes happens that the press of deadlines and of other assignments forces students to leave much of their writing unrevised. Other writers, including the author of this chapter, revise constantly as they write. These people probably spend more time reading what they have just written than they spend writing during the drafting phase. The result is that they write at a relatively slow pace, but they have to spend much less time in a discrete revision stage. In either case, though, the major thrust of revision should be on the ideas that are expressed instead of on the surface features of the writing. This is not to say that we advocate ignoring surface features (e.g., punctuation, agreement) but the real task of revision is to reconsider and evaluate ideas.

The traditional way to encourage revision is to ask students to submit a draft of their writing for review by the teacher or by a peer response group. Except with the most mature and most committed students, we have found this relatively unsuccessful in encouraging genuine revision. Students are seemingly conditioned to consider an assignment "finished" when they turn it in. When we have made comments, sometimes very extensive ones, on drafts of papers, we have found that most students make only perfunctory attempts to incorporate our suggestions into their papers. They generally "correct" deviations from standard usage, and they may even add a sentence or two to clarify a point or elaborate on an idea. By and large, though, most students look upon revision as nothing more than "fixing" problem spots in their papers.

The relative unwillingness of students to genuinely revise their writing is probably a function of their lack of maturity. They haven't discovered for themselves the joy of discovery that revision promotes, so they value it much less than more mature writers do. The teacher can encourage genuine revision by frequently calling it to students' attention and by stressing it in instruction; however, serious revision might well be beyond the grasp of most adolescents.

Types of Writing Assignments

The traditional writing assignment on a work of literature at the college level is a critical analysis and interpretation of a text. This is the kind of writing most college English professors do for professional publications, and this is the type of assignment they typically give their English-major students. Most of these students continue the tradition when they become teachers, but often middle school and high school students are not ready to take on this task.

We maintained in the previous chapter that the reader-response orientation ultimately leads to interpretation and that analysis, through close reading, is an important part of the responding process. We don't intend to repudiate this claim here, but we do want to offer alternatives to the formal interpretive essay that enable students to discover and refine their responses to the literature they read. In this section we offer suggestions about writing assignments in two broad areas that, for convenience, we will call *academic* and *creative*. This distinction is arbitrary, and the two categories certainly overlap. Academic assignments, by our definition, are those which ask students to write about their ideas about a work or their feelings toward it. Academic assignments will take the form of ordinary expository prose. Some of these will be written in the third person and some in the first person. They will essentially consist of statements of opinion about the work. Creative assignments, again by our definition, will take the form of works in the same form as the original work of literature. In other words, if students read a poem, a creative assignment on the poem might be to write a poem in response to the one they read.

Academic Assignments The most useful academic assignment is the response paper. As the name implies, students describe their responses to a work of literature or to some aspect of the work. In Chapter Six we described several exercises (e.g., the most important word) that are well suited for this type of writing assignment. Any of the questions we listed in Chapter Six are also suitable for response papers, as are a great many other aspects of works of literature that the works themselves will suggest.

Response papers can vary in length and formality, all the way from a single paragraph written in class as an impromptu exercise to a piece of 500 or more words written at home over several days. What distinguishes the response paper from the critical essay is its purpose. The purpose of the critical essay is to develop an argument about the interpretation of a work of literature; the purpose of the response paper is to explain the writer's response to a work of literature and to explain the reasons for that response. In many instances the response paper will include interpretive statements but in a manner that is much less formal than the critical essay. The response paper permits students to explain how the work makes them feel, as well as the ideas the work stimulates in them. The critical essay is much more objective than that, and a discussion of the feelings of the writer of the essay is almost always inappropriate.

The response paper can serve as the basis of class discussion of the work, especially if it is written before discussion begins. When response papers are used for this purpose, it often helpful for the teacher to type and distribute copies of several response papers for the students to consider. There will be a strong tendency among students to evaluate the quality of the responses. This can be a tricky situation for teachers because the only valid criterion for evaluating a reader's response is the extent to which the author of the paper considered all relevant aspects of the work of literature in articulating the response. Nevertheless, with this criterion in mind, evaluation of the response papers by students in class discussion can be very productive in helping them sharpen and refine their own responses. It is always necessary to get the permission of the writers of the papers before using them in class discussion, and, where possible, papers from other classes on the same subject should be used to avoid hurt feelings and embarrassment.

The second type of academic assignment is the reconstruction of a work of literature in the student's own words. This assignment can be very useful in determining how students perceive a work of literature. David Bleich describes how he uses this technique to determine a reader's subjective perception of a poem in the hope of being able to point out patterns of perception to the reader.[13] In other words, he attempts to make students more aware of their own responses. If a detailed individual analysis of every reader's reconstructions of poems or other works of literature seems impossible for a middle school or high school teacher of literature because of the time involved, the principle can be applied in class discussion with the whole class. The reconstructions of three or four students can be typed and reproduced for the whole class, and discussion can focus on how the perceptions differ from one another. In all probability, members of the class will realize that their own perceptions differ from the perceptions of others in the class, and they can begin to analyze what in themselves caused them to see the work differently from others.

This type of activity differs from the response paper in that it requires students to recast the ideas and the other aspects of the work in their own words, rather than to comment on them directly or to comment on their feelings about them. The discussion that follows the writing is extremely useful in helping students understand the work.

A third type of academic writing assignment that is useful in helping students articulate and clarify their responses is the reading journal. A reading journal is a record of the responses students make to their reading as they are reading or immediately after they finish reading. It can be kept in a notebook or on looseleaf pages stapled together to form a booklet. In any case, the content is the thoughts and feelings students experience as they read.

The assignment of the reading journal can take a number of forms depending on the literature that students are reading. For example, if the text is a novel, the teacher can ask students to write a description of what they think will happen next after every twenty pages of text. Or, the teacher can select several key events in the novel and ask students to explain why they think the events occurred or what the significance of the events might be. Or, the teacher can ask students to explain what they would say or do after one or more significant events if they were present in the novel as a character. If the text is a short story, the same sorts of assignments can be made at various points in the story. If the text is a poem, the assignment can be a reconstruction of the poem.

The reading journal is extremely flexible in form and content, and it serves the useful purpose of causing students to express their responses *as they experience them.* In other words, it causes students to think about their reading before they discuss it in class. With initial responses already established in the reading journal, the time in class can be spent discussing the initial responses and helping students clarify how they feel about what they have read. As a practical matter, it is sometimes necessary for teachers to set minimum length requirements to ensure that students actually do think about what they have read. Some students, when faced with a requirement to produce a specified number of words, will argue that they don't have anything to say. In those cases, teachers can require that they reconstruct the work. Often reconstruction stimulates responses that were present all along below the level of conscious thought.

The fourth type of academic assignment consists of letters written by students to various people, including friends, teachers, parents, characters in the work, and the author of the work. Letters to friends, teachers, and parents can take the form of "Let me tell you about this novel/play/ poem/story." If students like the work they are writing about, they should tell why they liked it. If they disliked the work, they should explain their reasons for this reaction as well.

In either case, the letter constitutes a response to the work, and it has the added advantage of having a very specific audience that students can readily comprehend. It is entirely appropriate for teachers to assign several such letters on the same work and to discuss with students how their awareness of audience influences the choices they make as they write. Letters to characters are even better adapted to the teaching of an awareness of audience in that students must understand the character in order to address the letter to him or her in a way that is appropriate. A discussion of letters to the same character written by several members of the class can serve to help clarify students' understanding of who the characters really are. A letter to an author is likely to have a purpose that is different from the purposes of letters to anyone else. Again, by assigning several letters with different purposes, teachers can help students realize how an awareness of purpose affects choices in subject matter, detail, diction, and other aspects of writing. It goes without saying that letters to authors can actually be mailed to them (if the authors are alive, of course) through their publishers. Some authors, such as the Young Adult novelist Robert Cormier, routinely answer letters from students, and some, such as Cormier, are willing to accept telephone calls from individual students or whole classes.

The fifth type of writing assignment of an academic sort is the traditional formal critical essay. This assignment should be reserved for older and more advanced students, but it is entirely appropriate as part of a response-oriented literature curriculum. In fact, literary criticism is really nothing more than the responses of critics to the literature they read. True, it is a good bit more formal than response papers, journals, letters, and the like, but it is, nevertheless, a response to literature.

Most of the better composition textbooks include a section or chapter on writing critical analyses, and these are adequate for most students. However, one serious weakness in most of the textbooks we've seen is their failure to provide a model of what a critical analysis looks like. It is perhaps ironic that most teachers ask their students to write formal papers without ever letting them read one. The college English major eventually acquires an awareness of what formal critical writing *sounds* like by reading criticism for term papers and for other purposes in college courses, but high school students are rarely required to read anything more formal than their textbooks. Furthermore, the process of using quotations from a text to support critical points is foreign to students until they have been exposed to it. If teachers were asked to perform some complicated task—fabricating a stained glass window, for example—without benefit of seeing a demonstration of how the task is done, they would probably strenuously object, and rightly so. However, teachers often ask their students to perform complicated writing tasks without giving them the benefit of a *demonstration* of how to perform them.

One of the best ways of providing a model for students to follow is for teachers to write a critical analysis essay for their students to read and study. The essay should not be on the same work as the one students will be asked to write on, but it should be on a work that students are familiar with. The practice of writing for students is useful in helping teachers remember the struggles writers go through when they try to express themselves on paper, and students are usually relieved to know that even their teachers have trouble reducing their thoughts and feelings to the written word.

The sixth and final type of academic writing assignment we will consider is the research paper. This assignment is usually the scourge of the senior year, but with greater frequency students are being assigned research papers at lower grades as well. Many teachers assign research papers on general topics, such as the warming of the earth's atmosphere, environmental pollution, censorship, and the like, and what we have to say about research-based writing really doesn't apply to this type of assignment. Other teachers, especially those who, like the authors of this book, live in states that have curriculum standards that require a research paper which incorporates analysis and interpretation, require students to write their research papers on works of literature. Our comments are addressed to these teachers.

One reason students dread the research paper as much as they do is that research papers require much more than simple reading and writing. The factor that makes these papers different from other critical analyses is, of course, the research. Unfortunately, some students get so involved in locating sources of information and so bogged down in manipulating bibliography cards, note cards, preliminary outlines, and the other paraphernalia of research writing that the actual writing takes second place or is given only cursory attention. Locating sources is never a simple matter, but the problem is of truly massive proportions for high school students. There is obviously a finite number of works of literature that students can write about, and students often find that several other students in their class or school may be working on the same subject. Since most libraries allow students to check out books and keep them out for several weeks, it often happens that the student who gets to the library first is the only one who has access to the best and most useful information. The other students who are writing on the same subject are forced to resort to periodicals for their sources, but they quickly discover that most school and public libraries don't subscribe to very many scholarly journals, if any at all. These students, in their naivete, turn to their friend *The Readers' Guide to Periodical Literature* for sources, only to discover that *The Readers' Guide* only indexes book reviews and not scholarly discussions of works of literature. Other students want to write about an obscure work for which little or no criticism exists anywhere, or they select works that are too recent for much criticism to have accumulated.

The question of doing library research for a research paper on a work of literature is one that every school and every English teacher has to deal with sooner or later. On the one hand it is desirable for students to learn to use the library and the specialized reference materials that large libraries contain, but on the other hand it hardly seems fair to evaluate a student's research paper if the student does not have access to sources. Furthermore, in evaluating a research paper, the quality of the argument and the scope of the discussion are tied to the quality of the information the student was able to discover. If a student makes a bad choice of works to write about and can't find much information, the paper is likely to be poor. To solve these problems and to permit students to devote their complete efforts to reading the criticism and writing the paper, some schools have adopted casebooks for research papers. A casebook usually contains the text of a work of literature, often a novel or long play, and criticism from a variety of sources. Not many casebooks are published on a regular basis, but the Norton Critical Editions published by the W. W. Norton Company, while not really casebooks as such, are useful for this purpose. There are drawbacks to the use of the Norton books (for example, the pagination of the original sources is lost), but these drawbacks are greatly outweighed by the advantages these books offer.

One obvious advantage of the casebook approach is that students are guaranteed of having access to enough critical material to write their papers. The criticism is usually the best available on each work, and in the case of the Norton Critical Editions, contemporary reviews and other background information is provided. A second advantage to casebooks is that the teacher has access to the same material that students have access to. This makes it possible for the teacher to judge whether students actually understand the criticism, and it makes it much easier for the teacher to investigate suspected plagiarism.

Most composition textbooks provide at least one chapter on the mechanics of writing a research paper, and these are usually adequate for basic instruction. However, most high school composition texts assume that students will be assigned general topics rather than topics based on literature. It is usually up to the teacher to make the point that a topic on a work of literature requires a different type of thesis statement than a topic of general interest. Specifically, the thesis statement should be a critical *opinion* that the writer will attempt to support in the course of the paper. Students should also be made aware that it is entirely possible they will observe aspects of the work they're writing about that they don't find in the criticism they read. Many students need reassurance that they are free to make these points, provided they support them with evidence from the text.

The research paper is often overwhelming to students, and they need careful guidance and support as they tackle it. The first reaction of most is that it is an impossible task to write a research paper on a work of literature, but as they get involved in the process most of them realize that it can be done and that the work is usually very satisfying. It is often a good idea to follow up a research paper with some sort of sharing activity. Students who do a good job on their papers are proud of their accomplishment and want to share it with others. They should be given that opportunity.

There are a number of other types of academic writing that students can be engaged in. For example, students can be assigned extended definition essays on a complex concept (e.g., tragedy, comedy, Romanticism), character analyses, explications of poems or passages of long works, and the like. All of these kinds of writing assignments force students to think about the literature they read, and all of them elicit responses. Our concept of academic writing is an essential activity in the study of literature.

Creative Writing Assignments In addition to academic writing assignments, another way in which teachers can encourage students to express and to clarify their responses to literature is through writing assignments which require and permit students to write creatively. The creative writing assignments we suggest in this section are of two types. The first type asks students to try their hands at writing original works of fiction and poetry modeled on the works they read. The second type asks students to respond to texts by adding to or changing part of the literary works they study.

In our years of teaching we have discovered that a surprisingly large number of students write poetry and fiction for their own entertainment or to express some deeply felt response to their own experiences. This natural interest in writing can be used advantageously in the literature classroom by asking students to write poems, short stories, and plays as class assignments. The real value of this kind of creative writing is that it enables students to experience the same kind of joy and frustration that artists experience when they write. Furthermore, it gives students first-hand experience with the strengths and limitations of various genre.

After reading and studying poetry, as a rather obvious example, students who are asked to write a poem must learn to cope with the issues of rhyme and meter in a way they could never appreciate simply through reading. Students tend to take for granted that the rhyme and meter of traditional verse forms exist at all, but when they write a traditionally structured poem they quickly learn that producing one takes a great deal of hard work. Students who struggle with the Italian sonnet form, for example, may never actually produce one that meets all of the requirements of the form, but they leave the experience with a deeper awareness of the constraints of the form and a deeper appreciation—sometimes bordering on awe—for the artistry and craftsmanship of writers who do use the form successfully. A student once asked the author of this chapter how poets are able to get the form to come out right and still say what they want the poems to say. When the student was told that it happens through hard work and not through chance, as he had apparently assumed before he tried to write a sonnet of his own, he said that he guessed that's why poetry is considered art. This reaction is typical of the insight students achieve when they are asked to write creatively, and we suspect that reading alone would never have produced it.

Teachers who assign creative writing should be prepared to be pleasantly surprised at how well a great many students handle the assignment. At the same time, teachers should not be disappointed if no Whitmans or Audens emerge in their classes. The experience of writing literature is what matters, and teachers should be prepared to encourage and reward effort as much as accomplishment.

The second type of creative writing involves an expansion of texts that students read and study in class. The Australian teacher Peter Adams has identified five types of assignments which require what he calls *dependent authorship*. According to Adams, dependent authorship requires students "to take on *the role of the author*, and to write from 'inside' the world of the text."[14] Adams sees this type of writing as being dependent in two ways: first, dependent writing requires a familiarity with the original text; and, second, dependent writing is based on the resources and constraints of the original text. As he explains it,

> The original work . . . supports and constrains and amplifies the student's imaginative entry into the life of the text *in the role of author*. It is my experience that dependent authorship not only enables a surprisingly wide range of students to write about literature with an unusual depth and power of response, but that it is the means by which they can discover and explore elements of their response to the work that they could not grasp or articulate in any other way.[15]

The first type of assignment Adams suggests is called imaginative reconstruction of a text. By this he means that students are assigned to write sequences of narrative to fill in gaps that exist in stories. Adams gives examples from Colin Theile's *Blue Fin* and Richard Hughes's *A High Wind in Jamaica*,[16] but an example that is perhaps more widely known can be drawn from Emily Brontë's novel *Wuthering Heights*.

There are several noteworthy gaps in the text of *Wuthering Heights*, at least two of which have been imaginatively reconstructed by professional writers. The first gap that is worth attention is the three-year period in which Heathcliff is absent from Wuthering Heights, hence from the novel itself. After Catherine Earnshaw announces that it would degrade her to

marry Heathcliff, he disappears, only to return three years later transformed from the vulgar, uneducated, poverty-stricken adolescent he was
at his leaving into a wealthy, educated young gentleman. Brontë makes no
comment whatever about how this transformation occurs, and how
Heathcliff spent his time during the period is never brought up by him or
by any other character. The novelist Jeffrey Caine has taken advantage of
this gap to create his novel *Heathcliff*, in which he describes Heathcliff's
adventures during his absence from Wuthering Heights.

Another gap in the novel which has occasioned an imaginative reconstruction by a professional writer occurs in connection with Catherine
Earnshaw's diary. Mr. Lockwood is forced to spend the night at Wuthering
Heights because of a winter storm, and during the night he discovers some
old books in which Catherine has written a diary in the margins of the
pages. The diary entries are quite revelatory concerning both conditions at
the Heights after Mr. Earnshaw's death and the relationship between
Catherine and Heathcliff. But the diary and the rest of the text of the novel
leave unanswered a number of provocative questions: Why is Mr. Earnshaw so fond of Heathcliff? Why is Hindley spirited off to college so
suddenly? What is Ellen Dean's real relationship to the Earnshaw family?
Why does Catherine think it would degrade her to marry Heathcliff?

These questions, and a great many more, are answered in John
Wheatcroft's imaginative reconstruction of Catherine's diary in a novel
entitled *Catherine, Her Book*. Wheatcroft does a superb job of using tiny
threads of evidence (hints, really) from the text of *Wuthering Heights* to
create a work that is at once fine prose fiction and literary criticism. His
work is especially remarkable in that the language of *Catherine, Her Book* is
amazingly faithful to Brontë's original.

Both *Heathcliff* and *Catherine, Her Book* are good examples of the kind
of writing Adams means by imaginative reconstruction. Obviously, teachers would not assign students whole novels to write in response to their
reading, but brief episodes are certainly appropriate. This kind of writing
enables students to enter texts in ways that no response paper, critical essay,
or character sketch could possibly do.

Adams calls the second type of assignment that he describes adding
to the text.[17] This type of assignment is similar to imaginative reconstruction
in that it requires students to write new adventures for a character that are
similar to adventures found in the text (Adams' example is Wart's adventures in T. H. White's *The Sword in the Stone*) or to write continuations of
texts (Adams cites Greg Matthews' *The Further Adventures of Huckleberry
Finn* as an example of a continuation). Both kinds of assignments require
students to enter the world of the text and to actually *be* the characters they
write about.

The third type of assignment Adams describes is the epilogue.[18] Adams gives an example from *Lord of the Flies* in which students were asked to select a character and to write a brief passage depicting that character years after the boys are rescued from the island.

The fourth type of assignment, dreams, is particularly provocative. Adams makes this point:

> Since dreams are highly condensed symbolic representations of inner experience, not only can they provide a very useful way of focusing students' attention upon a character's inner response to the experiences he or she has undergone in the course of the novel, but they can encourage the poetic evocation, through image and symbol, of meaning and insights that could otherwise not reach formulation.[19]

In this assignment students are asked to write a dream that one of the characters could have. Any number of works are suitable for this kind of assignment. The example Adams gives is from *The Slave Dancer* by Paula Fox.

Finally, Adams describes an assignment he calls altering the text: rewriting the ending.[20] This is the kind of assignment that is appropriate for a large range of literary works. Like imaginative reconstruction and adding to the text, it requires complete absorption with the characters and the events of the story.

In addition to the five types of assignments described by Adams, another type of assignment that is capable of engaging students' attention and enhancing their involvement with a literary work involves shifting genres. Earlier in this chapter we described Readers Theatre as a form of oral response to a literary work. We said at that time that scripts for Readers Theatre can be written by students based on novels, short stories, and narrative poems. This kind of writing involves shifting from one literary genre to another, and in order to accomplish this task students must be thoroughly immersed in the literary work they are rewriting. The same sort of rewriting can be done in the other directions. For example, a ballad or other narrative poem can be rewritten as a short story, and a passage from a play can be rewritten as a dramatic poem.

Conclusion for Written Responses As the foregoing discussion illustrates, the days of an arbitrary distinction between composition and literature instruction are gone forever. The literature teacher must be a teacher of writing, and the composition teacher can work best when literature is the basis of the composition curriculum. Common sense suggests this marriage, and the reader-response orientation to the teaching of literature demands it.

Notes

1. David Bleich. *Readings and Feelings: An Introduction to Subjective Criticism.* Urbana: National Council of Teachers of English, 1975, p 3.

2. Shirlee Slayer. *Readers Theatre: Story Dramatization in the Classroom.* Urbana: National Council of Teachers of English, 1982, p 5.

3. Peter Slade. *An Introduction to Child Drama,* 1958. Quoted in Frank Whitehead. *The Disappearing Dais: A Study of the Principles and Practice of English Teaching.* London: Chatto & Windus, 1966, p 123.

4. Whitehead, *The Disappearing Dais,* p 125.

5. Whitehead, *The Disappearing Dais,* p 124.

6. Dwight L. Burton. *Literature Study in the High School.* Third Edition. New York: Holt, Rinehart and Winston, 1970, p 81.

7. Madelaine Myers. "A Talk Show with Class." In Patricia Phelan, ed. *Talking to Learn Classroom Practices in Teaching English,* Vol 24. Urbana: National Council of Teachers of English, 1989, pp 20–21.

8. Andrew W. Wilkinson. "The Implications of Oracy." *Educational Review* (Univ. of Birmingham) 20(2): 123–135, February 1968. Reprinted in Dwight L. Burton and John S. Simmons, eds. *Teaching English in Today's High School: Selected Readings.* 2nd ed. New York: Holt, Rinehart & Winston, 1970, pp 221–135.

9. James M. McCrimmon. "Writing as a Way of Knowing." In *The Promise of English.* Champaign: National Council of Teachers of English, 1970, pp 117–130.

10. Quoted in Donald M. Murray. "Internal Revision: A Process of Discovery" In Charles R. Cooper and Lee Odell, eds. *Research on Composing: Points of Departure.* Urbana: National Council of Teachers of English, 1978, p 101.

11. Murray, "Internal Revision," p 86.

12. Murray, "Internal Revision," p 86.

13. Bleich, "Internal Revision," p 21.

14. Peter Adams. "Writing from Reading—'Dependent Authorship' as a Response." In Bill Corcoran and Emrys Evans, eds. *Readers, Texts, Teachers.* Upper Montclair, NJ: Boynton/Cook Publishers, Inc., 1987, p 121.

15. Adams, "Writing from Reading," p 121.

16. Adams, "Writing from Reading," pp 122 and 123.

17. Adams, "Writing from Reading," pp 128–136.

18. Adams, "Writing from Reading," pp 136–140.

19. Adams, "Writing from Reading," pp 140–141.

20. Adams, "Writing from Reading," pp 145–151.

CHAPTER EIGHT

Broad-Range Approaches to Curriculum Organization in Literature

The literature program, like any other area of the curriculum, has to be organized in some way. A good organizational plan will ensure that students come in contact with a wide variety of literature, that they progress from less difficult and complex material to more difficult and complex material as they mature, and that they avoid repeated exposure to the same works as they move through the secondary grades. No single organizational pattern is perfect for all courses or for all students, but some ways of organizing the literature curriculum are decidedly better than others.

In this chapter and the next one, we will offer a set of general principles for curriculum organization and several organizational patterns which have emerged through the years. In this chapter we will focus on what we call *broad-range* approaches to curriculum organization, and in the next chapter we will concentrate on *focused* approaches.

General Principles for Curriculum Organization

The principles we list and explain in this section are based on what we believe are the fundamental goals and purposes of literature study in middle school and high school. The goals and purposes themselves are discussed at length in Chapter Two, and individual teachers or English departments in schools may want to add other principles to our list to accommodate goals specific to their programs. As they stand, however, these principles can serve as both a guide to establishing an organizational pattern and a set of criteria for judging the value of existing patterns.

1.   **The organizational pattern should promote interest in literature.**
     This may seem to be so obvious as to be self-evident, but in our experience many literature curricula seem to ignore this point altogether. Whether teachers like it or not, not all literature is equally interesting to adolescents, and this includes some of the literature considered to be among the very best by critics and mature readers. This seems to be especially true of the earlier works of British and American literature. We don't deny the importance of such writers as John Milton and Jonathan Edwards to the development of *belles-lettres*, but their works usually have little appeal to contemporary American teenagers. In some organizational patterns, notably the much-honored chronological survey, Milton and Edwards appear fairly early, and concentration on their works at the beginning of a semester can have the effect of casting a deadly pall of boredom on literature study at the outset.

2.   **The organizational pattern should promote extended involvement with long works (i.e., novels and full-length plays).**
     Longer works of literature, especially novels, provide an opportunity for immersion into an imaginative world—an immersion that is necessarily longer, and probably more complete—than any number of short stories or lyric poems can provide. For this reason we believe students at every grade and of every ability level should have the opportunity to read and study long works as part of their English courses. In some high school programs, students take literature and writing in separate semester-long courses, but even in this arrangement novels and full-length plays can be included every semester. In fact, writing is enhanced through literature study, and, as we imply in Chapter Seven, long works studied in a writing course can serve as the basis for writing instruction and writing assignments.

3.   **The organizational pattern should provide opportunities for the appropriately intensive study of individual works.**
     This principle has to do with the pacing of instruction. At one extreme is the temptation to gallop through one, and sometimes more than one, work a day in order to "cover" the textbook or reading list. At the other extreme is the temptation to conduct what

amount to graduate-level seminars on major works. The plays of Shakespeare especially seem to cry out to some teachers for long, intense, and, alas, tedious analysis, but the works of many other authors are also often stretched out unmercifully over four or more weeks of class time.

The compulsion to "cover" the material at the expense of intensive study results in glossing over works that should be explored, savored, and understood over several days of class activity. We have known and worked with teachers who satisfy this compulsion near the end of a semester or year by showing videotapes and filmstrips based on short stories, novels, and plays that their students haven't read so the students will, in their words, "at least know what they're about." How any student can even remember the plots of many literary works "experienced" through nonprint media in a short period of time is beyond our comprehension, to say nothing of the violence done to the literary works themselves.

On the other hand, some teachers go overboard in the other direction and bore their students with weeks of background material and minute analyses of some works. One favorite subject for such over-treatment is the architecture of the Globe Theatre. Shakespeare's plays have been successfully produced countless times in places that don't even vaguely resemble the Globe, yet in the minds of some afficionados, no reading of *Julius Caesar* or *Macbeth* would be complete without a plank by plank study of "this wooden O." As early as 1927, research by Nancy Gillmore Coryell proved that this type of overly detailed study of literature cooled students' interest and produced no improvement in skills.[1] Still, some teachers persist in ferreting out every inconsistency in *Hamlet* and every mythological reference in *Romeo and Juliet* at the expense of time that could be spent on additional works.

4. **The organizational pattern should provide opportunities for extensive reading exploration and for individualization of reading assignments.**

This principle may at first seem to contradict our third principle, but, in fact, it complements it. While time should be set aside for in-depth study of some works, other time should be allocated for wide collateral reading. For example, in a unit on the short story, part of the time can profitably be spent in class discussing stories students read in common, but part of the time can also be spent reading stories selected individually by students with the teacher's guidance. In this way, the teacher can help students satisfy their personal interests and can help students find stories that are more closely matched to their interests and ability levels.

5. **The organizational pattern should provide at least some opportunities for students to read and study works of recognized cultural importance.**

   Our position throughout this book is that a great deal can be done in literature study with works that are not ordinarily included on lists of world literary classics. However, we also feel that it would be just as unfortunate to ignore the classics entirely as it would be to force reluctant students to read them exclusively. We believe that one of the functions of a literary education is to provide students with a sense of who they are within the larger framework of a particular culture, and classic works of literature can help accomplish this. Furthermore, the study of works of literature which have cultural significance can develop a fund of knowledge that will enrich students' understanding of the literary allusions they will meet throughout life.

   The question of what constitutes a classic has been widely debated for generations, and a complete discussion of this issue is outside the scope of this book. For our purposes, a work of "recognized cultural importance" is one which has been, or is currently, widely taught in schools and colleges. It should be obvious that not every work that meets these criteria is appropriate for every grade or every level of ability.

Broad-Range Approaches to Curriculum Organization in Literature

The term *broad-range* as we use it here describes ways of arranging units or whole courses so that students are exposed to many literary genres or to many different works of the same genre, with no attempt made to focus in depth on a particular writer, literary period, or idea. The emphasis in broad-range approaches is usually on some goal other than a detailed or exhaustive examination of specific literary works. The four broad-range approaches we will describe in this chapter are (1) the free reading approach, (2) the chronological survey approach, (3) the genre approach, and (4) the mythic approach.

Free Reading

The most broad-ranging of the broad-range approaches is free reading. This approach is based on the idea that students will read more, with

Do the Broad-Range Approaches Conform to Principles for Curriculum Organization?

	Principles				
Approaches	Interest	Long Works	Intensive Study	Extensive Study	Cultural Significance
Free Reading Chronological	Yes	Yes	No	Yes	Yes
Survey	No	No	No	No	Yes
Genre	Yes	Yes	Yes	Yes	Yes
Mythic	Yes	Yes	Yes	Yes	Yes

Figure 8.1

greater pleasure, if they are given time to read in school, if they have access to interesting and worthwhile works, and if they have the benefit of professional guidance from teachers in selecting works to read. The point of the free reading approach is to get students involved with works of literature at a level that suits their ability and to encourage them to read as widely as possible with little or no regard for "covering" any of the usual concepts associated with the formal study of literature.

Programs of this type are organized in a variety of ways, but in most cases students are required to read a set number of works—usually novels—and to respond to them in some way specified by the teacher or negotiated individually between the teacher and the student. One free reading course we have worked with was a high school semester elective course called Hooked on Books, after the program developed by Daniel Fader and Elton McNeil.[2] The structure of this course is representative of the way effective free reading courses can be organized.

The students in the course were required to develop a contract with the teacher in which they stated the grade for the course they wanted to work toward. Point values were assigned to each grade (A=200 points, B=150 points, C=100 points, and so forth), and books and magazine articles were also assigned point values by the teacher. In order to earn an A, a student had to read and respond to works which had a total point value of at least 200 points. Longer and more difficult works naturally carried higher point values than shorter and easier works.

The responses to the books generally consisted of some sort of written report, but at least two of the responses had to be oral and two had to be a project other than a written or oral report. For example, project responses could be art work, student-made films, scrapbooks, models, posters, and the like. The points assigned to a work were not awarded until the reading was done and the response completed.

The beginning of each class period (five to ten minutes) was devoted to oral or project responses whenever these were scheduled. During the remainder of the class, students read silently, selected new books from the large number of paperbacks available in the classroom, or discussed their reading with the teacher.

While any student can benefit from the free reading approach, it is especially valuable for two specific groups of students at opposite ends of the academic achievement continuum. First, unmotivated, reluctant readers who are often unable to benefit from a more structured literature class that involves formal essays, class discussions, deadlines, and tests are free to set their own goals and to move at their own pace. Second, highly motivated, superior readers who are capable of independent work are given the freedom to pursue their own reading interests unhampered by the constraints of a syllabus.

The role of the teacher in the free reading approach shifts from that of dispenser of information to that of organizer and motivator of learning. First, the teacher has to establish some sort of process for assigning grades, keeping records, and determining how students will make responses. Second, and most importantly, the teacher has to provide guidance in the selection of books and other works students read. This second function is far more difficult than it may appear. For one thing, the teacher has to know the students quite well in order to know what will appeal to their interests and abilities; and, for another thing, the teacher has to have a wide knowledge of literary works at every level of sophistication in order to recommend books appropriately.

A well-organized free reading program can meet a variety of needs in a school, but it is not a cure-all for every problem in the literature curriculum. This approach violates our third principle (appropriately intensive study of works by the whole class); thus, by our criteria it would have to be used in conjunction with some other approach that would permit large-group interaction. However, as a unit of six or nine weeks' duration, or even as a one-semester component in a more structured program, free reading offers enormous potential for students.

Chronological Survey

Of all of the approaches to curriculum organization we discuss in this book, the chronological survey approach is probably the best known and most widely used in the schools, especially at the high school level. The reason for this popularity is the traditional importance of American and British literature in the high school curriculum. Since these national literatures developed over time, it is quite natural to assume that they should be studied in the same order in which they developed. This idea is reinforced for most future English teachers in college when they are required to take survey courses that are usually organized chronologically. Teachers tend to teach the way they are taught, so it is not surprising that the chronological survey would hold a place of honor year after year.

We believe that the traditional chronological survey is the least effective way of organizing the literature curriculum in the secondary grades. This idea is far from new or original; in fact, Robert Pooley made the same point in an article in the *English Journal* in 1939.[3] Nevertheless, teachers hold on tenaciously to the chronological survey despite compelling arguments against it.

In its simplest form, the chronological survey approach requires students to begin with the earliest American or British literature and to work their way through to the present. Frequently the works studied are assigned to rather arbitrary literary periods, and the edifice of the national literature is erected using the periods as building blocks.

Three reasons are often cited to justify the chronological approach, and, since this approach is so important in most literature curricula, it is worthwhile to examine these reasons in some detail.

The first reason some people give to justify the chronological approach is that it allows students to see firsthand how literary forms developed and how authors influenced one another across the ages. We don't deny that it is possible to perceive development and influence across the centuries, but to really see this occur would require much wider reading than high school students, and most undergraduate English majors, are capable of handling. Consider the English novel as an example. It is a long and difficult march from Defoe's *Moll Flanders* to, say, D. M. Thomas' *The White Hotel*, with many distracting side excursions along the way. To really see the way the novel developed, such a course would have to include the likes of *Tom Jones, Tristram Shandy, Pride and Prejudice, Wuthering Heights, Middlemarch, Great Expectations, The Return of the Native, Women in Love, Ulysses, To the Lighthouse,* and *The Power and the Glory,* and that would only get students up to 1940. One of the things about this list or similar lists that should be immediately recognizable is that these works bear very little resemblance to one another. In fact, they stand out as "great books" precisely because they are fresh, original, and innovative. Virginia Woolf might have been influenced by Emily Brontë in some vague way, but the kind of analysis it would take to demonstrate this is the stuff of doctoral dissertations and scholarly journals, and not the stuff of high school literature courses.

A second reason some teachers give to support the chronological survey approach is that it helps students understand the characteristics of the various literary periods. However, literary periods are often little more than arbitrary groupings based on historical accident. Let's return to our list of novels for illustrations of this point. Jane Austen's *Pride and Prejudice* was published in 1813 after a major rewrite in 1812 of a previously-rejected earlier draft. The year 1813 is in the middle of the Romantic period of British literature, but there are none of the features of romanticism in this novel. Furthermore, *Great Expectations* and *Wuthering Heights* are both Victorian pieces, but they resemble neither each other nor the works of the great Victorian poets Tennyson and Browning (whose works, incidentally, aren't similar, either). What often happens in chronological survey courses is minor works that "fit" the periods are taught instead of the more important major works that don't fit very well, and students are led to believe that literary periods exist as pre-established schools of thought that dominated all of the literature written during their duration.

A third reason some teachers often give for the chronological approach is that it enables students to see the relationship between political/social history and literary art. This is the weakest reason of the three we discuss here, but it is, unfortunately, the one that is most often used to justify chronological surveys. We don't deny the existence of topical references in many literary works, nor do we deny the importance of an idea like the Great Chain of Being in understanding some aspects of some of Shakespeare's plays. But no enduring literature depends on a detailed knowledge of history, philosophy, art, or any other field of endeavor for its meaning or beauty. This is also true of allusions to mythology and the Bible. It goes without saying that any reading of a novel like Kurt Vonnegut's *Player Piano* is greatly enriched if readers recognize the mythological and other classical allusions in the book, and readers are better off with John Knowles' *A Separate Peace* if they recognize the similarity between the tree in the novel and the biblical Tree of the Knowledge of Good and Evil. However, it is possible to read and study these works, and any other work of literature, as independent works of art that speak to readers directly, without the mediation of elaborate historical or philosophical or mythological or biblical information.

This leads us back to what Pooley calls "the grave danger of chronology in literature," which is "the tendency to teach the history of literature rather than the literature itself."[4] This danger is especially acute in the reader-response orientation we advocate. The history of literature consists of facts that are easily reduced to multiple choice questions that require very little thought and produce no significant responses. We have already discussed at length the relative unimportance in the reader-response orientation of facts about the author and about the historical context of a work. We are not willing to say that a chronological organization makes response-based teaching impossible, but we have serious questions about the validity of selecting a work because of its historical importance instead of its potential to engage students.

In terms of our general principles for curriculum organization, the chronological survey approach violates all but the last one, that is, opportunities to study works of cultural significance. This approach usually fails to promote interest in literature (Principle One). It tends to limit extended involvement with long work (Principle Two) and appropriately intensive study of individual works (Principle Three) because the time required for activities related to these principles often can't be "spared." Finally, the chronological survey approach makes it difficult or impossible to allow extensive collateral reading or individualization in selecting works (Principle Four). After all, even if teachers are willing to pause in their progress through literary history long enough to allow their students time for extensive, individualized reading in, say, the Elizabethan Age or the Transcendentalist Movement, no students but the most able are likely going to want to stop.

Genre Approach

The third broad-range approach, that of arrangement of works by genre, is widely used in secondary school literature curricula, especially in grades 7 through 10. This approach to curriculum organization is based on the idea that students can best learn to comprehend and enjoy literature by studying the elements of literature and the relationship of these elements in a work. The goal is to help students develop tools they can use in later life to approach serious literature on their own. Although this method of organization violates none of our general principles for curriculum organization, the way the genre approach is presented in most secondary school literature textbooks is not consistent with our understanding of the reader-response orientation to the teaching of literature.

The genre approach was a particular favorite of the New Critics because it provided a way of arranging literature for analysis. A typical chapter in a textbook that subscribes to the principles of New Criticism discusses a literary concept, plot, for example, and then presents several stories for students to read and analyze to practice their skills of analyzing the plot of a short story. If the stories happen to appeal to students and if the stories are such that a genuine transaction between reader and text can occur, so much the better, but the reason the stories are included has everything to do with their potential for permitting practice in analysis and very little, or nothing, to do with their potential for engaging readers. The same is true of chapters devoted to poetry and drama. We mention these facts because teachers who want to engage in response-based teaching will encounter selections in secondary literature anthologies that simply do not elicit responses from adolescents as well as other selections do. One example of a story many students don't respond particularly well to is James Thurber's classic "The Secret Life of Walter Mitty." This story is extremely well known, and when it was published during the Second World War it drew enormous praise from readers. But the references are dated, and most adolescents have trouble identifying with the protagonist. "The Secret Life of Walter Mitty" is an excellent vehicle for teaching certain elements of plot, but a teacher committed to response-based teaching may want to omit it in favor of a more engaging story.

The same advice applies to textbook material on the technical elements of literature. In Chapter Five we noted that the skill of close reading is one of the beneficial by-products of the reader-response orientation to teaching because students should be encouraged to ask what in themselves caused their response and what in the text caused their response. Clearly, close reading of this sort leads to an awareness on the part of students of the literary devices writers consciously employ in their work. Students need a vocabulary with which to describe these elements of texts, and the traditional literary terms serve this purpose well. Studying literature genre by genre helps focus attention on the devices peculiar to various literary forms, and the genre approach provides natural opportunities for teachers to teach the vocabulary of literature study. What the teacher must always remember, though, is that the literature and students' responses to the literature are the subject matter of instruction, not vocabulary terms. When discussions of technical literary terms in textbooks are useful, they should be used; when they aren't, they should be omitted. The vocabulary serves the students, and not vice versa.

The key to success in using the genre approach in curriculum organization is the order in which the genres are studied and in which the literary elements are introduced. We know of no research to look to for enlightenment in this matter, but the nature of the genres themselves offers some help. Our guiding principle here is movement from least abstract to most abstract and from least complex to most complex. By this principle, the novel should come first, followed by the short story, drama, and poetry, in that order. This is, of course, a *general* principle. Obviously, some novels are considerably more abstract and more complex than some poems. Our assumption is that given a body of literature in these four genres appropriate for students at a particular grade level and a particular level of ability, they will find novels easier to handle than short stories, short stories easier to handle than plays, and plays easier to handle than poetry.

The first genre in terms of our concrete-to-abstract/least-complex-to-more-complex continuum is the novel. Adolescents, like the general reading public, prefer the novel to any other literary form. The reasons for the popularity of the novel include the following: (1) the novel allows fuller character development than is possible in the short story; (2) the novel offers the opportunity for a psychological exploration of characters that is not ordinarily afforded by drama; (3) the novel consists of an extended elaboration of conflict that translates into longer and more complicated plot development; and (4) the novel requires considerably more time for reading than short stories do, and the extended time makes possible a more complete immersion into the imaginative world of the work, which in turn permits more reflection on the causes and effects of the conflict, the motives of the characters, and the possible outcomes of the plot.

In recent decades the line between fiction and nonfiction has blurred considerably, and readers now find themselves faced with the phenomenon of the *nonfiction novel*. Everything we say here about the novel applies equally to these nonfiction works, as well as to biographies, autobiographies, and other works whose authors employ the techniques of fiction.

The short story should follow the novel in the organization of the unit or course. Ordinarily, the reverse occurs; however, we believe the short story is a more difficult (hence less popular) genre than the novel, and students have an easier time understanding such abstract concepts as plot, setting, characterization, point of view, and the like when they see them first in their more obvious and more fully developed form in the novel.

The difficulty inherent in short stories arises from their compression. The time frame of a short story, as in the case of a story like John Updike's "A & P," is often no longer than the time required to read the story, and in some short stories, such as Faulkner's "A Rose for Emily," the time involved in the story is not clear or is irrelevant. The plots of many short stories revolve around conflicts that are only implied in a general way (such as Eudora Welty's "The Petrified Man" or Hemingway's "A Clean, Well-lighted Place"), and setting is often of little or no importance. Finally, characterization in short stories is usually severely limited because of the limitations of the length of the story. Critics often speak of "round" or "flat" characters in short stories, but even round characters in short stories lack the depth and growth of characters in novels.

Even though novels and short stories differ considerably in their difficulty, the same elements of fiction apply to both. The most important literary elements include plot, characterization, setting, point of view, and the rhetorical or stylistic matters of symbolism and tone.

With regard to plot, students should learn to recognize the four basic conflicts or relationships: the individual and nature; the individual and other people; the individual and self; and, the individual and cosmic forces, variously defined as God, fate, the inevitable, and so forth. Older and more advanced students may also be interested in the so-called stages of plot development: the exposition, the complication, the climax, and the denouement. While it may be necessary to consider these aspects of plot individually, the study of plot should never be undertaken in a vacuum. For, as Henry James points out, "What is character but the determination of incident? What is incident but the illustration of character?"

The second element, character, should therefore be discussed in relation to the events of the plot. The concepts of *static* and *dynamic* as they relate to character development are useful ways of discussing how a character's growth or lack of growth contributes to the action and helps resolve the conflict. Similarly, E. M. Forster's terms—*round* and *flat*—describe the extent to which a given character is fleshed out by the author. Students should be introduced to these terms and should be encouraged to use them in discussions of fiction.

Setting is much more important in some works than in others, and often too much is made of the setting for works in which it is not important. However, students should learn to recognize when the setting is important in establishing the tone for the entire work. For example, Poe establishes the atmosphere in the very first sentence of "The Fall of the House of Usher" by describing the landscape surrounding the mansion:

> During the whole of a dull, dark, and soundless day in the autumn of the year, when the clouds hung oppressively low in the heavens, I had been passing alone, on horseback, through a singularly dreary tract of country, and at length found myself, as the shades of evening drew on, within view of the melancholy House of Usher.

The fourth element, point of view, often presents difficulty for students, but the problems are more often with the technical vocabulary used to describe point of view than with the concept itself. Older and more advanced students learn to use the technical vocabulary associated with this element, but students at every grade level are able to understand the concepts underlying the relationship of the narrator to the characters and events in a story.

Finally, students should develop a vocabulary to describe how an author creates effect and meaning in a work of fiction. An understanding of such rhetorical techniques as symbolism and tone can add enormously to a reader's enjoyment of a fictional work, and these aspects of literature, especially tone, have significant carryover to other types of reading. Symbolism is relatively easy for all but the most literal-minded to grasp, but there is a real danger of turning otherwise sensible students into obsessive symbol-grubbers. Tone, on the other hand, is generally much more difficult, even for very able students. However, concepts such as the difference between denotation and connotation, sentence length, the use of formal latinate words, and the like should probably be considered, at least with older students.

The concept of theme is often considered to be one of the elements of fiction, and anthologies organized by genres often give one or more selections which "feature" theme. We believe that what is often spoken of as theme is actually the meaning of a work, or, as William Kenney describes it, "the necessary implications of the whole story, not a separable part of a story."[5] Too frequently discussions of theme degenerate into exercises in finding the "moral" of a work or in formulating aphorisms that sound good but that violate the uniqueness and integrity of the work of art. No discussion of a work is complete without attention to the overall effect it creates or to the original insight it provides into the human condition. But, as a distinct element, theme should be left to drama where the term makes more sense.

The next genre in the order imposed by our least-complex-to-most-complex and least-abstract-to-most-abstract principle is drama. The compression of the short story is substantially increased in this literary form, and, because the descriptive material in short stories is eliminated, readers are left to their own devices to visualize the setting and much of the action that occurs in a play. The result is talk in the forms of dialogue and monologue (soliloquies), with occasional sketchy stage directions. The typographical conventions employed in scripts take some getting used to, and they sometimes create substantial reading problems for otherwise able readers.

The first important element to consider in a study of drama is character. The concepts of static and dynamic, and round and flat characters that apply in fiction apply in drama, but students must learn to infer these aspects of character from the content of what the characters say rather than from the narrator's comments about the characters. This requires reading skills that many uninitiated students don't possess, but the teacher can help them develop these skills through a series of carefully designed reading readiness activities.

The first type of readiness activity can involve Readers Theatre productions based on a novel or short story the students have already studied. Readers Theatre basically consists of rewriting a short story or scene from a novel into a kind of play and then having students read the script with appropriate emphasis and meaning. Students who already know the "play" are able, with practice, to read the parts in character, and they are then better able to understand how the characterizations are created. Obviously not every short story lends itself to this kind of activity, but more do than might at first be evident.

A second readiness activity can involve using excerpts from whatever play the students are going to read. If a professional recording of the play is available, the students can listen to the first scene or even the first act as they follow the text. If a recording isn't available, a few of the more proficient readers in the class can be asked to prepare a reading of the first part of the play in advance and present it while the rest of the class follows along. In either case, the presentation should be followed by a discussion of who the main characters are and of what they are like. It might be tempting to have students listen to the complete recording of a play instead of having them read it on their own. However, one of the obvious goals of teaching drama is to help students learn how to approach a work of dramatic literature independently, and this goal will never be met if they are always allowed to listen to the interpretation of the text given by professional actors on a record or tape.

The second important point to consider in teaching drama is theme. A theme in a play is an idea that underlies the action and that is often repeated in several places in the play. One of the most common themes in drama is the difference between illusion and reality. In *Hamlet*, for example, King Claudius gives the illusion of being a kind and just ruler, but the reality is that he has murdered his brother in order to marry his sister-in-law Gertrude and to seize the throne of Denmark. Hamlet himself gives the other characters the illusion of being mad when he assumes his "antic disposition," but by acting insane he is able to uncover the truth of the corruption of the King. Other themes are present in *Hamlet* and in other plays. For example, the theme of betrayal runs throughout Eugene O'Neill's tragedy, *Long Day's Journey into Night*. In this play, the wife and mother, Mary Tyrone, feels betrayed by her husband, who is too stingy to provide her and the children with a decent home. Mr. Tyrone and the sons, in turn, feel betrayed by Mary's drug addiction; Mr. Tyrone feels betrayed by the younger son's illness that will drain the family financially; and the younger son feels betrayed by his older brother, who led him into a dissolute life that helped ruin his health.

In both of these plays the themes we briefly touch on contribute to the meaning and effect of the works, but in neither case do the themes alone create the full impact of the plays. As we implied in our discussion of theme in connection with fiction, the term *theme* is rather ambiguous, and it is best applied to a repeated idea in drama than to the overall artistic impact of a novel or short story. In drama, a theme is like a melody that is repeated, with variations, in a symphony, and students can learn to identify these in the plays they read, study, and attend.

The other elements of literature, for example, plot, point of view, rhetorical strategies, and so forth, are also present in drama, of course, and they should certainly be considered and discussed whenever a play is read and studied. However, the ideas we discussed in relation to fiction with regard to these elements apply to drama as well.

The last genre in order of complexity and abstractness is poetry, and within this genre the natural progression is from narrative poetry to dra-

Continuum of Literary Genres

Concrete Least Complex						Abstract Most Complex
Novel	Short Story	Drama		Poetry		
			Narrative Poetry	Dramatic Monologue	Lyric Poetry	

Figure 8.2

matic monologue to lyric. The steps in learning to read poetry progress from identifying what the poet says on a literal level to understanding what the poet implies on a figurative level.

One reason students have difficulty reading poetry is that they insist on reading it line by line, instead of sentence by sentence. Most poems are written in sentences. While sometimes the sentences are long, with many subordinate clauses and much convoluted syntax, they are sentences nevertheless. When this concept is first introduced, it is sometimes helpful to ask students to copy the poem as a set of sentences, instead of a set of lines, and to read what they have copied. This is a bit tedious, perhaps, but once students grasp the idea, their reading of poetry improves immensely.

A second reason students find poetry difficult to comprehend is that they are unaware that many poems must be read more than once in order to understand them. Students can be taught to use a reading plan like the one following as they begin to approach poetry. When they use such a plan, they are often surprised to discover that a poem that once appeared vague and opaque is actually quite comprehensible. The steps in the plan are as follows:

1. Begin with a silent reading of the poem.
2. Proceed to the oral reading of the poem by student volunteers or by the teacher if no volunteers are forthcoming.
3. Paraphrase the poem word by word, line by line, or sentence by sentence.
4. Conclude with a second oral reading with appropriate emphasis.

Once this is accomplished, students usually have a grasp of the literal meaning of the poem. From here students can move on to a consideration of the implied or figurative meaning of the poem.

Most literature anthologies that are organized by genres provide explanatory material on the basic figures of speech, poetic diction, rhyme, meter, and other technical aspects of poetry. Some teachers get carried away with the more "objective" aspects of the study of poetry and spend weeks having students scan poems, determine rhyme schemes, and identify figures of speech. These activities often become ends in themselves rather than means to deepening understanding and appreciation of poetry. Students should learn about the mechanical aspects of poetry for the same reasons and to the same extent that they should learn about color pigments and brush strokes in an art appreciation course. Detailed study of poetic techniques beyond a basic familiarity tends to give undue importance to these matters.

The genre approach to organizing the literature curriculum seems to lend itself to creative writing better than other patterns of organization, and the study of poetry seems to be a good time to ask students to try their hands at producing literature of their own. There is almost no limit to the types of poetry students can write, and the simpler forms, such as haiku, are usually the easiest ones to begin with. In writing poetry, students learn how poets create meaning by doing so themselves, and the results are often surprisingly good. Of course, students can write short stories, plays, and even novels, but poetry often comes to life for the first time for many students when they become poets themselves. The use of creative writing as a means of eliciting and deepening responses to literary work is dealt with extensively in Chapter Seven.

The genre approach to organization reached its heyday during the reign of the New Critics because it is obviously so well suited to the kind of analysis New Criticism demands. This approach can be useful in a response-based curriculum as well, and through it students' attention can be drawn to various elements of texts as they seek the textual source of their own responses. Many middle school and high school literature anthologies are organized by genre, and, with caution and sensitivity, these books can serve as a valuable resource for teachers who are committed to the reader-response orientation to the teaching of literature.

The Mythic Approach

Our final broad-range approach to the organization of the literature curriculum is based on the organizational scheme described by Northrop Frye in his essay "Archetypal Criticism: Theory of Myths," in the seminal volume, *The Anatomy of Criticism*.[6] Frye divides literature into *comedy, romance, tragedy,* and *irony-satire,* and these four divisions can serve as useful ways of grouping works of literature in the secondary grades. This approach violates none of our general principles for curriculum organization.

In the mythos, or plot, of comedy, according to Frye, we usually find "that a young man wants a young woman, that his desire is resisted by some opposition, usually parental, and that near the end of the [work] some twist of plot enables the hero to have his will."[7] This basic structure is best seen in dramatic pieces, but it also appears in novels and short stories. Jane Austen's *Pride and Prejudice,* for example, follows this basic structural format with the exception that the story is told from the young woman's (Elizabeth Bennet) point of view.

Comedy usually has a happy ending, and this almost always includes a marriage followed by a party to celebrate the occasion. At the party, everyone is reconciled, and the opposition unites with the side of the hero to create a new society of fellowship. The humor in comedy results, in part, from the destruction of some absurd or irrational obsession that attempts to keep the hero and heroine apart. In *Pride and Prejudice* it is Darcy's pride in his social status that causes him to consider Elizabeth beneath him, and it is Elizabeth's prejudice toward Darcy's pride that causes her to consider Darcy too haughty for her. In Shakespeare's *The Merchant of Venice,* Shylock's obsession with his pound of flesh almost prevents Bassanio's happiness with his wife Portia. While most modern readers tend to pity Shylock and to see him more as a victim than a villain, the audience in Shakespeare's day was delighted when Shylock's obsessive vengeance in demanding Antonio's death is used against him in the absurd requirement for obtaining his payment imposed by Portia, disguised as the young lawyer Balthasar, in the trial scene. In fact, read from the Elizabethans' point of view, the reunion of Portia and Bassanio at Belmont at the end of the play seems anticlimactic.

In more general terms, the plot pattern of comedy involves some attempt at achievement on the part of youth, an attempt by age to prevent this achievement, and the final triumph by youth in the end. *The Adventures of Huckleberry Finn* fits this pattern as Huck tries to live by his own lights by first trying to escape the harsh civilizing rules of the Widow Douglas and later by trying to lead Jim to freedom. He eventually succeeds in being able "to light out for the Territory," but his triumph comes only after much interference from the "civilized" world of adults. *The Adventures of Huckleberry Finn,* like most other mythic comedies, illustrates the conflict between the illusion of wisdom associated with age and the reality of wisdom associated with youth.

One productive area of study related to comedy is the stock characters who people both comic literature and the sit-coms on TV. Once definitions are provided for the stock character types, students enjoy citing examples of them from their reading and viewing experience. The most common stock characters include the ingenue (or female protagonist), the villain, the rogue, the parasite, the pedant, the braggart, the dowager, the shrew, the dunce, and the eccentric.

Romance is the second plot type that Frye identifies. In romance, the archetype is the successful quest in which the hero sets out to achieve some goal but is hindered by obstacles that must be overcome along the way. The prototype of the romance is the story of Perseus, who sets out to slay the Gorgon Medussa. After overcoming many obstacles, Perseus fulfills his mission and, after even more adventures, lives happily ever after with his wife Andromeda. In the Perseus story, as in all romance, a conflict exists between the protagonist, or hero, and an antagonist who is the enemy of the hero.

The primal conflict of romance between forces of good and evil can have many plot variations. Many novels, including some of the novels of initiation we consider in Chapter Ten, follow this basic pattern. For example, *The Old Man and the Sea* by Ernest Hemingway fits this pattern of romance, although the enemy of the old man lies within himself in the natural human tendency to give up when the struggle to define the self becomes intense. The marlin that the old man catches is symbolic of this struggle, but the real conflict is within Santiago. He eventually succeeds even though his success cannot be measured by the shark-eaten skeleton of the fish.

The third mythos—tragedy—is concerned with the question of why evil exists in the world.[8] In these terms, students can approach traditional tragic drama, as well as other tragic works, through a thoughtful consideration of how this question is answered by various authors.

In a traditional tragedy like *Oedipus Rex*, the question focuses attention away from the murder of Oedipus' father and his marriage to his mother as the cause of his downfall onto his own failure to examine the consequences of acts before he commits them. This failure is a manifestation of Oedipus' pride, which is his tendency to see his judgments as correct even when they aren't. On the road to Thebes, Oedipus kills an old man who refuses to get out of the way, and he later marries an older woman, both without entertaining the possibility that these people could be his parents. Later he rashly insists that the Thebans get to the bottom of what is causing the plague on the city without once considering that he may be the cause. Thus, in our terms, the real tragedy of Oedipus—and thus one of Sophocles' answers to the question of why evil exists—is his mania for acting on impulse. In *Hamlet*, Shakespeare says that Hamlet's downfall occurs because he thinks he can set Denmark—and, by extension, the world—aright by his own deeds. Hamlet's tragic flaw isn't his inability to act (he acts quite effectively when he kills Polonius, when he changes the letter carried by Rosencrantz and Guildenstern, and when he stabs Claudius); rather, his tragic flaw, hence the cause of his downfall, is his pride in thinking that human action can be effective in rooting out corruption. In other words, if Hamlet hadn't taken seriously the Ghost's statement that revenge would purge Denmark of evil, his own downfall would never have occurred.

By this standard, many other works can be considered tragic. George Orwell, for example, in *1984* probes the origins of the evil of totalitarianism in the human tendency to manipulate language dishonestly and to remake history to suit the purposes of the state. Robert Cormier tells readers that greed and obsession can corrupt even men of the highest religious ideals in *The Chocolate War,* and Harper Lee explores the source of racial prejudice and irrational behavior in *To Kill a Mockingbird.*

Finally, the mythos of irony-satire offers a view of human foibles and failings. Frye makes several rather subtle and technical distinctions between irony and satire, and he concludes that "the chief distinction between irony and satire is that satire is militant irony."[9] We will deal with irony and satire as a single form and will rely on the more traditional distinctions among satiric forms and types as organizational divisions.

The chief characteristic features of satire, according to Gilbert Highet in *The Anatomy of Satire,* are these: "it is topical; it claims to be realistic (although it is usually exaggerated or distorted); it is shocking; it is informal; and (although often in a grotesque or painful manner) it is funny."[10] The topical nature of satire quite naturally dates it rather quickly, and its shock-value, often manifested in disgusting, vulgar, and obscene language and references, makes some of it inappropriate for all but the most mature readers. Nevertheless, students, many of whom are natural satirists themselves, usually enjoy satire as well as, or better than, any other type of literature, and the importance of satire in the literature of every nation and age demands a consideration of this form in school.

Satire comes in three basic forms and is of two basic types. This is a generalization, of course, and satirists often use all three forms and shades of both types in a single work. Nevertheless, for convenience we will discuss the forms and types as though they existed in a pure and unmingled state.

The three forms of satire are monologues, parodies, and narratives. In monologues, "the satirist . . . addresses us directly. He states his view of a problem, cites examples, pillories opponents, and endeavors to impose his view upon the public."[11] Some of the stand-up comedians who entertain in nightclubs and on TV are examples of practitioners of the art of satiric monologue, as are satiric newspaper columnists like Art Buchwald, and many students know their style well.

Parody, the second satiric form, involves the re-working of a serious literary or other artistic work for a comic purpose. Sometimes the purpose is to ridicule the form itself, and sometimes it is to ridicule the ideas in the work. In 1970, the National Lampoon Group published a brilliant and sophisticated paperback called *This Side of Parodies*,[12] which included, among other gems, "The Polaroid Print of Dorian Gray" by Michael O'Donoghue, and Sean Kelly's "Swan Song of the Open Road" and "The Love Song of J. Edgar Hoover." William Zaranka edited *The Brand-X Anthology of Poetry* (Burnt Norton Edition),[13] and this book includes parodies of British and American poetry by the likes of Ezra Pound, Charles Lamb, Max Beerbohm, and others. Students who have some familiarity with the works parodied in these and similar collections enjoy reading these parodies and are sometimes moved to write parodies of their own.

The third form of satire—and by far the most common form studied in literature courses—is satiric narrative. A satiric narrative, as the term implies, is a satiric story. *Gulliver's Travels* certainly fits into this category, as do some of works of such diverse authors as Chaucer, Mark Twain, and Aldous Huxley.

The two types of satire—Horatian and Juvenalian—bear the names of the Latin writers, Horace and Juvenal, who first perfected the forms. These two types of satire represent opposite ends of a continuum, and individual works of satire lean toward either end of the continuum, depending on the purpose and attitude of the author.

The Horatian satirist, in Highet's words, "likes most people, but thinks they are rather blind and foolish. He tells the truth with a smile, so that he will not repel them but cure them of that ignorance which is their worst fault."[14] Horatian satirists realize that they are subject to the same human weaknesses as the rest of the race, so they write from the perspective of someone who has, or easily could have, the same problem they are pointing out in others. Chaucer is a Horatian satirist in "The Nun's Priest's Tale" when he warns readers through the rooster Chanticleer of the dangers of vanity and of ignoring intellectual insight and reason. Kurt Vonnegut uses Horatian satire in his works, as does Aldous Huxley in *Brave New World* and Joseph Heller in *Catch-22*.

The second type of satirist—the Juvenalian—"hates most people, or despises them. He believes rascality is triumphant in his world.... His aim therefore is not to cure, but to wound, to punish, to destroy."[15] The Juvenalian satirist is a pessimist who believes he or she is superior to ordinary human beings, who are incapable of improvement. Jonathan Swift is a Juvenalian satirist at the end of *Gulliver's Travels* when he has Gulliver prefer the company of horses to that of his family, and Swift writes as a Juvenalian throughout "A Modest Proposal." Mark Twain in some of his later pieces, notably *The Mysterious Stranger*, is a Juvenalian satirist as well.

The real appeal of satire lies in its humor. Adolescents are naturally critical of themselves and of adult authority figures, and the criticism of adult society inherent in satire, coupled with its often biting humor, makes this form naturally appealing to secondary school students.

The mythic approach to curriculum organization allows teachers to create units that incorporate literature from all genres, from both British and American literature, and from all time periods. Because of its flexibility and its potential for in-depth study of both significant literary forms and significant individual literary works, the mythic approach deserves much broader attention than it typically receives in middle schools and high schools.

Conclusion

The broad-range approaches to curriculum organization discussed in this chapter provide exposure to many types of literature. The chronological survey approach, despite its shortcomings, and the genre approach are by far the most widely used approaches used in schools. A balanced literature program in the middle and upper grades should include one or more of the better of these approaches, but breadth without depth is not without its weaknesses. Therefore, teachers and other curriculum decision-makers should seriously consider incorporating one or more of the focused approaches to curriculum organization discussed in the next chapter into the overall design of the literature program.

Notes

1. Nancy Gillmore Coryell. *An Evaluation of Extensive and Intensive Teaching of Literature: A Year's Experiment in the Eleventh Grade.* Teachers College, Columbia University, Contributions to Education, No. 275. New York: Teachers College, Columbia University, 1927.

2. Daniel N. Fader and Elton B. McNeil. *Hooked on Books: Program and Proof.* New York: Berkley Publishing Company, 1968.

3. Robert C. Pooley. "Varied Patterns of Approaches in the Teaching of Literature." *English Journal,* 28: 345, May 1939.

4. Pooley, "Varied Patterns," p 345.

5. William Kenney. *How to Analyze Fiction.* New York: Simon & Schuster, 1966, p 91.

6. Northrop Frye. *Anatomy of Criticism.* Princeton: Princeton University Press, 1957.

7. Frye, *Anatomy of Criticism,* p 163.

8. William McAvoy, ed. *Dramatic Tragedy.* New York: McGraw-Hill Book Company, 1971, p ix.

9. Frye, *Anatomy of Criticism,* p 223.

10. Gilbert Highet. *The Anatomy of Satire.* Princeton: Princeton University Press, 1962, p 5.

11. Highet, *Anatomy of Satire*, p 13.

12. *National Lampoon/This Side of Parodies*. New York: Warner Books, Inc., 1974.

13. William Zaranka, ed. *The Brand-X Anthology of Poetry*. Cambridge: Apple-Wood Books, Inc., 1981.

14. Highet, *Anatomy of Satire*, p 235.

15. Highet, *Anatomy of Satire*, p 235.

CHAPTER NINE

Focused Approaches to Curriculum Organization in Literature

The broad-range approaches to organizing the literature curriculum that we described in Chapter Eight are designed to provide a wide overview of literature, rather than a deep and exhaustive examination of any one aspect of a body of literary art. Most school literature curricula have traditionally been organized according to one or more of the broad-range approaches, usually the genre approach in the lower grades and the chronological approach in the upper grades. The major textbook companies help keep this tradition alive by employing these approaches in their anthologies. While the broad-range approaches may provide comfort and a sense of security to teachers and parents, there are other approaches to curriculum organization that meet the five organizational principles we described in the previous chapter and that are capable of providing students with deeper, more intense literary experiences.

Each of the four focused approaches we describe in this chapter zeroes in on one of the following: brief but important periods of literary history, the works of a single major writer, the literature associated with a single literary movement or major literary idea, and literature that deals with a single theme that is important in literature and in the lives of human beings. The basic goal of these approaches is to develop a deeper and richer understanding of a limited aspect of literature by experiencing that aspect from the perspective of several different works that are representative of the time period, the major writer, the movement or idea, or the theme.

Do the Focused Approaches Conform to Principles for Curriculum Organization?

Approaches	Interest	Long Works	Principles Intensive Study	Extensive Study	Cultural Significance
Focused Chronology	Yes	Yes	Yes	Yes	Yes
Major Writer	Yes	Yes*	Yes	Yes	Yes
Major Idea	Yes	Yes	Yes	Yes	Yes
Thematic	Yes	Yes	Yes	Yes	Yes

Figure 9.1
*Some units organized according to the Major Writer Approach will focus on lyric poetry. However, given writers of novels or plays, the approach conforms to this principle.

Most of the focused approaches don't come commercially packaged, and teachers who use them may find themselves doing more preparatory work than teachers who use only standard literature textbooks. However, these approaches can be as exciting as they are challenging, and often teachers who use them experience the immense satisfaction of watching the units or whole courses they invent awaken students to the excitement of intellectual discovery.

The most important element in planning successful units that are based on one of the focused approaches is the judicious selection of the literature that students will read and study. This obviously requires that teachers who plan these units have wide knowledge of the body of literature that is appropriate for possible inclusion in a particular unit. In Chapter Six we recommended that the most important criterion in choosing works for study in a reader-response oriented program is the potential for the works to permit authentic transactions between students and texts. In other words, the best works are those that facilitate response.

In addition to this criterion, the five principles of curriculum organization we enumerated in Chapter Eight are also useful in guiding the selection of works. In summary form, these principles are as follows: (1) Selections should promote interest in literature. In other words, works should be selected because they interest students. (2) Selections should include long works, that is, novels and full-length plays. (3) Selections should be complex enough to warrant intensive study. (4) Selections should include some less complex works that students can read, enjoy, and respond to on their own. (5) Selections should include works of recognized cultural significance.

The Focused Chronological Approach

We call the first of the four focused approaches the Focused Chronological Approach because it concentrates on the literature of a very brief segment of literary history. This approach is an adaptation of the excellent American humanities curriculum developed by Brooke Workman of West High School, Iowa City, Iowa, and published by the National Council of Teachers of English in 1975 as *Teaching the Decades.* The Workman curriculum consists of three semester-long units. Two of the units cover single decades (the 1920s and the 1930s), and the third covers the period 1945 to 1960. Each of the three long units is broken down into smaller parts dealing with the following: the concept of culture; the history (especially the social history) of the period; popular culture of the period as reflected in radio programs, movies, and best sellers; architecture and painting of the period; poetry and drama of the period; and music and dance of the period.

Obviously, Workman encompasses a great deal more than literature study, and the enormous variety of activities and materials he provides are designed to meet goals that are different from the goals of a literature curriculum. However, while much of Workman's curriculum may be of relatively little usefulness in a literature course, the idea of focused concentration on the literature of a single decade or slightly longer period is entirely appropriate for high school students. It is obviously not necessary to concentrate exclusively on American literature or on the twentieth century, as Workman does.

Clearly, some decades lend themselves to this approach better than others, but a little research will reveal a great many decades or slightly longer periods that would be rich sources of material for units organized according to the Focused Chronological Approach. Consider, for example, the decade of the 1850s.

In America the 1850s saw the publication of some of the most significant and enduring novels in all of the literature of the United States: Hawthorn's *The Scarlet Letter* (1850), *The House of the Seven Gables* (1851), and *The Blithedale Romance* (1852); Melville's *Moby Dick* (1851); and, Harriet Beecher Stowe's *Uncle Tom's Cabin* (1852). This last book, while not generally considered high art, was extremely popular, was influential in encouraging the Abolitionist movement, and is usually considered a work of cultural significance. In poetry this decade gave birth to the first edition of Whitman's *Leaves of Grass* (1855), Longfellow's *Hiawatha* (1855), *The Courtship of Miles Standish* (1858), and Whittier's *Songs of Labor* (1850). In literary criticism Poe's lecture entitled *Poetic Principle* was posthumously published in 1850, and in journalism *Harper's Magazine* was established in 1850 and *The Atlantic Monthly* in 1857. Finally, the decade saw the publication of important essays by Emerson (*Representative Men*, 1850) and Oliver Wendell Holmes (*The Autocrat of the Breakfast Table*, 1858).

The American literary events of the 1850s are sufficient in both quantity and quality for a significant unit in a high school or college literature course. Such a unit would certainly raise the question of why this single decade produced so many works and literary events of lasting significance, and the answer to this question would likely lead to some consideration of the social and political history of this decade.

In British literature the decade of the 1850s is equally rich. Novels published during that time include Dickens's *Bleak House* (1852), *Hard Times* (1854), *Little Dorrit* (1855), and *A Tale of Two Cities* (1859); Thackery's *The Virginians* (1857); Trollope's *Barchester Towers* (1857); and, George Eliot's *Adam Bede* (1859). In poetry the decade gave birth to, among many other notable poetic works, Elizabeth Barrett Browning's *Sonnets from the Portuguese* and Tennyson's *In Memoriam* in 1850; Arnold's *Poems* in 1853; and Tennyson's *Idylls of the King* in 1859. In the area of significant nonfiction, the decade of the 1850s saw the publication of Ruskin's *Stones of Venice* (1851), Newman's *The Idea of a University* (1852), Charles Darwin's *The Origin of Species* (1859), and John Stuart Mill's *On Liberty* (1859).

While the political history of this period is relatively unimportant with respect to British literature, the social history of the age is fascinating and can be enlightening regarding the social problems of the period that still plague industrialized countries. One work that we feel is ideally suited for study by high school students that explores social conditions for the Victorian Age is Charles Dickens's brilliant novel *Hard Times*. This novel is relatively unknown, but it deserves attention. It is Dickens's shortest novel (some 250 pages in most paperback editions), a fact that never detracts from a Victorian novel's teachability, and at least one major critic thinks it is Dickens's masterpiece.[1] *Hard Times* deals with the typically Romantic concern with the relationship between reason and emotion in human life, and, in the process of working out this theme, the author sheds light on Victorian problems in the areas of education reform, environmental pollution, housing conditions, factory owners' abuse of workers, the effects of urbanization and the mechanization of industry on the proletariat, and the powerlessness of the poor. The novel was originally serialized in Dickens's magazine *Household Words*, so groups of chapters can be assigned to correspond to the original installments. The effect of assigning the novel this way is to create in students the same suspense at the end of each day's reading that Dickens's original audience must have felt. The study of *Hard Times* could well serve as an introduction to a unit on the 1850s in British literature and open the way to deeper understanding of the other literature of the decade.

Whether the concentration is on the 1850s or the 1950s, on American literature or British literature, the Focused Chronological Approach offers students an opportunity for in-depth study of individual works and of significant periods in literary history. This approach lends itself well to a semester of work or less, but to concentrate on a single decade in a single country for an entire year is to run the risk of having students lose interest. However, a year-long course in which the first semester concentrates on American literature of the 1850s, say, and the second semester focuses on American literature in the 1950s, or a course in which the first semester deals with American literature in the 1850s and the second semester with British literature of the same decade could be an exciting experience for teacher and students alike.

The Illustrative Unit which follows, like the other Illustrative Units in this chapter, is intended to provide a model of how the Focused Chronological Approach can be used in organizing a unit of study.

Illustrative Unit on a Focused Chronological Period
The Harlem Renaissance of the 1920s

Grades: 9 to 12
Time Required: 2 to 3 weeks
Introduction

The Harlem Renaissance is the name given to a burst of literary activity during the 1920s in New York City's Harlem section. Set against the background of the Roaring Twenties and Prohibition, African-American writers of that period asserted their own voices in clear, distinct tones. The unit concentrates on the works of four writers, and most of the literature is poetry. All of it deals with the experience of Americans of African ancestry, but many of the ideas and sentiments expressed in the works are universal human concerns.

A short unit on the Harlem Renaissance might be especially appropriate in conjunction with a study of the works of Hemingway, Fitzgerald, and other writers of the so-called "Lost Generation." The writers of the Harlem Renaissance attempted to assert their individuality and their unique sense of racial identity, and their work deserves greater attention than it usually receives in chronological surveys.

Goals:

1. To read works of literature of the Harlem Renaissance period by James Weldon Johnson, Langston Hughes, Claude McKay, and Jean Toomer.
2. To understand the growing self-awareness of African-Americans during the 1920s as expressed in the works.
3. To grasp the significance of the oppression of African-Americans during that period of history.

James Weldon Johnson

First published in 1927, James Weldon Johnson's poetic sequence *God's Trombones* is an attempt, in the poet's words, to "take the primitive stuff of the old-time Negro sermon and, through art-governed expression, make it into poetry." The seven "sermons" in the work deal with major events in biblical literature, such as creation, the crucifixion of Jesus, and the last judgment.

Readings

Any of the passages from *God's Trombones*, but especially "The Crucifixion" and "The Judgment Day."

Langston Hughes

Hughes is the most prolific of the Harlem Renaissance authors, and, along with Richard Wright, Ralph Ellison, and James Baldwin, is one of the most highly regarded African-American writers of the first half of the twentieth century. Hughes' poetry is widely anthologized, and his short stories featuring his character Simple have achieved considerable fame.

Readings
Poetry

"A Note on Commercial Theatre"
"Theme for English B"
"Motto"
"A Dream Deferred"
"Harlem"
"Ballad of the Landlord"
Short Stories
"Thank You, Ma'am"
"On the Road"

One-act Play
"Soul Gone Home"

Claude McKay   Claude McKay was a Jamaican who moved to the United States in 1912. Although he published novels during the latter part of his career, he is best known for his poetry, especially his sonnets. All four of the sonnets listed below deal in some way with the strength and dignity of African-Americans in the face of oppression.

Readings

"Baptism"
"If We Must Die"
"The Lynching"
"America"

Jean Toomer   Although Toomer did not sustain literary activity throughout his lifetime, his novel *Crane* was one of the best known works produced during the Harlem Renaissance. *Crane* is not a traditional novel; rather, it is a series of prose vignettes woven together by lyric poems. This fact makes it relative easy to extract selections from it for use with students. It is a kind of initiation novel that deals with the coming to awareness of African-Americans.

Readings

Selections from *Crane.* If possible, students should read the entire novel.

The Major Writer Approach

The second focused approach to curriculum organization consists of units of study, some perhaps as long as a semester, that deal with the work of a single major writer. The goal of these units is to enable students to get to know a writer in much greater depth than would ever be possible in a survey course and to experience the writer's development over the course of his or her career. Courses of this sort are quite common in college English curricula, especially at the upper levels, and the idea can be modified and adapted to be appropriate to many different grade levels in middle school and high school.

One fine model for using the Major Writer Approach is Brooke Workman's *Writing Seminars in the Content Area: In Search of Hemingway, Salinger, and Steinbeck.*[2] Like Workman's *Teaching the Decades*, this curriculum includes goals, lesson plans, schedules, handouts, and a variety of resources that can be reproduced (permission to do so is given in the text) and used directly with students. Workman's three units are each designed to cover a ninety-day semester, but each can be shortened to accommodate other time frames. In each unit students write seven sharply focused papers, and each student is expected to undergo peer evaluation of his or her writing at least twice during the unit.

In Workman's Hemingway seminar, in addition to the papers of their peers, students read three novels (*The Sun Also Rises, A Farewell to Arms*, and *The Old Man and the Sea*), seventeen short stories, and approximately 100 pages of biographical material. In the Salinger seminar, students read two novels (*The Catcher in the Rye* and *Franny and Zooey*), thirteen short stories, biographical material, and the papers of other students. The literature in the Steinbeck seminar includes four novels (*The Red Pony, Tortilla Flat, Of Mice and Men*, and *The Grapes of Wrath*), eight short stories, biographical material, and student papers. The composition component of each seminar is handled through handouts and direct instruction by the teacher. Each of the seven papers emphasizes one or more new writing skills.

Brooke Workman has done a great service for teachers who are interested in using the Major Writer Approach to curriculum organization by providing a wealth of material on three writers who are obvious candidates for intensive study. More than that, he has provided a model of how such a unit can be organized. However, as Workman himself implies, a great many writers are appropriate for study in this way, including many writers of Young Adult fiction. Teachers who are interested in helping their students become deeply involved with a significant portion of a major writer's body of work will find this approach useful.

Illustrative Unit on a Major Writer
The Versatile Mark Twain

Grade: 11
Time Required: Varies depending on works chosen; 3 to 4 weeks
Introduction

There are a number of ways in which American literature can be taught other than the conventional chronological survey. One possible approach would be a regional one, with a Great Writer(s) component providing a culmination. One such unit could be "New England in Literature," with Hawthorne, Frost, Melville, or O'Neill providing the ultimate component. Another could be "The South in Literature," with Faulkner or Alan Tate or Flannery O'Connor providing a similar function. The unit described here, however, is designed to be a culmination to a larger unit on "The Midwest in Literature."

This unit is directed at eleventh graders with at least average to *slightly* below average reading ability. The unit on the Midwest would include the following subtopics:

1. Realism in American fiction
2. Regional literature—the *local colorists*
3. The Frontier (including the frontier town)
4. Elements of native American humor
5. The cowboy: a western bumpkin/hero

It is not within the province of this Illustrative Unit to do more than mention these subtopics; for those who wish to develop them, there are numerous literary works and secondary sources with which to do so. What *is* provided, however, is a brief overview of a study segment on Mark Twain. Twain's works will be used to illustrate how this major American literary figure reflected, to one degree or another, all of the subtopics considered in the broader unit on the Midwest in literature.

Goals:

1. To familiarize students with one of the most celebrated authors in American literature.
2. To demonstrate Twain's multifaceted talent.
3. To illustrate a distinctly *American* voice in literature.
4. To offer cultural background through the eyes of a creative literary artist, rather than through the eyes of a sociologist or historian.
5. To read and discuss works that show Twain to be a realist, a local colorist, a creator of an image of the frontier, a humorist, and a creator of genuinely American literary characters.

Mark Twain as Realist Mark Twain was initially, and in some ways perennially, a journalist. His great capacity for careful observation, his ability to enjoy through travel the odd corners of the landscape of the West, and his extraordinary capacity to reproduce the speech patterns of people of all walks of life all contribute to his realistic style. Twain was a spontaneous realist. He had a unique ability to portray people, communities, and events as he encountered them, without editorial commentary; his journalistic power added to his spontaneity. At a time when fiction writers in France, Germany, Russia, and England were displaying the capacity to create objective, almost clinical, perspectives on reality in their work,

Twain stood out as an author who could faithfully display the American cultural milieu as it developed west of the Mississippi River and far from the urban sophistication of nineteenth-century Boston, New York, and Philadelphia.

A number of Twain's works illustrate his realistic bent, and the following list is only a partial compilation of them. All of these works are book length, and it would be impossible for students to read all of them. It would perhaps be wisest to select relatively short excerpts from several of them that illustrate Twain's contribution to the evolution of realism in Western literature in general and American literature in particular.

Readings

Roughing It
Life on the Mississippi
The Innocents Abroad
A Tramp Abroad
The American Claimant

Mark Twain as Local Colorist In an era when a large number of writers were discovering, describing, and analyzing the small communities that were sprouting almost daily and then struggling to survive, Mark Twain can be identified as one of the most accomplished. The work of Bret Harte, Hamlin Garland, E. W. Howe, Thomas Bailey Aldrich, Mary Catherwood, Edward Eggleston, and Henry Blake Fuller, to name a few, put the West on the map, but none did so with the finesse and fine ear for local dialect as Mark Twain. His ability to create memorable images from ostensibly nondescript localities represented a new direction in world literature. As the noted American literature scholar Bernard DeVoto has claimed, in his creation of the microcosm of the Western small town, Twain could be credited with being the first truly *American* writer. He was a literary artist who, unlike his predecessors and peers from the eastern United States, was not imitative of the stylistics of the mother country. His was a pioneering spirit, and his genius in the raising of local color writing to an elevated plane established him as foremost among American authors who sought to convey the uniqueness of this entirely new lifestyle.

As before, the following list presents a number of titles that are appropriate to illustrate Twain's talents as a local colorist. The teacher can select a single work from the list for study by the whole class, or students can select works from the list for individual reading.

Readings

The Adventures of Tom Sawyer
The Adventures of Huckleberry Finn
Life on the Mississippi
Roughing It
Pudd'nhead Wilson and Those Mysterious Twins
The Celebrated Jumping Frog of Calaveras County and Other Sketches
(short stories)

Mark Twain as Creator of the Frontier In all of the works mentioned thus far, Twain helped to develop the distinctive image of the frontier, a panorama of Western geography as seen through the eyes of those who were discovering and settling it. He also contributed a significant portrait of the frontier town in its immediacy, its transient populations, its violence, its vulgarity, and its romantic charm. His descriptions of towns similar to his native Hannibal, Missouri, provided the literary world with a totally different kind of setting and an original lifestyle, which in turn provided an inspiration to an unending stream of popular literature, in the form of the Western adventure tale, that readers can find in any bookstore and that has served as the subject matter for commercial films and television dramas. In a radically different direction, it was Twain's portrayal of the frontier, more so than that of any literary contemporary, which influenced such American scholars as DeVoto, Henry Nash Smith, Alfred Kazin, Walter Blair, Constance Rourke, and Van Wyck Brooks to write numerous volumes on the American frontier as the locale of a great New World symbol and zeitgeist.

The frontier subtopic can be studied through the work of the local colorists mentioned earlier, but Twain's novels, nonfiction sketches, and short stories all contain a number of striking examples of his treatment of the frontier. A teacher need only look through the titles already listed in order to identify a large number of useful examples. Also of use in this or any other treatment of Twain is the recording "Mark Twain Tonight!" (Columbia Records) in which Hal Holbrook plays the role of Mark Twain. This recording contains several highly pertinent readings from Twain texts, as well as from his autobiographical writings.

Mark Twain as Humorist Just as Twain's treatment of the frontier is an original contribution to world literature, so, too, is his brand of humor. It can be quickly and easily distinguished from the clever, subtle, verbose, urbane humor of previous British and American writers. As DeVoto, Blair, and others have noted, it can be identified as native American humor, complete with the vulgar anecdote, the gross exaggeration (the *tall tale*), the often grotesque caricature of the cowboy, the incongruous justification of urbanity and crudeness, the recurrent pratfall, and the belly laugh. Much of the humorous effect is achieved through the deliberate and accurate recreation of the frontier dialect, which was also totally new to both the sophisticated literary scholar and the casual reader in the United States and in Europe. Thus, Twain's humor took both verbal and physical forms. It could be coarse, but it could also be subtle, as found particularly in some of his satiric works. It is present in virtually all of his "American" novels and short stories already listed, but it is frequently used as a device in several of his "European" works. The "European" works include *A Connecticut Yankee in King Arthur's Court*, *The Mysterious Stranger*, *Personal Recollections of Joan of Arc by the Sieur Louis de Conte*, and *The Prince and the Pauper*. Twain considered the last two of these novels his best work. An exhaustive study of the "European" novels is probably inappropriate as a culmination to a unit on the Midwest in literature, but selected passages can be chosen to illustrate Twain's humor.

Mark Twain as Creator of "American" Characters Much has already been said in the foregoing sections of this unit about Twain's originality in the evocation of a new American personality. In dealing with the local color, the frontier, and the humor subtopics, consideration of his characters, both major and minor, is inevitable. Also, as previously stated, the dialects spoken by the people in the "American" works are faithful reproductions of the speech patterns of his region and era, and, as such, are worthy of discussion. In conveying these dialect features, the Hal Holbrook recordings would be most useful; his portrayal of Huck Finn's language is particularly valuable. In any event, Twain's creation of the Western individual, both as courageous pioneer and unsophisticated rube, should constitute an important part of the work teachers can do with Twain's selections.

The Major Idea Approach

The third of the focused approaches is called the Major Idea Approach. This approach to curriculum organization concentrates on a major idea or movement in literature (e.g., transcendentalism, naturalism, tragedy) and calls for in-depth study of literature from a variety of periods, in a variety of genres, and across national lines. In this approach the goal is to enable students to grasp a major aspect of intellectual history through the study of both representative works of literature and significant critical and theoretical works. The use of this approach should result in a detailed knowledge and understanding of the major idea in question, in better than average familiarity with the works of a relatively small group of writers, and in a methodology that can be applied to the study of other major ideas.

One way that the study of a major idea can proceed is deductively. If the deductive method is chosen, students begin with a definition of the major idea and then evaluate the literary works they read in terms of the degree to which these works conform to the definition. This method can help students realize that the philosophical inclination of most writers changes and grows over the course of their careers. For example, the poet George Gordon, Lord Byron is always listed as a romantic poet, yet many of his works, most notably the satires, are decidedly neoclassical in stance and tone. These works are closer to the works of the great writers of the eighteenth century, especially Alexander Pope, than they are to the works of William Wordsworth. Students studying a unit on romanticism deductively would have to evaluate Byron's work in terms of the definition of romanticism they are given and decide the extent to which Byron can legitimately be called a romantic poet.

A second method of approaching the study of a major idea is inductively. Using this method students gradually develop a definition of the idea under consideration by analyzing the characteristics of the works they read. In a sense, this method is an application of the scientific method to the study of literature, and it most closely resembles the way scholars and literary critics work. In essence, when students work inductively, they examine data (the works of a writer) and formulate a tentative hypothesis (definition) to describe the qualities they expect to find in the works of subsequent writers who are supposed to be representative of the major idea under discussion. As additional writers' works are read, the hypothesis undergoes revision and expansion to account for new aspects of the major idea that were not previously observed. Obviously, any definition students develop, like any definition professional critics develop, must remain tentative and subject to revision as new data present themselves.

No matter which method of study is used, an important benefit to students—in addition to an understanding of the major idea and knowledge of the works they read—is the experience of learning and applying a formal intellectual methodology for studying literature. Furthermore, both methods require an above-average tolerance of ambiguity, and both demand intellectual honesty beyond that which is routinely asked of high school students. These intellectual, psychological, and moral values are important parts of the foundation of any educational program.

As a further benefit, a detailed understand of a major idea can provide a basis for seeing the relationships that exist among other major ideas. The major ideas that serve as the underpinning of literary schools and movements never spring fully grown from the head of their inventor. Instead, they result from the gradual evolution of thought over time. A good example of this concept is the idea of tragedy, which began with the Greeks and continues to serve modern writers. Another example is romanticism, which, while generally thought of as a revolt against the concept of the ordered universe cherished by neoclassical writers in the eighteenth century, was actually long in coming into existence. The neoclassical notions of balance, harmony, and symmetry are based on prescientific concepts of a well-ordered world symbolized by the geocentric universe described by Ptolemy in the first century A.D. and by the metaphor of the Great Chain of Being (i.e., a system of rigid rankings that places every created entity on a link of a metaphorical chain) which justified the highly stratified social structure of Europe. Yet the Ptolemaic universe had been essentially disproved by Copernicus in 1543, and the Protestant Reformation (1517 and following) had essentially severed the roots of the inherent hierarchy of human society (e.g., God reveals Himself to king and peasant directly and equally). Thus, the ideas that undergird romanticism were almost three hundred years old by the time Wordsworth wrote his 1800 preface to the second edition of *Lyrical Ballads*, in which he set forth the basic premises of the romantic movement.

Furthermore, in large measure, realism is a direct outgrowth and refinement of romanticism. In the 1800 preface, Wordsworth states his intention of "bringing my language closer to the language of men." In other words, Wordsworth proposed to use language that was realistic. From here it was a relatively short step to realism in setting, conflict, and characterization. A thorough understanding of romanticism will certainly assist students in understanding the ideas that went before it and came after it.

The Major Idea Approach requires fairly intense work on the part of students, and it is probably best reserved for older and more able youngsters. When this approach is used, though, the result can be an intense understanding of one or other of the main currents in intellectual history.

Illustrative Unit on a Major Idea
The Evolution of Tragedy

Grade: 11 or 12
Time Required: 6 to 9 weeks
Introduction

Tragedy has been an important literary form during three significant ages: Greece during the Golden Age of Pericles, England during the Elizabethan Age, and the United States during the post–World War I period. While seemingly unrelated to one another, all three ages share a concern for establishing new answers to age-old questions, especially the question of the nature and source of evil. Tragedies written in these three ages share many elements in common, yet they obviously differ from one another in more than superficial aspects. The purpose of this unit is to expose students to tragic plays written in each of these period and to assist them in arriving inductively at a definition of tragedy that is capable of describing the essence of tragedy as it evolves through history.

During the Golden Age of Greece, approximately 500 B.C. to 400 B.C., thinkers were concerned with trying to reconcile fate and a belief in gods who routinely meddled in human affairs with a growing awareness of human free will. Thus, Sophocles used Oedipus as a man who desperately wants to avoid the horrible fate of killing his father and marrying his mother but who ends up doing precisely that when he attempts to take his fate into his own hands. In other words, when Oedipus tries to assert his free will in order to avoid evil, he unwittingly causes evil to occur.

During the Elizabethan Age in England, Shakespeare and his contemporaries were attempting to explain the nature and source of evil in a world in which the old order was rapidly disintegrating. In the medieval scheme of things, order and rank were established by God, and any attempt to disrupt this system of order and rank was sure to end in chaos on a grand scale. But the Elizabethans were witnesses to changes in ways of viewing the universe that shook the very foundations of their beliefs. First, explorers of several nations were proving that the earth was round, and not flat, as had previously been assumed. Second, astronomers were proving that the sun, and not the earth, was the center of the solar system. The concept of order, which had been based on an ordered universe in which planets and other heavenly bodies embedded in crystal spheres revolved around the earth, was beginning to fall apart. Third, religious upheaval brought about by the Protestant Reformation began forcing people to rethink the system of rank that had been previously taken for granted. The chief reason for this was the realization that if God could and did reveal Himself directly to people at every level of society, without regard to the hierarchy of the Catholic Church, perhaps in God's eyes the king is not inherently of higher rank than the peasant.

Shakespeare responded with characters like Macbeth and King Lear. Macbeth destroys order by murdering King Duncan and seizing his throne, and chaos and suffering ensue for Macbeth and his whole kingdom. King Lear destroys the concept of rank by abdicating to his daughters, and the result is disaster.

Finally, during the decades following the First World War, playwrights like Eugene O'Neill, Arthur Miller, and Tennessee Williams attempted to deal with the loss of certitude and traditional values that the Great War and the succeeding flu epidemic of 1918 to 1919 brought about. These authors chose tragedy as the appropriate vehicle to show human beings caught in the fog of illusion that ultimately destroys their lives.

Tragedy has endured as a literary form because it is flexible enough to permit a variety of world views to be expressed. It always deals with serious issues, especially the nature and source of evil, and it is no less appealing to adolescents at the end of the twentieth century than it was to the citizens of Athens during the Golden Age.

Goals:

1. To read representative tragedies from the Golden Age of Greece, the Elizabethan Age of England, and the post–World War I period of the United States.
2. To compare and contrast the nature and motivation of the tragic hero as portrayed in each age.
3. To inductively arrive at a tentative definition of tragedy that describes tragedy in all three ages.

The Golden Age of Greece

Readings

Edith Hamilton. *Mythology*, Chapter 18, "The Royal House of Thebes."
Edith Hamilton. *The Greek Way to Civilization*, Chapter 11, "The Idea of Tragedy."
Aristotle. *The Poetics*, the definition of tragedy.
Sophocles. *Oedipus Rex*.

Introduce this part of the unit by asking students to read "The Royal House of Thebes" from *Mythology* by Edith Hamilton. This chapter is the story of the founding of Thebes and of Oedipus and his children. Explain that Sophocles' audience would have been thoroughly familiar with the story of Oedipus and that Sophocles takes advantage of his audience's knowledge of the story to create dramatic irony.

Before assigning the reading of the play, ask students to identify a situation in their own lives in which they genuinely thought they were doing the right thing but in which they later learned, after it was too late to do anything about it, that they had done the wrong thing instead. This could be as simple as packing the wrong clothes for a trip: because the student failed to heed the warning of the weather forecast, the student took warm weather clothes, only to discover later that cold weather clothes were needed. Or, a student failed a test in school because he or she ignored the teacher's advice to study a particular body of material. Ask students to comment on how these situations made them feel.

After recollecting a situation from their own lives, ask students to respond to the following questions by telling whether they agree or disagree with each statement.

Opinionnaire

1. Most people would leave a particular place if they thought they would get into serious trouble by staying there.
2. Most people would do everything in their power to avoid killing someone else.
3. People who do things that are morally wrong usually know they are wrong but do them anyway.
4. Most people think through all of the consequences of their actions before they perform them.
5. When bad things happen to people, it is usually their own fault.

Once an attempt is made to establish collateral experience by having students recall past experiences and respond to the opinionnaire, the reading of the play can proceed. This can be done in class, with class members reading the various roles. In order to avoid distracting stumbles in the text, the readers should practice reading their parts ahead of time. More advanced students can read the play on their own, but students often have difficulty with poetic texts like this one when they read them silently.

After the play is read, discussion should focus first on whether Oedipus is morally guilty or innocent. A great deal has been written on both sides of this issue, so it should not be surprising if the class is unable to arrive at consensus. At first, most students will probably argue in favor of innocence. They should be reminded that Oedipus himself thinks he's guilty, as do the townspeople of Thebes.

Next, students should be asked to read Aristotle's definition of tragedy. A number of modern translations are readily available. Discussion should then focus on the factors that contributed to Oedipus's downfall. Aristotle wrote his famous definition of tragedy using *Oedipus Rex* as the model of a perfect tragedy. Students may not understand what Aristotle considered Oedipus's tragic flaw to be. It is hubris, or pride, of course, and Aristotle believed Oedipus's pride caused him to think he could outsmart his fate by leaving Corinth before the action of the play begins. In this sense, Oedipus placed his own will above the will of the god Apollo, as revealed by the Oracle at Delphi.

This part of the unit should conclude with the reading and discussion of the chapter entitled "The Idea of Tragedy" from *The Greek Way to Western Civilization* by Edith Hamilton. This chapter should help clarify some of the basic ideas of the nature and purpose of tragedy.

The Elizabethan Age of England

The leap from the Golden Age to the Elizabethan Age encompasses more than two thousand years. During that time Greek drama gave way to philosophy as a way of attempting to answer the fundamental questions of human existence. Greece fell to Rome, and Christianity, with its emphasis on free will and divine mercy, replaced the ancient religion of Greece. The Emperor Constantine suppressed drama in the Roman Empire, and, for five or six centuries, drama was unknown. It reemerged in the liturgy of the Catholic Church and developed steadily through the medieval period until it reached its full flowering with William Shakespeare during the English Renaissance.

The historical development of drama is interesting but of relatively little importance to an understanding of tragedy except in one important detail: the influence of Christianity. Shakespeare and his contemporaries saw the world and the problem of evil very differently from the Greeks. To them, evil was a direct result of human depravity; moral evil was freely chosen because of the human tendency to sin.

Readings

E. M. W. Tillyard. *The Elizabethan World Picture*, especially Chapters Two ("Order"), Three ("Sin"), and Four ("The Chain of Being").
William Shakespeare. *Macbeth*.

The material from Tillyard will be helpful in understanding the way the Elizabethans conceived of the world. The material is not easy for high school students to read, and the teacher may wish to highlight the main points in lecture form rather than assign the chapters for every student to read.

Before beginning to read *Macbeth*, ask students to reflect on times when they tried to get away with something but were caught by their parents or others in positions of authority. Did they ever feel comfortable concealing their deed? Did one deed lead to another and then another, as they tried to cover up the first deed?

Ask students to consider whether a suggestion by someone has directed their thinking along lines they had not previously considered. What role has pressure from their friends played in making them do something they really wanted to do but were afraid to try on their own? Why is it easier to go along with others to do something that we know is wrong and that we probably wouldn't do on our own?

Discussion of these and similar questions should help students key in on their own experiences that are relevant to the story of Macbeth. These questions, and others that will present themselves after the reading is under way, should prepare students for a deeper comprehension of the play.

The reading of a Shakespearean play is always challenging for high school students. The play should probably be read orally in class, and the readers should be encouraged to practice their parts ahead of time to enhance fluency. Many teachers prefer to play taped readings of the play by professional actors and to allow students to follow the text. Others prefer to show a videotape or film of a production of the play before reading begins so that students can become familiar with the plot before they read the text and so they can have a visual image of the action as they later read the play.

After reading, discussion should focus on the following areas:

1. What causes Macbeth's downfall?
2. Is Macbeth a tragic figure by Aristotle's definition?
3. What can be considered Macbeth's tragic flaw?
4. What, according to Shakespeare, is the source of evil?

Post-World War I Period of the United States

America had already produced major world poets, novelists, and short story writers by the beginning of the twentieth century, but until 1920, with the production of Eugene O'Neill's play *Beyond the Horizon*, the United States had produced no drama of lasting importance. This fact generally parallels the overall decline in drama as a literary art form throughout the Western world during the Eighteenth and Nineteenth Centuries. Ibsen created a sensation in Europe with *A Doll's House* in 1879, but, except for Ibsen, tragedy was little more than a relic of past ages.

The big change came as a result of the First World War. As mentioned earlier, the period after the war was characterized by a general hopelessness and a sense of alienation and isolation among writers and other intellectuals. The so-called Lost Generation of writers in Paris and elsewhere reflected the loss of certainty and traditional values that followed the great cataclysm of the war. Like the Greeks and the Elizabethans, the playwrights of the period turned to tragedy to see new answers to the timeless questions.

Readings

Arthur Miller. *Death of a Salesman*.
Arthur Miller. "Tragedy and the Common Man."

Before assigning *Death of a Salesman*, ask students to respond to the following opinionnaire by saying whether they agree or disagree with each statement.

Opinionnaire

1. A successful person is one who earns a lot of money.
2. Working with one's hands (e.g., carpentry, farming, mechanics) is less dignified that working with people or ideas (e.g., teaching, selling goods, banking).
3. Our society judges people by what they possess, regardless of whether they have the money to pay for what they buy.
4. Parents want their children to have more affluent and more comfortable lives than the parents have.

These statements, as well as a general discussion of consumerism and materialism, should prepare students to read the play. While *Death of a Salesman* presents reading challenges because of the flashbacks and the *imaginary* character of Ben, most older students are able to handle a silent independent reading of the play once these features are pointed out and explained to them.

After reading the play, discussion should focus on the following areas:

1. Is Willy Loman tragic, or merely pathetic?
2. Does the audience experience Aristotle's fear and pity for Willy?
3. What is Willy's tragic flaw?
4. How does Willy compare with Oedipus and Macbeth? What personality features do all three characters share?

After the play has been discussed in class, students should be asked to read Miller's essay, "Tragedy and the Common Man." After the essay has been discussed, ask students to write their own definition of tragedy, taking into consideration all three of the plays read in this unit.

The Thematic Approach

The fourth and most important of our focused approaches to teaching literature is the Thematic Approach. In this approach units of study are organized around an idea, or theme, that students find interesting and that they consider important in their lives. In such units the literature isn't limited by genre, period, nationality, or even artistic merit. The goal is to help students focus concentrated attention on the theme of the unit and to examine the theme from the viewpoints of a variety of works.

An interest in the Thematic Approach began in the 1920s when colleges began deemphasizing prescribed reading lists as prerequisites for college admission and when so-called "progressive" educators began advocating wide reading in the schools. These factors, along with the obvious economy of a single literature anthology rather than multiple volumes of single texts for each student, gave rise in the 1930s to the widespread use of literature textbook series. Many of these textbooks organized their contents according to theme. Thus, it became increasingly common for students to study literature centered on such themes as war, courage, justice, family relationships, and the like.[3] While a few textbook series still use the thematic approach, this organizational scheme is now relatively rare.

The most important advantage of the Thematic Approach is that it allows teachers to take full advantage of students' interests. Reading interest studies over the years have provided a wealth of information on what students like to read, but conventionally structured literature curricula tend to emphasize "worthwhile" literary works rather than works students actually enjoy. Carefully planned thematic units are able to offer the kinds of novels, stories, poems, and plays that students at various ages want to read.

A second important advantage of the Thematic Approach is that it permits a great deal more flexibility in how instruction takes place. As every teacher eventually learns, there is usually a wide range of reading ability in most English classes, including those classes that are tracked by ability. This range makes it difficult to find literary works that are accessible to less able readers and still of interest to readers of greater skill. In the Thematic Approach, where discussion can be centered more on the theme of the unit than on individual works, students can read a variety of different works that are suited to their ability and still participate in class discussion. A more common practice is to assign small groups of students of similar ability the same work or works and to conduct small-group discussions on both the theme and the works the students have read. In either case, though, the effect is the same: individual differences in reading ability are accommodated.

A third advantage of the Thematic Approach is that it permits a great deal of guided individualized reading. We have maintained throughout this chapter and the previous one that a good organizational pattern for the literature curriculum must provide opportunities for the study of literary works with entire classes, and we certainly have no intention of repudiating that principle here. However, we have also consistently maintained the importance of personal, individualized reading within the framework of the literature course. The Thematic Approach is well suited to meet both of these requirements. While one or two works in a unit can be discussed in common, students can profitably spend the rest of their time in sustained silent reading of works on the theme.

The importance of wide reading is underscored by research findings from the National Assessment of Educational Progress (NAEP) which are cited by Margaret Early and Bonnie O. Ericson. According to Early and Ericson, students who demonstrated mastery of higher order reading skills on the NAEP "were the ones who read widely, choosing books of fiction and nonfiction beyond those required in school."[4] They then go on to explain why guided individual reading produces this effect.

> To acquire sufficient prior knowledge to read new texts easily, students must read widely because only a fraction of knowledge about the world can come from other experiences in their short lives. Since prior knowledge includes familiarity with varying modes of discourse as well as with concepts and their labels, we realize why students who do not read (even though they have no trouble with decoding words) are severely handicapped when required to approach literature (especially that suggested by others) through reading on their own.[5]

To underscore the value of the Thematic Approach in fostering the kind of wide reading that they advocate and that the NAEP data support, Early and Ericson go on to say,

> Personal reading, guided by a teacher who knows the student's reading abilities, attitudes, and interests, must occupy a large share of time in class and out of class. Organized around themes, such reading contributes to common goals and is by no means unstructured and random. What is being argued for here, of course, is the thematic unit, supported by research and theory for more than sixty years and still widely ignored by teacher, publishers, and curriculum makers.[6]

Thematic units are best developed by teachers for specific groups of students because teachers are in the best position to know what their students like and how well their students read. However, teachers looking for published units to adopt or adapt for their students have several resources at their disposal.

The first resource is a set of commercially published thematic unit from Scholastic, Inc., that first began publishing thematic units in 1960 and that began reissuing those units (updated, of course), in 1990. The first four thematic units published in this new effort are entitled "Adventure & Suspense," "Relationships," "Values," and "Tomorrow." Each unit consists of an anthology based on the theme and sixty paperback books in a classroom library that also deal with the theme. The number of paperbacks ranges from twelve to fifteen titles, with four or five copies of each title. The units also include a teacher's manual and study guides for each of the books in the library. The anthology makes possible the study of some works in common, and the library makes possible individual reading and small-group study of texts. Most of the titles in the library are Young Adult novels, but such writers as Stephen Crane, C. S. Lewis, George Eliot, George Orwell, Thornton Wilder, Lorraine Hansberry, H. G. Wells, Ray Bradbury, Jack London, Daniel Defoe, John Steinbeck, and Louisa May Alcott are also represented.

A second resource is the work of the Committee on Thematic Units in Literature and the Humanities of the National Council of Teachers of English. This group published units in a volume entitled *Thematic Units in Teaching English and the Humanities,* edited by committee co-chairpersons Sylvia Spann and Mary Beth Culp,[7] and in three supplements to the original book. Sadly, these documents went out of print in 1989, but they may still be available in English department professional libraries. The units in these volumes are flexible and appropriate for a variety of grade and ability levels. The units can also serve as excellent models for teachers who may wish to develop their own.

Of all of the approaches to curriculum organization described in this chapter and the last one, the Thematic Approach offers more in terms of our five principles of curriculum organization than any other. This approach is suited to every grade level in the middle school and high school, and it can be used effectively with students of every level of ability. Unlike most of the other approaches, this one has the added advantage of offering genuine opportunity for students to provide input in the selection of works, and the units can be expanded and changed with relatively little effort. We concur with Early and Ericson, quoted earlier, that this approach should be much more widely used than it is.

Illustrative Thematic Unit
Nature and the Human Animal

Grade: 7
Time Required: 2 to 4 weeks
Introduction

It is important to choose a theme for middle school/junior high students that is within their emotional, social, and experiential range. The fundamental conflict between people and the forces of nature meets these criteria. In fact, in a Project English curriculum study completed in 1968,[8] a unit on this theme was field tested successfully with seventh grade students of average ability in six junior high schools. Such a unit places an emphasis on outer (physical) activity and includes a generous portion of action, suspense, and adventure. Moreover, the literary selections in *this* unit are all relatively short, in keeping with the more restricted attention spans of twelve-year-old students.

The unit features several perspectives on the relationships between people and nature. They are as follows:

1. nature as a being of neutral, amoral force
2. nature as having a spirit
3. nature as being both a friend and a foe of human beings
4. people's abuses of nature

These perspectives will be developed through the reading of various literary selections and will be the focal point of a writing assignment which will represent the culminating activity of the unit. Through them, students will gain the opportunity to consider the unit theme in breadth and in depth.

The teacher can introduce the unit through the display of several slides of natural scenes taken from the *Life Nature Library* series or any other resource (e.g., posters, calendar illustrations, magazine photos) which may be available. Once these illustrations have been viewed and briefly discussed by students, the teacher can have students read three short selections from the *Life* nature series, such as "The Forest," "The Sea," and "The Desert." Students will relate these passages to the illustrations they have just viewed. The teacher can then discuss with the class the *objective* nature of these illustrations and passages (i.e., natural elements are portrayed here as being neutral in terms of their relation to people). Some assignment which has the students write a few sentences on each illustration or passage reflecting this neutral state might be a good idea at this point. These can be written in notebooks and do not necessarily have to be graded.

The teacher can then introduce a series of short poems, all of which depict some aspect of nature. Several of these will be haiku. The following list is representative of the kinds of poems that are appropriate. Most of these poems can be found in *Reflections on a Gift of Watermelon Pickle and Other Modern Verse*, Stephen Dunning, Edward Leuders, and Hugh Smith, eds. (Glenview, IL: Scott Foresman, 1967).

Salvatore Quasimodo, "And Suddenly It's Evening"
Ch'en Yun, "Twilight"
Nakatsukasa, "If It Were Not for the Voice"
Kiyowara Fukuyala, "Because River-Fog"
Matsuo Rasho, "The Old Pond" and "A Crow in a Bare Branch"
Sappho, "Round About Me" and "Love"
Heine, "A Pine Tree Stands Alone"
Hesse, "In the Fog"

Ruth Lechlitner, "Kansas Boy"
Carl Sandburg, "Lost"
William Allingham, "Four Ducks on a Pond"
Dan Jaffe, "The Forecast"
Eleanor Averitt, "November Day"
Curtis Heath, "Wild Goose"
Jeanne McGahey, "Oregon Winter"
Christopher Morley, "Legacy"
H. D., "Dread," "Heat," and "Orchard"

Each poem offers a brief description, often a single image, of some natural phenomenon. The teacher can deal with them in any way that seems appropriate. The ultimate goal of this activity, however, is to lead students to assimilate a number of objective views of natural phenomena as found within the poems. The teacher may wish to have students try their hands at writing some haiku, thus adding to the collection of nature images to be considered.

The class can then move on to another perspective on nature. Students should read "I Wandered Lonely as a Cloud" by William Wordsworth and "The Lake Isle at Innisfree" by William Butler Yeats. In each of these poems there are key lines that point to the conviction of each of the poets that nature has a *spirit*; that the presence of nature affects people, stays with them, and influences their outlooks on life. The key lines should be emphasized in these two poems and in any others the teacher may select.

Next, students should read Robert Frost's "To the Thawing Wind." This poem implies that nature is friendly to people, that it in fact inspires them to enjoy life more fully. This theme should be pursued with the class through discussion. When it has been established as being a friendly perspective on the people-and-nature relationship, students should read Frost's "Storm Fear." In this poem nature is depicted as being hostile to people. The verbs in the poem help create the sense of hostility. Additional poems, such as Frost's "An Old Man's Winter Night" and Adrienne Rich's "Storm Warning," can help clarify the point that nature is both friendly and hostile to human beings.

In moving from poetry to prose, the teacher can use a commercial film to present yet another view of nature's influence on people. A good choice for such a film is the classic *Stanley and Livingston*. Other choices include *Northwest Passage* and *King Solomon's Mine*. All three of these are older, but they have been colorized and do provide excellent examples of nature-people relationships. Any number of other films can also be used for this purpose.

A prose selection that reflects the sometimes adversarial relationship between people and nature is Carl Stephenson's short story, "Leningen

Versus the Ants." This story is quite short, fast paced, and clearly illustrates the adversarial theme. It also has the advantage of providing a useful link to the Frost poems mentioned earlier. Next, Jack London's renowned story, "To Build a Fire" can be assigned. In this selection, the posture of nature is somewhat more subtle and complex than that found in the Stephenson story. Some questions like the following may be helpful in assisting students to perceive the adversarial relationship:

1. What hints are given that this trip will end in disaster?
2. When and why does the dog decide to leave the man?
3. Explain what the man's last words mean to you. Do they change your attitude toward him? To whom does he address them?
4. Is the man responsible for his own death, or is nature at fault?
5. Does the author want you to assume that nature is an enemy of human beings? Why or why not?

A third prose selection that can be included here is E. B. White's humorous essay, "Walden." Before having students read it, however, it would probably be wise to provide some background on Thoreau, his philosophy of nature, and how he illustrates his philosophy in *Walden*. White's essay is a satire on the deterioration of people's commitment to the preservation and beautification of nature. In essence, it represents a contemporary environmentalist's position on people's mindless abuse of nature, even though it was written in 1948 and is couched in a gently critical tone. The background on Thoreau mentioned earlier is especially important because White addresses his piece to "Henry." It might also be helpful to provide a map of eastern Massachusetts so students can have a sense of where Walden Pond is located.

In the discussion that follows the reading of White, the teacher or knowledgeable students can provide input on contemporary environmental problems in the United States. Students should be asked to share their own concerns about the environment and to discuss specific environmental problems in their region. If the students seem ready to handle it, the teacher can introduce some ideas about satire. Since such a concept is rather complex and, as satire, White's essay is quite understated, this may not be appropriate for all seventh grade classes.

The unit can include a variety of written and oral assignments, but a good culminating activity is an essay entitled "Learning to Live with Nature: Some Problems and Ideas." In this paper students should be encouraged to allude to any of the selections, as well as the film, that they have studied in the unit. This paper can help students clarify their responses to the literature they read and to the issues they discuss.

Illustrative Thematic Unit
The Literature of War

Grade: 12
Time Required: Varies; 4 to 6 weeks
Introduction

An appropriate literary theme for twelfth grade students is the literature of war. High school seniors face the direct or indirect effect of war and/or the possibility of war as part of their entrance into adult life. Today's seniors are members of the third generation to live under the constant strain of possible nuclear holocaust. While a major conflict may not be part of their immediate experience, threats of war and guerilla uprisings constantly threaten the peace of their world in Africa, Central and South America, the Middle East, and Southeast Asia. More countries have the capacity to spread nuclear destruction than any of them care to think about, and it is virtually impossible to turn on the 6 o'clock news without seeing someone in a military uniform preparing for, or carrying out, armed conflict.

Since the Universal Military Preparedness and Training Act of 1948, most American young men face military service as a real possibility in their lives. Since 1960 young women have joined the armed forces and have applied for admission to the service academies in increasing numbers, and in 1989 female troops first participated in combat in the United States invasion of Panama. Furthermore, the cry in the decade of the 1980s for improved cultural literacy among the nation's youth had made knowledge of America's engagement in major armed conflicts, both from an historical and a literary perspective, a need of growing importance.

The topic of war is truly one of the oldest and, arguably, one of the most enduring of any found in the history of global literature. *The Iliad*, after all, was primarily a war story. Poems, plays, novels, and short stories have featured armed struggles in all languages down through the centuries. Today Americans are constantly reminded of the military disaster of Vietnam through novels—later made into films—entitled *Apocalypse Now, Platoon, The Deer Stalker,* and *The Killing Fields,* among others. A teacher who wants to teach a unit on war will never lack for adequate text materials, both celebrated and popular. The description of this unit is, therefore, a bare bones representation of works that are available.

Thrust of the Unit

The major thematic thrust of the unit presented here is that one of the distinctive characteristics of twentieth century literature is the changing attitude toward war evident in the works of writers in several cultures since the end of World War I. To establish this contrast clearly, teachers can present their students with any of a series of whole texts, or excerpts from longer ones, that illustrate the *before* attitude. *The Iliad*, particularly in its earlier sections, can provide some highly pertinent passages. The history plays, and some of the tragedies, of Shakespeare offer several more. *Henry V* contains some eloquent passages, as does *Richard II*. Celebration of heroism and achievement in the armed struggle can be found in *Macbeth, Julius Caesar, Antony and Cleopatra,* and *Coriolanus*. Battle scenes from *Paradise Lost* furnish more, and several of Browning's poems offer still further possibilities. It would be most effective, however, to be sure to include some of the poems written just before and during the early days of World War I. Rupert Brooke's "The Soldier" is virtually a must. Kipling chips in with some lyrical words redolent of Nietzchean chauvinism: "Gunga Din," "Tommy," "Fuzzy Wuzzy," and "Mandalay" all bespeak the glory of war and, in "Tommy," proclaim the real hero of Western civilization (at least as Kipling saw things at the time) to be the common foot soldier, the individual ignored and even abused by society in peace but to whom society turns in time of war.

After these poems and others similar in tone have been shared with students, the teacher can move to another series of poetic selections, this time written in the latter phases of the war or just after it. Poems by Siegfried Sassoon, Wilfred Owen, C. H. Sorley, Thomas Hardy, and e.e. cummings will do the job nicely. They speak of the horror of war, the psychological trauma it creates, the indelible imprint it makes both on the bodies and the minds of those who endured and survived, the impersonal nature of killing in an increasingly technological endeavor, the loss of faith in The Cause, and other such pronouncements of revulsion, rejection, disillusionment, and despair. Two novels which both reflect this *new look* at the phenomenon of people's attitudes toward war are Erich Maria Remarque's *All Quiet on the Western Front* and Ernest Hemingway's *A Farewell to Arms* (Hemingway's *The Sun Also Rises* presents a somewhat more indirect example in its preoccupation with the significance of The Wound as a result of modern warfare). The study guide that follows is representative of the kind of questions that can be developed for the study of a novel in this unit.

Study Guide for
All Quiet on the Western Front

1. What is the relationship between the war and the people at home?
2. Identify several instances of naturalistic description in the novel and explain their purpose.
3. What does the protagonist feel that the war has done to his life?
4. How does his leave affect Paul?

5. Cite several examples of soldiers' attitudes toward superiors. Why do they have these attitudes?
6. Did Himmelstoss do a good job of training young recruits? Why or why not?
7. What does the impersonal, sometimes casual, attitude toward death suggest about the effects of war?
8. Why does comradeship mean so much to the characters in the novel? Cite examples of comradeship.
9. Do you feel the story would have been better told from the omniscient, rather than the limited, point of view? Why or why not?
10. Does Paul Baumer best exemplify character presentation or character development? Why?

In addition to the novels, Siegfried Sassoon's "Attack" and "Does It Matter" both exemplify the new attitude quite vividly. There are other short poems that provide the same perspective. These can be found in numerous anthologies of poetry.

The continuing feelings of negativism, despair, and resistance to the erstwhile noble causes in wars and the participation of common people in them characterize most of the war literature from the 1930s to the present. Novels, plays, short stories, and poems written during this period illustrate that spirit almost unanimously. Teachers can, by choosing among them and presenting them for class discussion, reinforce the concept of changing attitudes toward war. The basically negative attitude is exacerbated by the addition of a series of subthemes which have appeared since World War II and which extend through Korea, Vietnam, and localized struggles elsewhere. Some of the more prominent among these *new* feelings are as follows:

1. The fear of possible nuclear destruction (*Lord of the Flies, On the Beach, Hiroshima*, and works by Ray Bradbury).
2. The plight of the displaced person (works by Kafka, Nevil Shute's *The Pied Piper, Jacobowsky and the Colonel*, Auden's "Refugee Blues").
3. The cause as related to *limited wars* and *police actions* (*The Bridges of Toko-Ri, Platoon, Coming Home*).
4. The reality of the Holocaust (*Exodus, The Diary of Ann Frank*, works by Sholem Asch, Elie Wiesel).
5. Frustrations of human beings in high tech combat (*The Deer Stalker*, Pyle's *Here Is Your Way, Fail Safe, The Killing Fields*).

The topics listed above could be used for small group work or for individualized reading. The works listed, plus a great many more, can serve as texts for this part of the unit.

A great deal of poetry has been written on the conflicts following World War I. Overwhelmingly, it represents the changing spirit discussed earlier. Some of the respected poets whose works reflect this theme are W. H. Auden, Randall Jarrell, Henry Reed, Theodore Roethke, Stephen Spender, Dylan Thomas, Ezra Pound, Howard Nemerov, David Gascoyne, and Richard Eberhart. This is a partial list; the teacher may well have an equally pertinent set of authors.

A number of significant novels have been written expostulating modern attitudes toward war over the past fifty years. Those listed below could be used effectively for study with the whole class or for individualized reading.

Adult Novels

Erich Maria Remarque, *A Time to Leave and a Time to Die*
James Jones, *From Here to Eternity* and *Whistle*
John Hersey, *A Bell for Adamo*
Norman Mailer, *The Naked and the Dead*
Ernest Hemingway, *For Whom the Bell Tolls*
Pierre Boulle, *The Bridge Over the River Kwai*
John Steinbeck, *The Moon Is Down*
Herman Wouk, *The "Caine" Mutiny*

Young Adult Novels

John R. Tunis, *Silence Over Dunkerque*
Sue Ellen Bridges, *All Together Now*
Bette Greene, *Summer of My German Soldier*
Robert Cormier, *After the First Death*
Harry Mazer, *The Last Mission*
Sarah Patterson, *The Distant Summer*
Robert Westfall, *The Machine Gunner* and *Fathom Five*
James Forman, *Ceremony of Innocence*

There is also an imposing amount of high-quality drama written about the wars. One generally overlooked play is Robert E. Sherwood's Pulitzer Prize winning *There Shall Be No Night* (1940). This play, concerning one family's fate in the brutal Soviet conquest of Finland in 1939 to 1940, provides an eloquent expression of the pacifistic attitude toward war. It is stated in direct and moving tones by the protagonist, Dr. Erik Valkonen, in the next to last scene of the play, immediately before his family and his

Finnish comrades are overwhelmed by the Russian army. It would be difficult to find a more emphatic, unequivocal denunciation of global conflict than the one expressed in this play. Other worthwhile plays on the war theme are as follows:

Robert E. Sherwood, *Idiot's Delight*
Arthur Miller, *All My Sons*
Tennessee Williams, *Period of Adjustment*
Stallings and Anderson, *What Price Glory?*
William W. Haines, *Command Decision*
Irwin Shaw, *Bury the Dead*
Lillian Hellman, *Watch on the Rhine*
Berthold Brecht, *The Private Life of the Master Race*
Konstantin Simonov, *The Russian People*

The unit on literary perspectives on war can be developed through a variety of genres and with works from several decades. It offers to older adolescents a chance to examine an aspect of modern life that is significant, terrifying, and possibly imminent. It can be used to link the past with the present and to make a number of meaningful comparisons and contrasts. It can easily be used as a vehicle for introducing some of the truly significant literary works of this century.

Conclusion

No single approach to curriculum organization can ever hope to meet the needs of all students, and it is often necessary to combine approaches, or even invent new ones, to solve specific instructional problems and to accomplish specific instructional goals. We believe that the five principles of curriculum organization we described in Chapter Eight and reiterate in this chapter can help keep curriculum makers on a even course, regardless of the problems and goals.

Notes

1. F. R. Leavis. *The Great Tradition*. London: Chatto and Windus, 1948, p 227.

2. Brooke Workman. *Writing Seminars in the Content Areas: In Search of Hemingway, Salinger, and Steinbeck*. Urbana: National Council of Teachers of English, 1983.

3. Arthur N. Applebee. *Tradition and Reform in the Teaching of English: A History*. Urbana: National Council of Teachers of English, 1974, pp 128–130.

4. Margaret Early and Bonnie O. Ericson. "The Act of Reading." In Ben F. Nelms, ed. *Literature in the Classroom: Readers, Texts, and Contexts*. Urbana: National Council of Teachers of English, 1988, p 35.

5. Early and Ericson, "The Act of Reading," p 35.

6. Early and Ericson, "The Act of Reading," p 35.

7. Sylvia Spann and Mary Beth Culp, eds. *Thematic Units in Teaching English and the Humanities.* Urbana: National Council of Teachers of English, 1975. First Supplement, 1977; Second Supplement, 1980; Third Supplement, 1980.

8. U. S. Office of Education, Final Report, Project No. H-026. *The Development and Testing of Approaches to the Teaching of English in the Junior High School.* Washington, D.C.: U. S. Dept. of Health, Education, and Welfare, 1968.

CHAPTER TEN

Literary Topics of Special Importance

Introduction

The world of imaginative literature is a vast one, and teachers sometimes don't know where to begin in selecting topics, themes, and individual works of literature that will be appealing to their students. In this chapter we deal with four topics that we have found to be of special interest to adolescents. They are the topics of coming of age, of utopia, of social criticism, and of literature by and about women and minorities. Each of these topics can be fashioned into thematic units, or works on each topic can be incorporated into some other curriculum design. Regardless of how they are used, though, these topics represent issues that adolescents are interested in and that they respond to.

Coming of Age

The major task of adolescence is coming of age, of moving from childhood to adulthood. Some adolescents make this transition relatively smoothly and comfortably, but for some the task is difficult and challenging. Between the ages of roughly eleven and twenty, young people must accomplish at least the following:

1. Accept and integrate into their personalities the physical changes they go through during adolescence. Some children experience a rapid growth spurt early in adolescence, some experience gradual growth over several years, and some experience a growth spurt near the end of high school. With few exceptions, the growth

237

associated with adolescence is a problem for teenagers. The girl who suddenly finds herself a head taller than everyone else in her class feels awkward, conspicuous, and self-conscious. She may refuse to stand up straight out of fear that she will call attention to herself and that some well-meaning adult will comment on how tall she is. The boy who is a late bloomer must stand by and watch his classmates surpass him in height, strength, and coordination. He feels inadequate and out of place among the bigger boys who continually better his attempts in athletics. Even the boy or girl who experiences steady growth over several years feels that something must be wrong with them as they watch their larger friends achieve adult height years before they do.

Many adolescents have weight problems that add to their burdens of growing up. Some teenagers are thinner than they would like to be, and some even suffer from eating disorders, such as bulimia and anorexia nervosa. Most adolescents with weight problems suffer from obesity, and they are often the butt of cruel jokes and of thoughtless teasing by their friends and classmates.

An increasingly large number of adolescents need the attention of orthodontists, and some of them are quite self-conscious about having to wear braces on their teeth. Others have orthopedic problems, such as scoliosis, that require back braces, body casts, and sometimes even spine surgery. In addition to being terribly uncomfortable, these orthopedic appliances and procedures often exacerbate the adolescent's feelings of being abnormal and inferior.

The development of secondary sex characteristics provides all sorts of problems for both boys and girls. Boys have to endure the humiliating experience of the change of voice, which almost invariably calls attention to them at a time in their lives when they would just as soon be invisible. Most boys worry about the size of their genitals, and a good many are concerned about the onset of facial hair. Girls worry about the size of their breasts and about developing other aspects of a womanly figure.

Adults tend to forget the torment of facial acne, hair that won't cooperate, and the awkwardness they experienced as adolescents, but for students in middle school and high school these aspects of development are painful realities. Many coming of age novels feature protagonists who go through all of the painful stages real kids have to put up with in their physical development toward adulthood, and many times these works of fiction help them see their problems in a more realistic perspective than they otherwise would.

2. Accept and integrate into their personalities their developing sexuality. Coming to terms with sex is one of the most difficult and
   most important tasks adolescents face. Adolescents have an enormous curiosity about sex, of course, and they seem never to get
   enough information to satisfy them. More importantly, though,
   they have sexual feelings and desires that they have never known
   before, and many of them are confused and embarrassed about
   these matters.

   Friendships become increasingly important to adolescents
   during their middle school and high school years, and youngsters
   have to learn to integrate their new friends into their lives. Some
   parents complain that their children spend more time with their
   friends than they do with their families, and often friendships
   established in adolescence last a lifetime. Making and keeping
   friends isn't always easy, and many adolescents have to learn to
   deal with rejection by other adolescents they thought were their
   friends.

   During the first two years of high school, most adolescents
   begin making friends with members of the opposite sex for the
   first time, and many of them also begin dating. Adolescent crushes
   can be quite serious and intense, and more than a few young men
   and women fall in love with their high school sweethearts and end
   up marrying them. A good many high school couples enter into
   sexual relationships that sometimes result in unwanted pregnan-
   cies, which in turn sometimes cause them to seek abortions, to drop
   out of school, or to marry before they're ready to do so. In any of
   these cases, the emotional burdens of their situations are enormous, and the results are often disastrous. Even when pregnancy
   is not an issue, adolescents who are involved in a sexual relationship must deal with the growing problem of sexually transmitted
   diseases.

   For some adolescents, coming to terms with their sexuality
   means discovering and accepting their homosexual orientations.
   Despite increased tolerance, American society is still largely homo-
   phobic, and gay teenagers often find themselves rejected by their
   families and friends. Many other adolescents experience confusion
   and uncertainty about their sexual orientations, and these youngsters sometimes suffer considerable anxiety and pain.

   Once again, the developing sexuality of the protagonists is a
   major concern of coming of age fiction. In fact, since the 1960s,
   coming of age novels have tended to treat sexuality in very realistic
   terms, and this has created problems for some teachers who want
   to use contemporary coming of age novels with their classes but

have trouble identifying titles that are acceptable within the standards of their communities.

3. Develop a sense of separateness and individuality apart from parents and other adults. This task is the source of much of the rebellion that is associated with adolescence as young people go about the task of defining themselves apart from others. Parents and teachers often misinterpret rebellion as a rejection of them and of the values they hold dear, but this is rarely the case. In fact, most adolescents eventually turn out to be remarkably similar to their parents, but they must arrive at this point on their own.

Sometimes the conflict between parents and their teenage children revolves around the question of how much independence they have at any given moment in their lives. Some parents demand good grades in school, and their adolescent offspring assert their independence, subconsciously no doubt, by making poor grades and pretending not to care about them. Some parents set strict curfews and other restrictions on how much freedom their children have to come and go as they please, and many adolescents test the limits of their parents' authority over them by failing to conform. Some parents are concerned about the people their adolescent children spend time with, and some teenagers flagrantly choose boyfriends/girlfriends their parents don't approve of, saying, in effect, that their parents can't control their emotions any longer.

Sometimes teenagers appear to rebel by experimenting with lifestyles, or at least the trappings of lifestyles, to see how they fit. Attire that may be considered outrageous by parents may be considered just as outrageous by their children and their children's friends, but bizarre outfits are a way of announcing one's desire to be considered off-beat or unconventional, and some adolescents may want to try out that image of themselves to see how they like it. The use of obscene and vulgar language may be another way of proclaiming one's contempt for "hypocritical" conformity, as may be an interest in music that their parents find loud and offensive. Some adolescents become politically conservative if their parents are liberal, or liberal if their parents are conservative. The areas for possible *rebellion* against conventional standards are almost limitless, but the need some teenagers have to try out new ways of acting points to the more basic need to define themselves as unique, independent people.

Coming of age fiction is filled with characters who rebel against authority and who try out new personae in the search for their own identity. One need only think of Frankie Addams/F. Jasmine Addams/Frances Addams of Carson McCuller's *The Member of the Wedding*, who changes her name to suit her new sense of who she is, or of Holden Caulfield in J. D. Salinger's *Catcher in the Rye*, who can't stand the phoniness of the adults he encounters at every turn, for evidence of this fact. This aspect of the coming of age novel makes it highly appealing to most adolescents, especially those who would prefer to try out new lifestyles and personae vicariously rather than taking the risk of trying out new identities on their own. Teachers should be aware that some people object to books that feature overt adolescent rebellion. These people claim that such books *encourage* teenagers to rebel against their parents and others in authority, as though teenagers need encouragement to rebel. In fact, books about rebellious adolescents may provide enough vicarious experience that they have quite the opposite effect the would-be censors fear, but rational arguments seldom have much effect on book-banners.

4. Make decisions about the future. Adolescence is the time in life when young people must begin making serious plans for their future vocations. Beneath the surface of most apparently carefree and irresponsible adolescents is the knowledge that sooner or later they are going to have to earn a living and support themselves. For some teenagers the question of whether they will attend college was decided for them by their parents when they were still in the cradle, and they have little or no trouble living up to their parents' expectations. Some adolescents think they want to go to college but have no idea of the type of career they want to pursue or of what they want to major in, and others want to go to college but know their families can't afford for them to go. A large number of students—a majority in many schools—know they aren't interested in college, but they don't have any concrete plans about the kind of work they would like to do. For them, the future is a big mystery, often a scary one. A disturbingly large number of students have been conditioned since birth to believe they can't possibly make anything of themselves and have no hope for the future. Many of these teenagers have been caught in the jaws of poverty all their lives, and for some of them the future consists of nothing more optimistic than staying out of jail. If they manage to remain in school until they graduate from high school, they feel their vocational choices will be severely limited.

The vocational crisis of adolescence often hits hardest during the senior year of high school, especially during the second semester. There is a prevalent myth in American high school culture that the senior year is the best year of school. Seniors start the school year in high spirits. They are the "bosses" of the school, they reason, the old hands who know all the tricks. In a few short months they will graduate and leave all of the petty rules and restrictions of high school behind them, and they will be *on their own*! Those who are going to college go through the process of filling out applications, obtaining references, perhaps visiting a few college campuses. By the end of the first semester they are still confident their futures have no limits, but they are beginning to get a little tired of school. After all, they're seniors. By the time April comes around, senior-itis has infected almost everyone, and then the college acceptances come in. Until then, going to college was a far-off adventure that knew no bounds, but all of a sudden real decisions have to be made. The luckier ones are accepted at three or four schools, and they have to face economic facts of life. "Well," their parents ask, "how do you propose to pay for this fancy school?" Suddenly the $80.00 they earn each week flipping hamburgers doesn't seem like much money. Or, their parents might say, "If you expect us to pay for college, you're going to have to set some career goals for yourself. Exactly what is it you want to be?" Life becomes a good bit more complicated at this point, and it isn't so much fun to be a senior any more.

The non–college-bound students don't fare any better. Many of them have to deal with the prospect of being turned out by their parents when they graduate. These students are typically even less goal-directed than their college-bound classmates, and, in an increasingly large number of communities, the factory jobs their parents moved into after high school no longer exist. As graduation approaches, many of them become noticeably depressed as they contemplate, perhaps for the first time, what adulthood and independence mean.

Many coming of age novels depict characters in the situations students face in having to make vocational choices. In American society of the twentieth century, what one does for a living amounts to what one *is*, and many coming of age novels recognize this fact.

5. Develop and integrate a personal system of values. Most people acquire a value system from their parents and other significant adults they come into contact with during the childhood years. Children rarely question why a particular deed is right or wrong, and they are largely unaware that they are being imbued with a system of morality. One of the inevitable consequences of adoles-

cence, though, is a growing awareness of the rights of other people and the development of a sense of justice. Many adolescents have trouble accepting what they consider to be the hypocrisy of their parents and other adults, and, more importantly, they are often unsettled when circumstances in their lives force them to confront their own capacity for evil. These teenagers often demand perfection of adults, including their teachers, and they play the game of using the failings of others, especially adults, to justify their own moral transgressions. While this appears to be hypocrisy on their part, it is probably part of the larger process of sorting out and internalizing their own moral values.

For a great many adolescents, religion is a significant fact of life that they must come to terms with. Most adolescents don't really understand the difference between *knowing* and *believing,* and nowhere is this distinction of more importance to them than in religion. As a result, they tend to want proof for such beliefs as the existence of God, and they are often skeptical when this proof isn't forthcoming. Other adolescents are deeply committed to religion, and the practice of religious observances occupies a significant part of their lives. Those who believe in the literal interpretation of scripture are sometimes quite adamant in wanting everyone to think the way they do, but often their unyielding stance is a cover-up of their own doubts and insecurities in their religious beliefs.

Coming of age literature is filled with adolescents trying to arrive at conclusions about the standards and values on which to base their lives. One thinks of Stephen Dedalus in James Joyce's *A Portrait of the Artist as a Young Man* and John Grimes in James Baldwin's *Go Tell It on the Mountain* as two outstanding examples of adolescents searching desperately for a foundation for their religious and moral principles. Other fictional characters experience similar crises as Stephen and John, and all of them tend to parallel in whole or in part the struggle for values that every adolescent undergoes.

In addition to the five developmental tasks described in the foregoing paragraphs, a great many adolescents have to deal with the issue of drugs and alcohol. Survey statistics that are released from time to time show that drug and alcohol use among teenagers varies slightly from year to year, but the problem never goes away. A detailed analysis of the causes and effects of substance use and abuse by adolescents would require a book-length treatment that is obviously outside the scope of this text, but the problem is often a significant one that teachers have to be aware of and deal with among their students. And, like other aspects of adolescent experience, the problem is dealt with repeatedly in coming of age fiction.

Many adolescents also have to deal with bias and prejudice for the first time in their lives. Whether the prejudice is based on race, religion, ethnic origin, gender, social class, lifestyle, physical or mental handicap, or some combination of these and other factors, the result is usually harmful to students' self-concepts. A large body of coming of age literature deals with prejudice, and it can sometimes be useful in helping students identify their own prejudices and in helping them accept themselves in spite of the prejudice they encounter.

Still other adolescents have to cope with destructive conditions in their homes. These conditions range from extreme poverty to brutal abuse by parents or other adults. Divorce often creates confusion and anxiety for adolescents, and sometimes they are caught in the middle of power struggles between their divorced parents. Other adolescents have psychological problems that require professional intervention, and some even go so far as to attempt, and even commit, suicide. All of these problems are confronted in coming of age fiction.

Coming of age literature is no substitute for psychotherapy or referral to social service agencies, but a great many students are comforted and encouraged by reading about adolescents with problems similar to their own. Establishing correlative experience is very easy in most instances, and imaginative entry into works occurs almost automatically. As a source of titles, coming of age fiction is rich indeed.

Types of Coming of Age Fiction

Thus far we have used the general term "coming of age literature" to refer to a very large corpus of works that deals with the vicissitudes of adolescence and young adulthood. This body of literature can be divided into two broad categories that are different from one another in the way the fiction, usually in novel form, is structured. These two categories are *initiation* fiction and *Bildungsroman* fiction.

Initiation Fiction

Initiation literature comes in all of the forms that other literature comes in—short stories, plays, poems, and novels—but of these forms the novel presents the best opportunity for teachers to employ the topic of coming of age in English classes. For this reason, our discussion in the remaining sections of this chapter will focus on novels.

Stages in the Initiation Process

Stage One	Stage Two	Stage Three
Separation ⟶ from childhood	**Transition** ⟶ from childhood to adulthood	**Reincorporation** into society as an adult
• often involves a wound, such as circumcision, tattooing, etc. • serves as a symbolic death	• requires a period of seclusion • includes instruction in the myths and taboos of the society • serves as a symbolic period of gestation	• serves as a symbolic rebirth

Figure 10.1

The initiation novel is a relatively recent phenomenon in literature in the English language. This parallels the fact that adolescence as a separate stage of life is of relatively recent origin. In the eighteenth and nineteenth centuries in England, when the novel was in its infancy and early development, society generally considered children to be "little adults," and children were often put to work as young as eight or nine years old in the mills, factories, and mines that grew up during the Industrial Revolution. Adolescence came into existence as an identifiable stage in life when compulsory school attendance laws decreed that young people remain in school into the teenage years. In the twentieth century, the period of adolescence has lengthened as the age of compulsory school attendance has increased and as the need for more education has made longer the time children remain dependent on their parents. In terms of the developmental tasks we outlined earlier, adolescence may well extend into the early twenties for many young people, even though by then they may have established themselves as contributing adult members of the society.

The first initiation novel in the United States was Thomas Bailey Aldrich's *The Story of a Bad Boy*, published in 1869. There had been earlier novels that featured an adolescent protagonist, of course, most notably the books of Horatio Alger, Jr., but these books presented highly sentimentalized views of adolescence, and the protagonists tended to act like younger versions of mature adults. In Aldrich's book, Tom Bailey, the protagonist, acts like a real teenager: he gets into trouble at school, joins a secret boys' club, and falls madly in love with an older girl. The novel ends rather realistically with Tom's disappointment at having to go to work instead of to college because of his father's death.[1]

The next initiation novel in America was *The Adventures of Huckleberry Finn*, published by Mark Twain in 1884. Henry James followed next with *What Maisie Knew* in 1897, and from there the canon of significant initiation novels has grown steadily.

The most important characteristic of the initiation novel is that it contains an adolescent protagonist who undergoes a series of adventures on the road to adulthood. The term *initiation* is appropriate for these works because their protagonists usually undergo a series of events that closely parallel the stages of the initiation rites of preliterate, so-called primitive, tribes throughout the inhabited world. Hugh Agee studied seven initiation novels published between 1940 and 1953, and found that all of them incorporate the three basic stages of initiation rites, namely *separation* from childhood, *transition* from childhood to adulthood, and *reincorporation* into society as an adult.

Anthropologists like Sir James Frazer have studied the initiation rituals of various peoples and have learned that the separation from childhood is often portrayed as a kind of ritualized death. Frequently, this "death" involves a wound of some kind, such as circumcision, and it is followed by a period of transition when the initiates are taken away from the rest of the tribe to a secluded place where they are instructed in the myths, taboos, and laws of the tribe. The transition period is followed by a ritualized rebirth, after which the initiates are reincorporated into the tribe as full adult members.[2]

The cycle of separation-transition-reincorporation of initiation rituals parallels the cycle of separation-initiation-return that Joseph Campbell says the hero experiences in world mythology. In fact, this pattern may well be part of the racial memory of all human beings that Carl Jung calls the *collective unconscious*. As Campbell puts it:

> Apparently, there is something in these initiatory images so necessary to the psyche that if they are not supplied from without, through myth and ritual, they will have to be announced again, through dreams, from within—lest our energies should remain locked in a banal, long-out-moded toyroom, at the bottom of the sea.[3]

As an example of the separation-transition-reincorporation cycle, *The Bear* by William Faulkner is especially important because, in the words of Hugh Agee, this novel "is the closest approximation in American literature to the pattern of initiation ceremonies in primitive societies."[4] In *The Bear*, the protagonist, Ike McCaslin, undergoes separation and transition between the ages of ten and sixteen on annual hunting trips into the woods to search for Big Ben, the bear of the novel's title. Ike's mentor on these trips is Sam Fathers, an old man well versed in the ways of the woods. Ike learns from Sam that he must enter the woods on the woods' terms and that he must leave behind the tools and values of civilization. Ultimately, only when Ike sets his rifle aside before entering the forest can he meet Big Ben face to face. The knowledge Ike gains is that nature, represented by the bear, and civilization, represented by the rifle, are incompatible. This knowledge compels Ike to relinquish the family fortune he inherits when he learns that it was acquired disreputably, and he becomes a carpenter, an occupation no doubt symbolic because of its association with Christ.

As Agee points out, Ike's initiation does not end in total reincorporation into the "tribe."[5] Instead, he rejects the values of society on the basis of the more profound and more enduring values he learns during his period of transition in the woods. As Agee further notes, many protagonists of initiation novels fail to achieve reincorporation to the extent that many of them experience a sense of alienation from their societies.[6]

Rather than pointing to an inherent flaw in the subgenre of the initiation novel, the failure of protagonists to achieve reincorporation into adult society by refusing to accept the prevailing values of society demonstrates its moral maturity. Huck Finn's refusal to compromise his principles regarding Jim's right to freedom, for example, is a strong indictment of slavery, but, more importantly, it is a strong testimony for the inviolability of individual conscience, regardless of the consequences. Huck's idealism is perhaps naive, but it is not unlike the idealism of many adolescents.

Not all initiation novels end with the alienation of the protagonist, of course. Agee's research revealed that some of protagonists succeed in achieving reincorporation as balanced, well-adjusted adults, and some do not. The novels Agee analyzed were as follows:

The Heart Is a Lonely Hunter (1940) and *The Member of the Wedding* (1946) by Carson McCullers
The Mountain Lion (1947) by Jean Stafford
Other Voices, Other Rooms (1948) and *The Grass Harp* (1951) by Truman Capote
The Catcher in the Rye (1951) by J. D. Salinger
The Adventures of Augie March (1953) by Saul Bellow

Agee's analysis confirmed the existence of the separation-transition-reincorporation pattern in all seven of these novels. However, three, arguably four, of the protagonists in these novels reach the reincorporation phase of the pattern and reject it, not all as nobly as Huck. For example, in *The Heart Is a Lonely Hunter*, Mick Kelly's "adjustment to adulthood is marred by the lack of any feeling of fulfillment."[7] In *Other Voices, Other Rooms*, Joel Knox's "denial of responsibility and independence is a denial of membership in the adult community, a refusal of normal manhood."[8] And in *The Mountain Lion*, "in slowly alienating herself from her environment, Molly [Fawcett] forgoes any chance of self-realization. Like the mountain lion, she has become an oddity and is doomed."[9] Holden Caulfield in *The Catcher in the Rye* is different from Mick, Joel, and Molly in that he understands the necessity of full incorporation into adulthood if he is to lead a reasonably balanced life, but "Holden's initiation is at best a stalemate. He has found no viable mode of confronting the realities of adulthood, and he is incapable, it seems, of making a separate peace."[10]

As alluded to earlier, the vast array of initiation novels that have been published in English since the appearance of *The Story of a Bad Boy* deal with one or more of the developmental tasks we discussed earlier in this chapter. In addition to the fact that there appears to be a basic human psychological need to participate, at least vicariously, in the separation-transition-reincorporation pattern of the initiation rituals, novels of initiation appeal to adolescents because they portray in objective terms the kinds of problems adolescents deal with.

The Bildungsroman

The second type of coming of age novel is the Bildungsroman. The German term "Bildungsroman" is usually translated "education novel," and its prototype and definitive example is *Wilhelm Meisters Lehrjahr (Wilhelm Meister's Apprenticeship)* by Johann Wolfgang von Goethe, published between 1794 and 1796. Like the initiation novel, the Bildungsroman deals with the adventures of an adolescent protagonist, usually male, who comes to some sort of reconciliation with the larger society. Unlike the initiation novel, the Bildungsroman usually follows the protagonist into young adulthood, and the Bildungsroman form prescribes several rather specific conditions and experiences for the main character.

One major study of the Bildungsroman subgenre is Jerome Hamilton Buckley's *Season of Youth: The Bildungsroman from Dickens to Golding.*[11] Buckley gives the following characteristics of the Bildungsroman:

> A child of some sensibility grows up in the country or in a provincial town, where he finds constraints, social and intellectual, placed upon the free imagination. His family, especially his father, proves doggedly hostile to his creative instincts or flights of fancy, antagonistic to his ambitions, and quite impervious to the new ideas he has gained from

unprescribed reading. His first schooling, even if not totally inadequate, may be frustrating insofar as it may suggest options not available to him in his present setting. He therefore, sometimes at a quite early age, leaves the repressive atmosphere of home (and also the relative innocence), to make his way independently in the city (in the English novels, usually London). There his real "education" begins, not only his preparation for a career but also—and often more importantly—his direct experience of urban life. The latter involves at least two love affairs or sexual encounters, one debasing, one exalting, and demands that in this respect and others the hero reappraise his values. By the time he has decided, after painful soul-searching, the sort of accommodation to the modern world he can honestly make, he has left his adolescence behind and entered upon his maturity. His initiation complete, he may then visit his old home, to demonstrate by his presence the degree of his success or the wisdom of his choice.

No single novel, of course, precisely follows this pattern. But none that ignores more than two or three of its principal elements—childhood, the conflict of generations, provinciality, the larger society, self-education, alienation, ordeal by love, the search for a vocation and a working philosophy—answers the requirements of the Bildungsroman. . . .[12]

The British novels that Buckley lists as examples of the Bildungsroman include some of the best known and most highly regarded novels in British literature. These include the following:

David Copperfield (1850) by Charles Dickens
The Ordeal of Richard Feveral (1859) by George Meredith
The Mill on the Floss (1860) by George Eliot
Great Expectations (1861) by Charles Dickens
Marius the Epicurean (1885) by Walter Pater
Jude the Obscure (1895) by Thomas Hardy
The Way of All Flesh (1903) by Samuel Butler
Tono-Bungay (1909) by H. G. Wells
Sons and Lovers (1913) by D. H. Lawrence
A Portrait of the Artist as a Young Man (1914) by James Joyce
Of Human Bondage (1915) by W. Somerset Maugham
Jacob's Room (1922) by Virginia Woolf
Free Fall (1959) by William Golding

Some more recent British Bildungsroman include Strike the Father Dead (1962) by John Wain and For Want of a Nail (1965) by Melvyn Bragg. American Bildungsromane include Look Homeward, Angel: A Story of the Buried Life (1929) by Thomas Wolfe and the Studs Lonigan trilogy by James T. Farrell.

The Bildungsromane is usually highly autobiographical, and the ending is often rather ambiguous. In some Bildungsromane, the protagonist dies; in others, the protagonist sets out into the future with no predictable results; and, in others, the protagonist achieves happiness and personal fulfillment. The absence of a father-figure is usually the starting point (one thinks of the orphan Pip in *Great Expectations* or the young Stephen Dedalus whose father lets him down as a role model in *A Portrait of the Artist*) in the hero's quest. This is important because the lack of a mentor forces the protagonists to seek their own education and development. Money, especially the lack of it, is often an important consideration of the plot, and the central conflict of the plot (e.g., Pip's relationship with Estelle) is usually the result of a personal failing on the part of the protagonist.[13]

With some exceptions, notably *Great Expectations* and *A Portrait of the Artist*, the Bildungsroman receives relatively little attention in most high school literature curricula. One reason for this is, no doubt, the considerable length and difficulty of most of those listed above. However, as coming of age literature, the Bildungsroman offers considerable potential, especially with more advanced students.

The Uses of Coming of Age Fiction

Coming of Age fiction can be used in a variety of ways in the secondary school curriculum. The most obvious of these ways is as novels for study by the whole class and as the main ingredient in thematic units.

Throughout this text we have advocated the study of some works of literature by the entire class at one time, and coming of age novels seem particularly well suited for this activity. First, many of the initiation novels are relatively short, and this factor makes these books less intimidating to students. Second, the subject matter is appealing to most adolescents. Third, there is usually no problem in establishing correlative experience for all the members of the class. And, fourth, there is a fairly large number of well known and highly regarded novels available.

Probably the greatest use of coming of age fiction, though, is in thematic units. Each of the developmental tasks we discuss earlier in this chapter can provide a central focus for a thematic unit, and there are plenty of novels to choose from that deal with one or more of these tasks. The large quantity of coming of age novels provides an opportunity for students to read about a particular aspect of one of the tasks that especially interests them. Likewise, coming of age novels can be included in thematic units that deal with broader topics, such as courage or death. Because they speak directly to adolescent experience, they can help make an otherwise abstract idea concrete.

Teachers who are interested in using coming of age literature will find two regular publications of the National Council of Teachers of Literature especially helpful. *Books for You: A Booklist for Senior High Students,* prepared by the NCTE Committee on the Senior High School Booklist, appears every few years in an updated edition. This book contains titles and annotations of recently published or re-released novels and nonfiction works listed by topic. Its counterpart, *Your Reading: A Booklist for Junior High and Middle School Students,* prepared by the NCTE Committee on the Junior High and Middle School Booklist, also contains titles and annotation by topic, and it, too, is updated periodically. In addition, the American Library Association publishes lists on a regular basis. None of these publications consists exclusively with coming of age fiction, but all of them have ample numbers of these books in their lists.

Coming of age is an inescapable task for everyone. Teachers who work with adolescents can take advantage of this fact to help engage their students in meaningful and worthwhile reading experiences. Coming of age literature is not the only solution to the problem of which works to teach, but it is certainly an important place to look for help.

Utopia

A second topic that is of interest to adolescents is utopia. While there aren't a great many utopian novels available in English, those that do exist are fun to read and offer an opportunity for students to examine some of the fundamental concepts on which society is based.

The term *utopia* comes from the title of a work by Sir Thomas More. More published his work in Latin in 1516 (it was published posthumously in English in 1551), and it was widely read throughout Europe. In *Utopia* More describes a mythical island (the word *utopia* comes from two Greek words that together mean *nowhere*) with a society modeled on a combination of medieval agrarianism and Plato's ideas of the ideal state. The citizens of Utopia lead a communal life, with shared goods and shared responsibilities.

More's *Utopia* is a model of an ideal civilization where violence and bloodshed, greed and selfishness do not exist. It is a disguised, albeit thinly so, criticism of the society that More found himself a part of in sixteenth century England. Another utopian society of this type is the one the American Edward Bellamy describes in his 1888 novel *Looking Backward: 2000–1887.* Instead of using an island as a means of isolating his society from the present, Bellamy sets his work in the future, in Boston in the year 2000. In *Looking Backward* Bellamy's protagonist awakens from a sleep of 113 years to a society in which everyone receives a well-rounded education, works at menial labor for three years after finishing school, and receives the same amount of money each year from the state regardless of the kind of work he or she does. Like More, Bellamy eradicates greed, theft, and poverty from his society and creates a place where everyone is fulfilled and happy. Bellamy's book was extremely popular all over the world, and a number of clubs were founded to attempt to implement some of the ideas he proposed. It remains the quintessential American utopian novel.

A fairly substantial body of utopian literature that is not very well known consists of utopian novels written by women about women. The oldest of these books is Mary Griffith's *Three Hundred Years Hence*, which was published in 1836 (and reissued by the Hall Publishing Company of Boston in 1975). In this novel women have earned the right to attend college and to own property. Mary Bradley Lane's 1880 novel entitled *Mizora: A Prophecy* (also reissued by Hall in 1975) is set at the North Pole. All of the inhabitants of the land are women, and they have perfected new forms of food. *Herland* (1915, reissued in 1979 by Pantheon) by Charlotte Perkins Gilman features another all-female society. More modern examples of utopias by women include Ursula K. LeGuin's *The Left Hand of Darkness* (1978), Marge Piercy's *Woman on the Edge of Time* (1976), Joanna Russ's *Female Man* (1975), and Joan Slonczewski's *The Door into Ocean* (1986).[14]

These works are all serious models of what society can become. There is implied criticism of current social and political conditions in these books, but their primary concern is with creating a picture of the possibilities open to human beings. These works represent the first type of utopian literature.

A typical work of the second type of utopian novel, the utopian satire, is Aldous Huxley's *Brave New World*. This book is set primarily in London six hundred years in the future. Bernard Marx, the protagonist, is a misfit in a society where everyone is "hatched" in test tubes and where everyone is conditioned to want only what he or she is given. Part science fiction, part social criticism, the brave new world is an extension of many of the trends and tendencies Huxley saw in America and England of the 1930s. In the new world marriage has been declared illegal, sexual relations are purely recreational, the drug soma is completely accessible to relieve any discomfort, the aging process has been conquered, and "everyone belongs to everyone else." While Huxley could hardly have known about such modern developments as in vitro fertilization and the sexual revolution, he nevertheless makes some rather startling predictions that make students think.

Brave New World is probably the most stunning piece of narrative satire in English in the twentieth century. Yet, despite the fact that it condemns promiscuous sex as being dehumanizing, it has consistently been the target of censorship. The censors are apparently incapable of reading the book as satire, or they are unwilling to do so. Teachers need to make sure that students and parents understand what the book is really about.

Another modern utopian novel by a British writer is George Orwell's *1984*. In this book Big Brother, an unseen personified force, controls everything that happens. Winston Smith, the protagonist, works in the Ministry of Information continually rewriting history to make it conform to the present policies of the government. Virtually every room in the country is monitored by a telescreen that permits the authorities to watch people all the time, and thought-crime is condemned and punished severely.

One of the most interesting features of *1984* is Orwell's ideas about language. The language of the government in the novel is called Newspeak, and this language, which is an abbreviated and highly truncated version of English, enables the government to control thought. In light of the growing concern about public doublespeak and the politics of using language as a tool of obfuscation, this aspect of the novel is a fertile field for discussion and analysis.

Taken together, *Brave New World* and *1984* present two visions of where society is headed. Unlike the works of More and Bellamy, which are serious attempts to set out principles to bring about reform in society in the direction of the models they present, these two books are obvious satires of the "good life" that most Americans aspire to and that the media seem to promote, if inadvertently. The Huxley text is useful in raising questions about the social responsibility of science and about the ultimate question of whether people can be truly free and truly equal at the same time. Orwell's book is useful in raising the question of dishonest uses of language and of the extent to which government should have power over individual liberties. In both cases, the novels present openings for thought and discussion about society and the principles on which it rests.

Utopian fiction in general presents opportunities for interdisciplinary study that few other topics in literature offer. The utopian movement in the United States has deep historical roots, and English and social studies teachers can easily cooperate on units that study the utopian ideal from both the literary and the historical perspectives. The communal living impulse of the 1960s and 1970s was recent enough that former commune members may be available in the community to serve as guest lecturers, and students can be asked to work together in groups to create their own utopian societies in writing.

Utopias have fascinated people since Plato first wrote *The Republic*, and they continue to interest students today. Once students willingly suspend their disbelief and enter into the world of the utopian novel, they are free to respond to the novel on its own terms. Often, students who read and discuss utopian fiction are better able to recognize strengths and weaknesses in their own society. Learning of this type will pay rich dividends throughout these students' lives.

Social Criticism

A third topic of interest to adolescents is social criticism as presented in literature. In a sense, all literature involves a kind of implied criticism of people and society in that all literature attempts to strip away illusion and to present reality. However, there is a body of work in both British and American literature that takes a critical view of social institutions with an eye toward bringing about change and reform. Charles Dickens wrote social criticism in many of his novels, and social criticism is an important part of many of the plays of George Bernard Shaw. The most important literature of social criticism, though, can be found in a group of American novels written in the 1930s.

The roots of American literature of social criticism originate in the work of Emerson, Thoreau, and Whitman. All of these writers protested conditions in their times and wrote eloquently about the need for change. Harriet Beecher Stowe's *Uncle Tom's Cabin* is an important nineteenth century work of social criticism. In the early years of the twentieth century Upton Sinclair produced *The Jungle*, a novel about social conditions among immigrants in Chicago who are forced to work for slave wages in the stockyards and meat packing plants. Frank Norris's contribution to the literature of social criticism is *The Octopus*, which deals with the conflict between wheat growers and the railroads.

James T. Farrell's contribution to the fiction of social criticism is his Studs Lonigan trilogy. In a sense, the novels in this series are more about the impoverished lives of immigrants in the lower middle class than they are about a clash between the economic system and human needs. However, by presenting the tragic story of Studs, Farrell succeeds in indicting the social institutions that should have been able to help the Irish immigrants, as well as other immigrant groups, settle into fulfilling lives in this country.

While the impulse toward social criticism has been present in American literature for almost two centuries, the great age of the novel of social criticism was the 1930s. During that decade, the United States, like much of the rest of the Western world, experienced the Great Depression. Writers like John Dos Passos explored the conditions of the times in novel form. Dos Passos's most famous work, the U.S.A. trilogy, is a mixture of news reports, biographies of famous people, and personal recollections, as well as a fictional account of his characters.

The most important novel of social criticism of the Depression era is John Steinbeck's *The Grapes of Wrath*. In this long and engaging novel, Steinbeck traces the misfortunes and hardships that the Joad family must endure as they travel from their native Oklahoma and attempt to settle in what they think will be the promised land of California. Students are usually able to become quite engrossed in this novel, and the rather overt symbolism and conflicts make this book very teachable. Another Steinbeck book that criticizes social conditions is *In Dubious Battle*. Shorter and more pointed than *The Grapes of Wrath*, *In Dubious Battle* concerns the struggles of striking fruit pickers in California during the Depression.

Native Son, by Richard Wright, and to a lesser extent his *Black Boy*, are powerful statements about the plight of African-Americans in the United States in the first half of the twentieth century. In *Native Son* Bigger Thomas, the protagonist, murders two people and is sentenced to death. As a product of the Chicago slums, Bigger is a prime example of the effects of bigotry and racial injustice.

Like the topic of utopian literature discussed in the previous section, the literature of social criticism presents excellent opportunities for inter-disciplinary work with teachers of American history. All of the novels of social criticism grew out of specific situations within society, and all of them incorporate history to some extent. In a cooperative effort with American history teachers, English teachers can help their students understand some of the major social forces in the history of the United States. A history teacher may be able to paint a very realistic picture of the Great Depression through facts and statistics, but John Steinbeck, in the hands of an enthusi-astic English teacher, can make that era alive in ways information alone never can.

Literature by and about Women and Minorities

The last of the special topics that adolescents respond well to consists of literature written by and about women and various minority groups in American society. In some ways singling out one or more groups of people for special consideration in a literature class may be construed to imply that these groups of writers are not worthy to be included in the regular list of writers that are ordinarily studied in school. In fact, one of the most persistent arguments against special courses or units on the concerns of women or minorities is that worthy material produced by these groups is, or should be, included in the regular curriculum. For example, with regard to women writers this argument says that really noteworthy women writers—like the Brontës, Jane Austen, George Eliot, Emily Dickinson, Virginia Woolf, Edith Wharton, Flannery O'Connor—are already studied alongside their male counterparts, and the inclusion of writers of lesser stature would weaken standards and open the way to the study of mediocre literature just because it happens to be the product of women. The same argument applies to African-American writers, and the proponents of this argument point to Langston Hughes, James Baldwin, Richard Wright, and Ralph Ellison as evidence that the best are already studied in school.

The fact that the lists of female and African-American writers that are taught in school is as short as it is should be the first evidence that perhaps the argument on literary merit has holes in it, especially when most of the people who decide which works are worthy of inclusion in the curriculum are white males. Obviously, for a writer to be judged worthy of inclusion in the traditional canon, the writer's work must be read and studied. But, if curricula never include any but the best know women and minority writers, how will other writers in these groups ever become known widely enough to be included?

A more significant point, though, with regard to the inclusion of a greater number of works by and about women and minorities rests with the nature of what literature study attempts to achieve. Literature is the best means available to broaden students' awareness of the experiences of human beings in every walk of life. As such, the unique perspective of women and members of minority groups on what it means to live in a world that is often hostile or indifferent to their special concerns is essential for students to genuinely experience literature. Margaret Anne Zeller Carlson says it best when she discusses the place of literature by and about women in school curricula, and her remarks apply to literature by and about minorities as well. Carlson comments:

> Feminine readers need to be able to see themselves in situations true to their own lives as they experience them, to be able to identify with their own goals in many circumstances. In the absence of such characterizations, the same sense of invisibility surrounds a woman as it does a member of a minority race. Invisibility creates a sense of powerlessness and actively undermines self-confidence to succeed and persist. As English teachers, we believe that role models in books, as in real life, make an important difference in readers' lives. We regularly choose characters who demonstrate qualities of heroism, or endurance, or self-discovery, or human caring, because we believe that they can be inspiring. . . . These

characters, then, need to be of both genders, to give both men and women the self-confidence they need to move toward these ideas. Women need heroic role models, just as men do, to see themselves as Doers and Thinkers. They need images of independence as well as dependence, of victory as well as loss. . . . Without such images, a woman can have difficulty even *imagining* herself in these situations.

Second, curriculum changes need to be made for the sake of men and boys. They, too, are being denied the women's voice and the chance to understand the concerns and feelings of the other gender. As we try to integrate women into all aspects of our society, especially in the working world, it is just as vital for men to know more about women. The negative role models that may be presented in schools can reinforce old prejudices that prevent, or at least slow down, a student's ability to see beyond them. Men, too, will have trouble imagining the kind of women they would admire without meaningful role models.[15]

In the case of literature by and about minorities, Carlson's argument can be extended to include the fact that many students have little or no contact with some minority groups, and exposure to literature by and about them can introduce students to whole cultures that they may never learn about first hand. Consider literature by Native Americans. Because Native American literature existed almost exclusively in the oral tradition until the publication of N. Scott Momaday's novel *House Made of Dawn* in 1968, the literature of the American Indian was, and is, largely unknown to non-Indians. Since the publication of Momaday's work, a fairly large body of literature by Native Americans has become available. Some literature textbooks pay lip service to the Native American literary tradition, but most students never experience this rich body of fiction and poetry. As a result, the images of Native Americans they tend to develop are those portrayed in television and movie Westerns, an image that is as distorted as it is trite. The same can be said of literature written by Hispanic-Americans, Asian-Americans, and other minority groups.

A full-scale treatment of literature by and about women and various minority groups is beyond the scope of this book. Our purpose in suggesting that teachers consider including these topics in their literature courses is to help raise awareness of the valuable contribution to the overall literature program and to the personal development of students that these topics offer. As people in the United States become increasingly sensitive to the needs and concerns of people who are nonmale, nonwhite, and non-English speaking, the literature of women and minorities will become increasingly important in secondary education. Teachers of literature can help increase this sensitivity by making a point of incorporating this literature in their curricula.

Conclusion

During adolescence, young people become aware of themselves and their world in ways that were impossible when they were younger. Literature teachers can take advantage of this growing awareness, and increase it, by selecting works that appeal to adolescent concerns. Coming of age literature appeals directly to adolescent problems and needs, and it should be a part of every student's experience in school. Utopian literature forces students to confront problems and institutions in their societies that they may never think about otherwise, and the literature of social criticism helps students understand historical forces that have shaped the nation. Finally, literature by and about women and minorities offers an opportunity to provide students with insight into human experience that may not be accessible to them in any other way. All of these topics are capable of expanding the emerging world of the adolescent.

Notes

1. William Hugh Agee. "The Initiation Theme in Selected Modern American Novels of Adolescence." Unpublished Ph.D. dissertation, Florida State University, 1966, pp 53–58, passim.
2. James Frazer. *The Golden Bough: A Study in Magic and Religion.* One-volume abridged edition. New York: Macmillan Publishing Co., 1979, p 805.
3. Joseph Campbell. *Hero with a Thousand Faces.* New York: The World Publishing Company, 1956, p 12.
4. Agee, "Initiation Theme," p 85.
5. Agee, "Initiation Theme," p 89.
6. Agee, "Initiation Theme," p 89.
7. Agee, "Initiation Theme," p 146.
8. Agee, "Initiation Theme," p 153.
9. Agee, "Initiation Theme," pp 151–152.
10. Agee, "Initiation Theme," p 159.
11. Jerome Hamilton Buckley. *Season of Youth: The Bildungsroman from Dickens to Golding.* Cambridge, MA and London: Harvard University Press, 1974.
12. Buckley, *Season of Youth,* pp 17–18.
13. Buckley, *Season of Youth,* pp 19–23, passim.
14. We are indebted to Jane Donawerth. "Teaching Science Fiction by Women." *English Journal* 79(3): 39–46, March 1990, for the titles of utopian novels by women.
15. Margaret Anne Zeller Carlson. "Guidelines for a Gender-Balanced Curriculum in English, Grades 7–12." *English Journal* 78(6): 30–31, October 1989

CHAPTER ELEVEN

Teaching Literature to Students with High and Low Academic Ability

A great many high schools, both public and private, serve populations of students that are as diverse and heterogeneous as the general population. A large school is likely to have students at every point on the continuum of intellectual ability, from the highest to the lowest. In this chapter we will focus on literature instruction for students at the opposite ends of this continuum. Most of what we say throughout this book applies to all students of all ability levels, but special considerations apply to students of high and low ability that aren't necessarily relevant to all students.

A Note about Tracking

One of the most controversial issues in education through the decades has been the issue of *tracking,* or grouping students by ability or achievement level. This issue will almost always arise whenever the teaching of high-achieving or low-achieving students is discussed. Tracking occurs in most programs that are designed specifically for low-achieving students, but there is usually very little controversy about separating low achievers from the masses because these programs are looked upon as being compensatory in nature, designed to make their clients equal to the rest of the students in the school. (There has been some concern among parents and teachers of handicapped students that these students be placed in so-called least restrictive environments, and this has given rise to the concept of *mainstreaming*, which holds that handicapped students who are capable of being educated in classes with their nonhandicapped peers should be placed in those classes whenever possible. Mainstreaming often affects English teachers in that students who are otherwise classified as mildly mentally retarded or as learning disabled in a specific way may be assigned to their classes, but a detailed discussion of this issue, and of the specialized teaching strategies mainstreamed students may need, is beyond the scope of this chapter.) Tracking often does become an issue with the education of high-ability students because it begins to look like elitism, and elitism is inconsistent with the philosophy of equal opportunity that the public schools of this country are supposed to subscribe to.

The arguments in favor of tracking generally proceed from pragmatic considerations. Believers in tracking point out that instruction can be handled more efficiently if students of equal ability are grouped together. In a heterogeneously grouped class, teachers can reasonably expect wide variation among students in interests, motivation, skills development, and, especially, reading ability. In order to meet the needs of every student in such classes, teachers often have to develop several alternate lessons, use textbooks and other materials on several reading levels, and deal with concepts with some students that other students mastered in lower grades. This leads to a great deal more work for teachers, but it also has potentially deleterious effects on students. Consider a curriculum component like the research paper. In a heterogeneously grouped class, some students may intend to go on to college, and their interest in learning how to write a research paper may be quite high. Other students in the same class may intend to enter the work force immediately after high school graduation, and the fine points of the research paper are of no interest to them. What does the teacher do? Does the teacher teach some students how to write the traditional research paper and give other students different instruction? Won't this create resentment among those who perceive their assignment as harder than the assignments of others?

The obvious solution to the problems created by heterogeneous grouping is extensive individualization of instruction. In a highly individualized program, the skills and interests of each student are assessed, and individual "prescriptions" are created to meet the assessed needs. During class periods students work individually or in small groups on the work they are assigned. The advocates of tracking point out that this system is very time consuming for the teacher and that it is unrealistic to ask a high school English teacher to individualize instruction for 150 or more students each day. Furthermore, while individualized instruction may work reasonably well with the skills associated with grammar, usage, spelling, vocabulary, and so on, it is not well adapted to literature study, which should usually include group discussions of works read in common. Proponents of tracking argue that it is far more efficient for teachers to give their full time and attention to preparing lesson to an entire class than to have their time and attention diluted by having to prepare four or five lessons for each class period.

The opponents of tracking tend to base their arguments on philosophical and theoretical considerations. In the first place they point out that tracking is inherently undemocratic. *Ability* and *achievement* in school is most closely related to language skills, and language skills are largely a function of the socioeconomic class to which students belong. Students from the lower socioeconomic classes tend to end up in the lower tracks, while students from the upper socioeconomic classes tend to end up in *average* or advanced classes. The result is de facto segregation by socioeconomic class and, often, by race.

In the second place, opponents of tracking point out that students tend to work toward the level of expectation set for them by teachers. If expectations are set low, as they almost always are in *basic*, or below average, classes, students work at that level. If expectations are set high, students work toward meeting them, and even if they don't fully meet expectations, their achievement is higher than it would otherwise be. Thus, rather than dragging down students of higher ability, heterogeneous grouping raises the achievement level of lower-ability students. This is an example of the so-called self-fulfilling prophecy at work: teachers expect students to behave/achieve in certain ways, so the teachers unconsciously create circumstances which force students to behave/achieve the way they expect them to.

It is not our intention to offer a solution to the problem of what to do about tracking. We have taught classes that were homogeneously grouped and classes that were heterogeneously grouped, and there are advantages and disadvantages to both systems. The approaches we outline in this chapter, with the exception of courses specifically intended for students with advanced skills, can be used in either grouping arrangement.

Teaching Literature to High-Ability Students

Our concern in this section is with the students whose achievement places them within the top ten or fifteen percent of all students in secondary school in the United States. These are the students for whom literature study is often unchallenging and routine. These are the students who have traditionally fallen through the holes of the web of special programs sponsored by federal, state, and local initiatives. Ultimately, these are the students who

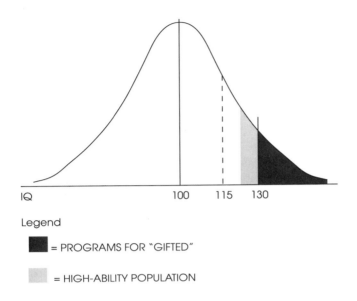

IQ   100   115   130

Legend

■ = PROGRAMS FOR "GIFTED"

▨ = HIGH-ABILITY POPULATION

Figure 11.1 The High-Ability Population on the Normal
Curve of IQ

will run our country and who will make up the bulk of the people in the
professions in the years to come.

In preparing to write this chapter, we searched the professional
literature in the hope of finding theory and research that would guide our
work. Unfortunately, our search turned up almost nothing written specifically about the teaching of literature to high-ability learners. In the section
that follow, we will necessarily have to draw heavily on our personal
experience, and that of colleagues who work with high-ability students. As
this chapter is being written, it would appear that teaching literature to
high-ability students represents a fertile field for research.

Characteristics of High-Ability Students

We have already defined high-ability students as those who fall in the
top ten or fifteen percent of the general high school population. These
students typically like school, and they have a genuine desire to be educated. School is the top priority in their lives, and they are usually supported in their desire to do well in school by parents and other adults who
are important to them. They come to school regularly, and they make a
point of obtaining notes and of doing make-up work when they do have to
be absent. These students are usually good test-takers, and their scores on

standardized achievement tests are generally above the 85th percentile. They are often active in extracurricular activities, including athletics, and they compose the bulk of the membership in school honorary societies and other organizations. They are the leaders of the school.

The students we have just described are relatively easy to spot in the student body of a school. However, there is another group of students who are potentially high achievers who, for a variety of reasons, do not succeed in school. These high-ability underachievers are often bored with the regular curriculum of the school and would rather spend their time reading or writing material that interests them than doing class assignments. Some of these students find the practices of instruction, especially in English classes where the emphasis is on basic skills, a waste of their time. This does not mean that these students have mastered the details of punctuation, spelling, usage, and the like; in fact, in most cases they have not. It does mean, though, that they see these areas of the curriculum as unimportant and that they think the time spent on them would be better spent on more intellectually challenging concepts. These students are not ''high-ability'' by our definition, but they definitely could be if they were to be truly engaged by what goes on in the classroom.

Some students who make high grades do so more because of their dogged determination and sheer hard work than because of their intellectual superiority. These students are overachievers in the sense that their success in school is dependent more on their effort than on their intellectual ability. These students may be slightly above average in IQ, and they typically do not share the intellectual characteristics of genuine high-ability learners.

Both high-ability and *potentially high-ability* students share several intellectual characteristics that set them apart from other students and that require that their educational experiences be different in some ways from the experiences of other students. These characteristics are listed and explained in a number of sources. We have chosen to follow the general outline provided by Gary A. Davis and Sylvia B. Rimm in their book *Education of the Gifted and Talented.*[1] The characteristics that seem to us to be most relevant to teachers of literature are as follows:

1. **Advanced Language Ability** Most high-ability students have language ability that is greater than their less able age mates. They start talking younger, their vocabularies are larger, and their writing is more complex and mature than students of lesser ability. Many of these students are capable of comprehending nuances of language that are beyond others their age. Their verbal facility often makes them appear older and more sophisticated than they really are.

2. **Advanced Thought Processes** Because high-ability students develop language earlier and more fully than others, they are capable of understanding more advanced concepts and of engaging in higher level thought processes at a younger age than their less able peers. This ability manifests itself in a greater ease in perceiving aspects of literature that are often lost on less intelligent students: cause-effect relationships, ambiguity in language, imagery, symbolism, allusions, tone, and so on.

3. **Advanced Reading Ability** High-ability students typically learn to read at a younger age than less able students, and they also read with greater comprehension than others. They enjoy reading and often spend a large part of their free time with books. Much of the time their reading is undirected, and they tend to amass a considerably greater fund of general information than other students. These students, when assigned the first three chapters in a novel for the next class period, may read the whole book in one night.

4. **Ability to Think Logically** High-ability students are capable of logical thinking far beyond their less able classmates. As young children they ask a great many questions, and they aren't content until they know the reasons behind the answers. This insistent desire to know *why* is sometimes annoying to adults when these children are young, but their curiosity may well be channeled into more socially acceptable forms by the time these students reach high school. In any case, the curiosity remains.

5. **Advanced Writing Ability** Given superior language development and superior reading skill, it is not surprising that high-ability students also tend to have advanced ability as writers. These students typically produce more writing on class assignments than less able students, and their writing "sounds" more like real writing. They also tend to write longer sentences that have more subordinate clauses, phrases, and other embedded structures than students with less ability.

6. **High Motivation and Persistence** These traits may not always be evident, especially in potentially high-ability students, but most high-ability students are capable of sustained hard work on projects that catch their interest. Some of these students are attracted to difficult work precisely because it is difficult (We know a high school senior who read James Joyce's *Ulysses* because she wanted a challenge.), and they often take great satisfaction in performing difficult tasks.

7. **Advanced Interests** Many high-ability students have interests and knowledge in subjects that don't generally attract students their age. This characteristic, in our experience, manifests itself most often in science and applied science (We have taught two students who operated successful computer consulting businesses while they were in high school, and we are constantly amazed at the sophistication of some of the science projects that appear in high school science fairs every year.), but we have known students who have taught themselves foreign languages, written professionally for publication, and developed patented inventions while they were in high school.

In addition to these intellectual characteristics, Davis and Rimm also list and explain several affective characteristics that are relevant to teachers of literature.[2] These characteristics are as follows:

8. **Advanced Moral Thinking** High-ability students tend to have greater sensitivity to moral values and issues than other students, although this doesn't mean that they are necessarily more moral in the choices they make. They may also be more interested in social issues, such as injustice to the poor, nuclear disarmament, environmental conservation, and the like.

9. **Greater Empathy and Perspective-Taking** High-ability students tend to be capable of seeing situations and problems from the point of view of other people to a greater extent than less able students, and this leads to an enhanced ability to empathize with others. They also tend to have greater sensitivity to others' feelings. Obviously, the qualities listed here and in No. 8 are both valuable assets in the reading and study of literature.

10. **Superior Sense of Humor** No doubt as a result of overall intelligence, high-ability students typically have a better sense of humor than less-able students. They can perceive humor in the works of authors like Charles Dickens and William Faulkner where other students are either confused or think that the situations or events described by these authors are "stupid."

Davis and Rimm, as well as other authors who list characteristics of able students, are quick to remind their readers that not every high-ability student possesses all of these characteristics or possesses them in the same degree as do others. We know from our experience of working with high-ability students for many years that this observation is true.

While all of the characteristics listed above are positive and appealing to teachers, we would hasten to add that teaching high-ability students is every bit as much work as teaching low-ability students, perhaps more. First, high-ability students demand academic competence, even excellence, from their teachers. If teachers are to gain the respect and attention of high-ability students, they must be extremely well prepared academically. Typically, these students do not "suffer fools gladly." They are usually more willing to accept a simple "I don't know" from a teacher in response to one of their questions than they are to accept a contrived answer that makes it obvious the teacher is faking knowledge.

Second, high-ability students learn much more rapidly than their less able classmates, and they are capable of dealing with literary works at greater depth. These students are not impressed with class discussions that never get beyond plot summary of a novel or story, and they may be capable of reading and studying three books in the time students of average ability read and study one. This means more work for the teacher.

Third, high-ability students often take a great deal of pride in their writing, and they expect detailed, substantive comments. A "well written" scrawled across an essay that took three or four hours to write isn't any more acceptable to them than it would be to an adult. While their writing is fairly free from surface errors in mechanics and usage, the task of reading and responding to a set of papers from high-ability students is demanding because of the thought required to comment intelligently.

Despite the additional work teaching high-ability students requires, they are usually very rewarding to work with. We have known teachers who asked to be relieved of teaching assignments that involved these students, but we suspect that these teachers took the assignments in the first place with a misconception of what they were getting into. If a teacher is willing to work hard and has a solid academic preparation, teaching high-ability students is a pleasure.

Principles of Teaching Literature to High-Ability Students

The methods of teaching literature to high-ability students are not substantially different from the methods used to teach literature to any other students. The need to establish correlative experience and to select works that interest students are as great with this group as with any other. The reader-response orientation we described in Chapter Six is as valid with high-ability students as it is with students of average or low ability, and the ways of expressing responses that we described in Chapter Seven are just as useful with high-ability students as they are with any students.

The most significant difference between teaching high-ability students and teaching those of lesser ability is qualitative, not quantitative, in nature. True, high-ability students read more, are capable of learning more in a shorter time, and produce more words in their writing assignments than average students, but these are essentially qualitative differences. It is entirely possible for a teacher to prepare a series of response questions on a short story that can be used with both high-ability and average-ability students. The average students may be capable of handling all of the questions in two or three class periods, but it may take the high-ability students two weeks to deal with all of them. This is an apparent contradiction to our contention that high-ability students learn faster, but the fact is that under most circumstances the high-ability students will have a great deal more to say in response to the questions than their less-able peers. They will raise issues that the teacher hasn't thought of, and they will see implications in literature that are far beyond their peers. Just as their writing is more prolific, more elaborated, and more mature than others', their responses in discussions are fuller and more detailed. What's more, it is likely that everyone in the group will have ideas to express, not just the handful who usually speak up among average and below-average students. To the extent that involvement of this sort represents learning, high-ability students learn more.

The fact that high-ability students learn quickly and at more depth than less able students has given rise to a pernicious belief on the part of some educators that high-ability students learn regardless of who teaches them or what they are exposed to. How anyone can expect students to learn to read inferentially if they are not encouraged to do so is beyond our comprehension. How anyone can expect students to learn to express their responses to literature if they are never given the opportunity to do so is also beyond our grasp. Yet, we have heard this idea voiced repeatedly, usually by people who apparently had not been among the high-ability group in school. These people are sometimes in positions to make teaching assignments and to determine the curriculum. The result can be disastrous: weaker teachers who cannot handle the behavior problems of students in classes with large numbers of low-ability students are assigned honors sections in the belief that "the smart kids will learn, regardless." We certainly don't advocate assigning low-ability students to weaker teachers; in fact, we are acutely aware that they need and deserve the best instruction available. However, high-ability students need strong teachers, too.

Given the need for strong teachers and strong curriculum for high-ability students, we offer the following principles for teaching literature to students with high intellectual ability. These principles are based on the characteristics of high-ability learners we discussed earlier in this chapter, on the nature of a reader-response oriented curriculum, and on our own perceptions that have developed through our work with high-ability students. Some of these principles, especially those regarding curriculum organization, may not apply to the Advanced Placement, International Baccalaureate, and college dual enrollment programs that we will describe later. However, they all apply through most of the middle school and high school grades. These principles are as follows:

1. **High-Ability Students Need Opportunities for All-Class, Small-Group, and Independent Work.** This principle applies for all students, but it is especially important for high-ability students. By teaching some works of literature to the entire class at the same time, teachers have an opportunity to demonstrate how one goes about formulating, articulating, and refining responses to literature. What's more, students need the opportunity to learn to listen to the responses of others, to evaluate them, and to modify their own ideas in terms of what they learn from their classmates. This is not especially easy for many high-ability students. They know what they think about a work, and they are sometimes impatient with others who don't grasp their ideas immediately or who have significantly different points of view. In Chapter Six we made the point that one of the benefits of the reader-response orientation is that it encourages a tolerance for ambiguity, but this occurs only if students have a chance to hear a variety of points of view. High-ability students may also have difficulty learning to respect the ideas of those they consider their intellectual inferiors, and, even in a homogeneous class of the very brightest students in the school, some will always be brighter than others. All-class instruction provides the right setting for accomplishing all of these objectives.

    Small-group work is important for several reasons. First, in heterogeneously grouped classes, small groups may be the best way of challenging high-ability students by putting them together for discussions and task-oriented activities. Second, in homogeneously grouped classes of high-ability students, there are usually some who try to dominate discussions carried on with the whole class. In small groups everyone has the opportunity to state opinions, to question others, and to *think aloud* in formulating responses. Third, small groups provide an opportunity for students to pursue individual interests within the context of a larger topic. In a thematic unit, for example, three, four, or five students may be interested in a particular book on the theme. They can form a natural small group based on their common interest, while others who are interested in other books can form other small groups. Finally, small groups can provide opportunities for students to develop and exercise leadership skills. More on this point later.

Individual activity is important because it provides a way to accommodate individual differences in interest and ability, even within a homogeneous class. Furthermore, individual activity allows students to become independent learners. Many high-ability students have already developed independence to some extent by the time they get to high school, but the skills they have developed on their own need to be expanded and refined. Individual assignments—and time in class to work on them under the guidance of the teacher—can greatly assist students in learning how to learn independently.

An important consideration for high-ability students, or of any students for that matter, is that independent learning isn't unstructured learning. Independent learning projects will be the most successful when the learning activities are directed toward some meaningful end and when deadlines and products are specified in advance. High-ability students typically take some of the more challenging courses offered in the school, courses that place heavy demands on students' time and energy. Without a specific plan, high-ability students are quite capable of spending the time they are supposed to be using for English on math, science, or history. Furthermore, high-ability students need direction from their teachers just as any other students do, and a specific plan, often formulated as a contract between student and teacher, can help provide this direction. Independent work also does not mean that teachers never monitor what students are doing. Periodic progress checks help keep students motivated and on schedule.

2. **High-Ability Students Need Opportunities to Become Expert in Specific Areas of the Literature Curriculum.** Earlier in this chapter we stated that many high-ability students have interests and knowledge in areas that are not usually within the ken of high school students. This happens because these students often have a real need to fully explore areas of knowledge, and many of them have the self-discipline and resources to accomplish this.

In the literature curriculum, this principle can be implemented by units of instruction that concentrate deeply on a curriculum component that might otherwise be given only cursory attention. For example, most high school students sooner or later meet Beowulf or Aeneas or Odysseus, usually in a very brief excerpt in an anthology, and this passes for an introduction to the epic. According to our second principle, students would be given an opportunity to really get to know what epic literature is all about.[3] They might read *The Iliad, The Odyssey, The Aeneid, Paradise*

Lost, and *The Divine Comedy.* Or, they might concentrate on some or all of the major national epics: *Beowulf* (Anglo-Saxon), *The Shah-Nameh* (Persian), *The Song of Roland* (French), *El Cid* (Spanish), *The Lay of Igor's Campaign* (Russian), *The Nibelungenlied* (German), and *The Kalevala* (Finnish). Or, the focus might be on American epics: *The Song of Hiawatha, John Brown's Body, Conquistador, The Mountain Men,* and *Paterson.*

In a unit of this type, all-class instruction could focus on one epic; for example, *The Aeneid,* and small groups could be assigned to investigate and read one of the groups of epics. Individuals who want to pursue the topic further can be allowed to do independent research and reading on other epics. A unit of this type might take two months or more, and it would certainly provide in-depth exposure to this important genre.

Other topics that are suitable for units designed to develop expertise are as follows:

- utopian and anti-utopian literature
- mythology
- an aspect of science fiction
- Transcendentalism
- Nobel Prize-winning authors
- Pulitzer Prize-winning authors
- Existentialism
- Theater of the Absurd
- Greek tragedy
- one type of Shakespearean play (e.g., the comedies)
- nuclear war
- The Holocaust
- writers from the student's home state

3. **High-Ability Students Can Benefit from Opportunities to Engage in Interdisciplinary Study.** Literature does not exist in a vacuum; it has an historical context and reflects the knowledge and values of the age in which it was written. A novel like *Uncle Tom's Cabin,* for example, grew out of a particular social situation in the middle of the nineteenth century in the United States, and it had a rather significant impact on the Abolitionist movement. The novel makes assertions about the conditions of slavery in the South, some of which may be exaggerations. An interdisciplinary study of this novel might include an investigation through primary and secondary sources of plantation life in the South, as well as the general

conditions of the times in northern cities where the novel had its greatest impact. For younger students, Farley Mowat's *Never Cry Wolf* could be studied as both a novel and as a scientific account of wolves in the north country.

Interdisciplinary study of this kind helps students see the basic inter-relatedness of all learning. Literature is supposed to give a picture of the way things *really* are, and sometimes this idea comes across most clearly when students can see how authors occasionally distort historical or scientific data on purpose in order to universalize their themes. Team-teaching is often a good way to teach an interdisciplinary unit, as when the history teacher directs students' study of the history of the pre–Civil War period and the literature teacher handles *Uncle Tom's Cabin.* Teachers who undertake interdisciplinary work often discover that the whole is truly greater than the sum of its parts.

4. **High-Ability Students Benefit from Opportunities to Engage in Creative Work.** In Chapter Seven we describe a number of creative writing assignments that can be used to elicit and refine students' response to literature. All of those activities are appropriate for high-ability students, but there are a great many more creative areas in which these students can excel.

Dramatic performance is a good place to begin. Readers Theatre offers many possibilities, especially if students are in charge of every phase of the production. The class can be divided into teams of writers, actors, production crew members, and publicity personnel. Class time can be spent profitably allowing students to organize themselves and to get about the business of planning and rehearsing their production. Drama productions of the more traditional kind are also within the scope of high-ability students. We know of a class of sixth graders who produced a scaled down version of the musical *Cats,* complete with costumes, singing, and dancing. They gave performances for students in their middle school, but they also took to the road and performed at several elementary schools in the area. The teacher of this class keyed in on the talents her students had developed through countless hours of music and dance lessons their parents had provided through the years, and she involved every student in the play. For some performances, a student may have worked the curtain, while for other performances that same student may have played the lead. Besides the fun and excitement these students had actually *doing* literature, they learned more than a little about some of the more popular poetry of T. S. Eliot.

Creative activity in literature classes can include the writing and publication of anthologies, newspapers, and novels. It can include art projects depicting scenes and characters from the works the students read. And it can include story telling activities for younger children and the elderly. There are virtually no limits to the kinds of creative activities teachers and students together can devise.

5. **High-Ability Students Need Opportunities to Develop and Exercise Leadership Skills.** One of the obvious side-effects of much of the creative work described above is that it provides a chance for students to be leaders. High-ability students need these opportunities, and the literature classroom is better suited than classrooms in most other school subjects.

As we pointed out earlier, high-ability students will be the leaders in society in the future. Their natural intelligence guarantees that they will have ideas about how things should be done and about how problems should be solved that people of lesser ability won't have. They will be more self-confident than the average person, and they will probably have the academic training and know-how it takes to implement their ideas. What they won't have, though, unless they are given a chance to develop them, are the experience, tact, and sensitivity that will make it possible for them to achieve positions of leadership as adults and to be effective in those positions.

Developing leadership skills isn't always easy for high-ability students. They often tend to be impatient with listening to the ideas of others when they are convinced that their idea is the best. In many cases, they need practice in delegating responsibility and in learning to live with a less-than-perfect job done by somebody else. They frequently prefer to do tasks themselves than to take time to explain to someone else how to do them. And, the more intense personalities among high-ability students often lose their tempers, thereby alienating potential allies.

We don't propose that literature teachers turn their courses into leadership training seminars or that Dale Carnegie's *How to Win Friends and Influence People* be a required text in English courses. We do propose, though, that the literature teacher who is aware of the need to provide opportunities for students to exercise leadership can do a great deal to make these opportunities available to students in the course of regular instruction. The small groups we have discussed in several places in this book are a good place to start. Group work should be structured to some extent, but even in the most highly structured group assignment somebody has to get the group started. In every group minds wander and conversational tangents develop, and somebody has to refocus the group's attention. These are opportunities for students to exercise leadership. Creative projects provide further opportunities for students to exercise leadership in a variety of ways, and teachers can make it a point to ensure that every student has a chance to be a leader from time to time.

6. **High-Ability Students Benefit from Opportunities to Make Meaningful Choices about Topics for Study.** This point is related to leadership development insofar as it requires mature consideration of alternatives. Everyone likes to feel that he or she has some say in what he or she is required to do, and nobody likes this more than the high-ability student. Far from a mentality that says, "Okay, kids, what do you want to learn next?" providing meaningful choices means allowing students to choose from worthwhile alternatives.

Students can be given meaningful choices in the works of literature they read. If the class is engaged in a thematic unit on war, for example, students can be allowed to select from a set of alternatives the novel or play that the class will study in common. If a writing assignment is at issue, meaningful choice can mean allowing students to select the topic they want to write about from several topics the teacher prepares. Or, meaningful choice in writing can mean allowing students to choose to write a short story or a poem instead of an essay.

In addition to helping students learn to make responsible decisions, permitting students to make choices in their learning activities underscores the fact that it is they who are ultimately responsible for their educations. Sooner or later every student who actually succeeds in becoming educated realizes that he or she is the only one to whom his or her education really matters. High-ability students catch on to this fact much younger than their less-able peers, but even they will want to blame someone else, such as their teachers, their parents, the school, and "them" when they don't succeed as they think they should. High-ability students won't become truly independent learners until they abandon this immature attitude, and providing meaningful choices in curriculum matters is one way literature teachers can help students overcome it.

7. **High-Ability Students Need Opportunities to Develop Intellectual Self-Discipline.** Intellectual self-discipline is a *sine qua non*

for genuine intellectual growth, and it does not occur naturally; it must be taught, developed, and encouraged. By intellectual self-discipline we mean such factors as the following:

a. Basing conclusions on fact and logic, rather than on whim or a desire to prove a point
b. Being willing to revise opinions when confronted with contradictory evidence
c. Considering opposing arguments and evaluating them honestly
d. Using language accurately and precisely
e. Avoiding unsupported generalizations
f. Refusing to oversimplify complex issues; and so forth

The teacher of literature is in an ideal position to encourage intellectual self-discipline by demanding that students think, and think clearly. In the chapter on the reader-response orientation to teaching literature, we emphasized the need for students to learn to identify which aspect of a text caused them to respond to the text the way they did. We said that this objective is met by encouraging close reading, and this concept applies to the development of intellectual self-discipline. If students are allowed to make statements they cannot support or defend, they will never learn to function independently as learners. If students are allowed to ignore contradictory evidence or to fail to take all of the relevant evidence into consideration in drawing conclusions, they will never develop self-discipline. And, if students are allowed to engage in sloppy thinking, they will never learn to really think.

As we pointed out at the start of this discussion, the principles we have outlined for the instruction of high-ability students are also valuable for all other students. We must emphasize that the only really significant difference between teaching high-ability learners and their less able classmates is qualitative, but this difference is of enormous importance.

Special Courses for High-Ability Students

Some schools have chosen to meet the academic needs of high ability students by establishing special courses for them. Three of the more common special courses are the Advanced Placement Program of the College Board, the International Baccalaureate program, and college dual enrollment.

Advanced Placement The oldest, largest, and best known program for high-ability students is the Advanced Placement Program sponsored by the College Board. This program came into existence in 1955 when a group of secondary-school and college educators began to realize that some of the brightest students in high school were capable of doing college-level work before high school graduation and that the ordinary secondary school curriculum was essentially unchallenging for them. One possible solution to this problem, of course, was early admission into college after the junior year of high school. While this solution may be appropriate for some students, many are not ready emotionally and socially for the independence of college life. Also, a student may be ready for college-level work in one area of the curriculum (English, for example) but not in every area. Furthermore, many secondary schools, especially independent private schools, are reluctant to relinquish their best and brightest students a year short of the four years of high school. The question, then, was how to meet the academic needs of high-ability students within the high school, the social setting where they belonged.

The answer to this question was Advanced Placement (AP). At the heart of AP is a set of national examinations in a variety of academic disciplines (sixteen disciplines as of this writing, with more planned for the future) that are administered by high schools during a two-week period in May each year. These examinations are scored on a five-point scale. A score of 5 is the highest and is supposed to mean that a student is "extremely well-qualified" in the subject in which the exam was taken. A score of 1 is the lowest and is supposed to represent "no recommendation" by the College Board.[4] A score of 3 or better is generally considered a passing score. At this writing, two AP exams are offered in English. The older and more widely taken exam is in literature and composition, and the newer exam is in language and composition.

Both of the exams in English consist of approximately sixty multiple choice items (the number varies slightly from year to year) and three essays. The multiple choice items are based on passages which are provided in the test, and the student's score on this portion of the exam counts for forty percent of the total grade. The total score on the essay portion of the exam counts for sixty percent of the total grade.

The essays are graded by readers who are assembled from the ranks of college and high school teachers from all over the country. The readers use a nine-point scale, and the essays are graded holistically. On the Literature and Composition exam, one essay is usually devoted to an explication of a poem, one to an analysis of a prose passage, and one to a work of literature of the student's choosing that is appropriate for the topic supplied by the exam. Students are given two hours to read the poem and prose passage and to write all three essays. The other hour of the three-hour exam is given over to the multiple choice questions. On the Language and Composition exam one essay question usually asks students to write a composition in which they agree or disagree with a position stated in a prose passage. Another question asks them to analyze the rhetorical strategies that the writer of a prose passage employs to create effect, and the third question usually asks students to describe something.

The scores on the examinations are reported to students near the middle of July each year, and transcripts are sent to the colleges students indicate they want the scores sent to. How the AP scores are used is entirely up to individual colleges. Some colleges grant no credit for AP scores, many grant full course credit for a score of 3 or better, while others require a 4 or even a 5 for students to receive credit. Other colleges grant placement in honors sections instead of credit on the basis of AP scores, and still others allow students to take an advanced course (e.g., the second semester of freshman English) during their first semester of college and grant credit in prerequisite courses retroactively if a student's performance in the advanced course meets a particular criterion set by the college. An increasing number of colleges grant sophomore standing to incoming freshmen on the basis of AP scores, but they usually require scores of 3 or better on several AP exams for students to be able to exercise this option.

The significant difference between AP and other credit-by-examination programs (such as CLEP [College Level Examination Program]) is that an Advanced Placement Course stands behind the exam. The concept of the AP course has been a part of Advanced Placement since the very beginning, and these courses, as well as the courses leading up to them, are often used by schools to meet the needs of their high-ability students.

One of the most appealing aspects of Advanced Placement is that the content of AP courses is not dictated by the College Board. Instead, the Board specifies a set of rather broad objectives for each course, and teachers are free to structure their courses however they wish in order to meet these objectives. Thus, there are no prescribed reading lists, no prescribed structures for courses, no prescribed methods of instruction, and no prescribed assignments. The College Board publishes two documents ("Teacher's Guide to AP Courses in English Language and Composition" and "Teacher's Guide to AP Courses in English Literature and Composition") that are useful to teachers who are planning an AP course for the first time, but readers of these guides (which include sample syllabi from several schools in various parts of the country) are struck by the enormous diversity of AP courses in schools all over America.

While AP continues to have wide acceptance by high schools and colleges, the program is not without its critics and detractors. In addition to criticism on a number of political issues surrounding the Educational Testing Service (which develops, administers, and scores the exams), standardized testing in general, and the use of the scores by colleges,[5] at least one critic of the AP English exams has pointed out that the tests violate the tenants of both the reader-response orientation to the teaching of literature and the writing-process orientation to the teaching of composition.[6]

In our opinion, these criticism of the AP exams are valid but not surprising. The AP exams predate the reader-response orientation and the writing-process orientation by two decades or more, and the AP exams have changed very little over the years because colleges and universities continue to see them as valid for their purposes. In our experience in working with both AP English exams for a number of years, students have not been adversely affected on the exams by either a reader-response orientation to literature study or a writing-process orientation to composition in the AP courses. It is likely that in time the AP exams will begin to reflect these two orientations, especially as they become firmly established in the English departments of increasing numbers of colleges and universities.

International Baccalaureate

The International Baccalaureate (IB) program is a world-wide curriculum leading to a Diploma that is accepted by institutions of higher education in over sixty-five countries. The sequence of courses takes two years, and students must demonstrate proficiency in six subjects by taking written and oral examinations. Exams in three subjects must be taken at the Higher Level and three at the Subsidiary Level.

In addition to the exams, students must submit an extended essay (4000 words), take a special IB course called Theory of Knowledge, and submit evidence of having participated in extracurricular activity (creative activity, physical activity, or community service activity) for the equivalent of a half day each week of the two-year sequence.

A major component of the IB curriculum is competence in the student's "best" language, usually the student's native language. In order to receive Higher Level credit in Language A, as it is called, students must take a four-hour written examination and a half-hour oral exam. The Higher Level written exam involves either an essay on a literary or general topic, or an analysis of a text the student hasn't seen before, or shorter essays of both types. The oral exam consists of a commentary on a passage taken from a text the student has studied in depth and questions on other aspects of literature the student has studied in the IB curriculum. Language A instruction must include works of world literature in translation.

The Language B component is a foreign language. The Higher Level exam in Language B consists of a one-hour test of comprehension and expression in the language and two essays on literature and culture. The thirty-minute oral exam consists of two parts for which the candidate may prepare ahead of time (for thirty minutes) and one part on literary texts the student has studied but not prepared in advance.

The other four subjects come from groups of academic disciplines. Group 3 (social studies) includes history, geography, economics, philosophy, psychology, social anthropology, and "organization studies" (i.e., business management). Group 4 (experimental science) includes biology, chemistry, physics, and physical science. Group 5 consists of mathematics. Group 6 includes art and design, music, Latin and Greek, and computer science.

The IB program is obviously much more demanding than AP or anything else offered in American high schools. This program must be adopted whole by a school, and the courses leading up to the two-year IB sequence probably need to start as early as sixth grade. As a program for high-ability students, IB is without peer.

High School–College Dual Enrollment

One means of offering challenging courses for high-ability high school students is dual enrollment programs. In these programs high school students take college courses taught on high school campuses by high school teachers. Students receive credit from the high school to use toward graduation, and at the same time they receive college credit in the course. This concept was first employed by Syracuse University in 1973, but since then it has been adopted by other institutions of higher learning.

Under the right circumstances dual enrollment can provide a challenge to high-ability students, but there appear to us to be some potential problems. First, dual enrollment credit is not always transferable from one college to another, so if students elect to attend colleges that won't accept transfer credit of this type, the program does not benefit them in terms of reducing college costs or college work loads. Second, by offering dual enrollment through a particular college, the high school implicitly endorses that college over others which may be more appropriate choices for their students. Third, in most dual enrollment courses we are aware of, high school teachers are expected to teach college courses with no additional compensation and no additional resources or support. Fourth, dual enrollment, unlike Advanced Placement and the International Baccalaureate, offers no opportunity for high schools (and the students themselves) to compare the performance of their students with the performance of students throughout the country. Finally, dual enrollment generally lacks the prestige of Advanced Placement, prestige that benefits students seeking admission to highly selective colleges and universities nationwide.

Of the programs for able students discussed in this chapter, Advanced Placement seems to us to lead the pack. The International Baccalaureate program offers a great deal to able learners, but it must be adopted in its entirety or not at all. Dual enrollment offers possibilities, but it is not without its dangers and drawbacks. Advanced Placement, while also not without its faults, is more flexible than IB and more carefully structured than dual enrollment. After a long history, Advanced Placement stands at the head of the line of opportunities for high-ability learners.

Helping High-Ability Students Deal with Stress

The topic of stress receives a great deal of attention in the mass media and other sources, and it is a topic that teachers should probably know more about. While the following paragraphs have nothing to do with teaching literature as such, they do have bearing on the needs of high-ability students that teachers of literature work with.

Stress is a fact of life for all adolescents who are in the process of finding out who they are. They must deal with pressure from their parents to conform to familial expectations. They must deal with peer pressure of all sorts. They must deal with the uncertainty of their futures. And, they must deal with the demands of their school work. Many adolescents complicate their lives even further by taking on part-time jobs (that often amount to full-time employment), serious romantic relationships, and heavy involvement in extracurricular activities. To meet all of the demands placed on them by others and themselves, they end up staying up later than they should, eating poorly, and not getting the physical exercise they need to stay fit. They get sick more often than they otherwise might, and this leads to absences from school, make-up work, more late nights, and more stress.

High-ability students are among the worst offenders. They typically take several honors or AP courses at a time, participate in more clubs and athletic activities, and spend more time on homework than other students. They also have the stress and anxiety associated with college admissions in their senior year, and this places an enormous burden on already-taxed nervous systems.

Teachers can help the stress experienced by their students in several ways without compromising their standards. Here are a few of these ways.[7]

1. **Improving Class Organization** Nothing is more stress-provoking than last minute assignments, and teachers can avoid this by planning their courses for six, nine, or more weeks in advance. For a number of years we have distributed a day-by-day syllabus of our high school courses to students on the first day of the school

year. The syllabus contains the dates that reading assignments, tests, and essays are due throughout the year. It is often necessary to make minor adjustments in the syllabus, but even with these minor aberrations students have the basic tool with which to plan their time. In a sense the syllabus serves as a kind of contract between teacher and students. By spelling out the contents and requirements of a course at the start of a semester or year, the teacher gives students who don't think they can handle the work, or who don't want to handle it, a chance to drop the course in favor of another course they might feel more comfortable in. Likewise, by staying in the course after the requirements are spelled out in detail, students implicitly agree that they will do the work asked of them. Students who have a syllabus are hard pressed to convince teachers they didn't know an assignment was due on a particular day because they had been absent, and parents appreciate knowing what their children are being assigned.

2. **Demystifying College Entrance Tests** In light of the great controversy surrounding standardized testing, one would expect that college entrance tests (particularly the ACT and the SAT) would be less important factors in the lives of students than previously. If anything, though, these tests have taken on even greater significance than they once had. The rising cost of a college education has made high scores imperative for students seeking scholarships, and some states, such as Florida, have created programs that include financial incentives for students who perform well on entrance tests. The result is a great deal of stress.

   One way teachers can help students cope with the stress of college entrance exams is by reviewing the tests with them in class and showing them some of the proven test-taking skills that are described in a number of publications. It isn't possible or desirable for teachers to try to prep their students by teaching a heavy load of vocabulary or reading comprehension skills just before the exams; these skills take years to develop. But, teachers can help reassure students that they won't be completely over their heads on the tests by working through one or more of the practice exercises provided by the testing companies.

3. **Discouraging Part-time Employment** In 1985 we conducted an informal survey among a group of high-ability twelfth-grade students and learned that 56% of them held some sort of part-time job. These students worked, on average, twenty hours a week, and only four percent said they contributed some or all of their wages to help support the family. These statistics present a rather clear

picture of kids who are wearing themselves out for very little reward. The stress factor must be enormous.

Obviously schools can't make rules prohibiting students from working, and there are circumstances under which part-time employment can help students develop habits of responsibility. However, when the opportunity presents itself, in group guidance sessions, in talks with individual students, in conferences with parents, for example, teachers can point out how much stress part-time employment can produce, and they can discourage students from taking on part-time jobs that demand too much of their time.

4. **Providing a Safety Net for the GPA** Some high-ability students avoid taking honors and Advanced Placement courses because they fear that their GPAs will suffer. Many schools have taken this fact into consideration and have given additional quality points for advanced courses. Most grade point averages are computed on a four-point scale, with an *A* being worth four quality points, a *B* three, and so on. When honors and Advanced Placement courses are given additional weight, an *A* receives five quality points, a *B* four, and so on. The weighted GPA doesn't help a student in college admissions because usually colleges want GPAs reported on a four-point scale, but the weighted GPA can help students with rank in class. They also provide a psychological safety net for anxious students who resent the fact that an *A* in, say, Weight Lifting I counts the same toward the GPA as an *A* in Advanced Placement English. Obviously, individual teachers can't decide whether a school will or will not grant additional quality points for advanced courses, but teachers are called upon from time to time to express opinions in such matters.

5. **Providing a Safety Net for Grades** Grading students is always a difficult and frustrating task. With high-ability students, though, the task becomes even more difficult. Work in advanced classes is almost always more difficult and more abundant than work in lower-level classes, and teachers of high-ability students sometimes feel a little uneasy about awarding a *C* to an essay in an advanced class that the same teacher would give an *A* in an "average" class. Furthermore, teachers who are aware of the stress most high-ability students live with realize that the student may well have written a much better essay if he or she had not had tests in calculus, physics, and Latin IV the day the essay was due. Many teachers help relieve some of the stress caused by the competition for high grades by allowing students to earn bonus points for

additional work in their courses. The bonus work may take the form of allowing students to write book reports on works not assigned for the course, permitting students to write one or more additional assignments with the understanding that grades on these assignments will replace low grades (if the new grades are higher, of course), or memorizing passages from Shakespeare or some other significant poet. This practice eases stress because students know they have a safety net should they fail to perform up to their own expectations on the work that is assigned, but it also makes it easier for teachers to give the grades they think students really deserve. Bonus work should be limited, of course, and bonus points should never be awarded except for additional work. Nevertheless, the opportunity for bonus work can make life a lot less stressful for students.

Teaching Literature to Low-Ability Students

A second group that has special needs in literature study is students of low intellectual and academic ability. This group is made up of students whose

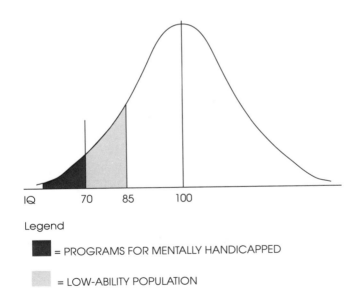

IQ   70   85   100

Legend

■ = PROGRAMS FOR MENTALLY HANDICAPPED

▨ = LOW-ABILITY POPULATION

Figure 11.2 The Low-Ability Population on the Normal Curve of IQ

academic achievement falls within the bottom twenty or twenty-five percent of students in the normal high school population. By our definition, it does not include students who are diagnosed as mildly mentally retarded, severely emotionally disturbed, severely learning disabled, or severely impaired in vision or hearing. It does include students with mild learning disabilities or other learning handicaps who are assigned to classes for nonhandicapped students. The kinds of students we are talking about are those who are likely to take courses labeled "basic" or "remedial" English.

Since the mid-1960s, various programs have been established by federal, state, and local mandate to provide compensatory education for students whose achievement is below grade level or below expectation, as determined by some objective means. These programs typically focus on so-called basic skills, which in English usually translate into language usage and mechanics. When reading instruction is included, as it often is, it usually deals with basic word recognition and comprehension skills, and the materials used for instruction are almost always specially prepared reading kits.

While compensatory education and basic English programs probably help narrow the gap between actual performance and potential performance for many students, too often students who are assigned to these programs or to basic classes never have much opportunity to study literature. English for them often consists of a steady diet of worksheets on grammar, usage, punctuation, spelling, and so on, and they are rarely, if ever, touched by the joy that literature study can bring into their lives.

Characteristics of Low-Ability Students

Low-ability students are as different from one another as high-ability students are, but there are several features they share that have an impact on their education in literature. Obviously, some basic students share more of these features than others, and the degree to which these characteristics exist in students varies greatly.

The first characteristic, and really the overriding one as far as the teacher of literature is concerned, is reading disability. Most of these students have been poor readers since the earliest years of elementary school, and the accumulated gap in reading skills has grown over the years to the point that ninth grade basic students may be as many as five years behind grade level in word recognition and comprehension skills. In addition to skills deficits, the reading disability of these students has helped create strongly negative images of themselves as learners. School has always been a place of failure for them, and every day is another illustration of the fact that they are poor learners. Some schools try to address these students' reading problems by assigning them to special classes in developmental or remedial reading, but these classes are usually too large for the kind of needed reading therapy to occur, teachers of these classes are often hampered by a lack of appropriate materials that interest these students, and the students often resent the fact that their lack of reading ability is so formally and publicly acknowledged by the school. We would be the last ever to argue against developmental and remedial reading programs at any level, but having worked in classes of this type, we realize how little they can accomplish for disabled readers, especially at the upper high school grades. Genuine reading therapy is another matter, but it is rarely available to older students.

A second characteristic of low-ability students is that they tend to be older than others in their grade, and the gap tends to widen as they move through high school. The reason for this, of course, is that they have been retained in elementary and middle school grades, and they tend to fail high school courses and have to repeat them. It is not at all uncommon to find seniors in basic English courses who are twenty, twenty-one, or even older. In addition to the embarrassment that these students often feel at being a good bit older than their classmates, the age difference creates considerable differences in what they are interested in. A junior or senior who is twenty or twenty-one years old may be married, may have children to look after and support, and may be struggling to meet adult financial responsibilities. These students are relatively rare because they often drop out before they ever get that far in school, but sixteen-year-olds in the seventh grade are not terribly uncommon. Students of this age have decidedly different interests than their twelve-year-old classmates.

A third characteristic of low-ability students is their general disaffectedness toward school and the entire educational enterprise. Their school attendance is often very poor, and they tend not to get involved in any aspect of school life outside the classroom. These students do not usually participate in athletics or in other extracurricular activities, they don't usually attend school dances and other social functions, and they usually have little pride in their school. They are truly marginal citizens of the school community, and they sometimes let their awareness of their status be known through sullen facial expressions and uncooperative behavior.

A fourth characteristic of low-ability students, especially at the lower grades, is disruptive behavior in the classroom. It stands to reason that students who have associated classrooms with failure, humiliation, and boredom through most or all of the years they've been in school should lash out against these places whenever the opportunity presents itself. Older basic students are frequently much more cooperative than their middle school counterparts because the ones who are most alienated from school typically drop out as soon as they are legally able to do so. New teachers are often assigned to basic classes because their older, more experienced colleagues have "served their time" with low-ability students and have moved on to more "desirable" assignments. New teachers are particularly vulnerable to assault by disruptive students because they lack the self-assurance and experience in defusing or preventing behavior problems that usually come with years of teaching. These new teachers often attempt to impose order by giving worksheets and drill exercises, and this often only exacerbates the problem and makes the students more rebellious.

Finally, low-ability students have very few interests that can be tapped in school. The traditional canon of British and American literature offers almost nothing of immediate interest to these students, and their relative inarticulateness makes it difficult for teachers to even find out what they enjoy doing. It is almost as though the world of the teacher and the world of the students don't intersect at any point. They don't see much value in school, and they really don't feel that school has anything to contribute to their lives. What's more, an appallingly large number of students of low ability come from families where education is not valued and where the tasks of school are not supported and reinforced. Often parents of these students see the school as their enemy as much as, or more than, the students do themselves.

The preceding paragraphs paint a fairly grim picture of the lives of low-ability students, especially as they relate to school in general and to English in particular. Years of failure, frustration, and misunderstanding leave deep scars on students' psyches, and the resentment they often demonstrate toward school is, in our opinion, entirely understandable. While the picture is grim and the chance of making major changes in the perspectives of many of these students may seem relatively slim, a dedicated teacher who is committed to providing the best education possible to every student can make a big difference in the lives of individuals. Teachers of literature probably have more working in their favor than teachers of any other academic subjects when it comes to arousing the interest of students with low ability, and, while these students don't learn as fast or as well as brighter students, they *can learn* if they are taught well. Many of the activities and methods we suggest in other chapters are as appropriate for low-ability students as they are for students of greater ability, especially the reading activities we suggest in Chapter Three and the reader-response activities in Chapter Six. In the rest of this chapter we will identify and describe some alternatives to traditional classroom activities that have the potential for engaging low-ability students.

Materials for Poor Readers

The fact that low-ability students have difficulty reading is the first and most significant hurdle to teaching literature to them, but this hurdle is not insurmountable. The folklore of education tells of the student who is classified as a nonreader at school but who manages to read and memorize the driver's handbook in order to pass the written test to acquire a driver's license. Whether this story is based in truth is irrelevant; the point behind it, though, is perhaps the most relevant fact in teaching basic students: students will read what interests them and what they perceive as important. If teachers try to motivate low-ability students to read literature that doesn't interest them, all of the pleading and all of the threats in the world won't succeed. If teachers provide exciting materials that speak to their students' needs and experiences, they will discover students who come to class early and who stay late to read.

This principle is a great deal easier to recite than it is to implement because selecting books for poor readers is often difficult and frustrating. There are a great many "easy" books on the market, but virtually all of them are intended for elementary school-age students. These books usually feature larger print than is used in books for older students, and the illustrations, especially on the covers, scream "juvenile" to anyone who comes near them. For these reasons secondary school students are sometimes embarrassed to be seen with them, and the stories and characters often do not interest them. These books are, after all, intended for children several years younger than high school, or even middle school, students. Appropriate titles do exist, though, and one excellent source of them is the booklist *High Interest—Easy Reading for Junior and Senior High School Students,* edited by Dorothy Matthews and published by the National Council of Teachers of English. At this writing, *High Interest—Easy Reading* is in its fifth edition, and more editions are planned for the future. This book lists some 300 titles in various categories, and all of the books are both appealing and accessible to at least some adolescent disabled readers.

The best general category of material for low-ability students is the genre of Young Adult (YA) fiction. We describe this genre in some detail in Chapter Five, and there are a number of sources of titles. The growing realism of YA fiction since 1970 has made this literary form more useful and more attractive than it ever was before to disabled and reluctant readers, and the novels always deal with the lives and problems of teenagers. Not all YA fiction is appropriate for poor readers because not all of it is written on a particularly low reading level. For example, a book like Robert Cormier's *I Am the Cheese* is challenging enough to give even high-ability students a workout. However, like the driver's handbook, the interest factor in some of these books may override difficulty. We had occasion to observe a first-year teacher laboring through an anthologized version of Dickens' *Great Expectations* with a class of ninth-grade low-ability students. The students were restless, distracted, and generally resistive to what the teacher was attempting to do. A month later on a return visit to the classroom the class was busy with Robert C. O'Brien's *Z for Zachariah*, and the difference in the students was amazing. They came into the classroom in an orderly fashion, picked up a copy of the book from the teacher's desk, sat in their places, and started reading—all before the final bell rang to signal the start of class. The teacher later said that the level of involvement was extraordinary and that their class discussions were exciting and challenging.

In addition to YA fiction written and published for a general audience, some publishers have produced YA novels specifically designed for students with reading problems. One such series is the Passages Reading Program published by the Perfection Form Company of Logan, Iowa. The novels in this series were all written by a former high school English teacher who originally wrote books for her own nonreading high school students. Some of the novels are written at the third-fourth grade reading level, and others are written at the fifth-sixth grade reading level. In addition to the novels, workbooks with vocabulary and comprehension activities are available to accompany the series. One of the most appealing aspects of these books is that they look like real books and not like material created for a special reading program.

Some companies, including Perfection Form, also offer books that have been rewritten to make them accessible to disabled readers. Usually these rewritten books consist of novels or short stories that are traditional favorites, even classics. Some of these series also come with workbooks, posters, and teacher's manuals.

Another important source of appropriate materials for low-ability students is the weekly magazines that are published by the Scholastic Book Company. *Scholastic Voice* and *Scholastic Scope* basically consist of rewritten stories, plays, and excerpts from novels and nonfiction works that are usually very appealing to low-ability students. In addition, these magazines contain skills activities related to the literature they contain and writing assignments based on the literature in them. In some schools classroom sets are kept on hand for use year after year—or at least until they fall apart.

Scholastic Voice and *Scholastic Scope* both feature a greater number of plays than would ordinarily be found in a traditional literature anthology. Sometimes the plays are keyed to current television shows or movies, and these seem to be especially appealing to students. The plays can serve as a vehicle for Readers Theatre (see the discussion of this useful technique in Chapter Seven), and students enjoy reading the parts aloud in class. The media tie-ins are almost always the favorite selections, and the use of these works in class can also give rise to some spirited discussions of other episodes of the same program.

Whether the reading material is a YA novel, a novel specifically written for poor readers, a rewritten classic, or a play from a Scholastic magazine, if students read it, the first and most difficult hurdle is crossed. For a student who has never read a book in his or her life, reading *any* book is a major accomplishment and should be treated as such. In causing this to happen, the teacher has begun to chip away at the wall of resistance that has been growing higher and thicker for years, and the success of reading a book paves the way for more success in the future.

The Language Experience Approach

An alternative to the use of commercially prepared materials is to have students create their own texts to read. This technique is often used in reading therapy and is called the *language experience approach.* In this approach students work alone or in groups to write their texts. The teacher may suggest a topic or even a general outline, and students write as much as they are able to on that topic. The students' texts then become the texts that they and others in the class read.

The theory behind the *language experience approach* is that the vocabulary and sentence structure students write are already accessible to them. It is highly unlikely that students will write words they don't know, and the sentence structure is likely to be the same as they use in speech. In addition, the content is virtually guaranteed to interest students, and the fact that they know the author or authors is an added incentive to read it.

This approach is very effective in stimulating interest in reading, and it has the added advantage of costing nothing—nothing, that is, except the teacher's time. Used correctly, this approach requires a good bit of time spent preparing authors' manuscripts for publication. The teacher should avoid the temptation to undertake major rewrites, but all of the manuscripts will probably require editing to correct spelling and punctuation errors. Errors in standard usage should be left untouched because to edit these out would be to destroy the "voice" of the author. If the teacher is lucky enough to have access to computers in the classroom, students can use them to write their works. Most word processor programs have spell-check features, and some even have usage-checks. The use of computers will eliminate much of the editorial work the teacher has to do, and students will probably end up producing longer and better-written manuscripts.

Again, while the reading of another student's story may not appear to be a major accomplishment, if one has never read anything before, reading that story begins to take on a great deal of significance. Once again, the cycle of failure and frustration is broken, and the ground is further prepared for more reading in the future.

Alternatives to Reading

English teachers who have spent years in college reading a vast amount of literature as an English major are likely to forget that oral literature was the very first literature to be composed and that it may still have a vital place in the literature curriculum, especially for low-ability students. Virtually everyone knows that *Beowulf, The Iliad, The Odyssey,* large sections of the Bible, and a great many other texts important in Western civilization had their start in the oral tradition. The rap music that became popular in the late 1980s is also very much in the tradition of oral literature, and some basic students may be practitioners of this literary form.

One effective way to tap the potential of the oral tradition in teaching literature to low-ability students is oral reading. This is a fairly obvious technique, but it is often used unproductively in many classrooms. Usually, oral reading is done by students who take turns reading a few paragraphs aloud. These students almost never practice their oral reading ahead of time, and many of them read so poorly that the oral reading experience is embarrassing to them and frustrating to their classmates. A far more effective method of using oral reading is for the teacher to read to the students. The teacher's reading may need to be practiced beforehand also, but even an unpracticed oral reading by a teacher is almost always better than an oral reading by a disabled reader. Most of the time students should probably be asked to follow the text as the teacher reads it out loud. This allows them to see and hear the text. Usually, learning increases as more senses are brought into play in the learning process, and, by following the text, students learn to associate sound with the printed words. Sometimes, though, oral reading in which students do not have a copy of the text can also be useful, especially in focusing on listening skills.

Another useful method of engaging students with literature through the oral tradition is storytelling. Since 1985 there has been a burgeoning of interest in this ancient art form all over the United States, and teachers of literature can use storytelling techniques in the classrooms.

The Nonprint Media

One of the oldest, and still one of the most popular, literary forms is drama. In the Athens of Sophocles and the London of Shakespeare, people flocked to the theaters to see plays, and one must assume that at least some of the members of the audiences of these playwrights would have been assigned to today's classes in basic English. What's more, television and motion pictures appeal to almost everyone, from people of the lowest ability to those of the highest. The reason is that these media present drama.

Teachers of literature have long known the importance of seeing productions of plays that are read and studied in class, but until fairly recently this was almost never accomplished. Teachers in the past who were committed to having their students view dramatic productions would, from time to time, go through the trouble of ordering a film and showing it in class, but using films was almost more trouble than it was worth. For one thing, films of full-length plays usually take several class periods to view, and invariably, it seemed, the film had to be returned to the film depository before the whole thing could be viewed by students. Also, film projectors had to be pampered, they had to be set up in the middle of the room away from the teacher's usual position, and they were noisy. Screens were a problem, too, if they were available at all, and the classroom somehow had to be darkened so the images on the screen could be seen clearly. More than a few teachers have been known to panic as they watched a film melt on the screen, spill out onto the floor, or pop in two when the projector acted up (as it always seemed to do).

The invention of the video cassette recorder has changed all of that, though, and now teachers can use films with a minimum of difficulty and expense. Literally thousands of videos are available (for example, the media center of one school we work with owns videos of four different productions of *Macbeth*), and productions of some classic works of literature can be purchased for less than $20.00. Teachers can take full advantage of this cornucopia of materials and can use them to teach literature to students who would not otherwise be able to read the text of the works.

The use of dramatizations of literary works always raises the question of interpretation. Obviously, the acting out of a work of literature means that the work is interpreted by someone other than a reader. In the case of plays, this is how the author intended the text to be treated, and the reading of the text of a play is a kind of added-on development that certainly Sophocles and Shakespeare never anticipated. Thus, in the case of drama, the question of interpretation by directors and actors is moot. Novels and short stories, though, are another issue. Obviously, these literary forms are intended to be read and interpreted by a reader, not acted out and interpreted by theater folk.

Our position is that dramatizations of novels and short stories *ordinarily* should not be substituted for a reading of the text. In fact, we have a problem with the use of dramatic productions of these genres even when the text is read. Some teachers like to have students read a novel or short story and then show them a video of a movie based on the work. This may occasionally be appropriate if the point of the activity is to show how the print and nonprint media must necessarily deal with a story differently. However, if the reading of a text is routinely followed by the viewing of a movie based on the text, students are soon conditioned to expect to have the text interpreted for them by the director and the actors. With few exceptions, the movie is never as engaging as the text, but students are often left with the impression of the work made by the movie rather than the text.

This is not to say, however, that movies based on novels and short stories may not be appropriate for nonreaders. This is especially true if the movies are used intelligently to help students visualize the characters and setting and to motivate them to read the work. For example, a teacher might show the first fifteen or twenty minutes of a video based on a novel to arouse the interest of the students and then ask them to read the text to find out what happens. Or, if a work contains a scene that is likely to be confusing to students when it is read, the dramatization of the scene can be used to help clarify what occurs.

The video revolution has helped bring drama to the classroom in a way film never could. Videos can serve as a powerful means of making literature available to students who would, in all probability, never read it. Videos can be overused, of course, and teachers who rely on them for everything they do in literature study will soon discover that students can be just as bored by a video as they can by sentence diagramming or punctuation exercises. However, used wisely, videos based on literary works can engage students and help them learn.

Reader-Response with Low-Ability Students

In Chapter Six we described the reader-response orientation to the teaching of literature and described several activities that teachers can use to elicit responses from students and help them refine those responses. In Chapter Seven we outlined a number of oral and written activities that can be used to help students express their responses to the literature they read. All of these activities, with the possible exception of the research paper and the critical essay, are appropriate for use with low-ability students. In fact, the reader-response orientation offers a freedom to teachers and students that other orientations do not provide.

In the reader-response orientation, there are no right or wrong answers to questions; instead, the criterion for judging the quality of the response is the extent to which it incorporates all of the relevant facts from the text. Furthermore, reader-response demands that students bring their own experiences to the reading act and that they take advantage of their unique vantage points in formulating their responses. Low-ability students are no different from students of greater ability in the experiences they have in life. In fact, because they are usually older than others in their grade, their experiences may be more extensive than others'. At any rate, students of low ability have just as much to offer in the reader-response orientation as anyone.

One problem that teachers may encounter with low-ability students that is perhaps less problematic with students of greater ability is a difficulty in articulating their responses. Low-ability students are not good with words; perhaps this is why they are labeled "basic." Writing is often very difficult for them, especially if the writing task involves dealing with abstract concepts and with emotions. Oral language is easier, but here, too, low-ability students often have trouble saying what they mean. One way teachers can help overcome this problem is through the use of more concrete responses.

These concrete responses can take the form of a variety of visual presentations that students can make at home or at school. The following list is by no means complete or exhaustive; rather, it is intended to be representative of the kinds of concrete responses students can be encouraged to produce.

1. **Book Jackets** After reading a novel, students can be asked to design a book jacket that suits the novel and that would attract the attention of someone who was shopping for a good book to read. The cover illustration can be an original drawing based on what the student considers to be the most important event in the novel, or it can consist of a photograph cut from a magazine or newspaper that illustrates some important aspect of the book. The inside flaps of the jacket can contain comments from "critics," (i.e., other students in the class who have read the novel). If biographical data are available about the author, the flaps can contain a paragraph or two of biography. The back of the jacket can contain a brief summary of the novel, a list of the characters with a brief identification of each, or a list of questions based on the book that might arouse the interest of prospective readers.

   The book jacket can become the basis of a class discussion. The teacher can ask the rest of the class to explain why (or why not) the illustration fits the book, why the critics reacted the way they did, and why (or why not) the plot summary is accurate. If several students make book jackets for the same book, the discussion can revolve around which jacket they like best and why. The book jackets can be used as classroom decorations or kept on file to be used in the future by students who are looking for a book to read.

2. **T-shirts** The T-shirt may be *the* popular art medium of the 1990s, and literature teachers can take advantage of their popularity to

encourage students to respond to literature. After reading a work of literature, students can be asked to draw and execute a T-shirt design that captures the essence of the work. This might involve using fabric paint to enliven a drawing, lettering to illustrate important words or quotations from the text, pictures of symbols that are found in the work, or fabric of various kinds glued on in meaningful patterns. The possibilities are almost limitless, and adolescents, who are very familiar with the T-shirt-as-art-medium, will have many ideas of their own. Again, the T-shirt, as a concrete response to the work, can be used to begin class discussions.

3. **Bumper Stickers** These are everywhere, of course, and students can use them to express their responses to a work of literature. The content of the bumper sticker is more limited than either the book jacket or the T-shirt, but they are perfect for one-sentence statements of meaning or for quotations from the text that students think are important.

4. **Headlines** Closely related to the bumper sticker is the newspaper headline. Students can write their own headline to capture the essence of a story or novel, or they can search magazines and newspapers for headlines that are appropriate. If students are motivated to do so, they can be asked to work in groups to produce a newspaper about the work. We have used this technique very effectively with Hemingway's *The Old Man and the Sea*. Students have written brief articles about aspects of the book, developed advertisements, and even produced an advice-to-the-lovelorn column.

5. **Posters** In this activity students are asked to imagine that they work for an advertising agency that has been given the contract to develop ads for the novel or play in question. They then draw pictures or cut photos from magazines to illustrate what they consider to be the most interesting or most important aspect of the work. A closely related activity is the collage. Students cut out words and pictures that illustrate the work. Again, these responses can serve as the center of class discussion, especially of why the student who produced the response chose to emphasize particular aspects of the work.

6. **Real Objects** Many works of literature contain any number of objects that are of importance, either symbolically or to the operation of the plot. Students can be asked to bring to class an object that appears in the work and then to explain the object's function. Or, students can be asked to bring in objects that remind them of some aspect of the work and to explain why they chose the object.

A word of caution is in order here. Many works contain objects that are dangerous, illegal, or otherwise inappropriate for students to have in their possession at school. If this activity is chosen, teachers should make it a point to remind students that some objects cannot be brought to school and to find out ahead of time which objects students plan to bring so that inappropriate objects can be kept off school premises. If teachers fear their students will not comply with these guidelines or will not exercise good judgment in this regard, students can be asked to bring pictures of the objects instead of the objects themselves.

As students develop confidence in their ability to respond to literature, verbal responses will become easier for them to make. As in every other aspect of teaching literature to low-ability students, and of teaching literature to students of every ability level, the teacher must be willing to begin where students are and to work with them with patience and kindness to help them deepen and broaden their responses to literary works. Success builds on success, and for students for whom success in school has been rare, every minute achievement is important. The reader-response orientation fosters the kind of environment that makes success possible.

Conclusion

The needs of high-ability and low-ability students in the study of literature are very different from one another, but both of these groups deserve the very best the American education system can provide. Instruction in literature that begins with an awareness of these needs will do more to improve the overall quality of the education of these populations than instruction in almost any other subject. Teachers of literature who are committed to this idea can truly change the lives of their students of any level of ability.

Notes

1. Gary A. Davis and Sylvia B. Rimm. *Education of the Gifted and Talented. 2nd ed. Englewood Cliffs, NJ: Prentice-Hall, Inc., 1989, pp 20–22. Adapted by permission.*
2. Davis and Rimm, *Education*, p 26. Adapted by permission.
3. An excellent resource for teachers interested in teaching epic poetry is Margaret Fleming, ed. *Teaching the Epic.* Urbana: National Council of Teachers of English, 1974. Another valuable resource, which includes discussion questions and a bibliography of paperback editions of a number of epics is Donna G. Rosenberg, "Mythology for the Gifted Student: A Recipe for Enjoyment and Self-Knowledge." *Illinois English Bulletin 75: 67–77, Winter 1988.*

4. "Advanced Placement Course Description: English." N.p.: College Entrance Examination Board, 1989, p 65.

5. For a full discussion of these and other political issues surrounding AP see James B. Vopat "The Politics of Advanced Placement English." in Gary A. Olson, et al, eds. *Advanced Placement English: Theory, Politics, and Pedagogy.* Portsmouth, NH: Boynton/Cook Publishers, a division of Heinemann Educational Books, Inc., 1989, pp 52–64.

6. David Foster. "The Theory of AP English: A Critique." in Gary A. Olson, et al, eds. *Advanced Placement English: Theory, Politics, and Pedagogy.* Portsmouth, NH: Boynton/Cook Publishers, a division of Heinemann Educational Books, Inc., 1989, pp 3–24.

7. The first three ways of reducing stress were suggested by Kay Jacob, "Stress and the Gifted Student of English." *Illinois English Bulletin* 75: 19–25, Winter 1988.

CHAPTER TWELVE

Censorship and Literature Study

Introduction to the Issue

In the opening chapter of this book, a series of objectives in the study of literature by young people are proposed. One has to do with developing critical reading skills, another concerns the expansion of students' cultural awareness, and so on. At the heart of any statement of objectives, however, lies the issue of relevance. Any literary text presents a portrayal of human experience. To comprehend such a portrayal beyond a superficial level, readers must be able to find some correlates in their experience with the imaginative situation found in the text. Of course, the experiences do not have to be literally the same. In the revised edition of *Literature as Exploration,* Louise Rosenblatt makes the following point: "In order to share the author's insight, the reader need not have had identical experiences, but he must have experienced some needs, emotions, concepts, some circumstances and relationships, from which he can construct the new situations, emotions, and understandings set forth in the literary work."[1] When the two experiences cross, the text can be internalized by the reader, sometimes intensively so. Readers will react to such a text in proportion to the degree to which they empathize with the situation they find. It is this correlation, to a large degree, which makes such a text *meaningful.*

Earlier in this book, in the chapter on literature and reading ability, the work of Harold Herber was discussed. Herber posed three levels of reading comprehension in his text *Teaching Reading in the Content Areas:* a literal level, followed by an interpretive one, and culminated by one of application. Relating this final level of Herber's to literature study, one could reasonably conclude that such study has its greatest impact on people who can gain new and helpful insights into ways they are living their lives by reflecting on themes implicit in the works they are reading. Such a level of comprehension is both useful and profound.

In still a later chapter, the issue of reading interest was reviewed. Much emphasis was placed on the degree to which the general interests of young people change as they move through adolescence into adulthood and on the ways in which those changing interests can be found in the newly formed reading interests of these young people. One of the consistent demands made by these adolescents during this evolutionary period, however, was that the materials they read reflect *reality*. Then it was noted that young people's definitions of what is *real* differ almost on a one-to-one basis. Still, the raising of the reality criterion has continued to be a consistent one with young readers. They tend to reject the world of magic, whimsy, and fantasy as their newly established penchant grows for texts to which they can relate their own life situations, as well as those of which they are becoming aware.

Literature teachers who attempt to provide their students with meaningful literary experiences, therefore, must search for texts with which those students can genuinely interact. That search should be accompanied by the criterion of literary realism so that the students encountering those works will feel they are involved in bona fide representations of life situations. Furthermore, these teachers will probably want to find texts which present the contemporary world, a world with which their young readers can most readily empathize. When such texts become the focus of classroom consideration, students can find their best opportunities to apply what they perceive in these works to their own lives.

Such a search, while being pedagogically sound, is not without risk. In the American system of education, schools are subject most directly and constantly to local control. While states, regions, and, to a much more limited degree, federal agencies influence what is taught, it is the local school board (or board of trustees in the case of private institutions) which really makes and enforces the rules. One of the major elements regulated by those boards is the curriculum.

School boards which function in communities large and small are elected by the people. The requirements for school board candidacy are typically minimal in terms of educational background and vocational affiliation. Actually, literary scholarship is virtually *never* an attribute sought in such candidates. What that leads to is considerable naivete among the overwhelming majority of board members who are currently deciding the overall curricula of schools in the United States, including what constitutes appropriate literature for study in school.

Communities do have mores which dictate their perception of what makes for a good education and what constitutes a bad one. (After all, they all went to school and turned out okay, didn't they?) Many citizens fret constantly over what is wholesome and what is objectionable in the curriculum. And many more are subject to persuasion by pressure groups which have a particular political, economic, spiritual, or social ax to grind. Thus, when certain curricular offerings are reviewed and certain texts within those curricula are scrutinized, the result can be anger, dissent, suspicion, and most of all, controversy.

One of the driving forces behind such controversy can be seen in the belief of a large number of Americans that the real objectives of public education should be those of training. That training should, in the eyes of such citizens, be characterized by narrowly concerned religious/spiritual values, conservative political orthodoxy, and those techniques which lead young people to a tranquil acceptance of their *place* in the work force. Closely related to those seldom overtly espoused objectives is the stubborn, persistent belief that the school system should not reflect the separation of church and state, that pluralism in deliberation of values and tastes is subversive, and that the true spirit of all school curricula should be a Christian one. When teachers choose books whose themes seem to reflect a departure from such orthodoxy, citizens have, over the decades, raised their objections, often in strident tones. The term used to denote most forms of those expressed objections is *censorship*.

While censorship incidents can be found throughout the history of education in our country, the years since 1975 have seen a significant increase in the activity of organized citizens' groups whose goal has been to review, to challenge, and to remove books from the schools within their communities. A substantial proportion of such books are literary in nature. Thus, the English teachers of the present must be both vigilant and judicious as never before in regard to what works are being distributed and/or assigned for all-class study.

A significant impetus for the new wave of censorship cases can be identified in what has come to be known as the *Hatch amendment*. In early 1979, the United States Congress passed, as part of an omnibus education bill, an amendment sponsored by U.S. Senator Orrin Hatch of Utah. This amendment made mandatory the granting of a request by any parent to examine—and possibly challenge—"all instructional materials used in any research or experimentation program supported by federal funds." While the expressed scope was directed toward those materials used for psychological testing in public schools, its implications were seized on by a number of late 1970s–early 1980s conservative pressure groups which were beginning their assault on several areas of public school programs. The *Hatch amendment* opened the door for those groups to scrutinize and often demand the removal of a number of curricular materials, a procedure they are still implementing as this book is being written.

The names of some of the more nationally prominent of such groups formed to challenge school textbooks are provided below. Many of them are familiar ones to even the casual observer; they have received a great deal of publicity in the media both in the United States and abroad.

1. The Educational Research Analysis Corporation formed by Mel and Norma Gabler of Texas
2. The Moral Majority (later the Liberty Forum) under Jerry Falwell
3. The Eagle Forum under Phyllis Schlafly
4. The Concerned Women of America under Beverly La Haye
5. The National Legal Foundation under Pat Robertson
6. The Citizens United for Responsible Education under Jimmy Swaggart
7. The National Association of Christian Educators under Robert L. Symonds [The goals of this organization are (a) to bring public education back under the control of Christians; (b) to take control of all local school boards; and, (c) to call for the removal of all counter-productive, secular humanist curricula from local schools.]

Kinds of Censorship

After looking at some of the censorship groups functioning in this country today, a logical question is: What kinds of censorship have been and are being practiced by concerned individual citizens and groups such as these? The catalogue includes five, all of which are related in one way or another to English teachers' decisions to involve their students in various aspects of the discipline. The first of these can be labeled *classic* because it includes the oldest and the most widespread censorship incidents.

1. **Classic Censorship** The most familiar type of censorship follows a predictable scenario: a teacher selects a work of literature for all-class consideration. A student in the class brings a copy of the text home. Then one or both of the student's parents notice the text; or, another citizen happens to learn that the text is being studied; or, another teacher mentions the text to an *interested* citizen. In any of these instances, the parent or citizen is incensed by the fact that the text in question is being taught in the school. That individual makes the objection known at the school where the text is being taught.

The citizen in question makes the school aware in one of several ways: by a letter to the teacher, by telephoning or visiting the teacher, by informing the teacher's department head or principal, or by contacting a school board member or the district superintendent. In one way or another, the teacher is asked to account for the selection of this text for all-class use. That may occur through a dialogue with the unhappy citizen. Such dialogues may include the department head and/or building administrator. The result of such a meeting may result in the withdrawal of the text or (less likely) the citizen becoming convinced that the text has genuine educational value. In a distressingly large number of cases, the principal will demand that the text be peremptorily removed from the classroom without further deliberation. Or the citizen's demand may be redirected to the superintendent's office or the school board's next agenda.

Most school districts have in place a fixed policy for dealing with citizens' complaints about texts being taught in their schools. Many of these policies have been adopted since the passing of the *Hatch amendment* and the use of that amendment by the groups previously identified to challenge books of all kinds and in all regions of the country. A sizable number of these policies have been patterned after the guidelines set forth in the National Council of Teachers of English (NCTE) publication, ''The Students' Right to Know'':[2]

Citizen's Request for Reconsideration of a Work

Paperback _____

Author _____   Hardcover _____

Title _____

Publisher (if known) _____

Request Initiated by _____

Telephone _____   Address _____

City _____   Zip Code _____

Complaint represents

_____ Himself/Herself

_____ (Name Organization) _____

_____ (Identify other group) _____

1. Have you been able to discuss this work with the teacher or librarian who ordered it or who used it?

_____ Yes   _____ No

2. What do you understand to be the general purpose for using this work?

a. Provide support for a unit in the curriculum?

_____ Yes   _____ No

b. Provide a learning experience for the reader in one kind of literature?

_____ Yes   _____ No

c. Other _____

_____

3. Did the general purpose for the use of the work, as described by the teacher or librarian, seem a suitable one to you?

_____ Yes   _____ No

If not, please explain. _____

_____

4. What seems, to you, to be the general purpose of the author in this book? _____

_____

5. In what ways do you think a work of this nature is not suitable for the use the teacher or librarian wishes to carry out? _____

_____

6. Have you been able to learn what is the students' response to this work?

_____ Yes   _____ No

7. What response did the students make? _____

_____

8. Have you been able to learn from your school library what book reviewers or other students of literature have written about this work?

_____ Yes   _____ No

9. Do you have negative reviews of the book?

_____ Yes   _____ No

10. Would you like the teacher or librarian to give you a written summary of what book reviewers and other sutdents have written about this book or film?

_____ Yes   _____ No

11. What would you like your library/school to do about this work?

_____ Do not assign/lend it to my child.

_____ Return it to the staff selection committee/department for re-evaluation.

_____ Other—Please explain. _____

_____

12. In its place, what work would you recommend that would convey as valuable a picture and perspective of the subject treated? _____

_____

Signature _____

Date _____

As can be inferred, this process can follow one of several progressions, can be relatively brief and simple or, as is often the case, can be lengthy and unpleasant. One unavoidable fact is that such encounters can and do put some teachers' careers on the line. Indeed, the classroom use of the novel *The Catcher in the Rye* by J.D. Salinger (1951) has cost more teachers their jobs than any other single publication in the history of U.S. education.

To attempt to catalogue even a representative number of censorship battles which have been waged in recent years over *objectionable* literary selections in public school classrooms would require a text longer than this one. For more information on this topic, the reader can consult the Bibliography (page 321) where a reasonably extensive listing can be found. One truly significant case will be reviewed, however; for several reasons, it is a crucial one for English teachers:

In 1976, the Island Trees School Board, representing a group of Long Island, New York communities, had a number of books, mostly modern fiction, removed from the library shelves of the high school in Leavittown. The Board charged that the books were

"anti-American, anti-Christian, anti-Semitic, and just plain filthy."
Among them were Kurt Vonnegut's *Slaughterhouse Five,* Desmond
Morris' *The Naked Ape,* and Alice Childress' *A Hero Ain't Nothing
but a Sandwich.* Backed by the American Civil Liberties Union, a
group of parents sued the school board under the First Amendment to the U.S. Constitution. The case wound its way through the
federal court system, ending up in the U.S. Supreme Court in 1983.
It is an important case for three reasons:

1. It was the first school censorship case to reach the Supreme
   Court in modern times.
2. It occurred in an affluent Northeastern suburb generally regarded as politically *liberal.* Leavittown is, in fact, a bedroom
   community for executive types who work in New York City.
3. It pitted two fundamental American rights against each other:
   the right of freedom of expression versus the right of local
   communities to control their schools.

For all of these reasons, the case drew national attention as it
followed its ponderous route through the courts. In April, 1983,
the Supreme Court ruled in a 5 to 4 vote that a lower federal court
had erred in dismissing the case without a trial. The crux of the
argument was that the school board had removed books from a
library without showing a compelling state interest in doing so.
The court granted a preliminary injunction to cause the board to
restore the books pending the outcome of the trial, but this point
had previously been mooted when a new board had restored the
books before the case got to the Supreme Court. The Supreme
Court really didn't deal with the substantive issue of whether or
not the books should be removed; they left that for the trial court
to decide. However, by voting that the original dismissal by the
district court had been an error, the Supreme Court upheld the
principle of free access to books *that had already been made available
by the school board for student use.* (Voting with the majority: Justices
White, Blackmun, Brennan, Marshall, and Stevens. Voting with the
minority: Justices Powell, Rehnquist, O'Connor, and Chief Justice
Burger.) The Court warned that their decision applied only to
school libraries. Writing for the majority, Justice William Brennan
stated, "This case is about a library, not a school's curriculum . . .
we freely concede that the school board has the right and duty to
supervise the general content of a school's course of study." Justice
Brennan's statement was indeed a prophetic one, as later events

Problems of Censorship

Type of Problem	Illustrative Text
Profanity	Salinger, *Catcher in the Rye*
Sexual Incidents	Orwell, *1984*
Sex and Violence	Steinbeck, *Of Mice and Men*
Attack on Family Life	Huxley, *Brave New World*
Criticism of Authority	Cormier, *The Chocolate War*
Unpatriotic Sentiments	Vonnegut, *Slaughterhouse Five*
Anti-Capitalism Sentiments	Steinbeck, *The Grapes of Wrath*
Anti-White Sentiments	Wright, *Native Son*
Anti-Semitic Sentiments	Roth, *Portnoy's Complaint*
Homosexual Activity	Baldwin, *Giovanni's Room*

Figure 12.1

will verify. Also to be noted is the fact that after the Island Trees decision Justices Burger and Powell retired from the Court to be replaced by Reagan appointees Antonin Scalia and Anthony Kennedy, and Justice Brennan, a consistent and eloquent advocate for First Amendment freedoms, has been replaced by President Bush's appointee, Justice Suter. These replacements have clearly added to the increasingly conservative/reactionary tone of the Court, a reality which will undoubtedly be felt in major censorship cases to be argued in the immediate future.

That school censorship cases are on the increase has been documented in the publication of People for the American Way's *Attacks on the Freedom to Learn*. In the 1988 to 1989 edition of this document, 172 reported cases of censorship were cited, up from 157 the previous school year. And the document further reminds us that these cases are only those which were *reported*. In all probability, many more occurred during that year without any official record of them. As this text is being written, the incidences of *classic* censorship are rising, with no end in sight.

2. **Proactive Censorship** This is a more subtle, but ultimately more powerful, form of censorship that has also been noted with increasing frequency over the past twenty or so years. This kind of censorship is different from the classic kind, but it is similar in intent. Outspoken, often extreme, citizens, state legislators, and

state department of education bureaucrats dictate both content and style of text materials for the public schools *before* these materials are even published.

For example, in Texas, an elderly couple, Mel and Norma Gabler, raise endless objections to the content of textbooks, sleuthing through them to ferret out *objectionable matter.* This has become a relentless crusade, inspiring attacks on texts by a number of communities and thousands of angered parents. The effect of the Gablers and those who imitate them has been heard by the publishing industry. If Texas education officials frown on certain textbooks, it is difficult for these books to be placed on the state adoption list. Texas, as publishers well know, is the second largest textbook-adoption state in the country, and to be shut out of Texas costs a lot of money.

When books fail to become adopted for specific reasons (*controversial* ideas, their un-American pronouncements, their questioning of Christian values, and so on), publishers have a clear-cut choice: go elsewhere with their books or change their editorial policies concerning objectionable matter in future editions of these texts. It is common to hear of editors combing through literature and language texts for such *objectionable* material before the updated revisions go to press in time for the Texas adoption. Because of the Gablers, the textbook industry makes judgments before the fact about what can and cannot go into the books they produce. Censorship expert Ed Jenkinson of Indiana University calls the Gablers "the two most powerful people in education today." That may be a bit extreme, but to believe that the Gablers have not caused publishers to engage in proactive censorship is naive.

Another group, usually liberal, has in fact joined the Gablers and their cohorts in prescribing what will and what will not get into textbooks. The following bill was passed by the 1978 California Assembly: 60044. No instructional materials shall be adopted by any governing board for use in the schools which, in its determination, contains:

a. Any matter reflecting adversely upon persons because of their race, color, creed, national origin, ancestry, sex, or occupation

b. Any sectarian or denominational doctrine or propaganda contrary to law

c. Any illustrations of any identifiable commercial brand names, representations, or corporate logos unless such illustrations are necessary to the educational purpose of the instructional material and that purpose cannot be achieved without using such illustrations, or unless such illustrations are incidental to a scene of a general nature. If, under these exceptions, a brand name, representation, or corporate logo is illustrated, prominence shall not be given to any one brand or corporation unless such illustration is necessary to the educational purpose of the instructional material and that purpose cannot be achieved without using such illustration.

While the intentions of civil rightists, feminists, Naderists, environmentalists, and other libertarian groups may be noble, their work has had an eviscerating effect on textbooks. The legislation they have fought so hard to pass in state after state then falls into bureaucratic hands in state departments of education. And bureaucrats make the rules publishers have to live by. The result is a series of ultimatums to publishers, bordering at times on the absurd.

Today, when writing a book for use in public schools, an author must be aware of:

1. The proportion of black faces in proportion to white faces
2. The use of names such as Carlos and Juanita in proportion to those of Billy and Sue
3. The use of pronouns that negate sex bias
4. Putting anyone in a stereotypical role
5. Paying obeisance to mandates of the consumer enlightenment moguls
6. Excluding materials that imply the rape of the natural environment
7. Any vaguely humorous, satiric, and/or critical treatment of anyone's religious preference
8. Any allusion to stereotypes of ethnic or national origins
9. Statements that may contain political bias
10. Reference to the use of drugs, tobacco, alcohol, non-nutritious foods, and so on.

These caveats have generally been spelled out in state legislation since 1975. Needless to say, writers who try to abide by them are cramped in thought and style. Then there are constraints imposed by those who demand subject matter which is true-blue

American, fundamentalist Christian, and redolent of pride in the free enterprise system.

So, as Southern vernacular expresses it, both the left and the right are getting in their licks on textbook publishing these days. Not surprisingly, both claim to be representing *the people* in their demands. The result is proactive censorship, a far more powerful and restrictive censorship than the *classic* variety. Textbook writers are denied latitude in what they can choose as themes and topics, the kinds of allusions they can use, and the way they convey their messages. In the emotional concern with individuals' rights, the forgotten people are the authors and text compilers. And the bland results are foisted off on the real victims—the students.

Proactive censorship will hinder most English teachers as they face the challenge of statewide testing. In the first place, the need to promote critical reading among secondary school students is becoming more and more evident. Large numbers of students appear to be limited in the ability to draw inferences, make judgments, arrive at conclusions, and test hypotheses as they read. The need for appropriate materials seems evident. But the prohibitive nature of the new wave of censorship may well deny publication of engagingly written materials about pressing issues. It isn't easy to develop critical reading abilities with beige selections. Students don't read reading; they read *something*, and the need for challenging materials has never been greater. Whether such materials can survive the Gablers, the ultrafeminists, the die-hard environmentalists, and others, and find their way into the textbooks becomes a serious question. Critical reading demands the use of critical positions implied in print. This kind of censorship greatly limits the availability of such texts to those teachers who badly need them.

3. **Abridgment and Adaptation** In the early fall of 1984, two discoveries occurred coincidentally. Daniel Blum, a student at Madison High School in Vienna, Virginia, had seen a Folger Theatre production of *Romeo and Juliet,* and when he sat down with his Scott, Foresman *America Reads* textbook to write a paper about Mercutio's Queen Mab speech, he noticed that some of the lines were missing. For example, the "fairies' midwife" who "gallops night by night / Through lovers' brains" is no longer characterized as the hag who "when maids lie on their backs,/ . . . presses them and learns them first to bear,/ Making them women of good carriage."

Around the time the story broke in Virginia, a parent in Minneapolis discovered that the same anthology had been altered as well as abridged. Romeo's line in Act V "Well, Juliet, I will lie with thee tonight," was changed to read, "Well, Juliet, I will be with thee tonight." Investigations by a Fairfax County textbook advisory committee, school boards, columnists, and People For the American Way revealed not only that more than 300 lines had been eliminated from Scott, Foresman's *Romeo and Juliet*—most of them sexual allusions—but that high school textbook publishers routinely expurgate Shakespeare. Some, including Scott, Foresman, note in teachers' editions that *abridgments* have been made. Many do not.

While acknowledging their abridgment, Scott, Foresman refused to restore the lines removed from *Romeo and Juliet*. Nor did the company show any willingness to restore some 100 lines which had been deleted from *Hamlet*, included in another of the company's anthologies. At this writing, the two plays remain abridged.

NCTE reacted quickly to this cutting of literary works. At the November, 1984 convention in Detroit, the membership unanimously passed the following Resolution:

ON OPPOSING ABRIDGMENT OR ADAPTATION AS A FORM OF CENSORSHIP

Background

Some publishers are producing texts in which abridgment and adaptation have become censorship. A well-known publisher's recent edition of *Romeo and Juliet* cut 404 lines, almost all of which contained sexual references. Although this publisher admitted the abridgment, the firm's statement did not explain the purposes of the cuts. Adaptation of a work, perhaps warranted in some cases, may also result in censorship. Publishers have a responsibility to provide information about the extent and nature of any alterations so that, when selecting texts, teachers can make informed choices. Be it therefore

RESOLUTION

RESOLVED, that the National Council of Teachers of English recommend that publishers present the complete text or sections of works which they choose to print whether in a single text or in an anthology; and that NCTE urge that if publishers do abridge or adapt a text, they clearly state that these alterations have occurred, and explain the nature and extent of the abridgment or adaptation in promotional information, teachers' guides, and other support materials.

Those publishing companies bent on continuing a policy of abridgement and adaptation have suffered a serious setback in California. In a November 1988 decision, the State Board of Education mandated that California schools replace carefully edited texts at all levels with *real* literature. The Board also demanded that publishers clearly label texts which had been abridged or adapted. The policy, which was initiated in the school year 1989 to 1990, serves as a bellwether for other states that use adopted textbook lists as a matter of policy. Since California, with eleven percent of the nation's annual textbook expenditure (roughly 1.5 billion dollars), has long been known as an educational trend setter, it is reasonable to assume that publishers seeking to sell books in that state have gotten the message. Moreover, it is likely that other states will note the California decision and rapidly follow suit as they have often done since the end of World War II. In an otherwise dreary outlook on censorship issues, this is a heartening sign.

4. **Censorship of School Journalism** While the publication of school newspapers does not precisely represent literary activity, a review of this problem does serve to demonstrate the multifaceted nature of censorship in school activities. Since most school newspapers are supervised by secondary English teachers, the issue is pertinent here.

In 1971, in St. Petersburg, Florida, an eleventh grade student on the school newspaper staff wrote an editorial questioning the practicality and, to some extent, the legitimacy of certain rules as stated in the student handbook. The student editor approved publication of the piece, as did the faculty advisor. The latter individual, however, decided to check with the principal *to be safe*. That decision was a wise one: the principal became incensed at the editorial and ordered its deletion from the upcoming edition of the paper. Stunned by the decision, the student discussed the matter with his parents who, in turn, encouraged him to submit the editorial to the St. Petersburg *Evening Independent,* a newspaper with a relatively broad regional circulation. The student did so, and shortly thereafter it was published. It brought an immediate, vitriolic reaction from the principal, who ordered the student suspended from school for a minimum of two weeks. He was to receive a failing grade on any tests or other graded assignments which he missed during that suspension. An honor student, the young man was also removed from the newspaper staff and the National Honor Society. Only when he submitted a written apology for his transgression was the suspension lifted. The failed grades and the two dismissals, however, were not rescinded.

In another case, a Pensacola, Florida, high school student, who was a member of the school newspaper staff in 1982, wrote an editorial criticizing school and county officials for renaming the school's football stadium after a revered former coach, ostensibly without consulting anyone. While waiting for a decision as to whether the editorial would be published in a later edition of the school paper, the writer showed it to a neighbor who happened to be a reporter for the Pensacola *News Journal*. When that reporter interviewed the principal and the elected district superintendent as to the validity of the charge, she was told that the name change was *not news* and that the editorial would not appear in the school newspaper.

This case dragged on for months, with the student's parents appealing to the principal and then the County School Board either to publish the editorial or explain their suppression of it. After much wrangling and stonewalling by the principal, the Board finally decided "for the good of the system" to quash the editorial. It was never published and, while the student writer was not directly punished, he was not allowed to submit for publication any further editorials to his school paper. He soon resigned from the journalism staff and graduated from the school, never having seen his questions concerning the arbitrary renaming of the stadium published or aired for open deliberation.

A more recent, and far more celebrated instance of censorship in school journalism took place in 1983. The editorial staff of the newspaper published by Hazelwood East High School decided in May of that year to publish two stories, one on teen pregnancy, the other on the effects of divorce on adolescents. Hazelwood is an affluent suburb of St. Louis, Missouri, not measurably different from the Island Trees school. In the Hazelwood instance, when the principal had both stories deleted, the students (all members of a course titled Journalism II) sued him under the First Amendment, and the case began its laborious journey through the federal court system. Just as in the Island Trees case, this one had its ups and downs.

The principal's decision was upheld in the U.S. District Court late in 1986, but that decision was reversed by the 8th U.S. Circuit Court of Appeals in the summer of 1987. Then, in January 1988, the U.S. Supreme Court voted 5 to 3 in favor of the principal's decision to censor the stories. (Justice Anthony Kennedy had just been confirmed to replace retiring Justice Lewis Powell and had not yet been seated on the court.) In doing so, the Court went against a 1969 decision which upheld the rights of a group of high school students in Des Moines, Iowa, to wear black armbands to school as a symbol of their opposition to the war in Vietnam. In that instance, Justice Abe Fortas wrote that the students "do not shed their constitutional rights to freedom of speech or expression at the schoolhouse gate." In 1988, however, Justice Byron White, writing for the majority, stated that "A school need not tolerate student speech that is inconsistent with its educational mission . . . School officials may impose reasonable restrictions on the speech of students, teachers, and other members of the school community." Editorial opinion, in this nationally celebrated case, was somewhat divided although probably sympathetic to the students to some extent. A most significant ramification of the Hazelwood decision, however, lies in the power which it placed in the hands of building principals to decide what can be included in their school's curricula and what cannot. Since broad curricular knowledge is not always a significant strength of such administrators, the long-range effects of this Supreme Court decision may be chilling indeed.

One effect of the decision just described was its use as precedent to decide a notorious censorship case in which classic works of literature were removed from a high school English course of study. In April 1986, a fundamentalist clergyman, supported by a number of aroused parents in Lake City, Florida, enjoined the school board to remove a book from the twelfth grade humanities course being taught at Columbia County High School. The text, *The Humanities: Cultural Roots and Continuities*, contained two selections that the clergyman and his followers deemed particularly offensive: Aristophanes' play *Lysistrata* and "The Miller's Tale" from Chaucer's *The Canterbury Tales*. With little hesitation, the school board gave the building principal absolute authority to remove the text and any other curricular materials which he felt might be objectionable. (The banished text was the only humanities book on the state-approved list at that time.) A Lake City parent, who was at that time a doctoral student in English at Florida State University, sued the school and the school board under the First Amendment. Once again, the case drew the attention of the national media.

In late January, 1988, U.S. District Court Justice Susan Black upheld the right of the school board to banish the text. In her decision, Justice Black cited as precedent the January 1988 (two weeks earlier) Hazelwood journalism case, laying emphasis on the powers bestowed by that decision on the building principal. Reacting to this decision, the plaintiff voiced the feelings of many people when she said, "It's one thing to censor seventeen-year-old writers in a school paper, but it's another thing to censor Chaucer and Aristophanes." Nevertheless, the decision of the District Court was upheld at the 11th U.S. Circuit Court of Appeals in January 1989. In his written opinion, Justice R. Lanier Anderson wrote, "Of course, we do not endorse the (school) board's decision . . . We seriously question how young persons just below the age of majority can be harmed by these masterpieces of Western literature. However, having concluded that there is no constitutional violation, our role is not to second guess the wisdom of the board's action." The court went on to point out that, in its opinion, in issues of curriculum, schools "have been accorded greater control over expression than they may enjoy in other spheres of activity." As this chapter is being written, the plaintiff has decided to carry the case to the Supreme Court despite both the two setbacks she has experienced and the unwillingness of the American Civil Liberties Union to continue their support of her petition.

Thus it would appear that federal judges, many of whom were appointed during the eight years of Ronald Reagan's presidency, are quite willing to support decisions of school officials to censor students' and teachers' activities in several areas of the curriculum.

5. **Censorship of Students' Creative Writing** One final kind of censorship needs to be identified and discussed, albeit briefly: that of suppressing students' creative expressions when those expressions appear in publications officially sponsored and financed by the school or district.

In the early 1960s, one of us served as the advisor to a high school literary magazine. A tenth grade student presented to the student editors a short story about a Jewish teenager who had just moved into a new neighborhood at Christmastime and was hurt by some anti-Semitic remarks made unwittingly by some of his new young neighbors. The editors accepted the story and the advisor concurred; it seemed to be a rather sensitive and restrained treatment of an ongoing social problem. About a week after the magazine was distributed, there came a telephone call from the education coordinator of the Twin Cities B'Nai Brith Council, expressing outrage at this "anti-Semitic piece" and demanding that either an apology be presented in writing to all readers or that all copies of the magazine be recalled. When the editors refused to do either, pointing out that the story was a sympathetic treatment of the issue, the caller threatened further, official action. He subsequently did confront the chief administrator of the school, who somehow persuaded him to let the matter stand and to pursue no further attempts to suppress the story. The lesson from this experience was this: what seems perfectly acceptable in student literary products to some may be offensive to others.

In the spring of 1968, an undergraduate at Florida State University who had just returned from a tour of duty as an infantryman in Vietnam submitted a short story to the school literary magazine, *Smoke Signals*. The story focused on the adjustment problems of a black Vietnam veteran upon his return to life in an urban ghetto. A sexual encounter was briefly noted, and several profane words were uttered by some of the characters. The Board of Publications Advisors of the University (three students and two professors) voted to publish the piece, by a vote of 4 to 1. The dissenting voter, a faculty member, was so disturbed by the decision that he went almost immediately to the University president, described the situation, and urged the deletion of the story. The president eventually did ban the story, much to the dismay of the Faculty Senate, which, after an ensuing heated debate, voted to censure the president for his action. Shortly after this censure, the president resigned, only to find that the State Board of Regents refused to accept his resignation and demanded that he resume his duties. A furor was raised, both on campus and in the community, over this chain of events. It was exacerbated by a barrage of regional media coverage. In due time, the story was published, and in February of the following year, the president resigned once more, bowing to a number of pressures. This time his resignation was accepted.

These two incidents took place a long time ago. Today, however, in the light of the Hazelwood East High School journalism decision of the U.S. Supreme Court, it is highly likely that student literary expression is again at risk. English teachers who are given supervisory responsibilities for such publications should take heed and act accordingly.

Censorship and Young Adult Fiction

In an earlier chapter on the nature and possible uses of YA fiction (Chapter Five), a transition in the thematic aspects of that genre was described. YA novels written before the late 1960s, the reader may recall, were generally tame. Dunning described them as "consistently wholesome and rigidly didactic," fervent apostles, on the whole, of white middle-class values and mores. With the publication of *The Outsiders* (Hinton), *The Contender* (Lipsyte), and *The Pigman* (Zindel) during the school year 1967 to 1968, however, a radical change took place, and the change has, at least to date, been a lasting one. Today, young adult novels deal with issues that are not so "consistently wholesome"—teenage sexual activity and pregnancy; drug and alcohol abuse; the actions of delinquent parents; racial hatred and violence; homosexuality; venereal diseases among young people; and other gripping contemporary social problems. Thus an updated review of most censored works will almost invariably contain several novels by Judy Blume, Cormier's *The Chocolate War* and *I Am The Cheese* (among others of his), some works by Richard Peck, Paul Zindel, Robin Brancato, and Paula Danziger, to name a few of the more prominent, frequently attacked YA authors.

In the light of this new thematic thrust, middle school and junior high teachers need to be just as judicious in choosing YA novels for all-class study as do their senior high counterparts in considering more *adult* texts. If those teachers pay heed to reviews published in *The ALAN Review*, note the analyses of current YA fiction presented in the *English Journal*, and stay in touch with their school's media specialists regarding the latest advisories of the American Library Association, they can avoid most of the pitfalls illustrated earlier in this chapter.

Some Suggestions for Classroom Teachers

Having shown the reader a great deal of the censorship darkness, it would seem not only appropriate but necessary to attempt to light some candles before closing out the discussion of censorship in the study of literature in secondary schools.

1. **Know Your Books.** Whether you are teaching a work well established as a literary classic (remember the Chaucer problem in Lake City) or a work of YA fiction, be sure you (A) have read it carefully, (B) have analyzed it critically on your own, and (C) have access to scholarly materials that support its literary value. Step "C" is more difficult with YA novels; thus, take seriously the previously noted suggestions about keeping up with *The ALAN Review*, and others.

2. **Keep Abreast of Policy Documents.** Make it your business to read and study current statements of curricular policy. Because these are almost invariably local policy statements—school and district ones—they may change frequently, as in the case of a new principal's appointment or the election of new school board members. It is a good idea to keep copies of the more pertinent documents (e.g., the "Citizen's Request for Reconsideration of a Work") in your desk drawer. When an irate citizen happens by, having such ammunition at the ready can well save you a lot of grief, at least for the moment.

3. **Develop Reading Lists with Care.** Be especially aware of selections you assign to the entire class and about which students will prepare graded responses. Share such lists with those individuals who are in charge of the school media center. Clear them with department heads, team leaders, and, where advised to do so, with building principals or their assistant principals for curriculum. Be sure these people are aware of selections you are listing and assigning. If there are language arts supervisory personnel on duty in district offices, send them copies of your lists and solicit their reactions. Don't try to conceal from your supervisors the fact that some of the works you are recommending to students may be controversial. They can support you only if they are informed ahead of time of what you're recommending.

4. **Develop Response Activities and Requirements Judiciously.** Besides being sound pedagogy, this suggestion is especially germane to the problem of potential challenge. Look closely at the focus of your writing assignments, your essay test questions, your all-class discussion topics, your group work tasks, and your role-playing scenarios. Be sure that they focus on main, pertinent thematic and stylistic elements of works to be studied. There are those citizens *out there* who want to believe that your tasks are aimed at titillation and the arousal of *hidden* prurient issues. Don't make such challenges so easy.

5. **Develop and Send Home Parental Consent Statements When This Seems Prudent.** Discuss this decision, as well as the statement itself, with department heads or senior departmental colleagues. When you feel the need to send such consent forms home with the students in one of your classes, send copies to principals (or administrators in charge of curriculum) as well. When you receive the signed, returned forms, file them in a safe, familiar place. You never know when you may have to show them to parents who are both indignant and forgetful.

6. **Develop an Alternative Text List.** This is closely related to Item 5, above. Whenever you are concerned that a selection may be controversial for any reason, and thus require a consent form to be sent home, prepare a list of texts on the same theme, in the same genre or mode, which can be assigned to the student whose parent objects to the one specified by the consent form. Although even this option doesn't placate some parents, it is usually an effective means of preventing the offended parent from demanding that all use of that text be halted. It also puts the ball in the parent's court in terms of significant educational goals, possibly opening the door for dialogue between the parent and the student (who may well want to read the original book).

7. **Elicit Feedback from Students.** A powerful antidote for the angry statements of a parent, or even a *concerned citizen,* can be the review of responses provided by students of what you have asked about their reading tasks, both in terms of what they have been asked to read and what kinds of responses they have been assigned to make. When intrusive individuals are shown that the students have been asked to stress the worthwhile, *clean* elements of the work considered rather than any inappropriate dimension, they may be more willing to accept the classroom text choices you have made. So take notes on students' contributions to pertinent class discussions. Better still, tape these discussions whenever possible. Save sample papers or sets of papers that the students submit in response to your assignments. Photocopy them before turning them back to their owners. Then have them ready for parent/citizen review. When such visitors are allowed to see or hear what use is made of literary materials in the classroom, they may be less willing to brand you as a purveyor of pornography, subversion, and the like.

8. **Get Involved in the Fight Against Proactive Censorship.** Contact publishers' representatives and state your opposition to deletion, abridgment, or adaptation of literary selections which you feel comprise an important part of your literature program of study. Speak through your affiliation with NCTE as well as your state and local professional organizations. If you live and work in a textbook-adoption state, contact the textbook evaluation committee. Or, better still, make an effort to be a candidate for these committees; they include several classroom teachers in their ranks. You, after all, are among any publishing company's prize customers. To date, they have been hearing almost exclusively from the Gablers and various pressure groups. If you speak with

an articulate, professional, and forthright voice, you may well overbalance those strident voices of narrow orthodoxy now heard throughout the country. In a very real sense, the teaching profession has not had its turn with those publishers. They will ignore teachers at their peril.

9. **Support Your Fellow Teachers.** When colleagues in your school or your district are being pilloried by the censorship vigilantes, come to their aid using any legal, professional, and influential way possible. Such teachers most often report that they feel terribly alone during such experiences. Testify for them when you are asked. Help them prepare their statements of rationale for choosing the texts they are being indicted for. Speak on their behalf to their department heads and/or building principals. Offer to accompany them if they are required to appear before the local school board or in any other forum. Be especially solicitous to those teachers who are new to the profession and/or community. History reveals that such traumatic experiences early in teaching careers can lead to decisions to quit the profession. Teachers can and should help other teachers unhesitatingly when they are facing censorship problems. The next time it may be you.

10. **Take the Initiative in Outreach Activities.** Identify key groups in the community. Those may include parent organizations, political groups (League of Women Voters, and others), ministerial associations, patriotic organizations (American Legion, Veterans of Foreign Wars, and others), Friends of the Library, and any other civic-minded groups. Meet them with persuasive professional materials which deal with the goals of literature instruction and the problems inherent in extremist censorship positions. Manifest your concern without being condescending or unnecessarily inflammatory.

    The ministerial groups are an excellent case in point. The great majority of their members are reasonable, fair-minded individuals, civic-minded and imbued with the ecumenical spirit. They usually have a great deal of experience in working with youth groups. Do not accept the stereotypic, generally inaccurate belief that such organizations are redolent of and dominated by arch-conservative, unresponsive, fanatical clergy who are totally unwilling to listen to reasonable arguments. When you reach out to these groups, retaining your poise, reasoning powers, and sense of humor during dialogues, you may be both amazed and highly gratified to discover what can be accomplished. This is the time to join in discussion with these individuals rather than castigate them in the teachers' lounge during your planning period each day. And remember that little helpful communication takes place when people are shouting at each other. In any case, teachers should be proactive here; such efforts could provide an insurance policy if and when the storms of censorship begin to blow.

In conducting the one-semester course offering titled *Teaching Literature in Secondary Schools,* we have always included the censorship topic in the syllabus. The students in this course have been, in the main, undergraduates who are seeking secondary certification in English (i.e., young people with interest and college preparation in academic English but without any prior teaching experience, at least none in public school classrooms). In fact, this course continues to be one of the prerequisites for the student teaching experience. During the consideration of the topic *censorship,* we *invite* (a euphemism for *require*) the class members to attend an evening panel discussion on the topic. The meeting is always held off campus, usually in the auditorium of one of the local churches. The panel includes the following five participants:

a. A high school principal
b. An elected member of the district school board
c. An experienced (and articulate) high school or middle school English teacher
d. A local citizen who, by his or her public statements, has expressed concern over text choices in the public schools
e. A local clergyman, usually one of a pronounced fundamentalist persuasion

The panel usually lasts two to three hours. We serve as moderator; each panelist makes a brief opening statement stating his or her perspective on the issue of censoring books in public schools; and, the remainder of the session is given over to questions posed to the panel by the audience. English teachers from the local secondary schools receive an open invitation to attend, and a few always show up. A social hour, restricted to coffee, soft drinks, and finger food, follows the formal presentation and question-and-answer period, allowing panelists and members of the audience to converse casually about issues raised in the formal session.

This censorship deliberation has been well-received every time it has been held. Most importantly, however, the undergraduates are given an opportunity to hear the thoughts and feelings of citizens who have concerns about censorship. It is usually an eye-opening occasion.

In all of the above, dialogue is the key. Whatever else it is, censorship does provide a significant issue which promotes interaction between community members and the schools which serve them. Perhaps the best advice we can offer is that teachers take the initiative in the conduct of such dialogue. The potential forums are several; the stakes, high.

11. **If All of the Above Have Been Attempted in One Way or Another, and the Problem Generated by the Irate Citizen(s) Persists, Stand Your Ground**   Most of these citizens, especially the members of the pressure groups mentioned earlier, regard compromise as a sign of weakness. State your convictions on the value of the literary experience in the preparation of young people for the complex, often bewildering adult world of today. Stress the need for developing critical thinking abilities for those students who are seeking entrance into that world. You might go so far as to suggest that the development of vigorous, independent thought helps to protect youngsters from being victims of various cults that seek to control their lives. Do make the distinction between training (as indoctrination) and education. Don't apologize and don't pander to anyone's prejudices. A sound literature study component is one of the bulwarks of a good education; such a component needs to be both defended and preserved.

Summary

For many reasons, several of which have been cited in this chapter, censorship of literary offerings is now and probably always will be a problem without a solution, at least when *solution* is defined in an absolute sense. The reconciliation of First Amendment rights and local control of the schools will remain a difficult one, and it will continue to be dealt with on a case-by-case basis. Too often, there are smoldering resentments and misunderstandings between school and community, and these tend to flare up angrily during confrontations about choices of books to be used in various courses of study in the English classroom. The task of mediating disagreements on these choices falls most typically on building principals.

Recent history testifies that their record of support for teachers in this issue is a most unimpressive one. The censorship challenges often come when they are least expected, and they can be both vitriolic and frustrating. Often they reveal the mean-spirited nature of some of the citizens teachers serve. But, as John Dewey explained, in order to solve a problem, the individual must first realize that a problem exists. The purpose of this chapter has been (1) to lay out the problem in its complexity, and (2) to offer some proposals for coping with it. Teachers should know their material and why they selected it; familiarize themselves with the communities in which they teach; and seek support from agencies which call themselves *support services* (i.e., librarians, media specialists, curriculum supervisors, and others). Moreover, they must keep cool when confronted by the *apostles of purity*. In a word, they should heed the Boy Scout motto, "Be Prepared."

Notes

1. Louise M. Rosenblatt. *Literature as Exploration.* 4th ed. New York: The Modern Language Association of America, 1983, p 81.
2. Lee Burress and Edward B. Jenkinson. "The Students' Right to Know." Urbana: National Council of Teachers of English, 1982, pp 44–45.

Bibliography

The works listed in the five sections of this bibliography are intended to be representative of the kinds of resources teachers of literature will find useful for their professional reading. This list is not intended to be exhaustive of the professional publications in the area of literature study.

I. Resources for Book Selection

Abrahamson, Richard F. and Betty Carter, eds. *Books for You: A Booklist for Senior High Students*. 10th ed. Urbana: National Council of Teachers of English, 1988.

Burgess, Anthony. *99 Novels: The Best in English since 1939*. New York: Summit Books, 1984.

Davis, James E. and Hazel K. Davis. *Your Reading: A Booklist for Junior High and Middle School Students*. 7th ed. Urbana: National Council of Teachers of English, 1988.

———. *Books for the Junior High Years*. FOCUS, Spring 1989.

Gilbar, Steven. *Good Books: A Book Lover's Companion*. New Haven: Ticknor & Fields, 1982.

Jett-Simpson, Mary, ed. *Adventuring with Books: A Booklist for Pre-K–Grade 6*. 9th ed. Urbana: National Council of Teachers of English, 1989.

Matthews, Dorothy, ed. *High Interest—Easy Reading for Junior and Senior High School Students*. 5th ed. Urbana: National Council of Teachers of English, 1988.

Stensland, Anna Lee. *Literature by and about the American Indian: An Annotated Bibliography*. 2nd ed. Urbana: National Council of Teachers of English, 1979.

Tway, E., ed. *Reading Ladders for Human Relations*. Urbana: NCTE and the American Council on Education, 1981.

Walker, Eleanor, ed. *Book Bait: Detailed Notes on Adult Books Popular with Young People*. 4th ed. Chicago: American Library Association, 1988.

II. Journals in English Education and the Teaching of Literature

The ALAN Review. Assembly on Literature for Adolescents, National Council of Teachers of English.

Arizona English Bulletin. Arizona English Teachers' Association.

Booklist. American Library Association.

College English. National Council of Teachers of English.

Connecticut English Journal. Connecticut Council of Teachers of English.

English Education. Conference on English Education, National Council of Teachers of English.

English Journal. National Council of Teachers of English.

The English Language Arts Bulletin. Ohio Council of Teachers of English.

The English Record. New York State English Council.

Florida English Journal. Florida Council of Teachers of English.

Focus. Southeastern Ohio Council of Teachers of English.

Horn Book Magazine. The Horn Book, Inc.

Illinois English Bulletin. Illinois Association of Teachers of English.

Iowa English Bulletin. Iowa Council of Teachers of English.

Journal of Reading. International Reading Association.

Journal of Reading Behavior. National Reading Conference.

Kentucky English Bulletin. Kentucky Council of Teachers of English.

Kirkus Reviews. Kirkus Service, Inc.

Language Arts. National Council of Teachers of English.

The Leaflet. New England Association of Teachers of English.

Missouri English Bulletin. Missouri Council of Teachers of English.

Publication of the Modern Library Association. Modern Library Association.

The Reading Teacher. International Reading Association.

Reading Research Quarterly. International Reading Association.

Research in the Teaching of English. National Council of Teachers of English.

School Library Journal. R. R. Bowker Co.

Virginia English Bulletin. Virginia Association of Teachers of English.

Wilson Library Quarterly. H. W. Wilson Co.

Wisconsin English Journal. Wisconsin Council of Teachers of English.

III. Selected Works of Literary Criticism

Bodkin, Maud. *Archetypal Patterns in Poetry: Psychological Studies of Imagination.* London: Oxford University Press, 1963.

Booth, Wayne C. *The Rhetoric of Fiction.* Chicago: University of Chicago Press, 1961.

Brooks, Cleanth and Robert Penn Warren. *Understanding Fiction.* New York: Holt, Rinehart & Winston, 1958.

————. *Understanding Poetry.* New York: Holt, Rinehart & Winston, 1960.

Cain, W. E. *The Crisis of Criticism: Theory, Literature, and Reform in English Studies.* Baltimore: The Johns Hopkins University Press, 1984.

Daiches, David. *Critical Approaches to Literature.* Englewood Cliffs, NJ: Prentice Hall, 1956.

Donelson, Kenneth L. and Alleen Pace Nilsen. *Literature for Today's Young Adults*. 3rd ed. Glenview, IL: Scott, Foresman and Company, 1989.

Eagleton, T. *Literary Theory: An Introduction*. Minneapolis: University of Minnesota Press, 1983.

Empson, William. *Seven Types of Ambiguity*. London: Chatto & Windus, 1930.

Frye, Northrop. *Anatomy of Criticism: Four Essays*. Princeton, NJ: Princeton University Press, 1957.

————. *The Educated Imagination*. Bloomington, IN: Indiana University Press, 1964.

Gardner, J. *The Art of Fiction: Notes on Craft for Young Writers*. New York: Vintage Books, 1985.

Geertz, C. *The Interpretation of Cultures*. New York: Basic Books, 1973.

Guerin, Wilfred L., et al. *A Handbook of Critical Approaches to Literature*. 2nd ed. New York: Harper & Row, 1979.

Lucas, F. L. *Literature and Psychology*. Ann Arbor, MI: The University of Michigan Press, 1962.

Perrine, Laurence. *Sound and Sense: An Introduction to Poetry*. New York: Harcourt, Brace and World, 1963.

Richards, I. A. *Practical Criticism*. New York: Harcourt, Brace and Company, 1929.

Rosenheim, Edward W. Jr. *What Happens in Literature*. Chicago: University of Chicago Press, 1963.

Santayana, George. *Reason in Art*. New York: Charles Scribner's Sons, 1924.

Stafford, William. *Friends to This Ground*. Champaign, IL: National Council of Teachers of English, 1967.

Wellek, Rene and Austin Warren. *Theory of Literature*. New York: Harcourt, Brace and Company, 1942.

Wimsatt, W. K. Jr. *The Verbal Icon*. New York: Noonday Press, 1958.

IV. Selected Texts on the Theory and Practice of Teaching Literature

Applebee, Arthur N. *Tradition and Reform in the Teaching of English: A History*. Urbana: National Council of Teachers of English, 1974.

Atwell, Nancy. *In the Middle: Writing, Reading, and Learning with Adolescents*. Portsmouth: Boynton/Cook, 1987.

Bleich, David. *Readings and Feelings: An Introduction to Subjective Criticism*. Urbana: National Council of Teachers of English, 1975.

————. *Subjective Criticism*. Baltimore: The Johns Hopkins University Press, 1978.

Burton, Dwight L. *Literature Study in the High Schools*. 3rd ed. New York: Holt, Rinehart & Winston, 1970.

Burton, Dwight L., et al. *Teaching English Today*. Boston: Houghton Mifflin, 1975.

Burton, Dwight L. and John S. Simmons. *Teaching English in Today's High Schools*. 2nd ed. New York: Holt, Rinehart & Winston, 1970.

Carlson, G. Robert. *Books and the Teenage Reader: A Guide for Teachers, Librarians and Parents.* 2nd rev. ed. New York: Harper & Row, 1980.

Carlson, G. Robert and Anne Sherrill. *Voices of Readers: How We Come to Love Books.* Urbana: National Council of Teachers of English, 1988.

Carter, Candy, ed. *Literature—News that Stays New: Fresh Approaches to the Classics.* Classroom Practices in Teaching English 1984. Urbana: National Council of Teachers of English, 1985.

Christenbury, Leila and Patricia P. Kelly. *Questioning: A Path to Critical Thinking.* Urbana: National Council of Teachers of English/ERIC, 1983.

Cooper, Charles E. *Measuring Growth in Appreciation of Literature.* Newark, DE: International Reading Association, 1972.

———. ed. *Researching Response to Literature and the Teaching of Literature: Points of Departure.* Norwood, NJ: Ablex, 1985.

Cooper, Charles E. and Alan C. Purves. *A Guide to Evaluation for Responding.* Lexington, MA: Ginn, 1973.

Cooper, Jan, Rick Evans, and Elizabeth Robertson. *Teaching College Students to Read Analytically: An Individualized Approach.* Urbana: National Council of Teachers of English, 1985.

Corcoran, Bill and Emrys Evans, eds. *Readers, Texts, Teachers.* Portsmouth: Boynton/Cook, 1987.

Creber, J. W. Patrick. *Sense and Sensitivity: The Philosophy and Practice of English Teaching.* London: University of London Press, 1965.

Crowley, Sharon. *A Teacher's Introduction to Deconstruction.* Urbana: National Council of Teachers of English, 1989.

Davis, Ken, ed. *The Responding Reader: Nine New Approaches to Teaching Literature.* Special issue of the *Kentucky English Bulletin* 32(1), Fall 1982.

Davis, Walter A. *The Act of Interpretation.* Chicago: University of Chicago Press, 1978.

Dixon, John. *Growth Through English.* Reading, UK: National Association for the Teaching of English, 1967.

Duke, Charles R. *Creative Dramatics and English Teaching.* Urbana: National Council of Teachers of English, 1974.

Fader, Daniel and Elton B. McNeil. *Hooked on Books: Program & Proof.* New York: Berkley, 1968. Reissued in 1976.

Fagan, Edward R. *Field: A Process for Teaching Literature.* University Park, PA: Pennsylvania State University Press, 1964.

Farrell, Edmund J. and James R. Squire, eds. *Transactions with Literature: A Fifty-Year Perspective.* Urbana: National Council of Teachers of English, 1990.

Favat, F. Andre. *Child and Tale: The Origins of Interest.* National Council of Teachers of English Research Report No. 19. Urbana: National Council of Teachers of English, 1977.

Fish, Stanley. *Is There a Text in this Class? The Authority of Interpretive Communities.* Cambridge: Harvard University Press, 1980.

Fleming, Margaret, ed. *Teaching the Epic.* Urbana: National Council of Teachers of English, 1974.

Fleming, Margaret and Jo McGinnis, eds. *Portraits: Biography and Autobiography in the Secondary School*. Urbana: National Council of Teachers of English, 1985.

Frye, Northrop. *On Teaching Literature*. New York: Harcourt Brace Jovanovich, 1972.

Hoetker, James. *Dramatics and the Teaching of Literature*. Champaign, IL: National Council of Teachers of English/ERIC, 1969.

Holland, Norman. *The Dynamics of Literary Response*. New York: Oxford University Press, 1968.

———. *5 Readers Reading*. New Haven: Yale University Press, 1975.

Iser, Wolfgang. *The Implied Reader: Patterns of Communication in Prose Fiction from Bunyan to Beckett*. Baltimore: The Johns Hopkins University Press, 1974.

———. *The Act of Reading: A Theory of Aesthetic Response*. Baltimore: The Johns Hopkins University Press, 1978.

Johnson, David M. *Word Weaving: A Creative Approach to Teaching and Writing Poetry*. Urbana: National Council of Teachers of English, 1990.

Judy, Stephen N. *Explorations in the Teaching of English*. 2nd ed. New York: Harper & Row, 1981.

Kahn, Elizabeth A., Carolyn Calhoun Walter, and Larry R. Johannessen. *Writing about Literature*. Urbana: National Council of Teachers of English/ERIC, 1984.

Klein, Marvin L. *Talk in the Language Arts Classroom*. Urbana: ERIC/National Council of Teachers of English, 1977.

Mallick, David. *How Tall Is this Ghost, John?* Adelaide: Australian Association for the Teaching of English, 1984. (A text on teaching Shakespeare)

Mandel, Barrett John. *Literature and the English Department*. Urbana: National Council of Teachers of English, 1970.

Miller, Bruce E. *Teaching the Art of Literature*. Urbana: National Council of Teachers of English, 1980.

Milner, Joseph O'Beirne and Lucy Floyd Morcock Milner, eds. *Passages to Literature: Essays on Teaching in Australia, Canada, England, the United States, and Wales*. Urbana: National Council of Teachers of English, 1989.

Moffett, James. *A Student-Centered Language Arts Curriculum, Grades K–13*. Boston: Houghton Mifflin, 1969.

Moran, Charles and Elizabeth F. Penfield, eds. *Conversations: Contemporary Critical Theory and the Teaching of Literature*. Urbana: National Council of Teachers of English, 1990.

Nelms, Ben F., ed. *Literature in the Classroom: Readers, Texts, and Contexts*. National Council of Teachers of English Forum Series. Urbana: National Council of Teachers of English, 1988.

Olson, Gary A., Elizabeth Metzger, and Evelyn Ashton-Jones, eds. *Advanced Placement English: Theory, Politics, and Pedagogy*. Portsmouth: Boynton/Cook, 1989.

Peck, David. *Novels of Initiation: A Guidebook for Teaching Literature to Adolescents*. New York: Teachers College Press, 1989.

Phelan, Patricia, ed. *Talking to Learn*. Classroom Practices in Teaching English, Vol. 24. Urbana: National Council of Teachers of English, 1989.

—————. ed. *Literature and Life: Making Connections in the Classroom*. Classroom Practices in Teaching English, Vol. 25. Urbana: National Council of Teachers of English, 1990.

Probst, Robert E. *Response and Analysis: Teaching Literature in Junior and Senior High School*. Portsmouth: Boynton/Cook, 1988. Originally published as *Adolescent Literature: Response and Analysis*. Columbus: Charles E. Merrill, 1984.

Purves, Alan C. *Elements of Writing about a Literary Work: A Study of Response to Literature*. Urbana: National Council of Teachers of English, 1968.

—————. *Literature Education in 10 Countries*. New York: John Wiley and Sons, 1973.

Purves, Alan C., et al. *How Porcupines Make Love: Notes on a Response-Centered Curriculum*. Lexington, MA: Xerox College Publishing, 1972.

Purves, Alan C. and Richard Beach. *Literature and the Reader*. Urbana: National Council of Teachers of English, 1981.

Purves, Alan C. with Victoria Rippere. *Elements of Writing about a Literary Work: A Study of Response to Literature*. National Council of Teachers of English Research Report No. 9. Champaign, IL: National Council of Teachers of English, 1968.

Rabinowitz, Peter J. *Before Reading: Narrative Conventions and the Politics of Interpretation*. Ithaca: Cornell University Press, 1987.

Rosenblatt, Louise M. *Literature as Exploration*. 4th ed. New York: The Modern Language Association of America, 1983.

—————. *The Reader, the Text, the Poem: The Transactional Theory of the Poem*. Carbondale: Southern Illinois University Press, 1978.

Scholes, Robert. *Textual Power: Literary Theory and the Teaching of English*. New Haven: Yale University Press, 1985.

Simmons, John S., Robert E. Shafer, and Gail B. West. *Decisions about the Teaching of English*. Boston: Allyn and Bacon, 1976.

Slatoff, Walter J. *With Respect to Readers*. Ithaca: Cornell University Press, 1970.

Sloyer, Shirlee. *Readers Theatre: Story Dramatization in the Classroom*. Urbana: National Council of Teachers of English, 1982.

Spann, Sylvia and Mary Beth Culp, eds. *Thematic Units in Teaching English*. Urbana: National Council of Teachers of English, 1975. First Supplement, 1977; Second Supplement, 1980; Third Supplement, 1980.

Squire, James R. *The Responses of Adolescents While Reading Four Short Stories*. National Council of Teachers of English Research Report No. 2. Champaign, IL: National Council of Teachers of English, 1962.

Standford, Barbara Dodds and Karima Amin. *Black Literature for High School Students*. Urbana: National Council of Teachers of English, 1978.

Stottlar, James, ed. *Teaching the Gifted*. Illinois English Bulletin, Winter 1988.

Suleiman, Susan R. and Inge Crosman, eds. *The Reader in the Text: Essays on Audience and Interpretation*. Princeton: Princeton University Press, 1980.

Tompkins, Jane P., ed. *Reader-Response Criticism: From Formalism to Post-Structuralism.* Baltimore: The Johns Hopkins University Press, 1980.

Turner, Darwin T. and Barbara Dodds Stanford. *Theory and Practice in the Teaching of Literature by Afro-Americans.* Urbana: National Council of Teachers of English/ERIC, 1971.

West, William W. *Teaching the Gifted and Talented in the English Classroom.* Washington: National Education Association, 1980.

Whitehead, Frank. *The Disappearing Dais: A Study of the Principles and Practices of English Teaching.* London: Chatto & Windus, 1966.

Wilson, James R. *Responses of College Freshmen to Three Novels.* National Council of Teachers of English Research Report No. 7. Champaign, IL: National Council of Teachers of English, 1966.

Wolf, Dennie Palmer. *Reading Reconsidered: Literature and Literacy in High School.* New York: College Entrance Examination Board, 1988.

Workman, Brooke. *Teaching the Decades.* Urbana: National Council of Teachers of English, 1975.

——. *Writing Seminars in the Content Area: In Search of Hemingway, Salinger, and Steinbeck.* Urbana: National Council of Teachers of English, 1983.

V. Censorship

Anderson, A. J. *Problems in Intellectual Freedom and Censorship.* New York: R. R. Bowker Co., 1974.

Anderson, R. C., et al. *Becoming a Nation of Readers.* Washington, DC: National Institute of Education, 1986.

Anderson, T. H. and B. B. Armbruster. "Studying," in Pearson, P. D., ed. *Handbook of Reading Research.* New York: Longman, 1985.

Anderson, T. H. and D. J. Foertsch. *On Making Frequent Predictions While Reading Expository Text.* Urbana, IL: University of Illinois Center for the Study of Reading, in press.

Beach, Richard. "Issues of Censorship and Research on Effects of and Response to Reading." In Davis, James E., ed. *Dealing with Censorship.* Urbana, IL: National Council of Teachers of English, 1979.

Burress, Lee A. *How Censorship Affects the School.* Special Bulletin No. 8. Wisconsin Council of Teachers of English. Stevens Point, WI: Wisconsin State College, 1963.

Burress, Lee, and Edward Jenkinson. *The Students' Right to Know.* Urbana, IL: National Council of Teachers of English, 1983.

Busha, Charles H. *Freedom Versus Suppression and Censorship; With a Study of the Attitudes of Midwestern Public Librarians and a Bibliography of Censorship.* Littleton, CO: Libraries Unlimited, 1972.

Craig, Alex. *Suppressed Books: A History of the Conception of Literary Obscenity.* Cleveland: World, 1963.

Davis, James E., ed. *Dealing with Censorship.* Urbana, IL: National Council of Teachers of English, 1979.

Donelson, Kenneth L. *The Students' Right to Read.* Rev. ed. Urbana, IL: National Council of Teachers of English, 1972.

Ernst, Morris and Alan U. Schwartz. *Censorship: The Search for the Obscene.*
New York: Macmillan, 1964.

Fellman, Davis. *The Censorship of Books.* Madison, WI: University of
Wisconsin Press, 1957.

Frank, John P. and Robert F. Hogan. *Obscenity, the Law, and the English
Teacher.* Urbana, IL: National Council of Teachers of English, 1966.

Haight, Anne Lyon. *Banned Books: Informal Notes on Some Books Banned for
Various Reasons at Various Times and in Various Places.* 3rd ed. New York:
R. R. Bowker Co., 1970.

Heintzman, R. "Liberalism and Censorship." *Journal of Canadian Studies,*
13(4): 1–2,120–122, 1978.

Hove, John. *Meeting Censorship in the School: A Series of Case Studies.* Urbana,
IL: National Council of Teachers of English, 1967.

Jenkinson, Edward. *Censors in the Classroom.* Carbondale, IL: Southern
Illinois University Press, 1980.

Karolides, Nicholas J. and Lee Burress, eds. *Celebrating Censored Books.*
Urbana, IL: National Council of Teachers of English, 1985.

Moffett, James. "Hidden Impediments to Improving English," *Phi Delta
Kappan* 67(1): 50–56, 1985.

Levine, Alan, et al. *The Rights of Students: The Basic ACLU Guide to a Student's
Rights.* New York: Avon Books, 1973.

Shugert, Diana P., ed. *Rationales for Commonly "Challenged" Taught Books.*
Connecticut Council of Teachers of English. Urbana, IL: National Council
of Teachers of English, 1983.

Index

Ability (*see* High-ability students;
        Low-ability students; Reading
        ability)
Abridgment, censorship by, 307–309
Abstract nouns, discussion, illustration,
        and application of, 53–54
Academic ability (*see* High-ability
        students; Low-ability students)
Academic writing assignments, 172–178
Accountability model, 23, 27
    and quantifiability of teaching goals,
        132
Action, young adult novel and, 100
Adam Bede, 208
Adams, Peter, 179, 180, 181
Adaptation, censorship by, 307–309
The Adding Machine, 13, 37
Adding to the text, as writing
        assignment, 180–181
Adolescents, 2 (*see also* Students)
    children versus, verisimilitude and, 8
    coming of age of (*see* Coming of age
        entries)
    fiction for (*see also* Young adult fiction)
        criteria for judging of, 117–120
    personal characteristics of, and
        reading interests, 85–86
    potential of, reading interests and, 88
    search for self-definition by (*see*
        Self-definition, search for)
    situation of, young adult novel and,
        100–101 (*see also* Young adult
        fiction)

temperament of, and interest in
        reading, 70, 75–76
Adulthood
    initiation into, theme of, 99, 244–248
    transition to (*see* Coming of age *entries*)
Advanced Placement English courses,
        40–41
Advanced Placement program, 274–277
    GPA and, 281
"Advance organizer," 48
Adventure, young adult novel and,
        100
The Adventures of Augie March, 247
The Adventures of Huckleberry Finn, 99,
        151, 199, 215, 246, 247
The Adventures of Tom Sawyer, 214
Advisory Group on History and
        Literature, 28
The Aeneid, 269, 270
Aesop's *Fables*, symbolism in, 15
"Aesthetic effect," 133
Aesthetics, study of, 38–40
Affective goals, 132
Affective learning, 147–148
African-American writers, 256
    Harlem Renaissance and, 209–211
African-American youth, integration of,
        21
After the First Death, 234
Age, of low-ability students, 284
Agee, Hugh, 246, 247, 248
Ah! Wilderness, 9
ALA (American Library Association), 89

329

ALAN (Assembly on Literature for Adolescents National), 89, 107
ALAN Review, 107, 108, 115, 314
Albee, Edward, 168
Alcott, Louisa May, 227
Aldrich, Thomas Bailey, 214, 245, 246
Alger, Horatio, Jr., 245
Allingham, William, 229
All My Sons, 235
All Quiet on the Western Front, 37, 232–233
All Together Now, 234
Altering the text, as writing assignment, 181
Alternative text list, censorship and, 316
Ambiguity, tolerance for, 145
"America," 211
American Civil Liberties Union, and censorship, 303, 312
The American Claimant, 214
American folk tales, symbolism in, 15
American Library Association (ALA), 89
American Memory, 28
America Reads, 307
Amusing Ourselves to Death, 46, 76–78
Analysis
    benefits of, 135
    problems with, 134–135
The Anatomy of Criticism, 198
The Anatomy of Satire, 201
Anderson, Maxwell, 13, 39
"And Suddenly It's Evening," 228
Angle of vision, in young adult novel, 103
Annixter, Paul, 6, 106
Anorexia nervosa, 238
Anthology(ies)
    and interest in reading, 71–72
    in thematic units, 226–227
    use of, 42–43
Antony and Cleopatra, 37, 48, 232
AP (*see* Advanced Placement *entries*)
"A & P," 193
Applebee, Arthur N., 139
Appreciation, self-conscious, 85–86
"Archetypal Criticism: Theory of Myths," 198
Argumentation, logical, 147
Aristophanes, 312
Aristotle, 220
Arnold, Matthew, 208
The Art of the Novel, 106

"As Best She Could," 144
Asch, Sholem, 233
Asimov, Isaac, 12
Aspects of the Novel, 106
Assembly on Literature for Adolescents National (ALAN), 89, 107 (*see also* *ALAN Review*)
Assignments (*see also* Response activities)
    additional, bonus points for, 281–282
    reading (*see also* Reading selections)
        individualization of, 185–186
    writing (*see* Writing assignments)
Atlantic Monthly, 91, 207
"Attack," 233
Attacks on the Freedom to Learn, 304
Attention, listening and, oral expression and, 165–166
Attention span, and interest in reading, 71
Attitude, and book reports, 90–91
Auden, W. H., 168, 233, 234
Austen, Jane, 190, 256
Authors, letters to, as writing assignment, 175
Authorship, dependent, 179
The Autocrat of the Breakfast Table, 208
Availability of young adult fiction, 102
Averitt, Eleanor, 229
The Awakening, 37

Back-to-the-Basics period, 23–24
    effect on teaching of literature, 132
    and young adult fiction, 105
Baez, Joan, 80
Baldwin, James, 210, 243, 256
"Ballad of the Landlord," 210
Banners at Shenandoah, 101
"Baptism," 211
Barchester Towers, 208
Basic English programs, for low-ability students, 283 (*see also* Low-ability students)
Basic Issues Conference, 20–21, 27, 107
The Bear, 246–247
Beauty, study of aesthetics and, 39
"Because River-Fog," 228
Beerbohm, Max, 202
Behavior, disruptive, low-ability students and, 284–285
Behavioral objectives, 132

Behavioral psychology, and
accountability model, 23
Bell, Terrell H., 24
Bellamy, Edward, 252
A Bell for Adamo, 234
Bellow, Saul, 247
"Benito Cereno," 87
Bennett, William, 28
Beowulf, 270
Beyond the Horizon, 223
"Big Little Books," 79
Bildungsroman, 248–250
Biloxi Blues, 38
Biographical and historical approach, 133
Black Boy, 255
Black writers (*see* African-American writers)
Black youth, integration of, 21
Blair, Walter, 215
Bleak House, 208
Bleich, David, 146, 149, 157, 173
The Blithedale Romance, 207
Blount, Nathan S., 106
Blue Fin, 179
The Bluest Eye, 36
Blum, Daniel, 307
Blume, Judy, 104, 314
Bonus points, for high-ability students, 281–282
Book clubs, 83
Book fairs, 84
Book jackets, design of, in reader-response with low-ability students, 292
Booklists (*see* Reading lists)
Book reports
and interest in reading, 89–91
oral, 164
Book reviews, in textual decisions, 91
Books, Van Wyck, 215
Books for You: A Booklist for Senior High Students, 251
Book swaps, 84
Book talks, 82
Boulle, Pierre, 234
Bowdlerization, young adult fiction and, 110
Boyer, Ernest, 25
Boys, attitudes toward reading of, 73–74
Bradbury, Ray, 12, 227, 233
Bragg, Melvyn, 249

Brancato, Robin, 109, 314
The Brand-X Anthology of Poetry, 202
Brave New World, 37, 202, 252–253
Brecht, Berthold, 235
The Bridge Over the River Kwai, 234
Bridgers, Sue Ellen, 101, 109, 234
The Bridges at Toko-Ri, 37, 233
Brighton Beach Memoirs, 38
Broad-range curriculum approaches, 183–203 (*see also* Curriculum organization, broad-range approaches to)
Brontë, Charlotte, 256
Brontë, Emily, 179, 189, 256
Brooke, Rupert, 232
Brooks, Cleanth, 135
Brooks, Gwendolyn, 9
Browning, Elizabeth Barrett, 208
Browning, Robert, 190, 232
Bruner, Jerome, 31
Buchwald, Art, 12, 201
Buck, Pearl S., 109
Buckley, Jerome Hamilton, 248–249
Buck Rogers, 13
Bulimia, 238
Bumper stickers, in reader-response with low-ability students, 292–293
Burroughs, Edgar Rice, 105
Burton, Dwight, 5, 10, 19–20, 105, 106, 163
Bury the Dead, 235
Bush, George, 28
Butler, Samuel, 249
Byron, Lord George Gordon, 217

Caine, Jeffrey, 180
The "Caine" Mutiny, 234
California, legislation for "real literature" in, 29
Campbell, Joseph, 246
Campbell, Patricia, 109
Camus, Albert, 39
The Canterbury Tales, 311 (*see also* Chaucer)
Capote, Truman, 247
Career Education, 23
Carlson, Margaret Anne Zeller, 256–257
Carnegie Commission, 25
Carnegie Report, 25–27
Casebooks, 177
Catch-22, 202

The Catcher in the Rye, 5, 9, 99, 112, 212, 241, 247, 248, 302
Cather, Willa, 87
Catherine, Her Book, 180
Catherwood, Mary, 214
Cats, 271
Catton, Bruce, 101
CEEB (College Entrance Examination Board), Commission on English of, 21, 107
The Celebrated Jumping Frog of Calaveras County and Other Sketches, 215
Censorship, 296–320 (*see also* Taboos)
  by abridgment and adaptation, 307–309
  and bowdlerization, 110
  and *Brave New World*, 253
  classic, 299–304
  discussion of, within course, 318
  Hatch amendment and, 298
  kinds of, 299–313
  organizations involved in, 299
  parents and, 74–75
    consent statements and, 315
  potential for, realism and, 88
  proactive, 304–307
    teachers and, 316–317
  publications about, 327–328
  of school journalism, 309–312
  of students' creative writing, 312–313
  and suggestions for classroom teachers, 314–319
  verisimilitude and, 10
  and young adult fiction, 313–314
Ceremony of Innocence, 234
Certainty, search for, realism and, 86–87
Character(s)
  letters to, as writing assignment, 175
  as literary element
    in drama, 195
    in fiction, 194
  readers' relationship with, 140–141
  in response-centered lesson, 150
  statements of, in young adult novel, 103
  stock, comedy and, 199–200
Chaucer, Geoffrey, 15, 202, 311, 312
Cheney, Lynne, 28, 31
"Cherrylog Road," 9
"Chicago School," 136

Childhood
  topics from, 95
  transition to adulthood from (*see* Coming of age *entries*)
Children
  adolescents versus, verisimilitude and, 8
  literature teaching for, secondary school literature teaching versus, 95–97
Childress, Alice, 303
The Chocolate War, 113, 201, 314
Choice (*see also* Reading interests)
  "Fifty-two Pick-up" and, 84
  for high-ability students, 273
  in recreational reading, 37, 38
Christenbury, Leila, 150–152
A Christmas Carol, 15, 56
Chronological approach, focused, 207–211
Chronological survey approach, 188–191
Cicero, 19
Citizens, in classic censorship, 299–304
Citizens United for Responsible Education, 299
Clarke, Arthur C., 12
Class discussion (*see* Discussion)
Classic censorship, 299–304
Classicism, after World War I, 19
Classics
  contemporary works versus, 42, 91
  empathy and, 4
  interest of readers and, 47
  junk versus, 42
  simplified, 80–82
  young adult novels versus, 105–107
Class organization, and stress in high-ability students, 279–280
Class response (*see* Response activities)
Classroom
  disruption of, low-ability students and, 284–285
  promotion of interest in, 88–93
Classroom libraries, and interest in reading, 82–83
Classroom teachers (*see* Teachers)
"A Clean, Well-lighted Place," 193
Clemens, Samuel (*see* Twain, Mark)
CLEP (College Level Examination Program), 276
Close reading, 142–145

Cognitive learning, 141–147

Coleridge, Samuel Taylor, 10

Colleagues, support of, censorship and, 317

College
preparation for, 40–41
secondary school and, dual
enrollment in, 278–279

College English Association, 20

College Entrance Examination Board
(CEEB), Commission on English
of, 21, 107

College entrance tests, stress in
high-ability students and, 280

College Level Examination Program
(CLEP), 276

Comedy, in mythic approach, 199–200

Comic books, 79

Coming Home, 233

Coming of age
developmental tasks in, 237–243
home environment and, 244
prejudice and, 244
substance abuse and, 243–244

Coming of age fiction
types of, 244–250
uses of, 250–251

Command Decision, 235

Commercials, oral book reports in form
of, 164

Commission on English, CEEB, 21, 107

Committee on Thematic Units in
Literature, 227

Communication, oral reading and, 160

Communication for Survival, 19

Community(ies)
correlative experience and, 6
groups in, censorship and, 317–319
mores of, 297–298
verisimilitude and, 10

Compensatory education, for low-ability
students, 283 (*see also* Low-ability
students)

Complexity, stylistic, young adult fiction
and, 103–104

Composition (*see* Written expression)

Comprehension (*see also* Reading
comprehension)
listening capabilities and, 65

Concerned Women of America, 299

Concrete responses, for low-ability
students, 292–294

Conflicts
between parents and adolescents,
240
in young adult novel, 104

*A Connecticut Yankee in King Arthur's
Court*, 216

Connolly, Marc, 13

Conquistador, 270

Conroy, Frank, 168

Consent, parental, censorship and, 315

Contemporary settings, young adult
fiction and, 101–102

Contemporary works
classics versus, 42, 91
older works versus, 42

The Contender, 100, 113, 314

Context, meaning through, 54–55

Contrivance, irony versus, 87–88

Coriolanus, 232

Cormier, Robert, 104, 109, 113, 175, 201,
234, 286, 314

Correct interpretation, concept of,
134–136

Correlative experience, 96, 296
empathy and, 4–7
importance of, 42
interpersonal problems and, interest
in reading and, 75–76
listening capabilities and, 64
reading selections and, 47–48
reflection on, 35–36
sources of, 6–7
symbolism and, 16

Coryell, Nancy Gillmore, 185

Council for Basic Education, and young
adult fiction, 105

Country music, 79–80

The Courtship of Miles Standish, 208

The Craft of Fiction, 106

Crane, 211

Crane, Stephen, 19, 87, 227

Creative work, for high-ability students,
271–272

Creative writing, censorship of, 312–313

Creative writing assignments, 172,
178–181
for high-ability students, 271–272
poetry and, 198

Credibility
of language, young adult fiction and,
102

willing suspension of disbelief and, 10–14
Critical analysis essay, 175–176
Critical reading, 34–35, 96
    abilities in, inadequacy of, 27
Criticism
    historical trends in, 133–136
    neo-Aristotelian, 136
    reader-response, 136–137
    selected works of, 322–323
    social, as literary topic, 254–255
Cross referencing, 55
"A Crow in a Bare Branch," 228
The Crucible, 37
"The Cub," 48
Culler, Jonathan, 147
Culp, Mary Beth, 227
Cultural awareness, 96
Cultural heritage, opportunities for study of, 36–37
Cultural importance, recognized, 186
Cultural Literacy, 27–29, 31–33
Cultural Literacy: What Every American Needs to Know, 29, 31–33
Culturally disadvantaged, 21
cummings, e. e., 232
Curricular policy, and censorship, 315
Curriculum(a)
    for high-ability students, 266–274
    middle school (*see* Middle school literature curriculum)
    response-centered, 137–140 (*see also* Reader-response orientation)
    testing, evaluating, and grading in, 153–155
    secondary school (*see* Secondary school literature curriculum)
    specific areas of, opportunities for becoming expert in, 269–270
Curriculum organization
    broad-range approaches to, 183–203
        chronological survey, 188–191
        free reading, 186–188
        genre approach, 191–198
        mythic approach, 198–203
    focused approaches to, 205–235
        chronological, 207–211
        major idea approach, 216–224
        major writer approach, 211–216
        thematic approach, 224–235, 250–251
    general principles for, 183–186

Cyrano de Bergerac, 39

Dad, 133–134
Danziger, Paula, 314
Dartmouth College, August 1966 debate at, 22
Darwin, Charles, 208
David Copperfield, 1, 249
Davis, Gary A., 263, 265
Davis, James, 112, 123
Death of a Salesman, 39, 223
Decades, in focused chronological approach, 207–211
Deductive study, in major idea approach, 217
The Deer Stalker, 233
Defoe, Daniel, 189, 227
Delight, unconscious, 86
Demosthenes, 19
Dependent authorship, 179
Depression era (*see* Great Depression)
Details
    excessive attention to, intensive study versus, 185
    and reading comprehension, 58
"Developmental," defined, 46
Developmental reading process, 45–64 (*see also* Reading)
Developmental tasks, in coming of age, 237–243
DeVoto, Bernard, 214, 215
Dewey, John, 19, 320
Dialect, listening comprehension and, 65
The Diary of Anne Frank, 233
Dickens, Charles, 1, 15, 19, 56, 104, 164, 208–209, 249, 254, 265, 287
Dickey, James, 9
Dickinson, Emily, 256
Dictionaries, cross referencing and, 55
Disaffectedness, in low-ability students, 284
Disbelief, willing suspension of, promotion of, 10–14, 99
Discovery, writing as process of, 167–168
Discussion (*see also* Oral expression)
    whole-group versus small-group, 158–160
    high-ability students and, 268
Disruptive behavior, low-ability students and, 284–285
The Distant Summer, 234

District policy documents, and censorship, 315

The Divine Comedy, 269

Divorce, 244

Dixon, John, 18, 22

"Does It Matter," 233

A Doll's House, 37, 152, 153, 163, 223

Donelson, Kenneth, 94, 110, 125–129

The Door into Ocean, 252

Dos Passos, John, 255

Drama
   expressionistic plays, suspension of disbelief and, 13
   in genre approach, 195–196

Dramatic activity
   for high-ability students, 271
   improvised, 161–164
   for low-ability students, 290

Drawings, in reinforcement, 61–62

"Dread," 229

"A Dream Deferred," 210

Dreams, as writing assignment, 181

Dreiser, Theodore, 104

Dual enrollment, high school–college, 278–279

du Maurier, Daphne, 38

Dunning, Stephen, 88, 99, 100, 101, 103, 104, 105, 111, 112, 114, 228, 314

Dylan, Bob, 80

Dynamic character development, 194, 195

Eagle Forum, 299

Early, Margaret, 85, 226

Early childhood literature curriculum, secondary school curriculum versus, transition concept and, 95–97

Eating disorders, 238

Eberhart, Richard, 234

Educational Research Analysis Corporation, 299

Educational Testing Service, and Advanced Placement Program, 276–277

Education of the Gifted and Talented, 263

Edwards, Jonathan, 184

The Effect of Gamma Rays on Man-in-the-Moon Marigolds, 9

Eggleston, Edward, 214

El Cid, 270

Elementary grades, use of literature in, 3

Eliot, George, 19, 208, 227, 249, 256

Eliot, T. S., 135, 271

Elizabethan Age of England, in major idea approach, 219, 222–223

The Elizabethan World Picture, 222

Elizabeth the Queen, 39

Ellis, W. Geiger, 107–110

Ellison, Ralph, 210, 256

Emerson, Ralph Waldo, 208, 254

Emotional range of readers, reading selections and, 47

Empathy
   in high-ability students, 265
   promotion of, 4–7

The Emperor Jones, 13

Employment, part-time
   correlative experience and, 7
   stress caused by, 280–281

Endings
   in comedy, 199
   search for certainty and, 86–87
   in young adult novel, 104

England, Elizabethan Age of, in major idea approach, 219, 222–223

English Journal, 105

English Language Arts, NCTE Curriculum Commission and, 20

Enjoyment
   reading for, in childhood, 95
   unconscious, 85

Entertainment
   sacrifice of literary understanding for, 70
   taste versus, 91

Environment, home (*see* Home environment)

Epics, romantic, willing suspension of disbelief and, 13

Epilogue, as writing assignment, 181

Erewhon, 37

Ericson, Bonnie O., 226

Escape reading, Teen Age Romances as, 78

Esquire, 78–79

Essays
   Advanced Placement, 275–276
   critical analysis, 175–176

Established texts, popular literature versus, 91

Ethnicity (*see* African-American *entries*;
    Minorities; Multi-ethnic literary
    elements)
Evaluation, in response-centered
    curriculum, 153–155
Evans, William R., 106
Events, ordering of, 62
    in young adult novel, 103
Exaggeration, suspension of disbelief
    and, 11, 12
Examinations (*see* Testing *entries*)
Exemplum, symbolism and, 15
Exodus, 233
Expectations, and tracking, 261
Experience
    correlative (*see* Correlative experience)
    shared, Herber exercises and, 51–52
An Experience Curriculum in English, 19
Expressionistic plays, suspension of
    disbelief and, 13

Facts, and reading comprehension, 58
Fader, Daniel, 37, 187
Fail Safe, 233
"The Fall of the House of Usher," 194
Falwell, Jerry, 10, 299
Family, correlative experience and, 6
Fantasy, children and, 95
A Farewell to Arms, 37, 212, 232
Farrell, Alyne, 83
Farrell, James T., 250, 254
Fathom Five, 234
Faulkner, William, 39, 103, 193, 212,
    246–247, 265
Feedback from students, censorship and,
    316
Female Man, 252
Feminist literary elements, demand for,
    27
Feminist Movement (*see also* Women)
    forerunners to, 37
Fiction (*see also* Novels; Short stories)
    for adolescents, criteria for judging of,
    117–120
    coming of age (*see* Coming of age
    entries)
    elements of, 193–195
    initiation, 244–248
    young adult (*see* Young adult fiction)
Fielding, Henry, 104
"Fifty-two Pick-up," 83–84

Film(s)
    impact of, on curriculum, 21
    for low-ability students, 290–291
    in thematic approach, 229
    thriller movies, 80
Fitzgerald, F. Scott, 20, 109, 209
Flash Gordon, 13
Flat characters, 194, 195
Flaubert, Gustave, 39
Flexibility, thematic approach and, 225
Florida statewide testing program, 23–24
    and critical reading, 35
Focused chronological approach, 207–211
    Illustrative Unit of, 209–211
Focused curriculum approaches, 205–235
    (*see also* Curriculum
    organization, focused
    approaches to)
Folk tales, symbolism in, 15
Footnotes, cross referencing and, 55
Forbes, Esther, 101
"The Forecast," 229
Foreign language, and International
    Baccalaureate program, 277–278
Formalism, 133
Forman, James, 234
Forster, E. M., 194
For Want of a Nail, 249
For Whom the Bell Tolls, 234
"Four Ducks on a Pond," 229
Fox, Paula, 181
Franny and Zooey, 212
Frazer, Sir James, 246
Freedom and Discipline in English, 21, 107
Free Fall, 249
Free reading approach, 186–188
Friendships, 239
From Here to Eternity, 234
Frost, Robert, 20, 58, 87, 212, 229, 230
Frye, Northrop, 198, 199, 200
Fukuyala, Kiyowara, 228
Fuller, Henry Blake, 214
Functional Literacy, as primary goal,
    23–24
Functional Literacy Test, 24
    and critical reading, 34–35
*The Further Adventures of Huckleberry
    Finn*, 180
Future, decisions about, coming of age
    and, 241–242
Future Shock, 7

"Fuzzy Wuzzy," 232

Gabler, Mel, 10, 299, 305
Gabler, Norma, 10, 299, 305
Gardner, David, 24
Gardner report, 24–25
Garland, Hamlin, 214
Gascoyne, David, 234
Gates-MacInitie Reading Test, 59
Gay adolescents, 239
Genre approach, 191–198
Genres, shifting, 181
Gifted students (*see* High-ability
        students)
Gilman, Charlotte Perkins, 252
Girlie magazines, 78–79
The Glass Menagerie, 36
Globe Book Literature, 80, 81
Glossaries, cross referencing and, 55
Goals, accountability movement and, 132
God's Trombones, 210
Goethe, Johann Wolfgang von, 248
Golden Age of Greece, in major idea
        approach, 219, 220–221
Golding, William, 36, 102, 144, 249
Goodbye, Columbus, 71
Goodbye, My Lady, 100
Gordon, Caroline, 135
Gordon, Lord George, 217
Go Tell It on the Mountain, 243
Grade point average (GPA), stress and,
        281
Grading
    in response-centered curriculum,
        153–155
    stress and, 281–282
The Grapes of Wrath, 36, 212, 255
The Grass Harp, 247
Great Books, 37
Great Depression
    curriculum changes with, 19–20
    opportunities for study of, 36
    and social criticism, 255
Great Expectations, 4, 19, 164, 189, 190,
        249, 250, 287
Great Testing Movement, 27
Greece, Golden Age of, in major idea
        approach, 219, 220–221
Greek tragedy, 39
The Greek Way to Civilization, 220
Greene, Bette, 234

Green Pastures, 13
Grey, Zane, 105
Griffith, Mary, 252
Groups
    for class discussion, whole group
        versus small groups, 158–160
    community, censorship and, 317–319
    for Herber exercises, 49
    high-ability students and, 268–269
    tracking and, 259–261
Growth spurt, and coming of age,
        237–238
Growth Through English, 18, 22
Guest, Judith, 99
Guidance counselors, teachers as,
        interest in reading and, 76
Guided individualized reading, thematic
        approach and, 225–226
Gulliver's Travels, 37, 202
"Gunga Din," 232

Haines, William W., 235
Hamilton, Edith, 220
Hamlet, 141, 145–146, 155, 185, 196,
        200–201, 308
Handicapped students, mainstreaming
        of, 259–260
Hansberry, Lorraine, 227
Hard Times, 208–209
Hardy, Thomas, 232, 249
"Harlem," 210
Harlem Renaissance, in focused
        chronological approach,
        Illustrative Unit of, 209–211
Harlequin series, 108, 110
Harper's, 91, 207
Harte, Bret, 214
Hatch, Orrin, 298
Hatch amendment, 298, 300
Hatfield, W. Wilbur, 19
Hawthorne, Nathaniel, 19, 207, 212
Hayakawa, S. I., 54
Headlines, writing of, in reader-response
        with low-ability students, 292–293
The Heart Is a Lonely Hunter, 247, 248
"Heat," 229
Heath, Curtis, 229
Heathcliff, 180
Hefner, Hugh, 79
Heine, Heinrich, 229
Heinlein, Robert, 12

Heller, Joseph, 202
Hellman, Lillian, 235
Hemingway, Ernest, 20, 39, 86, 109, 193, 200, 209, 212, 232, 234, 293
Henry V, 232
Herber, Harold, 48, 296
Herber exercises, 48–51
  creation of, 52
  rationale for, and nature of, 51–53
Here Is Your War, 233
Herland, 252
A Hero Ain't Nothing but a Sandwich, 303
Heroes/heroines
  in romance, 200
  suspension of disbelief and, 13
Herrick, Robert, 9
Hersey, John, 234
Hesse, Hermann, 229
Heterogeneous grouping, homogeneous grouping versus, 260–261
Hiawatha, 208
High-ability students, 261–282
  all-class work for, 268
  characteristics of, 262–266
  choices about topics for, 273
  creative work for, 271–272
  independent work for, 268–269
  intellectual self-discipline in, 273–274
  interdisciplinary study for, 270–271
  interest in reading and, 72–73
  leadership skills and, 272–273
  opportunities for becoming expert, 269–270
  principles of teaching literature to, 266–274
  small-group work for, 268
  special courses for, 274–279
    Advanced Placement, 274–277
    high school–college dual enrollment, 278–279
    International Baccalaureate, 277–278
  stress in, 279–282
Highet, Gilbert, 201, 202
High Interest—Easy Reading for Junior and Senior High School Students, 286
High School, 25–27
High school (*see* Secondary school *entries*)
A High Wind in Jamaica, 179
Hill, Grace Livingston Luce, 105
Hinton, Susan E., 112, 113, 137, 138, 314
Hipple, Theodore, 113

Hiroshima, 233
Hirsch, E. D., Jr., 29, 31–33
Historical–biographical approach, 133
Historical novels, young adult fiction and, 101–102
History, literary art and, chronological survey and, 190
The Hobbit, 38
Holmes, Oliver Wendell, 19, 208
Home environment (*see also* Parent[s])
  and coming of age, 244
  and interest in reading, 74–75
Homer, 81
Homogeneous grouping, heterogeneous grouping versus, 260–261
Homosexual orientations, 239
Honesty, intellectual, 145–146
Honor sampling, of young adult fiction, 125–129
Honors courses, GPA and, 281
Hooked on Books: Program & Proof, 37, 187
Horace, 19, 202
Horatian satire, 202
Household Words, 208
House Made of Dawn, 257
The House of the Seven Gables, 207
Howe, E. W., 214
Howells, William Dean, 8
Hughes, Langston, 210–211, 256
Hughes, Richard, 179
Human animal, nature and, thematic unit on, 227–230
The Humanities: Cultural Roots and Continuities, 311
Humor
  high-ability students and, 265
  satire and, 202–203 (*see also* Satire)
Humphrey, Hubert H., 22
Huxley, Aldous, 202, 252

I Am the Cheese, 9, 286, 314
IB (International Baccalaureate) program, 277–278
Ibsen, Henrik, 152, 223
The Idea of a University, 208
Idiot's Delight, 235
Idylls of the King, 208
"If It Were Not for the Voice," 228
"If We Must Die," 211
The Iliad, 231, 232, 269

Illustrative Units
    of focused chronological period,
        209–211
    of major idea approach, 218–224
    of major writer approach, 212–216
    of thematic approach, 227–235
Imaginative entry, 5, 10, 98
Imaginative reconstruction, 179–180
Improbable stories, children and, 95
Improvised dramatic activity, 161–164
Indifference, adolescence and, 70
Individual activity, for high-ability
        students, 268–269
Individuality, sense of, development of,
        240–241
Individualization
    heterogenous grouping and, 260–261
    of reading assignments, 185–186
    thematic approach and, 225–226
Individually Prescribed Instruction, 24
Individual teachers (*see also* Teachers)
    roles of, 41–43
In Dubious Battle, 255
Inductive study, in major idea approach,
        217
Initiation into adulthood, theme of, 99,
        244–248
In Memoriam, 208
The Innocents Abroad, 214
Institutional constraints, and teaching of
        literature, 131
Instruction (*see also* Teaching)
    flexibility in, thematic approach and, 225
Integration, 21
Intellectual ability (*see* High-ability
        students; Low-ability students)
Intellectual activity, writing as, 167–168
Intellectual honesty, 145–146
Intellectual self-discipline, high-ability
        students and, 273–274
Intensive study, organizational pattern
        and, 184–185
Interdisciplinary study, high-ability
        students and, 270–271
Interest in reading, 46, 69–84 (*see also*
        Reading interests)
    classroom promotion of, 88–93
    factors affecting, 70–82
        adolescence, 75–76
        "competitors" other than television,
            78–82
        home environment, 74–75
        reading ability, 70–74
        television, 76–78
    sex and, 73–74
    stimulation of
        methods for, 82–84
        organizational pattern and, 184
Interests
    of high-ability students, 265
    of low-ability students, 285
International Baccalaureate program,
        277–278
Interpersonal problems, and interest in
        reading, 75–76
Interpretations
    New Critics and, 133–135
    small-group discussion and, 159
    social learning and, 141
"In the Fog," 229
Iron Maiden, 79
Irony, contrivance versus, 87–88
Irony–satire (*see also* Satire)
    in mythic approach, 201–203
Irvine, Carolyn L., 110
Island Trees School Board, and
        censorship, 302–303
Ivanhoe, 19
"I Wandered Lonely as a Cloud," 229

Jackson, Shirley, 61
Jacobowsky and the Colonel, 233
Jacob's Room, 249
Jaffe, Dan, 229
James, Henry, 19, 87, 106, 194, 246
James, William, 19
Jarrell, Randall, 234
Jenkinson, Ed, 305
Jennings, Frank, 105
John Brown's Body, 270
Johnny Tremaine, 101
Johnson, James Weldon, 210
Jones, Donald, 144
Jones, James, 234
Journal(s)
    in English education and teaching of
        literature, 322
    as writing assignment, 174
Journalism
    literature versus, suspension of
        disbelief and, 11
    school, censorship of, 309–312

Joyce, James, 39, 243, 249, 264
Jude the Obscure, 249
Julius Caesar, 19, 37, 185, 232
Jung, Carl, 246
The Jungle, 254
Junior Novels, 20 (*see also* Young adult fiction)
  selected list of, 123
"Junk," classics versus, 42
Juvenal, 202
Juvenalian satire, 202

Kafka, Franz, 11, 103, 233
The Kalevala, 270
"Kansas Boy," 229
Kaufman and Hart, 38
Kazin, Alfred, 215
Keats, John, 39
Kelly, Patricia P., 150–152
Kelly, Sean, 202
Kenney, William, 195
Kidnapped, 19
"The Killers," 86
The Killing Fields, 233
King, Stephen, 38, 87, 99
King Lear, 219
Kipling, Rudyard, 232
Kleihauer, Lois Dykmann, 48
Knowledge, writing as intellectual activity and, 167–168
Knowles, John, 36, 190
Korean War, opportunities for study of, 37

"The Lady of the Lake," 4
La Haye, Beverly, 299
"The Lake Isle at Innisfree," 229
Lamb, Charles, 202
Landmark Series, 80
Lane, Mary Bradley, 252
Language (*see also* Vocabulary)
  credibility of, young adult fiction and, 102
  in reading selections, 47
  testing of, for International Baccalaureate program, 277–278
Language ability, in high-ability students, 263
Language experience approach, for low-ability students, 288–289
Language in Thought and Action, 54

The Last Mission, 234
Lawrence, D. H., 249
The Lay of Igor's Campaign, 270
Leadership skills, high-ability students and, 272–273
Learners (*see also* Students)
  teachers as, 139
Learning
  affective, 147–148
  cognitive, 141–147
  independent, high-ability students and, 269
  social, 140–141
  writing as process in, 167–168
Least restrictive environments, 259–260
Leaves of Grass, 208
Lechlitner, Ruth, 229
Lee, Harper, 201
The Left Hand of Darkness, 252
"Legacy," 229
LeGuin, Ursula K., 252
Leisure time, reading in, 37–38
"Leningen Versus the Ants," 230
Lessing, Doris, 39
Lesson(s)
  planning for, 139
  response-centered, 149–155
  sample (*see also* Illustrative Units)
    in reading, 59–64
Letters, as writing assignment, 174–175
Leuders, Edward, 228
Lewis, C. S., 227
Libertarian groups, and censorship, 306
Liberty Forum, 299
Library, classroom, and interest in reading, 82–83
Library resources
  cross referencing and, 55
  research papers and, 176–177
Life Nature Library, 228
Life on the Mississippi, 214, 215
Lifestyle(s)
  correlative experience and, 6
  experimentation with, 240
The Light in the Forest, 101
Lines, sentences versus, in poetry, 197
Lipsyte, Robert, 100, 113, 314
Listening, oral expression and, 165–166
Listening capabilities
  forms of oral interpretation and, 65–66
  reading and, 64–68

Literacy (*see* Cultural Literacy; Functional Literacy)
Literal recall, tests of, 154
Literary art, history and, chronological survey and, 190
Literary criticism
  historical trends in, 133–136
  works of, 322–323
Literary elements
  close reading and, 142–145
  feminist, demand for, 27
  in fiction, 193–195
  genre approach and, 192
  multi-ethnic, demand for, 27
Literary periods, chronological survey and, 190
Literary realism (*see* Realism)
Literary topics of special importance, 237–258
  coming of age, 237–251 (*see also* Coming of age *entries*)
  for high-ability students, 269–270
  literature by and about women and minorities, 255–257
  social criticism, 254–255
  utopia, 251–254
Literary understanding, sacrifice of, for entertainment, 70
Literature
  appreciation of, stages of, 85–86
  defined, 33–34
  history of, literature itself versus, 190–191
  journalism versus, suspension of disbelief and, 11
  oral, for low-ability students, 289
  popular (*see* Popular literature)
  reasons for teaching, 139–140
  selections of (*see* Reading selections)
  special topics in (*see* Literary topics of special importance)
  transition from reading to study of, 3–4, 94–99 (*see also* Young adult fiction)
Literature as Exploration, 296
"Literature for Adolescents—Pap or Protein," 105
Literature for Today's Young Adults, 94
Literature Study in the High Schools, 105
Little Dorrit, 208
Little men, little women works, 104–105

Little Rock Central High School, 21
Logical argumentation, 147
Logical thinking, in high-ability students, 264
London, Jack, 227, 230
Long Day's Journey into Night, 196
Longfellow, Henry Wadsworth, 19, 208
Look Homeward, Angel: A Story of the Buried Life, 250
Looking Backward: 2000–1887, 252
Lord of the Flies, 36, 102, 143, 144, 169, 170, 181, 233
Loring, Emily, 105
"Lost," 229
"Lost Generation," 209, 223
"The Lottery," sample reading lesson using, 59–64
"Love," 228
"The Love Song of J. Edgar Hoover," 202
Low-ability students, 282–294
  alternatives to reading for, 289
  characteristics of, 283–285
  language experience approach to, 288–289
  materials for, 286–288
  nonprint media and, 289–291
  reader-response with, 291–294
Lowell, Robert, 19
Lubbock, Percy, 106
"The Lynching," 211
Lyons/Carnahan Classmate editions, 80
Lyrical Ballads, 10, 218
Lyrics, popular music, 79–80

Macbeth, 19, 66, 102, 185, 219, 222, 223, 232, 290
McCrimmon, James M., 167
McCullers, Carson, 241, 247
McGahey, Jeanne, 229
The Machine Gunner, 234
McKay, Claude, 211
McNeil, Elton, 37, 187
Magazines, girlie, 78–79
Mailer, Norman, 234
Mainstreaming, 260
Major idea approach, 216–224
  Illustrative Unit of, 218–224
Major writer approach, 211–216
  Illustrative Unit of, 212–216
Male students, attitudes toward reading of, 73–74

"Mandalay," 232
The Man in the Gray Flannel Suit, 9
Man-versus-fate conflict, in young adult novel, 104
Man-versus-self conflict, in young adult novel, 104
Marius the Epicurean, 249
Matched pairs, in Herber exercises, 50
Matthews, Dorothy, 286
Matthews, Greg, 180
Maugham, W. Somerset, 249
Mazer, Harry, 234
Mazer, Norma Fox, 109
Meaning
    compression of, in anthologies, 71–72
    through context, 54–55
Media, nonprint (*see* Nonprint media)
Melville, Herman, 19, 87, 207, 212
The Member of the Wedding, 241, 247
Memorization, Cultural Literacy and, 32
The Merchant of Venice, 4, 199
Meredith, George, 249
"The Metamorphosis," 11–12
Metaphor, 55–57
    reading ability and, interest in reading and, 71
Michener, James, 37
Middlemarch, 189
Middle school literature curriculum (*see also* Curriculum *entries*)
    components of, 41
    thematic unit for, 227–230
    young adult fiction in (*see* Young adult fiction)
Middle school movement, effects on teaching of literature, 131
A Midsummer Night's Dream, 19
Mill, John Stuart, 208
Miller, Arthur, 219, 223, 224, 235
"The Miller's Tale," 311
The Mill on the Floss, 249
Milton, John, 184
Ministerial groups, censorship and, 317–319
Minorities, literature by and about, 209–211, 255–257
Misreadings, response-centered lesson and, 149–152
Mizora: A Prophecy, 252
Moby Dick, 207
Modern Language Association, 20

"A Modest Proposal," 12, 202
Moll Flanders, 189
Momaday, N. Scott, 257
Monologues, in satire, 201
The Moon Is Down, 234
Moral Majority, 299
Morals, symbolism and, 15
Moral thinking, in high-ability students, 265
More, Sir Thomas, 251
Mores
    censorship and, 297–298
    verisimilitude and, 10
Morley, Christopher, 229
Morris, Desmond, 303
Morrison, Toni, 36
Most important word technique, 149
    small-group discussion and, 159
Motivation, of high-ability students, 264
"Motto," 210
The Mountain Lion, 247, 248
The Mountain Men, 270
Movies (*see* Film[s])
Mowat, Farley, 270
Muller, Alfred P., 103, 114–115, 124
Multidimensional approaches, 2
Multi-ethnic literary elements, 42
    demand for, 27
Murray, Donald, 168, 169
Music
    popular, 79–80
    rap, 289
Myers, Madeleine, 164
The Mysterious Stranger, 202, 216
Mythic approach, 198–203
Mythology, 220

NAEP (National Assessment of Educational Progress), 226
Nakasukasa, 228
The Naked and the Dead, 234
The Naked Ape, 303
Narrative
    ability to follow, and interest in reading, 71
    satiric, 202
    structure of, and interest in reading, 71
Narrator, in young adult novel, 103
National Assessment of Educational Progress (NAEP), 226

National Association of Christian
     Educators, 299
National Center of Excellence in English,
     131
National Commission on Excellence in
     Education, 24
  ALAN and, 107
National Council of Teachers of English
     (NCTE), 20, 167, 300
  ALAN and, 89
  coming of age literature and, 251
  Curriculum Commission of, 20
  and young adult fiction, 105
  National Center of Excellence in
     English and, 131
  resolution on abridgment or
     adaptation as form of censorship,
     308–309
  thematic units and, 227
National Endowment for the Humanities
     (NEH), and Cultural Literacy,
     27–29, 31
National Lampoon Group, 202
National Legal Foundation, 299
National Science Foundation, 20
A Nation at Risk, 24–25
Native American literature, 257
Native Son, 255
Nature, and human animal, thematic
     unit on, 227–230
NCTE (*see* National Council of Teachers
     of English)
NEH (*see* National Endowment for the
     Humanities)
Neighborhood, correlative experience
     and, 6
Nemerov, Howard, 234
Neo-Aristotelian criticism, 136
Never Cry Wolf, 270–271
New Criticism, 133–136, 138
  and ambiguity, 145
  and close reading, 142, 143
  genre approach and, 191, 198
New England Puritan society,
     opportunities for study of, 37
Newman, John Henry, 208
Newspapers, school, censorship of,
     309–312
New Testament, parables from,
     symbolism in, 15
The New York Times Book Review, 91

The Nibelungenlied, 270
Nilsen, Alleen Pace, 94, 125–129
1984, 201, 253
Nixon, Richard M., 22
Nonfiction novel, 193
Nonprint media (*see also* Film[s];
     Television)
  correlative experience and, 6–7
  for low-ability students, 289–291
  text versions in, print versions versus,
     91–92
  use of, 42
Norris, Frank, 254
Norton Critical Editions, 177
"A Note on Commercial Theatre," 210
Note-taking, listening capabilities and, 67
Nouns, abstract, 53–54
Novels (*see also* Fiction)
  in genre approach, 192–195
  nonfiction, 193
  Novel of Initiation, 99, 244–248
  in Passages Reading Program, 287
  popularity of, reasons for, 192–193
  structure of, and interest in reading, 71
  utopian, 251–254
  verisimilitude and, 9
"November Day," 229
"The Nun's Priest's Tale," 202

Objective tests, 154
Objects, in reader-response with
     low-ability students, 293–294
O'Brien, Robert C., 287
O'Connor, Flannery, 212, 256
The Octopus, 254
O'Donoghue, Michael, 202
The Odyssey, 81, 269
Oedipus Rex, 200, 220
Of Human Bondage, 249
Of Mice and Men, 212
The Old Man and the Sea, 200, 212, 293
"An Old Man's Winter Night," 229
"The Old Pond," 228
O'Neill, Eugene, 9, 13, 20, 65, 196, 212,
     219, 223
On Liberty, 208
On the Beach, 233
On the Road, 210
Oral expression, 157–166 (*see also* Oral
     presentation[s])
  book reports in, 164

improvised dramatic activity in, 161–164
listening and, 165–166
oral reading in, 160 (*see also* Oral reading)
Readers Theatre in, 161
whole-group versus small-group discussion in, 158–160
Oral literature, and low-ability students, 289
Oral presentation(s) (*see also* Listening *entries*; Oral expression; Recordings)
and drama reading, 195–196
forms of, 65–66
practice of, 67
as reinforcement, 61
Oral reading, 160 (*see also* Oral presentation[s])
frequent use of, with children, 95
for low-ability students, 289
"Orchard," 229
The Ordeal of Richard Feverel, 249
Order, and reading comprehension, 58
Ordinary People, 9, 99
"Oregon Winter," 229
Organizational pattern, 184–186 (*see also* Curriculum organization)
The Origin of Species, 208
Orthodontia, 238
Orthopedic appliances, 238
Orwell, George, 110, 201, 227, 253
Other Voices, Other Rooms, 247, 248
Oui, 79
Our Town, 102
"Out, Out—," 87
Outreach activities, initiative in, censorship and, 317–319
The Outsiders, 112–113, 137–138, 314
Owen, Wilfred, 232

Paperback classroom libraries, 82–83
Parables, New Testament, symbolism in, 15
Paradise Lost, 232, 269
"The Pardoner's Tale," 15
Parent(s)
attitudes of, and interest in reading, 74–75, 83
censorship and, 74–75
consent statements and, 315
conflicts between adolescents and, 240
divorced, 244
verisimilitude and, 10
Parent-child cooperation, and interest in reading, 83
Parody, 201–202
Part-time employment
correlative experience and, 7
stress caused by, 280–281
Passages Reading Program, 287
Pater, Walter, 249
Paterson, 270
Paterson, Katherine, 101, 109
Patterson, Sarah, 234
"Paul's Case," 87
The Pearl, 106
Peck, Richard, 109, 314
Peck, Robert Newton, 101, 109
Peer evaluation of listening capabilities, 67
Penthouse, 79
People, nature and, thematic unit on, 227–230
People for the American Way, 304, 308
Perceptions, determination of, 149–152
Percy, Walker, 39
Perfection Form, books for low-ability students, 287
Period of Adjustment, 235
Perseus, 200
Persistence, high-ability students and, 264
Persona, and book reports, 90–91
Personality, integration of developing sexuality into, 239–240
Personal preferences (*see also* Reading interests)
of teachers, 43
Personal Recollections of Joan of Arc by the Sieur Louis de Conte, 216
Perspective-taking, in high-ability students, 265
Petitt, Dorothy J., 101, 104–106, 111–114, 117–122
"The Petrified Man," 193
Physical activity, overt, demand for, 87
Physical changes, in adolescence, and coming of age, 237–238
Pictures
children and, 95
secondary school students and, 96

The Pied Piper, 233
Piercy, Marge, 252
The Pigman, 113–114, 314
"A Pine Tree Stands Alone," 229
Planning, 139
Plato, 251, 254
Platoon, 233
Playboy, 79
Player Piano, 190
Plays (*see* Drama; Dramatic activity)
Pleasure, as goal of literary instruction, 37–38
Plot
    in comedy, 199
    in fiction, 193–194
    in romance, 200
Poe, Edgar Allen, 194, 208
"Poem," as event, 136
Poems, 208
Poetic Principle, 208
The Poetics, 220
Poetry
    as creative writing assignment, 178–179
    in genre approach, 196–198
    verisimilitude and, 9
Point of view, 194
    high-ability students and, 265
    in young adult novel, 103
"The Polaroid Print of Dorian Gray," 202
Policy documents, and censorship, 315
Political history, literary art and, chronological survey and, 190
Pooley, Robert, 189, 190
Poor readers (*see* Low-ability students)
Popular literature
    established texts versus, 91
    young adult novel and, 99–100
Popular music, 79–80
    rap, 289
A Portrait of the Artist as a Young Man, 243, 249, 250
Posters, in reader-response with low-ability students, 293
Postman, Neil, 46, 76–78
Potentially high-ability students, 263
    (*see also* High-ability students)
Pound, Ezra, 51, 202, 234
The Power and the Glory, 189
Practical Criticism, 72

Predictive statements, in Herber exercises, 50
Preferences (*see* Choice; Personal preferences; Reading interests)
Pregnancy, sexual relationships and, 239
Prejudice, 244
Preparation, oral reading and, 160
Prereading activities, 48–53
    rationale for, and nature of, 51–53
Presenting Robert Cormier, 109
Prewriting, 169–171
Pride and Prejudice, 73, 189, 190, 199
The Prince and the Pauper, 216
The Private Life of the Master Race, 235
Proactive censorship, 304–307
    teachers and, 316–317
Probst, Robert E., 144
Process of Education, 31
Professional organizations, and reading selections, 89
Progressive exercise, listening capabilities and, 67
Pubertal changes, 238
Publishers, abridgment and adaptation by, as form of censorship, 307–309
Pudd'nhead Wilson and Those Mysterious Twins, 215
Puritan society, opportunities for study of, 37
Pyle, Ernie, 233

Quality of young adult fiction, 104–111
Quantifiability of teaching goals, 132
Quasimodo, Salvatore, 228
"The Questioning Circle," 150–152
Questions, response-generating, 150

Racial integration, 21
Ransom, John Crowe, 135
Rap music, 289
Rasho, Matsuo, 228
Reader-response criticism, 136–137
Reader-response orientation, 130–156
    (*see also* Read-respond sequence; Response *entries*)
    affective learning and, 147–148
    cognitive learning and, 141–147
    critical reading and, 35
    criticism and, 136–137
    with low-ability students, 291–294

response-centered curriculum and, 137–140
response-centered teaching and, 148
social learning and, 140–141
Readers (*see* Students)
Reader's Digest editions, 80
The Reader's Guide to Periodical Literature, 176
Readers Theatre, 161
and drama reading, 195
Readiness activities, for reading drama, 195–196
Reading, 45–64
alternatives to, for low-ability students, 289
close, 142–145
content of, 47 (*see also* Reading selections)
correct, concept of, 134–136
critical (*see* Critical reading)
ease of
children and, 95
young adult novel and, 100
free, 186–188
individualized, guided, 225–226
interest in (*see* Interest in reading; Reading interests)
listening capabilities and, 64–68
metaphor in, 55–57
oral (*see* Oral reading)
pertinent competencies in, 53–55
prereading activities and, 48–53
recreational, 37–38
sample lession in, 59–64
silent, 96
study versus, transition to, 3–4, 94–99
Reading ability
in high-ability students, 264 (*see also* High-ability students)
and interest in reading, 70–74
in low-ability students, 283–284 (*see also* Low-ability students)
Reading assignments (*see also* Reading selections)
individualization of, 185–186
Reading comprehension
elements of, 57–59
Herber exercises and, 49
levels of, 296–297
sustained, 58–59
interest in reading and, 71

testing of, 154
Reading disability, 283–284
Reading exercises
ordering of events, 62
role playing activities, 62–63
written statements, 63
Reading interests, 69–70, 84–86 (*see also* Literary topics of special importance)
and development of literature appreciation, 85–86
personal characteristics of adolescents and, 85–86
realism and, 86–88, 297
thematic approach and, 225
Reading journal, 174
Reading lists (*see also* Reading selections)
alternative, censorship and, 316
for coming of age literature, 251
development of, censorship and, 315
for pleasure and recreation, 38
teacher-designed, 89
young adult fiction, 121–124
honor sampling, 125–129
Reading plan, for poetry, 197
Readings and Feelings: An Introduction to Subjective Criticism, 146
Reading selections, 47 (*see also* Reading lists; Text[s])
for children, 95
choices of, high-ability students' involvement in, 273
classroom libraries and, 82–83
correlative experience and, 47–48
emotional range of readers and, 47
gifted students and, 72
interest in reading and, 89
language of, 47
length of, 47
for children, 95
interest in reading and, 71
organizational pattern and, 184
for senior high school students, 96
young adult novel and, 103–104
of recognized cultural importance, 186
response-centered curriculum and, 137
teacher's knowledge of, censorship and, 314
in young adult fiction, 102
Reading skills, pertinent, 53–55

Reading vocabulary, enhancement of, 53–55

Read-respond sequence, 92 (*see also* Reader-response orientation)

Reagan, Ronald, 24, 28, 312

Realism (*see also* Verisimilitude)
reading interests and, 86–88, 297
young adult fiction and, 111–115

Reality, distortions of, suspension of disbelief and, 10–14

Rebellion, sense of individuality and, 240–241

Reconstruction
imaginative, 179–180
as writing assignment, 173

Recordings (*see also* Oral presentation[s])
listening capabilities and, 67
"Mark Twain Tonight!," 215
as reinforcement, 61
of students' oral responses, 68

Recreation, as goal of literary instruction, 37–38

The Red Badge of Courage, 87

"The Red Pony," 36, 212

Reed, Henry, 234

Reference sources, use of, cross referencing in, 55

Reflections on a Gift of Watermelon Pickle and Other Modern Verse, 228

"Refugee Blues," 233

Regional differences, correlative experience and, 6

Reinforcement
drawings in, 61–62
recordings in, 61

Relationships, and interest in reading, 75–76

Religion, coming of age and, 243

Remarque, Erich Maria, 232, 234

Remedial English programs, for low-ability students, 283 (*see also* Low-ability students)

Representative Men, 208

The Republic, 254

Research paper, 176–178

Resources
for book selection, 321
for thematic units, 226–227

Response(s), expression of, 157–181 (*see also* Response activities)
oral, 157–166 (*see also* Oral expression)

written, 166–181 (*see also* Written expression)

Response activities (*see also* Reader-response orientation)
children and, 96
development of, censorship and, 315
oral presentations and, 66
written, 96 (*see also* Written statements)

Response-centered curriculum, 137–140 (*see also* Reader-response orientation)
testing, evaluating, and grading in, 153–155

Response-centered lesson, 149–155

Response-centered teaching, 148–155

Response-expression cycle, 158

Response-generating questions, 150

Response papers, 172–173

"The Return," 51

The Return of the Native, 48, 189

Revision, in writing process, 169–171

Rice, Elmer, 13

Rich, Adrienne, 229

"Richard Cory," 80

Richard II, 232

Richards, I. A., 72

Richter, Conrad, 101

Right to Read, 23

The Rime of the Ancient Mariner, 79

Rimm, Sylvia B., 263, 265

Robertson, Pat, 299

Robinson, E. A., 80

Rock and roll music, 79–80

Roethke, Theodore, 234

Role playing activities, 62–63

Romance(s)
in mythic approach, 200
Teen Age, 78, 110–111

Roman Empire, opportunities for study of, 37

Romantic epics, willing suspension of disbelief and, 13

Romeo and Juliet, 185, 307

"A Rose for Emily," 193

Rosenblatt, Louise, 136, 140, 296

Roth, Philip, 71

Roughing It, 214, 215

"Round About Me," 228

Round characters, 194, 195

Rourke, Constance, 215

Royko, Mike, 12

"Rule of significance," 147–148
Rush, 79
Ruskin, John, 208
Russ, Joanna, 252
The Russian People, 235

Salinger, J. D., 5, 99, 112, 212, 241, 247, 302
Sample lessons (*see also* Illustrative Units) in reading, 59–64
Sandburg, Carl, 20, 229
Sappho, 228
Sassoon, Siegfried, 232, 233
Satire
 exaggeration in, 12
 in mythic approach, 201–203
 utopian, 252–253
Satiric narrative, 202
Saturday Review, 91
The Scarlet Letter, 37, 48, 100, 102, 207
Schlafly, Phyllis, 299
Scholarly texts, 97
Scholarship, preparation for, 40–41
Scholastic, Inc., thematic units from, 226–227
Scholastic Scope, 287–288
Scholastic Voice, 287–288
School boards, 297
School journalism, censorship of, 309–312
School policy documents, and censorship, 315
Science fiction, suspension of disbelief and, 12–13
Scientific thinking, 146
 in major idea approach, 217
Scott, Sir Walter, 19
Scripts, creation of, Readers Theatre and, 161
Season of Youth: The Bildungsroman from Dickens to Golding, 248–249
Secondary school, college and, dual enrollment in, 278–279
Secondary school literature curriculum, 18–43 (*see also* Curriculum *entries*)
 aesthetics in, 38–40
 Back-to-the-Basics period in, 23–24
 critical reading in, 34–35
 cultural heritage in, 36–37
 Cultural Literacy and, 27–29, 31–33
 Dartmouth debate on, 22
 dimensions of, options and, 33–41

early childhood teaching versus, transition concept and, 95–97
 Gardner report and, 24–25
 goals of, 25–26
 history of, 18–33
 pleasure and recreation in, 37–38
 as preparation for scholarship, 40–41
 recommendations for, 26–27
 reflection on correlative experience in, 35–36
 systems approaches to, 23
 thematic unit for, 231–235
Secondary sex characteristics, development of, 238
"The Secret Life of Walter Mitty," 192
Seeger, Pete, 80
Self-conscious appreciation, 85–86
Self-definition, search for, 240–241
 verisimilitude and, 9, 10
 young adult novel and, 101
Self-discipline, intellectual, high-ability students and, 273–274
Self-expression (*see* Oral expression; Written expression)
Self-knowledge, social learning and, characters and, 141
Sensationalism, realism and, 87
Sense of humor, high-ability students and, 265
Sentences, lines versus, in poetry, 197
Separateness, sense of, development of, 240–241
A Separate Peace, 9, 36, 190
Sequence
 exercise involving, 62
 and reading comprehension, 58
Setting(s), 194
 in young adult novel, 103
Sex, and interest in reading, 73–74
Sexuality, developing, personality integration of, 239–240
The Shah-Nameh, 270
Shakespeare, William, 19, 39, 48, 185, 190, 200, 219, 222, 232, 289
Shared experience, Herber exercises and, 51–52
Shaw, Geroge Bernard, 254
Shaw, Irwin, 235
Sherwood, Robert E., 234, 235
Shifting genres, 181
Shores, J. Harlan, 8

Short stories (*see also* Fiction)
    in genre approach, 193–195
Shute, Nevil, 233
Significance, rule of, 147–148
Silas Marner, 4, 5, 19, 106
Silence Over Dunkerque, 234
Silent reading, 96
Silhouette series, 108, 110
Simon, Neil, 38
Simon and Garfunkel, 80
Simonov, Konstantin, 235
Simplified classics, 80–82
Sinclair, Upton, 254
Slade, Peter, 162
Slaughterhouse Five, 303
The Slave Dancer, 181
Slonczewski, Joan, 252
Sloyer, Shirlee, 161
Small-group discussion, whole-group
    discussion versus, 158–160
    high-ability students and, 268
Smith, Dora V., 20, 105
Smith, Frank, 4
Smith, Henry Nash, 215
Smith, Hugh, 228
Social criticism, as literary topic, 254–255
Social history, literary art and,
    chronological survey and, 190
Social learning, 140–141
Socioeconomic class, and tracking, 261
"The Soldier," 232
The Song of Hiawatha, 270
The Song of Roland, 270
Songs of Labor, 208
Sonnets from the Portuguese, 208
Sons and Lovers, 249
Sophocles, 200, 219, 220, 289
Sorley, C. H., 232
Soul Gone Home, 211
Soul music, 79–80
Spann, Sylvia, 227
Special courses, for high-ability students,
    274–279
Spender, Stephen, 234
Sputnik, impact of, 20
Squire, James, 58, 86, 88
Stafford, Jean, 247
Stallings and Anderson, 235
Statements, in young adult novel, 103
Statewide testing programs, 23–24
Static character development, 194, 195

Stein, Gertrude, 73
Steinbeck, John, 20, 36, 106, 109, 212, 227,
    234, 255
Stephenson, Carl, 230
Stereotypes, in promotion of symbolism,
    14
Stevenson, Robert Louis, 19
Stock characters, comedy and, 199–200
Stones of Venice, 208
"Storm Fear," 229
"Storm Warning," 229
The Story of a Bad Boy, 245, 246
The Story of Ulysses, 81
Storytelling, for low-ability students, 289
Stowe, Harriet Beecher, 207, 254
Street, James, 100
A Streetcar Named Desire, 147–148
Street Scene, 13
Stress, in high-ability students, 279–282
Strike the Father Dead, 249
Students (*see also* Adolescents)
    creative writing of, censorship of,
        312–313
    emotional range of, reading selections
        and, 47
    feedback from, censorship and, 316
    high-ability (*see* High-ability students)
    interests of (*see* Interest in reading;
        Reading interests)
    low-ability (*see* Low-ability students)
    nature of involvement of, 42
    response of (*see also* Reader-response
        orientation)
        interest in reading and, 92
    teachers and, differences between,
        42
"The Student's Right to Know," 300
Studs Lonigan trilogy, 250, 254
Study of literature, transition from
    reading to, 3–4
    young adult fiction and, 94–99
Stylistics
    examination of, 97
    in young adult fiction, 102–104
Substance abuse, 243–244
Summer of My German Soldier, 234
The Sun Also Rises, 212, 232
Superboy/supergirl figures, 88
Supreme Court, and censorship, 303,
    310–311
Suspense, young adult novel and, 100

Suspension of disbelief, willing, promotion of, 10–14, 99
Swaggart, Jimmy, 299
"Swan Song of the Open Road," 202
Sweet Valley High romances, 110
Swift, Jonathan, 12, 202
Swiftwater, 6, 106
The Sword in the Stone, 180
Syllabus, and class organization, 279–280
Symbolism, 96, 194
  children and, 95
  promotion of, 14–16
Symonds, Robert L., 299
Syracuse University, and dual enrollment program, 278
Systems approach to curriculum, 23

Taboos (*see also* Censorship)
  violation of, in young adult fiction, 111–114
A Tale of Two Cities, 19, 48, 100, 208
Talk show format, oral book reports in, 164
Taping (*see* Recordings)
Taste, entertainment versus, 91
Tate, Alan, 212
Tate, Allen, 135
Teachers
  censorship and, 314–319
  demands on, high-ability students and, 266
  as guidance counselors, and interest in reading, 76
  individual concerns of, 41–43
  interest in reading of, and interest of students, 92–93
  as learners, 139
  oral reading by, for low-ability students, 289
  role of, in free reading approach, 188
  students and, differences between, 42
  in support of one another, censorship and, 317
  teams of, in middle school curricula, 41
"Teacher's Guide to AP Courses in English Language and Composition," 276
"Teacher's Guide to AP Courses in English Literature and Composition," 276

Teaching
  instructional flexibility in, thematic approach and, 225
  response-centered, 148–155
  theory and practice of, texts on, 323–327
Teaching as a Subversive Activity, 31
Teaching goals, accountability movement and, 132
Teaching Reading in the Content Areas, 296
Teaching the Decades, 207, 212
Teams, in middle school curricula, 41
  effects on teaching of literature, 131
Technology, opportunities for study of, 37
Teen Age Romances, 78, 110–111
Teenagers (*see* Adolescents; Students)
Television (*see also* Videos)
  correlative experience and, 6, 6–7
  impact of, on curriculum, 21
  and interest in reading, 76–78
  music videos on, 79–80
  verisimilitude and, 8
  and willingness to read, 46–47
Television commercials, oral book reports in form of, 164
Television talk show, oral book reports in form of, 164
Temperament, of adolescents, and interest in reading, 70, 75–76
Tennyson, Alfred Lord, 190, 208
Terkel, Studs, 7
Testing
  for Advanced Placement Program, 275–277
  college entrance tests, demystification of, 280
  for International Baccalaureate program, 277–278
  in response-centered curriculum, 153–155
Testing programs, statewide, 23–24
Text(s) (*see also* Reading selections)
  adding to, as writing assignment, 180–181
  altering, as writing assignment, 181
  alternative, censorship and, 316
  correct reading of, concept of, 134–136
  creation of, in language experience approach, 288–289
  established, popular literature versus, 91

as event, 136
imaginative reconstruction of, 179–180
print and nonprint vesions of,
interrelation of, 91–92
scholarly, 97
Textual decisions, 91–92
Thackeray, William Makepeace, 208
Thank you, Ma'am, 210
Theile, Colin, 179
Thematic approach, 224–235
Illustrative Units of, 227–235
Thematic focus of young adult novel, 104
Thematic units
coming of age fiction in, 250–251
resources for, 226–227
Thematic Units in Teaching English and the Humanities, 227
Theme
in drama, 196
in fiction, 195
"Theme for English B," 210
Theory of Literature, 33, 106
There Shall Be No Night, 234–235
Thinking (*see also* Scientific thinking;
Thought processes)
logical, in high-ability students, 264
moral, in high-ability students, 265
This Side of Parodies, 202
Thomas, D. M., 189
Thomas, Dylan, 65, 234
Thoreau, Henry David, 230, 254
"Those Were the Days," 80
Thought processes (*see also* Thinking)
in high-ability students, 264
Three Hundred Years Hence, 252
Thriller movies, 80
Thurber, James, 38, 192
Tillyard, E. M. W., 222
A Time to Leave and a Time to Die, 234
Tingle, Mary, 111, 112
"To Build a Fire," 230
Toffler, Alvin, 7
To Kill a Mockingbird, 201
Tolkien, J. R. R., 99
Tom Jones, 189
"Tommy," 232
Tone, 194
book reports and, 90–91
response-centered curriculum and,
138–139
Tono-Bungay, 249

Toomer, Jean, 211
Topics, important (*see* Literary topics of
special importance)
Tortilla Flat, 212
To the Lighthouse, 189
"To the Thawing Wind," 229
"To the Virgins To Make Much of
Time," 9
Tracking, 259–261 (*see also* High-ability
students; Low-ability students)
Tragedy
evolution of, in major idea approach,
218–224
in mythic approach, 200–201
"Tragedy and the Common Man," 223
Training material, literature as, critical
reading and, 34
A Tramp Abroad, 214
Travel, correlative experience and, 7
Treasure Island, 19
Tristram Shandy, 189
Trollope, Anthony, 208
T-shirts, design of, in reader-response
with low-ability students, 292–293
Tunis, John R., 234
Twain, Mark, 19, 202, 246
in major writer approach, 212–216
as creator of "American"
characters, 216
as creator of the frontier, 215
as humorist, 215–216
as local colorist, 214–215
as realist, 213–214
Twayne United States Authors series,
109
"Twilight," 228

Ulysses, 189, 264
Uncle Tom's Cabin, 207, 254, 270
Unconscious delight, 86
Unconscious enjoyment, 85
United States, post-World War I period
of, in major idea approach,
223–224
Universities (*see* College)
Updike, John, 39, 193
U.S.A. trilogy, 255
U.S. Supreme Court, and censorship,
303, 310–311
Utopia, 251
Utopia, as literary topic, 251–254

Values, personal system of, coming of age and, 242–243
Verisimilitude (*see also* Realism)
  promotion of, 8–10, 99
Videos
  for low-ability students, 290–291
  popular music, 79–80
Virgil, 19
The Virginians, 208
Visual media, in reinforcement, 61–62
Vocabulary (*see also* Language; Word *entries*)
  enhancement of, 53–55
  listening, 64
Vocational crisis of adolescence, 241–242
Voice, and book reports, 90–91
Vonnegut, Kurt, 190, 202, 303

Wain, John, 249
Walden (Thoreau), 230
"Walden" (White), 230
War, literature of, thematic unit on, 231–235
Warren, Austin, 33, 106, 133
Warren, Robert Penn, 135
Watch on the Rhine, 235
The Way of All Flesh, 249
Weight problems, and coming of age, 238
Wellek, Ren, 33, 106, 133
Wells, H. G., 227, 249
Welty, Eudora, 193
"We Real Cool," 9
Western civilization, lack of awareness of, 28–29 (*see also* Cultural Literacy)
Westfall, Robert, 234
Wharton, Edith, 256
Wharton, William, 133
What Maisie Knew, 246
What Price Glory?, 235
Wheatcroft, John, 180
"Where Have All the Flowers Gone," 80
Whimsy, children and, 95
Whistle, 234
White, E. B., 38, 230
White, T. H., 180
Whitehead, Frank, 162, 163
The White Hotel, 189
Whitman, Walt, 208, 254
Whittier, John Greenleaf, 19, 208

Whole-group discussion, small-group discussion versus, 158–160
  high-ability students and, 268
Wiesel, Elie, 233
Wilder, Thornton, 227
"Wild Goose," 229
Wilhelm Meisters Lehrjahr (Wilhelm Meister's Apprenticeship), 248
Williams, Tennessee, 36, 147, 219, 235
Willing suspension of disbelief, promotion of, 10–14, 99
Wilson, Sloan, 9
Winterset, 13, 39
Wolfe, Thomas, 250
Woman on the Edge of Time, 252
Women (*see also* Feminist *entries*)
  literature by and about, 255–257
  utopian novels, 252
Women in Love, 189
Woolf, Virginia, 39, 189, 249, 256
Word, most important (*see* Most important word technique)
Word clusters, 54
  listening and, 64
Word lists, in Herber exercises, 49–50
Word study skills, 53–55
Wordsworth, William, 217, 229
Working, 7
Workman, Brooke, 207, 211–212
Workman curriculum, 207–211
World War I
  curriculum following, 18–19
  opportunities for study of, 36–37
  study of period following, in major idea approach, 223–224
Wouk, Herman, 234
Wright, Richard, 210, 255, 256
Writing, creative (*see also* Writing assignments, creative)
  censorship of, 312–313
Writing ability, in high-ability students, 264
Writing assignments, 169–171, 172–181
  academic, 172–178
  creative, 172, 178–181
    for high-ability students, 271–272
    poetry and, 198
  in language experience approach, 288–289
  for low-ability students, 292, 293
Writing process, 168–171

prewriting in, 169–171
revision in, 171
Writing Seminars in the Content Area: In Search of Hemingway, Salinger, and Steinbeck, 211–212
Written expression, 166–181 (*see also* Written statements)
types of assignments and, 172–181
academic, 172–178
creative, 178–181
as way of knowing, 167–168
writing process and, 168–171
Written statements (*see also* Written expression)
as reading exercise, 63, 96
Wuthering Heights, 140–141, 179–180, 189, 190

Yeats, William Butler, 229
You Can't Take It with You, 38
Young adult fiction, 20, 94–116
action, suspense, and adventure in, 100
adolescent situation and, 100–101
availability in abundance of, 102
"best written" books in, 106, 121–122
censorship and, 313–314
characteristics of, 99–104

classics versus, 105–107
criteria for judging of, 106, 117–120
ease of reading and, 100
historical and contemporary situations and settings in, 101–102
identification as subliterary, 111–112
literary realism and, 111–115
for low-ability students, 286–287
popular fiction tradition and, 99–100
portrayal of search for self-definition in, 101
quality of, 104–111
reading lists in, 106, 121–124
honor sampling, 125–129
stylistic conventions and complexity of, 102–104
transition from reading to study and, 94–99
trends of, 108–109
well-written titles in, 121–124
Your Reading: A Booklist for Junior High and Middle School Students, 251
Yun, Ch'en, 228

Zaranka, William, 202
Z for Zachariah, 287
Zindel, Paul, 9, 113, 314